Page deliberately left blank

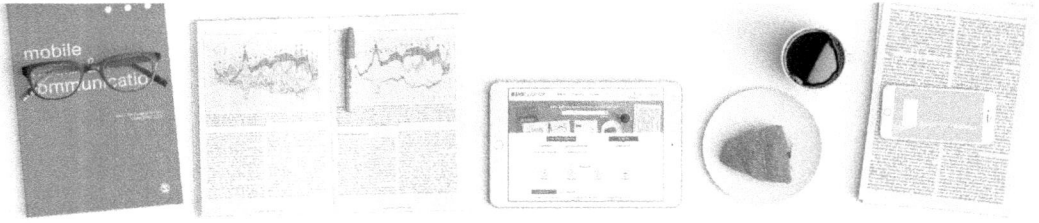

THE
ANNALS
of the American Academy of
Political and Social Science

VOLUME 687 | JANUARY 2020

Fatal Police Shootings: Patterns, Policy, and Prevention

SPECIAL EDITOR:

Lawrence W. Sherman
University of Cambridge, United Kingdom

SSAGE

Los Angeles | London | New Delhi
Singapore | Washington DC | Melbourne

The American Academy of Political and Social Science

202 S. 36th Street, Annenberg School for Communication, University of Pennsylvania, Philadelphia, PA 19104-3806; (215) 746-6500; (215) 573-2667 (fax); www.aapss.org

Origin and Purpose. The Academy was organized December 14, 1889, to promote the progress of political and social science, especially through publications and meetings. The Academy does not take sides in controverted questions, but seeks to gather and present reliable information to assist the public in forming an intelligent and accurate judgment.

Meetings. The Academy occasionally holds a meeting in the spring extending over two days.

Publications. THE ANNALS of The American Academy of Political and Social Science is the bimonthly publication of the Academy. Each issue contains articles on some prominent social or political problem, written at the invitation of the editors. These volumes constitute important reference works on the topics with which they deal, and they are extensively cited by authorities throughout the United States and abroad.

Subscriptions. THE ANNALS of The American Academy of Political and Social Science (ISSN 0002-7162) (J295) is published bimonthly—in January, March, May, July, September, and November—by SAGE Publishing, 2455 Teller Road, Thousand Oaks, CA 91320. Periodicals postage paid at Thousand Oaks, California, and at additional mailing offices. POSTMASTER: Send address changes to The Annals of The American Academy of Political and Social Science, c/o SAGE Publishing, 2455 Teller Road, Thousand Oaks, CA 91320. Institutions may subscribe to THE ANNALS at the annual rate: $1257 (clothbound, $1419). Individuals may subscribe to the ANNALS at the annual rate: $134 (clothbound, $197). Single issues of THE ANNALS may be obtained by individuals for $41 each (clothbound, $58). Single issues of THE ANNALS have proven to be excellent supplementary texts for classroom use. Direct inquiries regarding adoptions to THE ANNALS c/o SAGE Publishing (address below).

All correspondence concerning membership in the Academy, dues renewals, inquiries about membership status, and/or purchase of single issues of THE ANNALS should be sent to THE ANNALS c/o SAGE Publishing, 2455 Teller Road, Thousand Oaks, CA 91320. Telephone: (800) 818-SAGE (7243) and (805) 499-0721; Fax/Order line: (805) 375-1700; e-mail: journals@sagepub.com. *Please note that orders under $30 must be prepaid.* For all customers outside the Americas, please visit http://www.sagepub.co.uk/customerCare.nav for information.

THE ANNALS

© 2020 by The American Academy of Political and Social Science

Editorial Office: 202 S. 36th Street, Philadelphia, PA 19104-3806
For information about individual and institutional subscriptions address:
SAGE Publishing
2455 Teller Road
Thousand Oaks, CA 91320

For SAGE Publishing: Peter Geraghty (Production)

From India and South Asia, write to:
SAGE PUBLICATIONS INDIA Pvt Ltd
B-42 Panchsheel Enclave, P.O. Box 4109
New Delhi 110 017
INDIA

From Europe, the Middle East, and Africa, write to:
SAGE PUBLICATIONS LTD
1 Oliver's Yard, 55 City Road
London EC1Y 1SP
UNITED KINGDOM

International Standard Serial Number ISSN 0002-7162
ISBN 978-1-0718-1555-7 (Vol. 687, 2020) paper
ISBN 978-1-0718-1556-4 (Vol. 687, 2020) cloth
First printing, January 2020

THE
ANNALS
of the American Academy of
Political and Social Science

VOLUME 687 | JANUARY 2020

IN THIS ISSUE:

Fatal Police Shootings: Patterns, Policy, and Prevention

Special Editor: LAWRENCE W. SHERMAN

Introduction

Evidence-Based Policing and Fatal Police Shootings: Promise,
Problems, and Prospects . . . . *Lawrence W. Sherman*   8

Patterns of Fatal Police Shootings

Organizational Accidents and Deadly Police-Involved Violence:
Some Thoughts on Extending Theory, Expanding Research,
and Improving Police Practice . . . . *David Klinger*   28

Firearm Availability and Fatal Police Shootings . . . . *Daniel S. Nagin*   49

The Role of Individual Officer Characteristics in
Police Shootings. . . . . *Greg Ridgeway*   58

Predicting Bad Policing: Theorizing Burdensome and Racially
Disparate Policing through the Lenses of Social Psychology
and Routine Activities . . . . *Phillip Atiba Goff and Hilary Rau*   67

Network Position and Police Who Shoot . . . . *Linda Zhao*   89
and *Andrew V. Papachristos*

Policy-Making and Fatal Police Shootings

Police Killings as a Problem of Governance. . . . . *Franklin E. Zimring*   114

Social Interaction Training to Reduce Police Use of Force . . . . . . *Scott Wolfe,*   124
Jeff Rojek, Kyle McLean, and Geoffrey Alpert

Moving beyond "Best Practice": Experiences in Police Reform and a Call
for Evidence to Reduce Officer-Involved Shootings . . . . *Robin S. Engel,*   146
Hannah D. McManus, and Gabrielle T. Isaza

Reducing Violent Incidents between Police Officers and People with
  Psychiatric or Substance Use Disorders. . . . . *Harold A. Pollack*   166
                                                    and Keith Humphreys

Preventing Avoidable Fatalities

Police-to-Hospital Transport for Violently Injured Individuals:
  A Way to Save Lives?. . . . .*Sara F. Jacoby, Paul M. Reeping,*   186
                                                  and Charles C. Branas

Reconciling Police and Communities with Apologies, Acknowledgements,
  or Both: A Controlled Experiment. . . . . *Thomas C. O'Brien,*   202
                                        Tracey L. Meares, and Tom R. Tyler

Preventing Avoidable Deaths in Police Encounters with Citizens:
  Immediate Priorities. . . . .*Lawrence W. Sherman*   216

Afterword: A Policy-Maker's View

Five Years after Ferguson: Reflecting on Police Reform
  and What's Ahead. . . . . *Laurie O. Robinson*   228

Introduction

Evidence-Based Policing and Fatal Police Shootings: Promise, Problems, and Prospects

By
LAWRENCE W. SHERMAN

The promise of evidence-based policing is to reduce harm with better research for targeting, testing, and tracking police actions. The problems of using evidence-based policing to reduce harm are found in the emotional dimensions of ethics and risk. These problems are most pronounced with fatal police shootings, where the risks of injury to American police are often framed as a zero-sum choice in relation to the ethics of taking citizens' lives. Yet evidence-based policing offers good prospects for reframing the debate over fatal police shootings, in ways that could reduce harm to both police and citizens. This volume offers substantial new evidence for initiatives at all levels of U.S. government that could help to save lives in police encounters with citizens. Putting that evidence to work remains the major challenge facing the American police.

Keywords: evidence-based policing; fatal police shootings; guns; race; normal accident theory; police recruitment; training and governance; emergency medicine; mental health

A round 7:30 a.m. on a recent Monday in a large city, groups of young protesters placed food crates and other obstacles on main roads to block the rush hour traffic. When two traffic officers arrived, they ran at the protesters to move them up to the sidewalk. When one

Lawrence W. Sherman is director of the Cambridge Centre for Evidence-Based Policing, where he serves as editor-in-chief of the Cambridge Journal of Evidence-Based Policing. *He is also Wolfson Professor of Criminology Emeritus at the University of Cambridge Institute of Criminology, where he is chair of the Cambridge Police Executive Program. Until 2019, he served as a distinguished university professor at the University of Maryland. He was president of the American Academy of Political and Social Science and editor of* The ANNALS *from 2001 to 2005 and was elected a Thorsten Sellin Fellow of the Academy in 2009. He edited his first volume of* The ANNALS *in 1980, on Police and Violence. In 2017, he received Yale University's Wilbur Lucius Cross Medal, in recognition of his work as a pioneer of evidence-based practices.*

Correspondence: ls434@camb.ac.uk

DOI: 10.1177/0002716220902073

protester ran back into the street, one officer poked the barrel of his pistol into the protester's chest, then grabbed the protester with his left arm, while waving the pistol with his right hand. As they struggled, another protester—who was unarmed—ran toward the officer, who then shot the second protester in the abdomen. Later that day at police headquarters, high-level commanders announced that the shooting had been in compliance with the department's policy.[1]

The most striking fact about this shooting is that it happened in a city of 7.4 million people in which police killed no one at all in 2019. In general, cities where police shoot unarmed citizens with official approval tend to have high rates of shooting civilians. Given the total of 933 people killed by police shootings across the United States in 2019 (*Washington Post* 2020), the expected rate of fatal police shootings in the United States for that year was 2.8 deaths per million residents. In the city where the protester was shot, that rate translated to an expected number of twenty-one civilian deaths from police shootings for 2019. But that protester was not shot in the United States. He was shot by police in Hong Kong. He was shot in the one city that was declared by an Act of the U.S. Congress (2019), signed by the U.S. president, to be of concern to the United States because "the human rights of the people of Hong Kong are of great importance to the United States." Despite many good reasons for that concern, one of them cannot be the rate at which Hong Kong police kill residents of that city, which was zero in the year the president signed the law. The available evidence shows that U.S. residents are far more likely to be killed by their own police than Hong Kong residents are by theirs. Yet Hong Kong police have far lower public approval ratings than U.S. police, primarily over public reaction to police use of force.

While Hong Kong police were infinitely less likely to kill people in 2019 than U.S. police, the comparison points to three challenges that form the focus of this volume:

1. The central problem of police using lethal force in the United States is not *legality*, but perceived *necessity*: why can't more injuries from police use of force be avoided?
2. "Unnecessary" shootings have causes well beyond the split-second decision to shoot, found in wider systems and contexts that allow such moments to occur.
3. Police legitimacy can be lost even with low rates of fatal police shootings.

All three of these points show how understanding emotional reactions to policing can be central to the development and use of evidence to reduce overall harm from violence.

The Challenge of Fatal Police Shootings

Perceived necessity, not legality, of fatal police shootings

Evidence matters. But so do emotions. The taking of any human life is, and should be, a matter of great emotional significance. Even when police lives are at risk when they shoot, the public can and will ask why that risk to police was not managed better in advance.

If we analyze the November 11, 2019, shooting by the Hong Kong traffic officer, our emotions could point us to a conclusion that the shooting was "lawful but awful," if lawful it was. In the largely gun-free population of Hong Kong (whose murder rate is a tiny fraction of New York's), the necessity of using a pistol to disperse a crowd blocking traffic is highly questionable. Many observers, and perhaps most Hong Kongers, would have preferred that the police not use live ammunition at all when the underlying law to be enforced is a traffic violation. They might have preferred that two lone officers not have been allowed by superiors to go up against a large crowd, preferring to delay any enforcement action until a large number of police arrived with less-than-lethal weapons to disperse the crowd—perhaps even the much-maligned tear gas that the U.S. plans to ban for export to Hong Kong (U.S. Congress 2019, section 9). Critics might suggest that allowing such an asymmetrical engagement between two officers and hundreds of protesters would create a condition in which the officers would almost certainly perceive a threat of injury—one that would justify a shooting. These thoughts, and many others, underlie a widespread perception of police brutality in Hong Kong, despite its fatality-free record in 2019.

Emotions are just as important in this case to the local police employee federation. Had the top commanders publicly questioned the traffic officer's decision to take out his gun and shoot, there would likely have been fury at a failure to "back up" a courageous officer who put himself in harm's way to enforce the law—and who probably perceived the shooting as absolutely necessary. So, too, might any challenge to the shooting cause negative emotions toward the national leadership of this one country with "two systems": the Beijing leadership that repeatedly called on Hong Kong police to take "forceful action" against protesters. By November 11, 2019, protesters had injured many police officers, hitting some with metal rods, throwing flaming gasoline bombs in plastic bottles at others. Even a gun-free population can inflict a lot of damage on police officers, especially when police lack the legitimacy conferred by universal suffrage to elect the officials who oversee police actions.

Whatever the limitations of universal suffrage and the Electoral College in the United States may be, they are not a major issue in U.S. fatal police shootings. The United States has a police legitimacy problem, but it is not from having "one country with two systems." It is, rather, a problem that stems from one country with two cultures. When the President of the United States makes a public statement that encourages police to use excessive force with gang members (Sherman 2018), he was supported by members of one culture. When police chiefs across the nation issued statements criticizing the president's message (Rosenthal 2017), they were supported by members of another culture. Divisions of Americans along other lines, such as race and age, can also be identified in U.S. emotions about police use of force. Citizens and police on both sides of the cultural divide can become highly emotional on the question of when a shooting is necessary, versus when a confrontation can be avoided.

Reducing split-second decisions

Both Americans and Hong Kongers share the tendency to view police shootings in the framework of a zero-sum choice: if one wins, the other must lose. If officers do not shoot, they risk being injured or killed themselves. Stated this narrowly, harm to some seems to be inevitable. Even the U.S. Supreme Court, in decisions in both 1989 (*Graham v. Connor*, 490 US 386) and 2018 (*Kisela v. Hughes*, 138 S. Ct. 1148), has declined to regulate a police officer's perception that they are in imminent danger of death or serious injury. Under these rulings, a U.S. jury would have been able to uphold the legality of the November 11, 2019, shooting in Hong Kong.

The "inevitability" logic of these rulings concerns what Chief Justice Rehnquist called "split-second decisions," or what the authors of an *ANNALS* article a half century ago (Binder and Scharf 1980) called the "final frame" of a movie reel (see also Fyfe 1986). This conventional viewpoint places the policy for when to shoot in the context of the split second when an officer pulls the trigger—thereby ignoring all the contextual factors that shape (and limit) the choices of any officer who arrives at that split-second, final frame. Viewing a police encounter as a movie, we can rewind the movie to identify many previous "frames" in the reel of film, in which a different choice may have saved everyone from harm. In the case of the Hong Kong traffic officer, a decision to wait for further backup officers might have done just that. Split-second decisions are not inevitable. The need to make them can be reduced.

Legitimacy depends on more than number of fatal shootings

The United States and Hong Kong share a recognition that the police may shoot people sometimes without criminal prosecution, but never without risking a loss of legitimacy in the eyes of the public. Every time someone is killed by police, the basis for doing so can be contested. Legal principles notwithstanding, the argument that a shooting was "unnecessary" threatens the central claim of the state to a monopoly on the legitimate use of force (Weber 1946). If the police do not earn the moral right to use that force wisely, day in and day out (Bottoms and Tankebe 2012), the entire basis of the state may be undermined. It follows that even legal shootings pose a risk to both police and state legitimacy.

Yet legitimacy is hardly determined by the number of shootings alone. Even without killing anyone, the Hong Kong police suffered a rise from 5 percent to more than 50 percent disapproval in a few short months of 2019 (Lee 2019). This astonishing loss of legitimacy is widely blamed on injuries to protesters caused by police use of rubber bullets and tear gas, defined as excessive force by 69 percent of the population.

For reasons still unexplained, the number of fatal shootings by police in the United States declined by about 6 percent in 2019 compared to 2018 and compared to most preceding years (*Washington Post* 2020). This fact has attracted little attention in the United States. Nor has it changed the level of public concern when people are killed by police, or police killed by citizens. Just as evidence on crime trends takes a backseat to emotion-driving headlines about shocking individual cases of violence, much the same can be said about fatal police shootings. The goal of minimizing injuries caused by police may help to support police legitimacy. But achieving that goal is not enough.

In summary, the *general* goal of police killing fewer people is one that is widely shared across the various divisions and cultures within the United States. It is the *specific* circumstances in each case, tied to an individual officer who can be blamed or scapegoated for a shooting, that evoke the strongest emotions—and provide the greatest pressure for change. One way to avoid those emotions is to ask how shootings may be prevented well before the "final frame."

Answering that question requires a far broader understanding of the systems that determine the risk of fatal shootings than just the facts of each case. Identifying the full range of those systems, from police training to the emergency medical transport that takes wounded persons to hospitals, is hard enough (Sherman 2018); but understanding how they work, and how they can be improved to save lives, is even harder. The analysis needed to do that cannot be done by busy police executives who must manage many issues at all times. The reflective inquiry that is required must be undertaken by a range of talents, disciplines, and professions, working together to ask not just how each death might be prevented, but how patterns of death might be predicted and interrupted. This is exactly the kind of broad inquiry to which evidence-based policing and this volume are committed.

Evidence-Based Policing and Its Application to Fatal Police Shootings

In the last half century, police reform in the English-speaking world has increasingly been driven by research conducted by and with police officers. While police research was once a matter of academics "studying the police" from the outside, it has increasingly become a matter of academics working with police on the inside. In the most recent developments of this century, "pracademic" (practitioner-academic) police officers have led their own research projects, leading to publications in international journals (e.g., Williams and Coupe 2017; Andersen and Mueller-Johnson 2018; Massey, Sherman, and Coupe 2019). Driven in part since 2007 by thesis projects of hundreds of graduates of the master's degree program in evidence-based policing at Cambridge, pracademic research has been focused on the "Triple-T" conceptual framework of *targeting, testing,* and *tracking* police actions to make better use of police resources (Sherman 2013). This trend has even led (since 2010) to the formation of Societies of Evidence-Based Policing with thousands of members in the UK, Australia-New Zealand, the United States, and Canada.

The promise of evidence-based policing is not just that research can become more useful for police decision-making. It is also the promise that researchers in positions of power will be able to ensure that the research findings are used to improve police practices. One prime example of this has been the rapid adoption of a crime harm index (Sherman, Neyroud, and Neyroud 2016) to weight all crime counts according to the amount of imprisonment each crime category is assigned—either by sentencing guidelines or average sentences imposed. This practice alone can foster a wide range of evidence-based practices, consistent with investing the most policing in the most serious forms of crime.

With a greater emphasis on the differences in seriousness across all offence types, there may be better organizational systems for making policing more *proportionate*. That is, if police deploy minimal resources (and force) to low-harm crimes, and invest more time in preventing and detecting high-harm crimes, there may be reduced risk of violence in citizen encounters over minor crimes.

More important is the challenge to traditional practices that can be created by better targeting and testing, let alone tracking. Everything police agencies decide, from recruitment to assignments to discipline and dismissal, can be supported by better evidence. That promise is reflected in this volume by Greg Ridgeway's analytic *targeting* of the predictors of characteristics of officers who are more likely than others to shoot in situations of ambiguous (or contestable) necessity to do so. It is reflected in Linda Zhao and Andrew Papachristos's mapping the social networks of officers who are subject to complaints, which targets the officers in a "connector" role as somehow increasing police shootings of other officers when the connectors are reassigned.

The promise of *testing* police practices that could reduce fatal shootings is reflected in the article by Scott Wolfe and his colleagues on a randomized trial that assessed a new training program in how to de-escalate situations of potential violence. That promise is also reflected in the summaries by Harold Pollack and Keith Humphreys of a wide range of interventions that can reduce fatal police actions. Most ambitiously, it is tested by Thomas O'Brien, Tracey Meares, and Tom Tyler in their crowd-sourced experiment in the ways that police chiefs can apologize for fatal shootings.

The *tracking* of police practices and problems is reflected in the account offered by Robin Engel and her colleagues of how a police scholar was appointed to lead a large university police department in the aftermath of a fatal police shooting and applied research to develop a program of reform. It is also the nature of the article by Sara Jacoby and her colleagues about how few U.S. police agencies drive shooting victims to the hospital in police cars, despite some potential for saving lives using that practice. The promise of such tracking is to identify gaps in practice and in evidence that can be filled by more testing.

But there is more to police improvement than evidence alone. This volume features a fourth "T"—*theory*. In his opening article, David Klinger sets the theoretical stage for the entire volume. He shows how a change in theorizing about prevention of fatal encounters could generate the kind of evidence that is most needed to reduce the fatalities. Philip Atiba Goff and Hilary Rau show how a theory of identity threats can help to shape recruitment and selection of police officers and to appoint more of the kinds of people who are less likely to use force unnecessarily than many current police officers. Franklin Zimring offers a theory for national policy development that could provide more effective governance of police use of force.

Yet no theory is more compelling than the claim that the gun supply drives fatal police shootings. Tracking the variability in household gun ownership rates across the fifty states, Daniel Nagin provides strong evidence for that theory. This insight, as many others in the volume, reveals the problems in applying the research from this volume to reduce deaths in police encounters.

Applying Research in Practice: Problems and Opportunities

Rather than providing a conventional summary of the contents of the volume, this introduction offers a commentary on the problems of applying in practice the takeaway conclusions of each article. It does so in the spirit of resisting hubris about the promise of evidence-based policing, or indeed any kind of evidence-based practice based on rational behavior. As Ron Haskins (2018, 8), the special editor of a recent *ANNALS* volume on evidence-based social policy, observed in his own introduction to that volume, "We have miles to go before we can argue that [evidence-based policy] has been proven to . . . show clear progress in reducing the nation's social problems, most of which are complex and resistant to amelioration." As for some three centuries since the advent of the "enlightenment," the challenge to rational solutions has always been the attack on the idea of rationality itself (Davies 2019).

Patterns of fatal police shootings

David Klinger's article is the first and most comprehensive in the volume. Its aim is to map out the complex systems and contexts that shape each police encounter, long before and far beyond the "final frame." First and foremost is the organizational adaptation to a very high risk of the citizens killing police in any encounter. The uniquely American problem (among advanced economies) is that U.S. police officers are killed in the line of duty at a high rate. As Zimring (2017, 79) points out, from 2008 to 2012, U.S. police were thirty-five times more likely than German police to be killed in the line of duty. The difference in rates of killings *by* police between Germany and the United States was almost identical to the difference in killings *of* police. It could be proposed, then, that the internationally high rate at which police kill civilians in the United States is a rational adaptation to the internationally high rates of police dying in the line of duty. But the test of that proposition is whether there are alternative policies that the United States could adopt to reduce that massive difference.

Klinger goes far beyond that starting point of elevated danger to U.S. police. In his adaptation of Charles Perrow's *Normal Accidents* (1984), Klinger applies to policing a conceptual framework designed for high-risk, high-complexity organizations. Perrow's theory of "normal" accidents was developed from his detailed analysis of a 1979 nuclear power plant meltdown, followed by further analyses of aircraft, shipping, and other crashes of highly complex systems. His key idea is that "tightly coupled" systems with little slack are unable to absorb unexpected shocks, which makes them prone to a cascading spiral of system breakdowns resulting in complete failure of the system. When a citizen encounter occurs in which a police officer is killed, does kill, or both, there is often a good answer to "why and how did this happen?" The answer lies in the "tight coupling" of police practice.

One key feature of tight coupling that Klinger discusses is the sense of urgency police officers feel when they engage in citizen encounters. Often prompted from their radio dispatchers to go on to the next request for police service, officers may feel they do not have time for lengthy negotiations with, or even listening to, some noncompliant citizens they encounter. This need to meet "production demands" may compel them to push sensitive discussions with emotionally upset people faster than is wise—with a high risk of that quest for speed backfiring, and guns firing, in any struggle for immediate compliance with police orders. That is exactly what happened in Hong Kong on November 11, 2019: unable to wait for backup, nor expected to do so, the "systems" forced the officer into a situation where he decided to pull out his gun and shoot to protect himself. A system with less intensive "production demands"—one that would have required that he await a larger, team response—could have prevented that situation from arising, and the shooting that ended it.

As Klinger notes, the emotional resistance to delayed policing is very high in the United States. The delay-until-backup is an alternative system that might be justified in the United States with a large crowd breaking traffic laws—but not with a "shots fired" incident. When violence is in progress, delay looks like cowardice, as indicated by the disgrace heaped on the police officer assigned to the Stoneman Douglas High School in Parkland Florida in 2018 when it suffered a mass murder of seventeen people (Blinder and Mazzei 2018). While the officer delayed, people died. Yet mass murder is not a typical police situation. The culture of urgency in all tasks of American policing impedes strategies for delayed response. Urgency is overestimated, "just in case" the situation may be very dangerous. The paradox of this culture is that the failure to wait for a sufficient number of police may contribute to raising the danger level of the encounter—for the officer as well as the citizens.

Klinger's remedies are eminently sensible, but they face substantial challenges. His own training with the LAPD SWAT team suggests many alternative systems that could save lives. Selling, or even designing, those systems may only be possible if they are clothed in the rhetoric of courage, with the bravery and skill of a SWAT team as a model. Klinger's ideas are unlikely to sell themselves. But with a separate research agenda on how to persuade police agencies to design new systems, the fundamental rationality of Klinger's theory could still win out.

Daniel Nagin's article provides an essential analysis of the U.S. context for the redesign of policing systems. In sharp contrast to Hong Kong police killing no protesters in 2019, a gun-free city, U.S. police face a far more dangerous population. One indicator of that is how few suicides in Hong Kong are committed with guns, which are not even reported among all methods of suicides (Yip, Law, and Law 2003). Daniel Nagin's article in this volume uses the high, but varying, percentage of suicides committed with guns to indicate "gun density" across the fifty U.S. states, which has been validated as a predictor of the proportion of households with guns. He finds a substantial relationship between gun density and the rate per million people at which police shoot people fatally in each state. The greater the proportion of homes with guns, the greater the proportion of people who police shoot to death.

Nagin shows that this finding is consistent with what is called "statistical prediction" theory. That theory claims, when applied to this problem, that with more guns in a state, there is a greater chance that each person the police encounter may be carrying a gun. In the application of a zero-sum choice, Nagin suggests, the police may shoot more readily to preempt being shot themselves. Whether police *should* do that is an emotionally contestable question. Whether there is any way to prevent it, short of reducing the prevalence of gun possession, is an empirical question. Here again, there may be alternative systems of procedures, or even training and review, that could change the link Nagin finds between gun density and fatal police shooting rates. But a long program of trial and error testing would be needed to discover what works.

Nagin's article is also the first to report on the effects of something that can be changed by simply spending more money—and recruiting more doctors. That is, he finds that the more access to "trauma centers" there is, on average, within in a state, the lower the statewide death rate is from fatal police shootings. Trauma centers are enhanced versions of Emergency Medicine departments in major hospitals. They employ medical and support staff with much greater experience in treating gunshot wounds and with better equipment and special training. As Susan Jacoby and her colleagues report in their article in this volume, statewide average distances of homes from trauma centers has a strong correlation with higher statewide survival rates among people wounded by gunshots.

Nagin's finding, as he notes, is a correlation without proof of causation. States with more trauma centers may, for example, have more cautious police officers, or better police systems to minimize the perceived need to shoot to protect police. Yet the trauma center access correlation is powerful, and the theory is consistent with other data. If even one state that is a "trauma desert"—with no access to a trauma center anywhere in the state—were to create one, it would constitute an initial experiment in reducing lives lost to police shootings.

The problems of funding and staffing such centers in rural areas are of course substantial. Yet the idea would fall on common ground between propolice and antipolice constituencies. Everyone, including police officers shot in the line of duty, would stand to gain from "watering the trauma deserts." For people shot hundreds of miles from a trauma center, the impact may be limited, but helicopter ambulances and first aid using hemostatic bandages could enhance survival even across large distances from a trauma center. Nagin's data are clear about the correlation. It is now up to public health advocates to use the analysis to strengthen the case for better treatment of bullet wounds.

Despite this volume's emphasis on systems and context, there is a widespread concern about the kinds of people who wear badges and carry a gun. The attribution of blame, incompetence, racism, and other moral defects is more often focused on persons than on systems. But fatal police shootings are rare events, with little known about how different officers would deal with such situations—the same, or differently? Faced with the same facts, what percentage of officers would shoot, and what percentage would not? Most important, who are the people who can avoid shooting without getting shot, or without other harm resulting?

The research methods needed to answer these crucial questions require holding everything constant except the officers. Any study that compares officers across different situations is confounded by those differences. To study officers faced with exactly the same facts, Greg Ridgeway identified a unique dataset in the New York City Police. It offered detailed information on 291 officers present at a total of 106 shooting incidents, each incident involving multiple officers, in 2004 through 2006. In each of these incidents, at least one, but not all, of the officers at the scene discharged their firearms. Analysis of these incidents can identify the correlates of officers who shoot—or do not—in exactly the same situations as officers who make the opposite choice. The differences in characteristics of those officers provide the best possible research design for predicting which officers will be less likely to shoot—for better or worse.

The most striking finding in his analysis is the role of prior arrests made by the officers. Officers who had made ten or more misdemeanor arrests were 80 percent less likely to shoot than officers who had not made ten such arrests. But for felony arrests, the opposite was true: officers with 9.3 felony arrests were twice as likely to shoot as officers who had not made as many as 9.3 felony arrests. While the latter finding was a less certain (nonsignificant) finding, it suggests a very different orientation or work history between the two groups. Those with frequent experience in making "quality of life" arrests, possibly with persons suffering from mental illness, may be used to noncompliance and managing people through words and physical restraint. Those who make many felony arrests may expect to find weapons on the arrestees, giving them greater tendencies to make "statistical predictions" in Nagin's terms. The latter may shoot preemptively, for safety, in situations in which the misdemeanor arresters do not shoot.

Two other powerful and certain predictors in Ridgeway's New York study were (1) the officers who had repeated misconduct reports: these officers were three times more likely to shoot than those who did not; and (2) African American officers, who were also three times more likely to shoot than white officers. The prediction of more shootings by officers with more misconduct is one that could be dealt with by removing such officers from front-line assignments and removing their firearms. That policy was widely practiced in the New York City Police Department (NYPD) in the 1970s for alcoholic police officers, who performed such tasks as courier service or reception desk duty. But the prediction of more shootings by black officers is one that has no obvious application, except perhaps more research to understand it.

In this volume, Ridgeway shows that the findings for how many bullets are fired follow similar patterns to those who shoot or do not shoot, at least in the NYPD. But in a larger national sample of (only) officers who shoot, comparing how many bullets they fired, Ridgeway could not find the same predictors as he found in the NYPD. What that may mean is a need for this kind of study to be done in each large police agency and that all such studies should include data on officers present who did not shoot.

The article by Phillip Atiba Goff and Hilary Rau provides a more theoretically intensive approach to studying police use of force. Framing the question of individual officer differences in relation to "bad" policing, Goff and Rau include racism and excessive force in the target for prediction and explanation. Reviewing a wide range of laboratory experiments and field studies, Goff and Rau weave together various strains of situationist and identity psychology. Their review suggests that there may be much more powerful selection tools for appointing police officers than multiple choice tests and background investigations.

The tools that could be used to screen applicants for positions would be the kind of simulator technologies that are widely available for police training. These technologies generally create some kind of virtual reality experience for the officer, who is armed with a fake gun that can register when the officer would shoot (or not) in relation to a screening of a situation in which officers are treated as if they are present. These tools allow the trainee to be tested on whether they shoot too much, too little, or mostly right, in relation to risk. But in the research Goff and Rau review, the officers are provoked in various ways, to test how well they can control their temper.

The important point about this method is that training itself may do little to change (or improve) the personal conduct of any one officer. What could be more useful is to use such scenarios to screen out applicants whose reactions constitute "bad policing." As in many employment situations, it is much more effective to screen out people who are unsuited to the job than it is to try to increase their suitability once they are hired.

Perhaps the most surprising findings of Goff and Rau's review concern the "identity" theories being tested. One theory is that men react badly when their masculine identity is threatened and are more likely to pull the trigger than officers who are less threatened by aspersions to their masculinity. Predicting which men are more insecure about that identity may be something that the tests Goff and Rau review can accomplish. With long-term research to support the predictive value of the tests, they might withstand the inevitable court challenges brought by people excluded from police jobs on the basis of such evidence.

The more surprising finding is that "officers who are *concerned about* appearing racist are *more likely to use force* in racially disparate ways," as Goff and Rau report. Their evidence comes from surveying officers before they are tested with the simulators, so that their identity as people who are *not* racist is clearly established. If they both identify with being unbiased, and are insecure about whether they will be perceived that way, that condition seems to make them more prone to bad behavior. "In one 2012 study of officers from a large urban police department," Goff and Rau write, "the Center for Policing Equity found a correlation between stereotype threat and greater use of force against black civilians."

Here again, the problem of using this approach in training is that it may be too late after they have already been hired. Using it in hiring would pose legal challenges. But given the core importance of the personality traits needed to use deadly force with restraint, Goff and Rau's approach seems to be well worth exploring as a hiring technique. As long as there is a sufficient number of applicants for police jobs, and adequate pay to attract them, this approach may prove less problematic than the current hiring practices at reducing unnecessary shootings.

Once an officer accumulates a higher-than-usual number of complaints from the public, they may become prone to being transferred, or "shuffled," as Linda Zhao and Andrew Papachristos put it. Yet such "shuffling" of high-complaint officers may just make matters worse, at least in terms of their risk of shooting people—and of shootings by other officers in their social networks. That conclusion emerges from the Zhao and Papachristos article, which examines shootings of citizens between 2004 and 2016 by all 9,210 of the unique Chicago Police Department (CPD) police officers subject to one or more complaints, who collectively were the subjects of 38,442 complaints from 2000 and 2003.

By examining the links among officers who were identified in relation to the same incidents, the article counts the number of other officers to whom each "deviant" (complained-about) officer is linked, and by how many degrees of separation. The more links, and the fewer the average degrees of separation, the more likely the officer is to become part of a small "power few" of highly "central" people in these networks. Using standard terminology in social network analysis, Zhao and Papachristos call these power few officers "brokers"—because they are potential conduits for information, values, and reputations between different social networks.

As the authors put it, "Our findings show that although only a small percentage of all CPD officers shoot—those officers who do shoot appear to occupy a unique structural position, that of a network broker. This finding appears to hold even when considering *individual-level factors* such as age, race, gender, and activity. Our estimates suggest that each standard deviation increase in betweenness centrality predicts a roughly 1.17 higher odds of shooting net individual factors. The remaining association is strongly related to *organizational-level factors* such as shuffling."

The movement of high-complaint officers to other units may have two effects on the risk of their shooting. One is that these "brokers" themselves become more likely to shoot civilians. The other is that the brokers may "spread" their propensity to shoot people, so that transfers give them an opportunity to spread proshooting views among other officers who had not met them before. As the authors note, the correlational nature of the study limits their ability to conclude that transfers actually *cause* more shootings. But that is not, as they suggest, any reason to ignore social network analysis in making transfers, especially from one district to another. Social network analysis offers great prospects for improving police management, but only if the insights of the results can be specified and clearly linked to choices of optimal units to which high-complaint officers could be transferred.

Policy-making and fatal police shootings

While the first section of the volume reveals the complexity of the patterns of fatal police shootings, it merely hints at the difficulty of finding better policies to govern those patterns. Starting the second section of the volume at the highest level of governance, Franklin Zimring spells out the reluctance of all levels of government to take effective action that could save lives of both police and civilians. This problem is tied to the unique structure of American government, in which the federal government has scant obligation to govern policing, the states make scant use of their power to do so, and juries make scant use of often-strong evidence to convict police officers of criminal charges.

Zimring begins with the context of high murder rates of police by U.S. residents, but then shows how many more fatal police shootings are unrelated to the *actual* presence of guns. While Daniel Nagin's paper provides a statistical explanation for that in the evidence for a higher *probability* of guns being present in some states compared to others, that fact does not justify the deaths in some 40 percent of cases in which guns are not in the possession of the people police shoot. These are the arguably *unnecessary* fatal shootings against such risks as knives, in the kind of encounters faced by police in other countries (like the UK) that kill almost no one in such circumstances.[2]

Zimring quickly dismisses prosecution as an effective means of reducing unnecessary shootings, making the case for administrative reforms in policing. But his second theme sadly shows the limits of the first: the federal dispersion of powers makes administrative reforms unlikely to happen by systematic governance at the state level, where the power lies to create and destroy police agencies. With such rare exceptions as Camden, New Jersey—where the state abolished a failing police department and replaced it with a county-wide agency—the state legislatures have been reluctant to take decisive action to improve governance. And while some might say that federal oversight of local police reached an apex under President Obama, the rapid swings in federal governance make that level of intervention short lived.

Most readers will readily support Zimring's proposals for a more aggressive federal program of research and statistics on police use of deadly force, with a modest cost of $10 million per annum. Perhaps some policing organizations would even campaign for such an initiative, to save police lives. If the ever-changing gridlock of political parties in Washington after 2020 would allow it, the idea could actually become reality. Yet as former Assistant Attorney General Laurie Robinson observes in her article in this volume, the chances are still very low.

On a much smaller scale than national governance, Wolfe and his colleagues offer new evidence for hope in de-escalating risks of violence in police-citizen encounters. While "de-escalation training" recommendations from the Obama Task Force (President's Task Force on 21st Century Policing 2015) have been adopted in eighteen states (Sherman 2018), there is no consistent definition of either "de-escalation" or its training. Neither are there any impact evaluations of such training linked to police behavior in real-world settings.

Nonetheless, preliminary findings from a training experiment in Tucson (AZ) and Fayetteville (NC) suggest that a form of training called "social interaction skills" can help to reduce police use of force. Like so many policies, the devil may be in the details. Their careful documentation in this volume of how the program was implemented reveals much about the challenges of delivering any training in police agencies. Bluntly put, training is seen as a threat to operational performance of the police mission. To the extent that availability of police officers for operational work is reduced by time spent in training, abstracting officers for such courses may be seen as a threat to the safety of officers remaining on duty. Yet that is only a starting point.

What Wolfe and his colleagues show is a critical issue in all training: results may depend on the personality and skill of the trainer. In their words, "We conclude that the conceptual framework was generally well-received, but that results depended heavily on the selection and performance of each agency's own trainers." This conclusion provides evidence that training in policing is hardly as homogeneous a treatment as taking a pharmaceutical pill. States may require training with a certain label, but the effect of training on saving lives can be quickly undermined by a loose regulatory framework for delivering the training. Absent a state-level inspector-general of police to audit the delivery of such quality assurance strategies (Sherman 2015), the states may be unable to produce the effects they can agree should be sought by legislation.

Robin Engel and her colleagues carry us further into the organizational details of trying to reduce unnecessary use of force. Even in the wake of a nationally criticized fatal police shooting, the University of Cincinnati struggled mightily to find evidence-based guidance for reform. In her unprecedented appointment as an eminent police scholar leading a major university's policing, Engel provides a case study of looking for both ideas and evidence about those ideas. Ideas were far more plentiful than the evidence supporting them, as she recounts. The solution of generating new evidence was simply too slow for meeting the demand. The legitimacy of the police agency depended on taking action, regardless of whether such actions would work. Indifference is a worse sin than ineffectiveness. That, in an epigram, is what holds back generating new evidence when innovations are applied to fatal police shootings.

Engel's tenure in governance of a large police agency faced calls for five prominent reforms: body-worn cameras, de-escalation training, implicit bias training, early intervention systems, and civilian oversight. As the article observes, "These heavily endorsed interventions, however, are not based on a strong body of empirical evidence and may result in unintended consequences." Her efforts to decide whether to adopt these policies were hampered by the low statistical power that comes with rare events. Because her time was short, but time between shootings could last years, she was unable to test the ideas herself during her time in office. Many other police executives could say the same.

The time-to-evidence issue supports the conclusion that Engel and her colleagues reach: that university-based researchers should undertake long-term tests of policies to reduce fatal shootings. Even if these tests take years, the tenure of a university professor is very likely to outlast that of an agency police chief. In the end, the article suggests, only long-term scholarship can take the time to generate strong evidence on (thankfully) rare events.

One answer to the call by Engel and colleagues is the Pollack and Humphreys article. In a catalogue of policies for improving police encounters with persons with psychiatric or substance use disorders (PWPSUD), the evidence ranges from substantial to modest. Overall, their article suggests that the interventions reviewed might be the most rapid means of reducing fatalities nationwide. As Zimring (2017) points out, a high proportion of people shot fatally by police are mentally ill, if only transiently. Yet this appears to be one dimension of the problem that offers ample evidence for effective prevention of unnecessary shootings.

The Pollack and Humphreys review covers three categories of policies: (1) those intended to prevent violent confrontations between police and PWPSUD; (2) "in the-heat-of-the-moment" strategies, that is, how police can handle potentially dangerous situations involving people who are impaired in some way; and (3) long-term management strategies for PWPSUD who have been involved in the criminal justice system.

Most of these policies require coordinated action at various levels of operation. For police to take guns away from PWPSUD, for example, requires a state law to allow it, as well as local priorities to undertake it. The fact that the most aggressive such law in the United States—Indiana's—followed the death of a police officer suggests the widespread benefit of preventing violent confrontations in this way. They cite further evidence of lives saved from other states as well.

The heat-of-the-moment strategies connect to the evaluation described by the article in this volume by Wolfe and his colleagues. Strategies for keeping police out of harm's way while PWPSUD become less dangerous can be promoted and taught. But as the Camden, NJ, example Sherman (2018) discussed illustrates, the effective implementation of such strategies may depend on a police chief who is willing to terminate officers who reject such delay tactics.

The long-term management of PWPSUD offenders who are known to authorities may have the greatest potential of the three categories of innovations. Inexpensive tracking technologies for alcohol or drug use could trigger immediate interventions that would neutralize risks as soon as they begin to elevate. Alcohol use, in particular, seems subject to judicial oversight and mandatory monitoring for detection of violations, followed by immediate incarceration. The promising evidence for this approach, as reviewed in the Pollack and Humphreys article, points to much harm reduction beyond fatal police shootings; the policy may prevent accidents and domestic abuse at the highest proportions. Yet the publicity around any fatal police shooting may create windows of opportunity to introduce more expensive, and perhaps effective, day-to-day offender management.

Preventing avoidable fatalities

The topic of preventive policies in general leads to a highly focused, yet widely ignored, dimension of police fatal shootings. That dimension comes out of Zimring's framework of policies, starting at the end: how can more deaths be prevented even after people have been shot? Our invitation to Jacoby and her colleagues to start that discussion leads them to a cautious, if powerful, conclusion: "Prehospital transport known as 'scoop and run' . . . may shorten the time between injury and hospital care when emergency medical services are delayed or unavailable. Current evidence suggests that when comparing police hospital transport and emergency medical services transport, survival rates are at least equivalent, and in some studies, police-transported survival rates are better, for victims of violence."

The idea of scoop and run was pioneered in Philadelphia, a city with multiple trauma centers, in which police have routinely driven shooting victims to emergency rooms in police cars for nearly two decades. The authors cannot find evidence of any other police agency adopting such a policy. They also point out that the life-saving benefits in Philadelphia may depend heavily on the proximity to trauma centers, or even standard emergency rooms. As Nagin showed in his article in this volume, proximity to emergency medicine is a predictor (if not definitely a cause) of higher rates of death from police shootings. They note that "Pennsylvania, for example, has approximately 2.04 Level I and II trauma centers per million people and 99 percent of its population has access to a trauma center within an hour. In comparison, Arkansas has only recently received its first trauma center—just one in the entire state." Yet the policy has a clear theoretical basis in the biochemistry of blood loss.

Trying to persuade police officers to partake in scoop and run is a challenging task, as I personally experienced in Trinidad & Tobago. With more than three hundred murders a year, police were reluctant to risk disease, lawsuits, and bloodstains on the backseats of their cars. Despite urging by their Police Commissioner in 2014 to 2016, police in Trinidad & Tobago made very little use of either scoop and run or hemostatic bandages, which can substantially slow blood loss. When it came to people they had shot themselves, police were particularly morally reluctant to intervene. Some saw intervention in the deaths as a disruption of justice, especially where the wounded had shot at police officers. Similar dynamics may arise in U.S. cities.

The challenge of reducing the conflicts between police and community are also intensified after a fatal police shooting. Many police agencies refuse to issue any statements at all about the deaths that take place as a result of their officers. Some issue statements, but without an apology, or an apology without an acknowledgement of responsibility. The question of what kinds of statements can best promote reconciliation is an urgent one. It is especially urgent when African Americans are shot by white officers.

Testing alternative ways to address this challenge is difficult to do in field settings. O'Brien and colleagues offer the creative solution of randomly assigning written scenarios to hundreds of anonymous respondents on an internet crowdsource site. The respondents are surveyed for their reactions, and standard measures of police legitimacy are deployed. The method seems like a highly cost-effective way to test a range of statements police could make in the aftermath of fatal police shootings. It is the kind of approach that could benefit from multiple replications, as well as trial-and-error variations.

It is for the latter reason that the specific findings in this article are not nearly as important as the demonstration of the research method. If a program of research across tens or hundreds of such experiments could lead to a systematic review of what approaches work best, police executives could be much more evidence-based in how they respond to arguably unnecessary shootings.

Prospects for Reducing Fatal Shootings with Research

In the final article, the special editor offers a program for action. The program is tempered by the reality that public attention to police fatal shootings is limited. The daily blast of bad news from across the planet leaves little cognitive energy for thinking about American policing. The 2014 "Ferguson moment" of a second great awakening about fatal police shootings seems to have passed, with little concrete change in our national dialogue or policy choices about the problem.

Yet knowledge generated by research has a long lifespan. It does not have a use-by date, after which it should be discarded, unless it is contradicted by new research. The knowledge itself becomes no less reliable just because governments ignore it. Contexts shaping that knowledge may change, but facts from well-specified contexts do not. An army of researchers has been working away at cancer, plane crashes, and many other problems that have actually gotten better in the past half century. Policing may be different in character, yet the complexity in policing can be no greater than for those problems that have been getting better. What we can do is to lower expectations about how quickly our knowledge will grow. At the same time, we can focus on what we already do know can work.

The final article offers a takeaway about what can be done in the short term: do what can be done with the least resistance and with the greatest effect. In practical terms, this means that *campaigners for fewer police fatal shootings can form alliances with campaigners for fewer fatal shootings of police*. That is the message of the article by David Klinger. That is the basis for all the systems changes that he proposes to engineer, with the compliance of police cultures and organizations. The three top priorities suggested are as follows:

- Take away guns—legally—from vulnerable and dangerous people (the Indiana "red flag" law);
- Stop the bleeding—literally—in the seconds after each shooting; and
- Codify the interactional tactics that save lives in citizen encounters with police.

Each of these priorities I propose builds on the reflections offered by this volume's most eminent contributor, former Assistant Attorney General of the United States Laurie O. Robinson.

Reflections

Robinson's commentary addresses all the articles in the volume except the special editor's recommendations. Her comments offer candid assessments of a wide range of problems and prospects for the best use of the evidence in this volume. They draw on a great breadth and depth of political experience, especially in bridging research and policy. She remains cautiously optimistic that progress can be made on fatal police shootings, despite the enormous barriers to change.

Robinson's article identifies four areas of promise. One is the centrality of building trust between police and community and rebuilding it in the aftermath of fatal shootings. While evidence on how to do this best is limited, the substantial research on community policing offers some direction. A second area of promise that she sees is training, especially of the kind reported by Wolfe and colleagues. A third area is, more generally, operational police officers' buy-in for procedures and systems that would make everyone safer. The fourth is building better bridges between policing and academic institutions, which may in some sense be the most difficult. Starting with the very language used to present the research in much of this volume, there is a problem of communication between the two sectors.

The most important message she conveys is the need for scholars of policing to make their research more accessible to the general public, including police. Meaningful and helpful illumination of the dynamics of police shootings puts scholars under substantial pressure to use complex statistics and creative, sometimes complicated, research methods. In using the tools of experts, scholars may limit their audience to people who can take no action. So the research must also speak to those who can act.

Like Robin Engel in this volume, I offer an appeal to academics and "pracademics" of police practice: write a plain language summary of all the research that has implications for policy-makers. Spell out the policy implications, rather than pointing in a general direction. The true promise of evidence-based practice is that it focuses on concrete, applied solutions. By doing so, it can make research better able to serve democracy, even in a world roiled by "irrationality." Testing ways of saving lives can add much clarity, and rationality, to decision-making at all levels of governance. It is, after all, irrational to think that better evidence should win out, just because it is scientifically better than the alternative. Like police legitimacy, better evidence must sell itself in a public dialogue, every day, even with setbacks. The audience is ready and waiting. We need only reach out to it, with clarity and humility.

Notes

1. This shooting can be seen on YouTube at https://www.youtube.com/watch?v=acYz0ZTAtyE.

2. With the recent tragic exception of police shooting to death on London Bridge a convicted terrorist who had just murdered two Cambridge University criminology graduates on November 29, 2019. Even then, London police only shot him to prevent further deaths from what appeared to be his suicide vest full of dynamite.

References

Andersen, Helle Aagaard, and Katrin Mueller-Johnson. 2018. The Danish Crime Harm Index: How it works and why it matters. *Cambridge Journal of Evidence-Based Policing* 2 (1–2): 52–69.

Binder, Arnold, and Peter Scharf. 1980. The violent police-citizen encounter. *The ANNALS of the American Academy of Political and Social Science* 452:111–21.

Blinder, Alan, and Patricia Mazzei. 22 February 2018. As gunman rampaged through Florida school, armed deputy "never went in." *New York Times*.

Bottoms, Anthony E., and Justice Tankebe. 2012. Beyond procedural justice: A dialogic approach to legitimacy in criminal justice. *Journal of Criminal Law & Criminology* 102:119–70.

Davies, William. 5 December 2019. Let's eat badly. Review of *Irrationality: A history of the dark side of reason*, by Justin E. H. Smith. *London Review of Books*, 19–22.

Fyfe, James J. 1986. The split-second syndrome and other determinants of police violence. In *Violent transactions*, eds. A. Campbell and J. Gibbs, 207–25. Oxford: Basil Blackwell.

Graham v. Connor, 490 US 386 (1989).

Haskins, Ron. 2018. Evidence-based policy: The movement, the goals, the issue, the promise. *The ANNALS of the American Academy of Political and Social Science* 678:8–37.

Kisela v. Hughes, 138 S. Ct. 1148 (2018).

Lee, Francis. 16 October 2019. Our research in Hong Kong reveals what people really think of the protesters – and the police. *The Independent*.

Massey, John, Lawrence W. Sherman, and Timothy Coupe. 2019. Forecasting knife homicide risk from prior knife assaults in 4835 local areas of London, 2016–2018. *Cambridge Journal of Evidence-Based Policing* 3 (1–2): 1–20.

Perrow, Charles. 1984. *Normal accidents: Living with high-risk technologies*. New York, NY: Basic Books.

President's Task Force on 21st Century Policing. 2015. *Final report of the President's Task Force on 21st Century Policing*. Washington, DC: U.S. Department of Justice.

Rosenthal, Brian M. 29 July 2017. Police criticize Trump for urging officers not to be "too nice" with suspects. *New York Times*.

Sherman, Lawrence W. 2013. The rise of evidence-based policing: Targeting, testing, and tracking. *Crime and Justice* 42 (1): 377–451.

Sherman, Lawrence W. 24 February 2015. Reducing deadly force in US policing: A view from England and Wales. Statement to the Presidential Task Force on 21st Century Policing. Available from https://www.cam.ac.uk/research/news/police-use-of-force-white-house-told-us-must-learn-from-uk.

Sherman, Lawrence W. 2018. Reducing fatal police shootings as system crashes: Research, theory, and practice. *Annual Review of Criminology* 1:421–29.

Sherman, Lawrence W., Peter W. Neyroud, and Eleanor Neyroud. 2016. The Cambridge Crime Harm Index: Measuring total harm from crime based on sentencing guidelines. *Policing: A Journal of Policy and Practice* 10 (3): 171–83.

U.S. Congress. 2019. Public Law number 116-76, November 27.

Washington Post. 2020. Police shootings data base. Available from https://www.washingtonpost.com/graphics/2019/national/police-shootings-2019.

Weber, Max. 1946. Politics as a vocation. In *Max Weber: Essays in sociology*, trans. and eds. H. H. Gerth and C. Wright Mills. New York, NY: Oxford University Press.

Williams, Simon, and R. Timothy Coupe. 2017. Frequency vs. length of hot spots patrols: A randomised controlled trial. *Cambridge Journal of Evidence-Based Policing* 1 (1): 5–21.

Yip, Paul Siu fai, Chi-kin Law, and Frances Yik Wa Law. 2003. Suicide in Hong Kong: Epidemiological profile and burden analysis, 1981 to 2001. *Hong Kong Medical Journal* 9 (6): 419–26.

Zimring, Franklin E. 2017. *When police kill*. Cambridge, MA: Harvard University Press.

Patterns of Fatal Police Shootings

In recent years, violence by and against the police has been examined from the perspective of organizational accident theory. This article extends that work by reviewing some key ideas, identifying some limitations of organizational accident theory for understanding police-involved violence, and detailing some specific research topics for future empirical exploration. It concludes by offering some specific policy and practice recommendations to reduce police-involved violence.

Keywords: deadly force; police violence; normal accidents; high-reliability organizations; criminal justice policy; tactical reviews

Organizational Accidents and Deadly Police-Involved Violence: Some Thoughts on Extending Theory, Expanding Research, and Improving Police Practice

By
DAVID KLINGER

The production of this volume indicates that the social scientific community may be ready to take seriously Charles Perrow's (1984) work in *Normal Accidents* (and the larger body of academic literature in which it sits) in relation to deadly violence involving the police (Klinger 2005; Sherman 2018). There are sound empirical and theoretical reasons to believe that viewing deadly police-involved violence through the lens provided by Perrow's normal accident paradigm (and related works) holds great promise to accomplish many positive ends. These include (1) enhancing understanding of why and how violent interactions between police officers and citizens come to pass and how and why they play out, (2) reducing the number of police-citizen interactions that include the application of deadly force by police officers, and (3) reducing the number of serious injuries and deaths sustained by police officers.

David Klinger is a professor of criminology and criminal justice at the University of Missouri–St. Louis. Prior to pursuing an academic career, he worked as a patrol officer for the Los Angeles and Redmond (WA) Police Departments.

Correspondence: klingerd@umsl.edu

DOI: 10.1177/0002716219892913

The purposes of this article are to (1) show how looking at deadly police-involved violence through the lens provided by the normal accident paradigm and related social scientific work might accomplish these three goals, (2) identify some limitations of the normal accident and related intellectual traditions for accomplishing these goals, and (3) identify several places where work in these traditions should be extended to better understand and take action on deadly police-involved violence. The work begins with a brief overview of Perrow's (1984) normal accident framework and how this author (Klinger 2005) first applied it to the world of deadly police-involved violence.

Normal Accidents and Deadly Police-Involved Violence

Perrow (1984) developed the core of his normal accident thesis while serving as a consultant to the Presidential Commission investigating the near-catastrophic 1979 accident at the Three Mile Island nuclear power plant near Harrisburg, Pennsylvania. In seeking to understand how this accident came to pass, Perrow identified a pair of intertwined culprits: the incredible *complexity* of the techno-logical system that generated power via nuclear fission in the reactor that failed and the high degree of *coupling* between the complex, critical parts of this sys-tem. He came to believe that the accident in question occurred because the supremely complex and tightly coupled power generation system in place permit-ted an unimaginable series of technological and human failures to cascade out of control, dooming the highly engineered reactor. From this starting point, he developed a general theory of how and why bad things happen in high-tech sys-tems. He then illustrated its utility by applying it to account for disasters that had occurred in a broad array of fields beyond nuclear power generation, such as marine transport and commercial aviation.

Elegant in its simplicity, Perrow's theory holds that bad outcomes can be expected to occur in high-tech systems that involve a high degree of complexity and that are tightly coupled. The more complex the system, the greater the degree of interaction between its elements and the more likely it is that some-thing will go wrong. A problem in one aspect of a system will lead to additional problems in other system parts. Moreover, as systems become more complex, it becomes less likely that humans can quickly apprehend what is going wrong (or has already gone wrong) when something goes awry, which means that things can cascade out of control before the humans "in charge" can react to contain an initial problem. When the elements of a system are closely linked (coupled), only limited buffers exist between them. This means that failure can quickly spread as a problem in one element of the system propagates to other elements and a full-fledged disaster ensues. In asserting that bad outcomes are thus baked into highly complex systems that are tightly coupled, Perrow argued that they are a regular aspect of such systems. And so he dubbed the bad outcomes that he expects to sometimes occur in high-tech systems that are highly complex and tightly cou-pled, "normal accidents."

Klinger (2005) applied Perrow's ideas about complexity and coupling as the paired sources of bad outcomes in high-tech systems to the world of policing, arguing that many situations in which police officers shoot citizens—and where police officers are injured or killed by citizens—can be understood as normal accidents. He noted that when police officers interact with citizens, the parties involved constitute micro social systems that, by definition, have some degree of coupling and some degree of complexity. Those dimensions are a necessary consequence of at least two humans (at least one officer and at least one citizen) being located in a shared physical environment whose parts can interact with the involved human actors in many ways. During police-citizen encounters, then, both (1) how involved parties act and (2) features of the environment in which such events occur can influence the actions of the humans involved and the outcome(s) of these encounters. When officers are within arm's reach of suspected criminals who possess firearms, for example, it is more likely that they will shoot such suspects, that they will be injured or killed by such suspects, or that both outcomes will occur than would be the case if the involved officers were several yards away behind a barrier. So the tighter the coupling between citizen and officer, the greater the likelihood of injury to both.

On the complexity side, as the number of citizens and officers involved in police-citizen encounters increases, the greater the likelihood of unexpected interactions (1) between the humans involved and (2) with features of the physical environment, both of which can lead to citizen and officer injury.

Klinger (2005) identified the tragic 1999 incident in which four New York City police officers shot an unarmed man named Amadou Diallo as a classic instance of a normal accident police shooting. He explained how tight coupling and a high degree of interactive complexity during the incident led the involved officers to fire a total of 41 shots at a man who posed no threat whatsoever to anyone. Klinger also asserted that police officers' use of tactics that reduce coupling and complexity can reduce the likelihood that any given police-citizen encounter will involve deadly violence either by or against the police. For example, he noted that creating or keeping distance from armed citizens reduces the degree of coupling between officers and such citizens, detailed why having just one officer talking with and/or giving commands to armed citizens reduces the degree of complexity in the micro social systems created when multiple officers respond to such incidents, and explained how both tactics lower the odds that any of the police involved will discharge their firearms.

Deadly Police-Involved Violence and High-Reliability Organizations

Klinger's (2005) approach to the matter of understanding deadly police-involved violence and reducing negative outcomes was decidedly micro level; he focused on individual police-citizen interactions as the object of inquiry and analysis. More recently, Pickering and Klinger (2016) expanded the scope of inquiry and analysis of deadly police-involved violence in the normal accident tradition to include the meso and macro levels, incorporating a post-Perrow literature that developed the concept of "high-reliability organizations" (HROs; see, e.g., Roberts 1989, 1990). The focus of HRO analysis is to explain why many tightly coupled and highly complex human-created systems rarely, if ever, experience the sorts of accidents that Perrow wrote about. The HRO literature suggests that the key to avoiding bad outcomes in risky systems is to create cultures that promote and demand high performance at all levels of organizations whose work includes high-risk undertakings. Such HROs operate in many institutional fields—such as commercial aviation, the U.S. Navy's aircraft carrier fleet, and electrical grid operations—but all share certain cultural character-istics. Pickering and Klinger (2016) detailed these features, then argued that both individual police organizations and American policing writ large should adopt them, asserting that doing so would improve police performance and thereby reduce the amount of deadly police-involved violence in the United States.

At its core, Pickering and Klinger's (2016) argument is that police officers and organizations should develop what HRO theorists have dubbed "mindfulness," a proactive approach to dealing with risk that seeks to (1) prevent bad things from happening and (2) reduce the damage that is incurred on the rare occasions that such misfortunes come to pass (see, e.g., Weick and Sutcliffe 2001). Mindfulness consists of five interrelated attributes among members of organizations and organizational units:

1) *Preoccupation with failure*, which means not resting on one's laurels but, rather, seeking to identify and ameliorate any and all deviations from proper procedure, no matter how small and regardless of whether the deviation led to any sort of negative outcome.
2) *Reluctance to simplify interpretations*, which means consciously not follow-ing the natural human tendency to simplify the vast complexity in the world around us but, rather, keeping an open mind to alternative meanings of what might be going on in any given instance.
3) *Sensitivity to operations*, which means paying attention to the changes that are occurring or have occurred in any situation to adapt operations to address the new reality.
4) *Commitment to resilience*, which means (a) always being alert to the possibil-ity that problems will arise and (b) having the mindset and capacity to address problems before they grow, propagate, or lead to worse problems.
5) *Deference to expertise*, which means ensuring that the person, group, or unit possessing the greatest degree of expertise in a given arena possesses the authority and means to address challenges in that given arena when they arise.

Pickering and Klinger (2016) then drew on a related literature to argue that the key to developing that sort of mindful approach to police operations is the development of something called "safety culture." Reason (1997, 194) asserts that safety cultures are "informed cultures" that are "the product of individual and group values, attitudes, competencies, and patterns of behavior" that are per-petuated by "communications founded on mutual trust, shared perceptions of the importance of safety, and by confidence in the efficiency of preventative measures." Reason further asserts that for organizations to have the informed safety culture that will permit mindful, highly reliable performance in the face of high risk, they must possess four distinct subcultures:

1) A *reporting culture* in which organizational members feel emboldened to notify the powers that be when procedures are not followed or when something goes awry.
2) A *just culture* in which punishments for mistakes are rare (because few of them come from a malign heart), punishments that are meted out are fair, and organizational members are rewarded for providing information about problems.
3) A *flexible culture* in which the organization, subunits, and individuals have the freedom and the power to adapt to changing circumstances.
4) A *learning culture* in which safety-relevant information is available to all organizational members who might benefit from it, exchanged between those members who should possess it, and disseminated throughout the organization.

After laying out the elements of mindfulness and safety culture in the context of police operations, Pickering and Klinger (2016, 37) concluded "that if American police departments were to develop cultures of safety rooted in sound tactical and administrative practice that they would, over time, perform with notably higher levels of tactical proficiency, which would, in turn, lead to fewer officer injuries and fewer controversial shootings." In so doing, they challenged both individual police departments and American policing in its entirety to take these steps. By shifting the intellectual gaze from the micro level of Klinger's (2005) encounter-focused work to the meso (police departments and departmental subunits) and macro (American policing writ large) levels of analysis, Pickering and Klinger expanded the scope of theorizing about deadly police-involved violence in the normal accident tradition. They also made more concrete violence-reduction policy recommendations, extending well beyond those contained in Klinger's initial application of Perrow's (1984) paradigm to the high-risk world of police-citizen interactions.

Theirs is by no means the last word on viewing deadly police-involved violence through the lenses provided by Perrow and the HRO theorists, however. In fact, as evidenced by the publication of Sherman's (2018) aforementioned recent review of deadly police violence, there is much work to be done. The remainder of this article seeks to further that work.[1]

Affirming and Expanding the Scope of What Is Being Studied

Perhaps the first thing that needs to be done is to reiterate something that was explicit in the work of both Klinger (2005) and Pickering and Klinger (2016), but that Sherman (2018) treats as an afterthought: the utility of the work in the organizational accident tradition applies to *all* deadly violence that might occur in police-citizen interactions, not just the use of firearms by police officers. In his seminal piece, Klinger (2005) repeatedly stated that his application of Perrow's (1984) normal accident paradigm applied equally to the use of deadly force by the police and to deadly violence directed against police officers by citizens (and he spilt a good bit of ink on a case study of deadly violence against the police, detailing how the murder of Tacoma [WA] police officer Bill Lowry in August 1997 can be understood as a normal accident). While Pickering and Klinger (2016) did not include any detailed case studies, they devoted considerable attention to the matter of deadly violence against the police. Sherman (2018), on the other hand, mentioned the deadly risks that police officers face only in passing and never explicitly incorporated this aspect of deadly police-involved violence into either his theorizing or any of his policy recommendations. And this makes sense, because his essay was explicitly focused on reducing citizen death from police firearms. But as we move forward, we should not lose sight of the utility that the organizational accident literature holds for furthering understanding of and reducing deadly police-involved violence beyond police gunfire directed at citizens.

In this connection, there are at least two other forms of deadly police-involved violence where the organizational accident framework would appear to hold great promise. The first of these is situations where police bullets strike citizens that officers did not intend to shoot. Unfortunately, police officers sometimes shoot citizens they have no intention of striking with bullets. This can happen in three different fashions: (1) when police officers unintentionally discharge their firearms and a round (or rounds) hits a citizen, (2) when they intentionally fire their guns at suspected criminals and a wayward bullet (or bullets) strikes another citizen, and (3) when they otherwise intentionally fire their weapons at nonhuman targets (such as dogs) and a wayward bullet (or bullets) strikes a human.[2] As is the case with much about the use of deadly force by police officers, we do not know how often police officers shoot citizens they did not intend to shoot, but we do know that it sometimes happens. For example, Leen and Horwitz (1998) report that multiple citizens were killed in the 1990s by bullets accidentally fired by Washington, D.C., police officers. In 2015, officers in three different jurisdictions in three separate cases unintentionally killed citizens with stray bullets fired at suspected criminals (Klinger and Slocum 2017), and Los Angeles Police Department officers unintentionally killed two women in separate incidents in summer 2018—one during a shootout with a car-jacking suspect as he fled into a grocery store (Lloyd 2018); the other when officers shot at a man who was in the process of slitting a hostage's throat, and some of the bullets aimed at him struck her (Fedschun 2018). And where shots intentionally fired at things besides criminal suspects go, in 2015 a police officer in Iowa shot and killed a mother at a family dispute when he slipped on some ice as he sought to shoot the family dog that was approaching him (Clayworth 2018).[3]

A second area where it would appear that the normal accident framework has applicability is police fratricide (aka "friendly fire" or "blue-on-blue" shootings)—cases in which police officers shoot fellow officers. The New York State Task Force on Police-on-Police Shootings (Stone et al. 2010) identified twenty-six police officers who had been fatally shot by fellow officers during police operations between 1981 and 2009. Other officers had been killed in blue-on-blue scenarios before 1981, and others have been killed since, the last one at the time this article was completed (in March 2019) being Detective Brian Simonsen of the New York City Police Department. He was killed in February 2019 by a round fired by a fellow officer when several members of the NYPD responded to a robbery-in-progress call. The accounts of the twenty-six cases contained in the New York State Task Force report indicate that many (perhaps all?) of them involved Perrow's twin culprits of tight coupling and interactive complexity. News accounts of Detective Simonsen's demise (e.g., Katersky and Shapiro 2019) also indicate that both forces were present in this police fratricide.[4]

The fact that many unintentional police shootings of citizens and police by fellow officers can be understood as normal accidents means that Perrow's (1984) paradigm would appear to be relevant to all forms of deadly police-involved violence. Because the framework is so simple, with just two variables, it is also quite parsimonious. And because the hallmark of sound theory is parsimony and predictive power (e.g., Ekland-Olson and Gibbs 2017), it would appear that the application of Perrow's normal accident framework to deadly police-involved violence provides a theoretically sound basis for explaining how and why the small portion of the millions of police-citizen interactions that take place each year in the United States that turn extremely violent do so. And as we see below, it—coupled with the HRO literature—offers theoretically sound guidance for how to make these rare events rarer still.

Some Limitations and Challenges in Applying the Normal Accident Framework to Deadly Police-Involved Violence

It is important to note that I am not claiming that all instances where someone is seriously injured or killed during a police-citizen encounter are normal accidents. Perrow has observed (1984, 2012) that not all instances where bad things happen in high-tech systems occur because of tight coupling and high complexity; operators make errors and planners make conscious choices to cut corners and otherwise do things in ways that lead to disaster, for example, independent of system complexity and coupling. The same holds true for deadly police-involved violence: not all injuries and deaths suffered by police officers and citizens come from the tight coupling and interactive complexity present in police operations. Counted among the sources of avoidable shootings by police officers are negligent weapons handling (as appears to be the 2019 case where one St. Louis police officer shot another; Byers 2019) and basic criminal intent to harm independent of any justification (as in the 2015 shooting of Walter Scott by a North Charleston, SC, police officer; Edwards and Andone 2017). Injuries to police sustained during ambushes are further examples, as well as when officers are simply at the wrong place at the wrong time (e.g., a police officer driving into a gun battle between rival gangs on opposite sides of a city street). What we do not know is what portion of each of the various forms of deadly violence (i.e., officers being shot, officers intentionally shooting citizens, officers shooting citizens unintentionally, and police fratricide) can properly be considered normal accidents versus what portion arises from sources besides high complexity and tight coupling. So we need to (1) map out all of the logical sources of preventable shootings by police officers to understand what portion of them falls into each of the different categories identified and (2) classify situations where police officers or innocent citizens suffer serious injury or death as either normal accidents versus some other kind of event.

This effort to distinguish between various sorts of deadly police-involved violence must also include police shootings that under any reasonable construction of matters could not be avoided no matter what officers did (absent a willingness to permit assailants to seriously harm or kill them or innocent citizens). Among these sorts of situations would be those in which

- officers shoot gunmen who are in the process of seriously harming or murdering innocent citizens (e.g., during an "active shooter" event),
- officers return fire at assailants who ambushed or otherwise attacked them with no notice, and
- situations in which officers shoot hostage takers who threaten to kill a hostage(s) and have the capability to carry out the threat.

When police officers shoot suspects in circumstances such as these, they are simply reacting to life-threatening situations that they did nothing to create and fulfilling their mandate to protect innocent life (e.g., Fabre 2007; Klinger 2004). In terms of the normal accident shooting framework, the police can be logically viewed as causative agents regarding only those aspects of interactions with citizens that are in their control. Because actions of murderous citizens are simply beyond the control of the police, shootings of the sort discussed in this paragraph fall outside the bounds of what can be logically viewed as normal accidents.[5]

Returning to those shootings by and of the police that *can* be understood as normal accidents, we need to develop a better understanding of the particular aspects of coupling and complexity that matter most. Is it coupling of human beings (and of what "sorts" of people: police officers, suspected criminals, hostages, bystanders, and so on), coupling of humans with the physical environment, increased human complexity (and of what "sorts" of people; see above), increased complexity of the physical environment, or whatever else might be going on? Beyond case studies such as those discussed in Klinger (2005) and Sherman (2018), we have essentially no empirical evidence about the specific facets of complexity and coupling that tend to give rise to normal accident shootings. Similarly, we have little empirical information about which specific sorts of police decoupling and complexity-reduction actions are associated with avoiding shootings. So while we should move forward with the strong theoretical guidance provided by the normal accident framework, we should also seek to develop a strong empirical base that tests and refines any theoretically informed proposals for policies and practices. And consideration of the policing and organizational accident literatures suggests three additional matters that would appear to be worthy of specific attention in this effort. The first is "practical drift."

Practical Drift

The concept of "practical drift" was developed by Scoot Snook (2000) in his analysis of a 1994 incident that occurred in the skies above northern Iraq. Two U.S. Air Force pilots shot down a pair of U.S. Army helicopters in a no-fly zone when they mistook the aircraft for Russian-made helicopters flown by the Iraq military. As Snook sought to understand how the series of mistakes that led to this tragic friendly-fire incident occurred, he noted that there were well-established de-confliction/safety protocols in place to prevent such an occurrence. He also noted that they had not been wholly followed in the hours, minutes, and seconds leading up to the shoot down. His investigation into the matter further disclosed that the failure to follow protocols was not a one-off that suddenly appeared out of the blue. Rather, it was an established practice among U.S. military personnel that had evolved as flight operations in the area where the shoot down occurred went on over an extended period of time. As time passed and deviations from protocol produced no problems, the personnel involved came to view the deviations as acceptable ways of doing their daily work. Snook coined the term "practical drift" to describe this evolutionary process that involves "the slow steady uncoupling of local practice from written procedure" (p. 24).

As Klinger (2005) noted, police officers receive training in at least the basics of the sorts of tactics noted above in this article (e.g., keeping distance and using cover[6]) that are designed to keep them safe and reduce the odds of unnecessary shootings. As Sherman (2018) and others (see, e.g., especially Fyfe 1986) have noted, however, police officers do not always hew to the basics of their training. Why might this be? There could be several reasons, but practical drift might well be among the top sources.

After arguing for police officers to always use sound tactics, Klinger (2005) pointed out that in the vast majority of police-citizen encounters, it actually matters not one whit whether officers follow proper tactical protocol because the vast majority of the people they encounter would never seek to harm them. Thus, even when they perform poorly, officers the vast majority of the time will neither suffer any injury nor shoot their way out of some danger that could have been avoided by using sound tactics. This could be a major reason why officers do not always utilize sound tactics during interactions with citizens: it simply does not matter the vast majority of the time. Because it does not matter, because being tactically astute takes time and energy, and because police officers have many other matters that compete for their time and energy (e.g., community meetings, answering radio calls, filing reports), it might be quite tempting for officers to take tactical shortcuts.[7] Over time, as officers get away with taking tactical shortcuts, tactically unsound practices become the new norm. In other words, to slightly alter Snook (2000, 24), "the slow steady uncoupling of local [police] practice from . . . [sound tactical] procedure" may well take place, as for practical reasons officers develop ways to handle their business that deviate from their tactical training.

As efforts directed at improving police officers' tactical performance to reduce deadly police-involved violence move forward, the possibility that practical drift plays a role in police officers' not following training is worthy of serious attention. We know that police officers do not always follow their tactical training, so we need to figure out ways to improve police performance. The notion of practical drift gives us a powerful theoretical starting point for developing a sound understanding of the causes of police failure in this arena and for building ways to realize the improved performance that we need from our police. These twined points link directly to the HRO literature, especially its focus on "preoccupation with failure."

Revenge Effects

Another matter worthy of attention is the role that technology plays in the realm of deadly police-involved violence. The modern police operate in a world where technology is pervasive and where new technologies that are designed to advance the police mission are constantly coming online (e.g., the body-worn cameras and computerized evidence management systems that have become commonplace in the last two decades). But along with the intended positives that come from bringing technology into the world of policing comes a downside. In his 1997 book, *Why Things Bite Back: Technology and the Revenge of Unintended Consequences*, Edward Tenner discusses how technological innovations that are designed to accomplish positive ends ofttimes have the perverse effect of producing the negative occurrence they are designed to prevent. He calls such consequences "revenge effects." From antibiotics that give rise to resistant microbes that make fighting bacterial infections more difficult, to the widespread use of air-conditioning units in urban areas that raise outside temperatures and thus make city summers even more oppressive, Tenner describes how humans are repeatedly confronted with the fact that technologies we develop and apply to help us lead better, safer, and more productive lives can "bite back," wreaking unintentional havoc along with the benefits they provide.

In the world of policing, the potential for revenge effects is likely quite large. Serious scholarly digging is needed to unearth all of the many ways that new technologies might increase risks for police officers and citizens. But cursory consideration of the matter in light of Perrow's work discloses one arena worthy of immediate attention for deadly police-involved violence. Perrow (1984) notes that safety devices often turn out to have the paradoxical effect of actually increasing risk and sometimes leading to disaster. One species of police safety device are less-lethal weapons such as impact munitions and conducted energy devices (CEDs) such as Tasers. Officers can employ these tools to keep their distance from suspects who might well harm them if officers get in close proximity to them. In other words, these devices can reduce the degree of coupling between officers and potentially dangerous citizens until the police believe it is safe to approach and take into custody such individuals. But that theory does not always work in practice.

Klinger (2005) detailed the role that the presence of less-lethal impact munitions played in the murder of Tacoma SWAT officer Bill Lowry. Lowry was murdered by a barricaded gunman when he and some of his SWAT teammates left a point of cover after Lowry shot the suspect with a pair of impact munitions while the gunman stepped away from his rifle. Unfortunately, the gunman retrieved his rifle before Lowry and the other Tacoma SWAT officers could take him into custody. As Klinger noted, neither Lowry nor any of his teammates would have left their cover point absent their belief that the impact munitions had temporarily incapacitated the suspect. Because the less-lethal technology that the Tacoma SWAT team employed led Lowry and his teammates into the suspect's murderous gunfire, Lowry's death is a classic revenge effect: the "safety device" that was employed led to precisely what it was supposed to prevent: human death.

How many other police officers have been killed or seriously injured in the wake of the employment of some technology that was intended to keep them safe? How many citizens have been shot by police officers when some sort of nonlethal device failed to have its intended effect, when officers got closer than they normally would have to employ the device and then fired their service weapons when it did not work? These questions should be a pressing part of our research agenda.

Beyond seeking answers to these questions, there is other work on the subject of deadly revenge effects in police work that should be undertaken, work with a more directly pragmatic edge. Tenner (1997) asserted that many species of revenge effects are unknowable until they surface in whatever field a given technology is situated because humans cannot possibly envision all the potential implications of every technology. But he also noted that the history of technology is replete with cases where people did a remarkable job of thinking through the potential downsides of technologies and taking steps that prevent them from coming to fruition. In some cases this occurred prior to the initial application of the technology. More often, however, it occurred only after some specific disaster prompted people to consider where other potential revenge effects might lie. Given this, it would appear to be a worthy endeavor for police practitioners, policy-makers, and other interested parties to identify and catalogue the revenge effect injuries and deaths that have already occurred in policing and to seriously ponder the possible revenge effects that have not yet surfaced. Doing these two things, and then creating policy and practices based on the information gleaned, might well reduce the incidence of the deadly revenge effects that have already manifest and prevent others from surfacing.

The Human Factor: Fog, Friction, Fear, Fatigue, and Perception

While new technologies (and their attendant potential for revenge effects) will almost certainly continue to flow into the world of policing, three things that will not change are that (1) the officers who police our nation will remain human,[8] (2) the citizens with whom they deal will likewise remain human, and (3) the sorts of police-citizen interactions that give rise to deadly violence will therefore remain conflicts between human beings. The quest to understand and reduce deadly organizational accidents in police work must therefore include attention to certain features of the nature of human conflict.

Fog and friction

Students of war have long noted that humans in conflict often suffer from imperfect knowledge of their opponents, their opponents' capabilities, their own capabilities, and many other critical aspects of the conflict at hand. Commonly called *fog* (as in "the fog or war"), this imperfect knowledge can lead (and has led) to military disaster (e.g., Hale 1896). Fog has a close cousin that has also led to disaster during war: *friction*, that aspect of human conflict that renders the simple difficult and the difficult nearly impossible (Clausewitz 1873). As Heal (2000) notes, both fog and friction are forces that officers must battle to successfully resolve conflicts with citizens. To avoid normal accidents that might otherwise claim both police and citizen victims, scholars, policy-makers, and police practitioners should all examine the pernicious roles that fog and friction play in police-involved conflicts[9] and work to develop policies and practices that minimize their effects.

Fear

Another factor that can play a critical role in how conflict plays out is human emotion, especially fear. Klinger (2001, 2004), for example, has noted that a sizable percentage of police officers involved in shootings reported feeling fear at some point(s) during these events. Collins (2008, 2009) has argued that an emotion he calls "confrontational tension/fear (ct/f)" is typically present when humans find themselves in conflict with others, that it must be overcome for violence to occur, and that, when it is overcome, violence is "typically incompetent at hitting its desired targets" (2009, 567). The general notion that emotions play a critical role in human violence, and especially Collins's contention, would appear to be highly relevant to deadly police-involved violence of the normal accident variety (especially where errant police bullets go; see point three in the next paragraph).

As a general matter, a better understanding of how such emotions can drive events when police officers are in conflict with citizens might inform polices and training that can enhance the capacity of officers to avoid normal accident shootings. Developing ways for officers to be competent when they must use violence would on its face seem to enhance the capacity of officers to (1) avoid at least some shootings (e.g., using nonlethal force competently can sometimes forestall the escalation to lethal force); (2) protect themselves, fellow officers, and innocent citizens from harm at the hands of aggressors (by defeating the aggressor with gunfire before he or she can do harm); and (3) avoid collateral injuries to officers and citizens from errant police gunfire.

Fatigue and perception

Vila (2000) has noted that fatigue can greatly affect police officers' performance in various critical tasks, and Klinger and Brunson (2009) have noted that the vast majority of police officers involved in shootings experience perceptual anomalies (such as time slowing down, auditory occlusion, and tunnel vision). It is logical to suspect that both fatigue and perceptual anomalies could play roles in at least some normal accident shootings. Consequently, a more thorough understanding of these two phenomena and of the roles they play in deadly police-involved violence is warranted.

One point that Klinger and Brunson (2009) made about the presence of perceptual anomalies among police officers during shootings is that officers' actions during these incidents might sometimes be rooted in definitions of these situations that do not fully correspond with objective reality. That perceptual anomalies during encounters involving gunfire might alter officers' understandings of these events points to the larger fact that as human beings, police officers' actions will always be rooted in their definitions of the situations in which they are involved. There is a large volume of literature on how humans make sense of our world and how the mental models we create then guide our behavior (e.g., Thomas and Thomas 1928; Weick 1995). This literature includes a decent dose of work on how faulty sensemaking can lead people to act in ways that create disaster (e.g., Wieck 1993). In fact, the early pages of Perrow's (1984) seminal work includes multiple references to the role that faulty mental models play in creating normal accidents.

Perrow (1984) and others (e.g., Weick 1993) who have identified the construction of erroneous definitions of situations as a critical component of organizational accidents have also argued that disasters can often be avoided by helping individuals to make better sense of the situations they face. Some of the most egregious police shootings that fall into the organizational accident category include faulty sensemaking (see Sherman's [2018] discussion of the Tamir Rice shooting, for example). And at least some murders of police officers occur when officers misread details of the events in which they are enmeshed (recall that Bill Lowry and his SWAT teammates believed that the suspect who killed Lowry had been incapacitated by the impact munitions that Lowry fired). Given this, researchers and practitioners interested in better understanding and reducing deadly police-involved violence should look to both the general literature on sensemaking and the aspects of the organizational accident literature that address mental-model construction (e.g., refusal to simplify interpretations and sensitivity to operations) for guidance as they move forward.

Organizational and Institutional Contexts

The last several sections have focused on the micro-level matter of individual incidents. Our attention now turns to the meso and macro levels of analysis by applying James Doyle's informative 2010 essay, "Learning from Error in American Criminal Justice." Doyle's essay provides a helpful link between the organizational accident literature on one hand and the general issue of bad justice system outcomes on the other. Doyle noted that the American criminal justice system is imperfect and that practitioners throughout the system are well aware of these imperfections. He also argued that the social and political reactions to a 1996 U.S. Department of Justice (DOJ) report on wrongful convictions (Connors et al. 1996) created a cultural medium in which positive reforms to reduce the number of criminal justice errors might well be nigh. After reviewing the highlights of the DOJ report, Doyle discussed some of the reforms that came about to avoid additional wrongful convictions. He argued that many of the wrongful convictions identified in the report (as well as many other such cases) could be understood as organizational accidents.

Doyle (2010) then argued that the criminal justice system should change those aspects of their organizational and institutional cultures that give rise to mistakes as a means to reduce the number of errors that occur within the system. A key to accomplishing this sort of change was to shift the critical gaze of reform efforts away from punishment of *individual* workers who have done wrong (i.e., the proverbial "bad apple") and toward the specific aspects of the criminal justice *system* that lead to mistakes.[10] He further asserted that all elements of the system should make continual improvement of performance a core aspect of their work effort. He pointed to civilian aviation and medicine as two fields in the United States that had moved away from seeking to blame individual workers for all bad outcomes, had set continuous improvement as professional goals, and had thereby developed the above-mentioned safety cultures of which Reason (1997) wrote. In light of the successes of the medical and aviation industries, Doyle urged the American criminal justice system to follow suit and thereby reduce errors throughout its ranks.

Doyle (2010) identified careful reviews of incidents as a key driver of the development and perpetuation of the safety cultures built by the aviation and medical industries. After many fits and starts, both aviation and medicine developed systems that required or permitted (depending on the nature of the incident in question) detailed reviews of individual incidents that included, or *could have* included, negative outcomes (sometimes called "near misses"). These review systems also included looking across incidents to identify any commonalities or trends among them. Rooted in the notion that human beings are bound to make mistakes, these review systems seek to identify the *structural* sources of medical and aviation errors and then devise ways to correct them so that individual pilots and medical workers would make fewer errors.

Doyle's (2010) call for the American criminal justice system to learn from the review systems in medicine and aviation was focused on reducing wrongful convictions, but he argued that the ameliorative principles he extracted from these other fields and from the organizational accident literature could be applied to other issues in the criminal justice system. He even mentioned in passing officer-involved shootings (p. 134). Thus, Doyle set the intellectual table for both the initial musings of Pickering and Klinger (2016) and Sherman (2018) about examining cases where officers use deadly force to learn productive lessons and for the more detailed discussion of reviewing police-involved incidents that appears below.

Reviewing Police-Citizen Interactions

An initial question that must be answered regarding policing is what incidents get reviewed? In line with what gets reviewed in medicine and aviation, Doyle (2010) argued that criminal justice reviews should include not just bad outcomes but also near misses. This makes sense, for we should want to learn both from mistakes and from situations that *almost* had bad outcomes, instances where "but for the grace of God" a bad outcome would or could have happened. In medicine, and especially aviation, the parameters of what constitutes a near miss are spelled out. But this is not the case in law enforcement. So we will need to figure out what sorts of things in police operations constitute the near misses to be reviewed.

Even adding near misses to the review portfolio, however, still leaves our review gaze too narrow. We should also wish to review all instances in which police officers discharge their firearms, regardless of whether they included any sort of error by the officers involved. This is so because we should want to learn all we can about how to improve police performance (and perhaps even influence citizen behavior). And there may be small matters that did not contribute to the violent outcome but where the officers could do better and that might be relevant to future events.

We should expand our review gaze further still to *all* police encounters with citizens, for three reasons. First, because no police-citizen interaction is ever handled perfectly by the officers involved, each one offers an opportunity for identifying small matters that did not lead to either violence or a near miss but that, in some other context or situation, could have led to disaster. After all, as Perrow (1984) reminds us, normal accidents often arise from unexpected interactions between small mistakes that in isolation would not matter but that interact in specific circumstances to create disaster. The second reason all police-citizen interactions should be subject to review is that reviews of even the most mundane can identify the good things done by the officers involved, which can serve as reminders to both the involved officers and to other officers about the importance of following sound tactical procedures. The third potential value of the "review everything" approach is that such practice might just unearth a new tactic that an officer (or officers) used that prevented a situation from spinning out of control. Tactics in policing are not static. We have not identified the perfect way to handle each and every situation that officers might face. Some things that might arise in a given police-citizen encounter might have never been seen before. Tactics need to evolve to meet new conditions. Also, it may be that some problem that has long perplexed the police is resolved by a fresh tactical approach that some officer(s) took to a situation. Avoiding bloodshed through a new approach to a situation with a high potential for bloodshed is a good thing. But if knowledge about this new approach is not shared, it is a wasted opportunity for the law enforcement community to learn from good police work. The way to share positive developments is through a review process that will first identify it and then disseminate the knowledge gained far and wide in policing.

Ideas for Structuring Operational Reviews

In a nation with some eighteen thousand separate police agencies spread across fifty states and the federal government, and with officers involved in millions of encounters with citizens each year, it will not be an easy task to construct a review system that includes all of the pieces called for above. Fortunately, there are some tactical review practices in place in some realms of American policing that can be used as starting points. These can help to build the sort of robust tactical review system that can help reduce deadly police-involved violence.

Many police departments include reviews of the tactics used by the officer(s) on-scene whenever one or more officers in their employ discharges their firearm. Such reviews can result in critiques of the officers' performance, noting areas for improvement if any were uncovered.[11] Some police agencies already call in outside experts to review officers' actions in the wake of major incidents that result in police deaths, citizen deaths, or both (e.g., Stewart 2009). And many police training conferences include incident debriefs in which officers who participated in major incidents offer detailed information about what transpired, including "lessons learned." In short, there already exists a limited tradition in American policing of reviewing with an eye toward improving future performance incidents in which officers discharge their firearms and incidents in which officers are seriously injured or killed.

This tradition could be extended by developing state and/or regional tactical review bodies that would examine (1) every incident in which officers in a given region or state fired their guns and (2) every incident in which officers in that state or region were seriously injured or killed by purposeful citizen action. Staffing such review bodies and the scope of their charge would be important considerations, as police agencies would need to feel comfortable having an external body reviewing incidents involving their officers, and the reviews would need to be fruitful. One way to accomplish these goals would be to limit membership of these review bodies to experienced police officers who have demonstrated tactical acumen and to limit their charge to reviewing and reporting on the tactical aspects of the events reviewed.

But if postincident reviews are limited to instances where officers shoot or are injured or killed, many learning opportunities would be missed. This has long been recognized by at least one segment of the policing community: special weapons and tactics teams. SWAT teams have for many years commonly conducted informal reviews of all incidents they have handled to identify both where they performed well and areas where performance can be improved (Klinger and Rojek 2005). Some version of these sorts of reviews could be incorporated within other units of larger police departments. The proposed state/regional tactical review boards could also be used to review *samples* from smaller agencies of larger police operations in which no officers were injured or discharged their weapons. Just how such samples would be drawn would need to be determined. But the proposed tactical review boards could certainly be built to handle a substantial number of these sorts of cases. With the widespread use of in-car and body-worn cameras, the materials reviewed could include the video and audio of many encounters. In a similar vein, supervisors in individual police agencies could conduct tactical reviews of samples of in-car and body-worn camera recordings and interview the involved officers about what transpired.[12] Over time, regularized supervisory and external reviews of mundane incidents could help to build a culture of safety within police agencies, in regions and states, and throughout American policing writ large.

Another avenue for reviews of mundane police-citizen encounters could actually make for truly comprehensive reviews of all of the millions of interactions that occur each year. The line officers who are interacting with citizens can conduct self and group reviews of their tactical performances in the wake of each encounter. When I was a young police officer in Los Angeles in the 1980s, I was trained to both (1) review in my own mind each incident I handled to identify how well my tactical performance comported with what I was trained to do, and (2) discuss with whichever other officers were on-scene how well we tactically performed as a collective. As the years passed and I worked for and with other police departments, however, I was surprised to learn that this sort of regular tactical review was not common to American policing. It should be. And if this were to become a reality across the United States, American policing would have a grassroots-built version of the preoccupation with failure that HRO theorists maintain is a critical component of the safety culture that can forestall organizational accidents.

One challenge with these proposed reviews is disseminating the lessons learned from the reviews that would take place. While much of the knowledge gained from some reviews would necessarily remain local (e.g., within a given officer or groups of officers for the millions of mundane reviews), modern communication technology provides multiple opportunities to spread information in police departments, in regions and states, and across the nation. Already, various websites permit police officers to informally share lessons learned from their experiences on the job. The National Police Foundation has a Near Miss Reporting System where police officers can anonymously report cases in which they believe a bad outcome was narrowly averted. As time moves forward, more formal and more comprehensive reporting and dissemination systems than we have at the time of this writing could be developed that would allow for widespread sharing of lessons learned from line officer self and group reviews, supervisory reviews, departmental reviews, and reviews by regional and state tactical review boards.

Conclusion

The proposed areas of research, policy, and practice addressed above were offered in the spirit of furthering our understanding of the determinants of deadly police-involved violence and reducing injuries to both officers and citizens. They are offered as a direct response to Sherman's (2018) call for a "Second Great Awakening" in police efforts to reduce deadly police-involved violence (albeit with an explicit expansion of his vague mentions of police injuries). Putting in place the various sorts of reviews proposed in this article and maximizing the benefits of such reviews for improving police tactical performance are long-term goals that will likely take years to accomplish. But if they are seen as part of a push to improve the performance of the American criminal justice system overall—as Doyle (2010) has called for—they (or at least some parts of them) may be able to come on line sooner rather than later. And if that comes to pass, the police might come to be viewed as the institution that leads the way in the reduction of justice system organizational accidents that Doyle called for a decade ago.

As others contemplate the worth of specific calls made herein as means to effectuate what Doyle (2010) called for generally in the criminal justice system and what Sherman (2018) called for specifically in policing, there are matters that can be worked on immediately. In the realm of research, academics can further explore the utility of the organizational accident paradigm for understanding deadly police-involved violence. They can empirically investigate specific matters, such as

- which aspects of coupling and complexity matter most in the world of policing,
- the prevalence of revenge effects from technologies designed to make policing safer, and
- the role that practical drift plays in deadly police-involved organizational accidents.

In the practitioner realm, police supervisors, managers, and policy-makers can look to the organizational accident literature for guidance about how to develop the individual, group, organizational, and institutional mindfulness that can lead to the safety culture that can enhance police performance and thereby reduce the level of deadly police-involved violence in the United States.

In sum, if academics and practitioners take seriously the calls that Doyle (2010), Sherman (2018), a few others (e.g., Pickering and Klinger 2016), and this article have made for viewing some bad policing outcomes as organizational accidents and work to reduce them, we may just be able to save a multitude of lives.

Notes

1. From this point forward I use the phrases "organizational accident literature," "organizational accident tradition," and similar terms when referring to the both the normal accident and HRO literatures—a practice consistent with work in the normal accident and HRO traditions (e.g., Reason, 1997)—and use the appropriate specific term when referring to just one of them.

2. The term "wayward bullet" here refers to both bullets that miss what or whom the police are intending to shoot and bullets that strike an intended police target, pass through or bounce off of it, and then strike a human who was not targeted.

3. While it is beyond the scope of this article to take deep dives into any of these cases, the interested reader can use the following links to view body camera footage from the 2015 case in Iowa and the 2018 case in which Los Angeles Police Department (LAPD) bullets killed the female hostage: Iowa Case, https://www.youtube.com/watch?v=PhI00ElQ-JU; LAPD case, https://www.youtube.com/watch?v=BGxAly1TjgM. Even a cursory viewing of these videos indicates that both instances included tight coupling between the various parties involved (both police and citizens) and high degrees of interactive complexity between both the humans involved and the physical environment (and in the Iowa case an animal: the family dog). In other words, they can be understood as normal accidents.

4. While we have no real sense of how often it happens, we know that some citizens who are unintentionally shot by police officers survive their wounds and that some officers shot by their fellows do not suffer fatal wounds. See Simpson (2013) and Fedschun (2019), respectively.

5. At least as far as the police side of the equation goes.

6. Police field tactics are far more involved than the few matters mentioned in this article. A thorough discussion of field tactics lies far beyond the scope of this article. I recommend Heal (2000) as a starting point for those readers interested in obtaining some sense of the scope of police field tactics.

7. Sherman's (2018) discussion of production pressures would appear to be highly relevant here.

8. Unless some sort of dystopian future adumbrated by the film *Robocop* comes to pass, that is.

9. This would include blue-on-blue events in which officers mistake fellow officers for criminal suspects (see, e.g., Stone et al. 2010).

10. This gaze shift lies at the core of Sherman's (2018) call for a "Second Great Awakening" regarding efforts to control deadly police-involved violence.

11. Reviews of this sort are conducted in the wake of all shootings by both LAPD officers and all Los Angeles Sheriff's Department deputies.

12. One challenge here is that police departments typically do not promote people based on tactical acumen. This would have to change for this aspect of the proposed review process to be fruitful. See Pickering and Klinger (2016) for more on this point.

References

Byers, Christine. 29 January 2019. St. Louis officer accused of killing colleague in Russian roulette-like shooting is booked into jail. *St. Louis Post-Dispatch*. Available from www.stltoday.com.

Clausewitz, Carl von. 1873. *On war*. Translated by James J. Graham. London: N. Trübner & Co.

Clayworth, Jason. 12 September 2018. Police officer moments after fatally shooting Iowa mom: I'm "going to prison." *Des Moines Register*. Available from www.desmoinesregister.com.

Collins, Randall. 2008. *Violence: A micro-sociological theory*. Princeton, NJ: Princeton University Press.

Collins, Randall. 2009. The micro-sociology of violence. *British Journal of Sociology* 60 (3): 566–76.

Connors, Edward, Thomas Lundregan, Neal Miller, and Tom McEwen. 1996. *Convicted by juries, exonerated by science: Case studies in the use of DNA evidence to establish innocence after trial*. Washington, DC: National Institute of Justice.

Doyle, James. 2010. Learning from error in American criminal justice. *Journal of Criminal Law and Criminology* 100 (1): 109–48.

Edwards, Meredith, and Dakin Andone. 7 December 2017. Ex-South Carolina cop Michael Slager gets 20 years for Walter Scott killing. *CNN*. Available from www.cnn.com.

Ekland-Olson, Sheldon, and Jack P. Gibbs. 2017. *Science and sociology: Predictive power is the name of the game*. New York, NY: Routledge.

Fabre, Cecile. 2007. Mandatory rescue killings. *Journal of Political Philosophy* 15 (4): 363–84.

Fedschun, Travis. 1 August 2018. LAPD releases video of fatal police shooting of female hostage held at knifepoint. *Fox News*. Available from www.foxnews.com.

Fedschun, Travis. 13 January 2019. Indiana police officer accidentally shot by other cop in dramatic body-camera video. *Fox News*. Available from www.foxnews.com.

Fyfe, James J. 1986. The split-second syndrome and other determinants of police violence. In *Violent transactions*, eds. Anne Campbell and John J. Gibbs, 207–25. Oxford: Basil Blackwell.

Hale, Sir Lonsdale Augustus. 1896. *The fog of war*. London: Edward Stanford.

Heal, Charles "Sid." 2000. *Sound doctrine: A tactical primer*. New York, NY: Lantern.

Katersky, Aaron, and Emily Shapiro. 27 February 2019. NYPD may never determine who fired fatal shot in detective's friendly fire death. *ABC*. Available from abcnews.go.com.

Klinger, David A. 2001. *Police responses to officer-involved shootings*. Final report to National Institute of Justice. Washington, DC: National institute of Justice.

Klinger, David A. 2004. *Into the kill zone: A cop's eye view of deadly force*. San Francisco, CA: Jossey-Bass.

Klinger, David A. 2005. *Social theory and the street cop: The case of deadly force*. Ideas in American Policing, Essay no. 7. Washington, DC: Police Foundation.

Klinger, David A., and Rod Brunson. 2009. Police officers' perceptual distortions during lethal force situations: Informing the reasonableness standard. *Criminology and Public Policy* 8 (1): 117–40.

Klinger, David A., and Jeff Rojek 2005. *A multi-method study of police special weapons and tactics teams*. Final report to National Institute of Justice. Washington, DC: National Institute of Justice.

Klinger, David A., and Lee Ann Slocum. 2017. A critical assessment of an analysis of a journalistic compendium of citizens killed by police gunfire. *Criminology and Public Policy* 16 (1): 349–62.

Leen, Jeff, and Sari Horwitz. 18 November 1998. Armed and unready: City pays for failure to train officers with sophisticated weapon. *Washington Post*.

Lloyd, Jonathan. 24 July 2018. Round fired by officer killed Trader Joe's store manager in Silver Lake shootout: LAPD. *NBC Los Angeles*. Available from www.nbclosangeles.com.

Perrow, Charles. 1984. *Normal accidents: Living with high risk technologies*. Princeton, NJ: Princeton University Press.

Perrow, Charles. December 2012. Getting to catastrophe: Concentrations, complexity and coupling. *The Montreal Review*.

Pickering, Jordan C., and David A. Klinger. 2016. Enhancing police legitimacy by promoting safety culture. In *The politics of policing: Between force and legitimacy*, 21–39. Bingley: Emerald Group Publishing.

Reason, James. 1997. *Managing the risks of organizational accidents*. Burlington, VT: Ashgate Publishing Company.

Roberts, Karlene H. 1989. New challenges in organizational research: High reliability organizations. *Organization and Environment* 3 (2): 111–25.

Roberts, Karlene H. 1990. Some characteristics of one type of high reliability organization. *Organizational Science* 1 (2): 160–77.

Sherman, Lawrence W. 2018. Reducing fatal police shootings as system crashes: Research, theory, and practice. *Annual Review of Criminology* 1:421–49.

Simpson, Connor. 15 September 2013. New York cops accidentally shoot two bystanders in Times Square. *The Atlantic*. Available from www.theatlantic.com.

Snook, Scott. A. 2000. *Friendly fire: The accidental shootdown of U.S. Blackhawks over northern Iraq*. Princeton, NJ: Princeton University Press.

Stewart, James K. 2009. *Independent board of inquiry into the Oakland Police Department March 21, 2009 incident: A public report of findings and recommendations*. Arlington, VA: Center for Naval Analysis.

Stone, Christopher, Zachary Carter, Thomas Belfiore, Ella M. Bully-Cummings, Rev. Dr. Herbert, Michael J. Farrell, George Gascon, Arva Rice, Lew Rice, and Damon T. Hewitt. 2010. *Reducing inherent danger: Report of the Task Force on Police-on-Police Shootings*. Albany, NY: New York State Task Force on Police-on-Police Shootings. Available from https://www.hks.harvard.edu/sites/default/files/centers/wiener/programs/pcj/files/Police-on-Police_Shootings_with_appendices.pdf.

Tenner, Edward. 1997. *Why things bite back: Technology and the revenge of unintended consequences*. New York, NY: Random House.

Thomas, William I., and Dorothy S. Thomas. 1928. *The child in America: Behavior, problems and programs*. New York, NY: Alfred Knopf.

Vila, Bryan. 2000. *Tired cops: The importance of managing police fatigue*. Washington, DC: Police Executive Research Forum.

Weick, Karl E. 1993. The collapse of sensemaking in organizations: The Mann Gulch disaster. *Administrative Science Quarterly* 38 (4): 628–52.

Weick, Karl E. 1995. *Sensemaking in organizations*. Thousand Oaks, CA: Sage Publications.

Weick, Karl. E., and Kathleen M. Sutcliffe. 2001. *Managing the unexpected: Assuming high performance in an age of complexity*. San Francisco, CA: Jossey-Bass.

Firearm Availability and Fatal Police Shootings

Do states with more guns have higher rates of fatal police shootings? This article uses a validated measure of firearm availability (the percentage of suicides committed with a firearm) to examine the relationship between gun proliferation and fatal police shootings. It expands on existing research to include (1) measures of access to Level I and II trauma centers, (2) interpretation of the findings from the lenses of "statistical prediction," and (3) tests for structural differences between models for black decedents versus nonblack decedents. Findings confirm the correlation between statewide prevalence of gun ownership and fatal police shootings for both all decedents and unarmed decedents. It provides partial support for "statistical prediction" by police and finds that greater access to trauma centers is associated with lower rates of citizen deaths. The analysis suggests a far broader range of policy options for saving lives, such as better enforcement of legal restrictions on firearm possession, than focusing solely on policing systems.

Keywords: fatal police shootings; firearm availability; trauma services

By
DANIEL S. NAGIN

"An unarmed police depends, of course, upon an unarmed citizenry."
—Albert J. Reiss, Jr. (1971, 182)

Since 2014, highly publicized instances of fatal police shootings have reopened scrutiny of the factors that trigger deadly encounters with the police. Research on this issue has been limited, in part, because data from government sources cataloguing even a count of instances of fatal police shootings in the United States is woefully

Daniel S. Nagin is Teresa and H. John Heinz III University Professor of Public Policy and Statistics at Carnegie Mellon University, an elected fellow of American Academy of Political and Social Science, and the recipient of the Stockholm Prize in Criminology in 2014 and National Academy of Science Award for Scientific Reviewing in 2017.

Correspondence: dn03@andrew.cmu.edu

DOI: 10.1177/0002716219896259

incomplete (Barber et al. 2016; Zimring 2017). The research that has been done has focused on community factors such as racial composition and levels of violence (Klinger et al. 2016; Takagi 1974; Goldkamp 1976) or the impact of police adoption of less lethal technologies than firearms (Ferdik et al. 2014). The research of Zimring (2017) and Sherman (2018), however, set the stage for a broadening of the inquiry into putative causes of this pressing but neglected problem.

This analysis focuses on another possible contributing factor to the problem—the availability of firearms. Hemenway et al. (2018) reported a strong state-by-state relationship between rates of fatal police shootings and the household prevalence of firearms availability. Using the *Washington Post* multisource database, the authors found a pronounced positive relationship across the fifty states between state rates of fatal police shootings and firearm prevalence. The analysis in this article expands on the Hemenway et al. study by adding new data, new concepts, and new models. The evidence presented here suggests a far broader range of policy options for saving lives—such as better enforcement of legal restrictions on firearm possession and rapid transport of shooting victims to trauma centers—than focusing solely on police behavior, or even police systems.

Analytic Context

Deadly force is justified when an individual poses a serious threat to the safety of the on-scene officers or bystanders (Harmon 2008). An armed individual is a prime example of such a threat. Klinger et al. (2016), in an analysis of police shootings in St. Louis, MO, report that in 79 percent of incidents in which police discharge their weapon, at least one of the suspects possessed a firearm. Zimring (2017) analyzes a dataset assembled by *The Guardian* of fatal police shootings in the United States in 2015 and reports that in 56 percent of those instances, the decedent possessed a firearm. For the data used in this analysis, which was assembled by the *Washington Post* and covers the period 2015 to 2018, the percentage of decedents possessing a firearm is the same as in the *Guardian* data—56 percent.

Because firearms, unlike most other weapons, provide the capacity to inflict bodily harm at a distance, suspects possessing firearms pose a particularly high risk to police officers. Zimring (2017) argues that weapon availability is the only plausible explanation for the vastly higher rates of fatal police shootings in the United States compared to European countries. Still, the linkage between firearm availability and fatal police shootings is not obvious. As described in Cook (2018), presently only 31 percent of U.S. households possess firearms. For the vast majority of those owners, there is no realistic prospect of their using the weapon for an illegal purpose. But Cook (2018, 360) goes on to observe, "In jurisdictions in which gun possession is common, offenders may find it easier to access a gun in the informal or underground market. Indeed, the stock of guns in private possession serve as a reservoir from which most problematic transactions originate." By this mechanism, higher overall firearm availability may translate into more frequent encounters between police and armed suspects, even though most guns are held by law-abiding individuals. The general availability of firearms may also affect the probability of fatal shootings in circumstances in which the decedent is later ("ex-post") found to be unarmed. Police officers must make judgments about the risk of harm at the beginning of each encounter ("ex-ante"). In places where gun availability is higher, police officers may surmise (ex-ante) that they are at greater risk of harm via what economists and statisticians call statistical prediction/discrimination and act accordingly. Police officers' concern about encounters with armed suspects is real. Zimring (2017) reports that in more than 90 percent of killings of police officers in the line of duty, the killer inflicted the fatal injury to the officer with a firearm.

Data

This study uses statewide estimates of the rate of fatal shootings based on data assembled by the *Washington Post* on instances of police use of deadly force nationwide over the period 2015 to 2018. The data were assembled to remedy the shortcomings of data available from government sources, which underreport fatal police shootings by the police by at least 50 percent (Tate et al. 2016) or are limited to only a small subset of states (Barber et al. 2016). The *Post* created their dataset by searching local news reports, law enforcement websites, and social media; and monitoring relevant independent databases. For this analysis, the data for 2015 to 2018 were combined to create statewide rates over this period.[1]

Two Centers for Disease Control and Prevention (CDC) sources were used to estimate two alternative estimates of gun prevalence by state. The primary estimate, which derives from the CDC's WISQARS fatal injury reports, is the *percentage of suicides statewide that are committed with a firearm*. This percentage, which is commonly referred to as the FSS, is a widely used and validated measure of firearm availability (Cook and Ludwig 2006) and is calculated for each state for the period 2012 to 2014. A secondary CDC estimate is based on the 2004 Behavioral Risk Factor Surveillance System (BRFSS). Miller et al. (2013) used these data to calculate by state the percentage of households in which an adult is reported to possess a firearm. This survey-based prevalence estimate precedes the fatal shootings rates used in this analysis by a decade, but it is the latest available estimate based on the BRFSS.

Also included in the analysis is an estimate of the percentage of the state's population residing within one hour of a Level I or II trauma center (American College of Emergency Physicians 2014). As discussed in detail in Jacoby, Reeping, and Branas (this volume), proximity to a trauma center is often a decisive factor in whether a badly injured individual survives. Because the *Washington Post* data do not account for all violent encounters (they only record violent encounters with police that end in death), the proximity of trauma services is

TABLE 1
Summary Statistics for 50 States

Variable	Mean	Median	SD
Rate of fatal police shootings 2015–2018 (000000)	1.41	1.22	0.778
% of suicides with firearm 2012–2014 (FFS)	51.7	53.0	12.6
% of households with an adult possessing a firearm (BRFSS)	39.0	32.0	14.2
Homicide rate 2014	4.05	4.00	1.93
% urban 2010	73.6	73.8	14.6
% within 1 hour of a Level I or II trauma center	81.7	89.7	20.6

important to an accurate analysis. The analysis also includes the statewide homicide rate in 2014 and the percentage of the population living in urban areas. Table 1 reports summary statistics on all these variables.

Analysis

As indicated at the outset, an armed citizen in a confrontational encounter with the police is a prime example of a circumstance where the citizen may be posing an imminent threat to the police and therefore is more at risk of being shot by the police. Thus, the first step in the analysis is to examine the correlation across the fifty states between firearm prevalence and the percentage of fatal encounters where the decedent possessed a firearm. That correlation is indeed positive and very pronounced: .54 for the primary firearm suicide proportion measure of firearm prevalence. But does this positive correlation translate into higher overall rates of fatal police shootings? Figure 1 suggests that it does. It plots the association of the natural logarithm of the rate of fatal police shootings with the natural logarithm of firearm suicide proportion (FSS). Superimposed on the scatterplot is the corresponding regression of firearm prevalence on the fatal shootings rate.

Table 2 reports a detailed technical analysis: a series of regressions in logarithmic form with robust standard errors. The most basic specification includes only the FSS and trauma care proximity measures. The percent urban and homicide rate variables are next added to the specification, followed by a specification expanded to include regional dummy variables distinguishing the four largest census regions—East, South, Midwest, and West. The regional dummy variables are intended to serve as catch-all variables measuring socioeconomic and demographic characteristics other than urbanization and the homicide rate to distinguish regions that are correlated with both the rate of fatal shootings and gun prevalence. Inclusion of the regional dummies is important because there are distinct differences across regions in gun prevalence, with eastern states tending to have the lowest prevalence rates and western states the highest prevalence rates.

FIGURE 1
Fatal Shootings Rate 2015–2018 (natural log) versus Percentage of Suicides with
Firearms 2012–2014 (natural log)

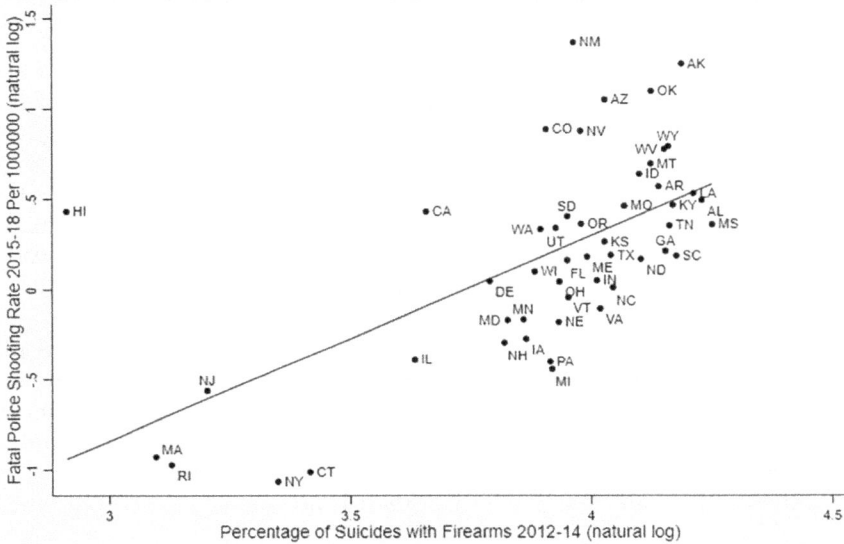

In all specifications, the FSS has a positive, statistically significant association with the fatal shootings rate (.05 or lower). The magnitude of that association, however, is sensitive to specification. Inclusion of the regional dummy
variables reduces the association, which can be interpreted as an elasticity, from
a 1 percent increase in gun prevalence being associated with about a 1 percent
increase in the rate of fatal shootings to instead about a 0.5 percent increase in
fatal shootings.

Trauma unit proximity is also associated with the rates of fatal shootings by
police. Absent the regional dummy variables, this association is negative and
significant—greater proximity of the population to trauma units is associated
with lower fatal shootings rates. Inclusion of the regional dummies, however,
reduces the magnitude of the proximity association by more than a half and
leaves the association significant for only a one-tailed test at the 5 percent
level.

Table 3 reports counterpart regressions splitting out rates for individuals who
were and were not found to have been in possession of a firearm when police
shot them fatally. The gun prevalence elasticities are larger for the regressions
based on rates of individuals with firearms than those without firearms. In all
specifications, the elasticity estimates for individuals with firearms are significant (.05). Higher firearm prevalence is positively and significantly associated
with the rate of fatal violence against individuals who were found not to possess
a firearm, when analyzed without the regional dummies.[2] Inclusion of the

TABLE 2
Regression Results for Natural Logarithm of Rate of Fatal Police Shootings

Variable	Est	t-Ratio	Est	t-Ratio	Est	t-Ratio
ln (FFS)	0.987	3.07	1.19	2.96	0.495	2.12
ln(%1hr)	−0.442	−2.33	−0.512	−2.55	−0.219	−1.75
ln(%Urban)	—	—	0.585	1.85	−0.669	−2.30
ln(Hom14)	—	—	−0.007	−0.07	0.152	1.48
Midwest	—	—	—	—	0.228	1.64
South	—	—	—	—	0.385	2.18
West	—	—	—	—	1.08	6.23
Constant	−1.74	−0.92	−4.71	−1.60	1.46	0.81

regional dummies, however, leaves the coefficient estimate, while positive, insignificant at conventional levels of significance. These findings lend credence, albeit limited, to the statistical prediction/discrimination hypothesis advanced in the introduction of this article. That is, higher gun prevalence is associated with higher rates of police officers possibly anticipating a greater likelihood that suspects possess a firearm even when suspects had no gun.

Race and Rates of Fatal Shootings

As with most measures of contact with the police, blacks are disproportionally represented among the decedents in the *Washington Post* data—24.5 percent of decedents were black, about twice their representation in the overall U.S. population. These data do not have nearly the detail required to make credible inferences about the influence of race independent of other characteristics of the encounter. The data, however, do potentially illuminate whether the association of firearm prevalence and fatal police shootings varies across race. Tests of differences in the coefficients of the FFS variable between separate regressions for black and nonblack decedents identified no significant difference, which implies that firearm availability does not differentially affect rates of fatality across race.

A variety of supplementary analyses were conducted to test the sensitivity of the results to an alternative measure of gun availability, the percentage of households in 2004 by state in which at least one household member reported owning a firearm, and to outliers. Regressions based on the alternative measure of gun prevalence yielded similar findings to those reported in Table 2 and residual analysis revealed no influential outliers, including, specifically, Hawaii, which can be seen in Figure 1 as a potential outlier. Negative binomial regressions based on the counts of fatal encounters by state yield similar results.

TABLE 3
Regression Results Distinguishing Decedents with and without Firearm

Variable	Rate with Firearms (natural log)				Rate without Firearms (natural log)			
	Est	t	Est	t	Est	t	Est	t
ln (FFS)	1.50	3.34	0.744	2.40	0.878	2.24	0.246	1.16
ln(%1hr)	−0.499	−2.33	−0.194	−1.14	−0.507	−2.31	−0.221	−2.10
ln(%Urban)	0.580	1.75	−0.689	−1.77	0.581	1.64	−0.698	−2.81
ln(Hom14)	0.023	0.23	0.165	1.21	−0.043	−0.36	0.145	1.56
Midwest	—	—	0.333	1.75	—	—	0.103	0.75
South	—	—	0.479	2.11	—	—	0.271	1.68
West	—	—	1.12	4.68	—	—	1.06	7.49
Constant	−6.60	−2.04	−0.207	−0.09	−4.30	−1.49	1.80	1.13

Discussion

The analysis identifies a pronounced, highly significant association between the statewide rate of fatal police shootings and the statewide prevalence of firearms. This association is not dependent on a statistical model with statistical controls or dependent on the presence or not of an outlying state. It is, however, an association based on a cross-sectional analysis of the fifty states. It, thus, begs the question of whether it can plausibly be interpreted as reflecting a causal effect of the availability of firearms on fatal police shootings. Confronting that question requires that we consider alternative interpretations.

Alternative interpretations include (1) reverse causality (hypothesizing that police use of deadly force might be the cause of firearm proliferation in the population), (2) suicide-by-cop (the prevalence of citizens who behave in ways threatening enough to cause the police to use lethal force), and (3) omitted variable bias (failure of this analysis to include the causal variable). Reverse causality would require that citizens are arming themselves for self-protection in anticipation of encounters in which the police might shoot them. This interpretation strains credulity. Rather than providing self-protection, arming oneself in police encounters is more likely a strategy for getting oneself killed. That fact brings us to the suicide-by-cop interpretation.

Undoubtedly, there are some instances in which the decedent was intent on provoking police officers to shoot them. Brandishing a firearm in the presence of police officers serves the aim of making the police the instrument of one's demise. Thumbnail sketches of the fatal incidents at the *Washington Post* website, however, suggest that overt attempts to provoke the police for the purpose of committing suicide are rare. Unintended actions that may have that effect, however, are more frequent. In about 25 percent of the incidents, the decedent was judged to be mentally ill. The sketches of some incidents involving a mentally ill decedent involve aggressive behavior on their part with no apparent instrumental purpose beyond acting out delusional impulses. However, even in these circumstances, if the individual were not in possession of a firearm, the aggressive behavior is less likely to pose an imminent threat to the officer or bystanders, and thereby use of fatal force may be less likely. In this sense, the presence of a firearm may heighten the risk of fatal shootings independent of the intentions of the individual who is acting out. Most incident descriptions, however, involve circumstances that cannot plausibly be interpreted as reflecting a desire by the decedent to be killed by the police.

The third alternative interpretation is "omitted variable bias," or the absence of another explanation that may actually cause the outcome and is highly correlated with the variables we have measured. This risk is always a concern in analyses of observational data, particularly in a cross-sectional analysis such as this one that includes only a limited number of observations. The risk in this case, however, begs the question of what those unmeasured causes might be. Figure 1 shows that the bivariate correlation between state-level rates of fatal shootings and the FSS-based measure of gun prevalence is pronounced. A counterpart figure based on the BRFSS-based measure of prevalence is comparably pronounced. Gun prevalence across states is not random—prevalence is lowest in more urbanized eastern states and highest in more rural western states. However, as the regressions reported in Table 2 show, the association between gun prevalence and fatal shooting rates persist even with the addition of urbanization and regional dummy variables to the regression and controls for proximity of trauma services and the homicide rate.

Other sources of omitted variable bias may, of course, remain. Of particular concern are the very large regional differences in fatal shootings rates. Potential confounders not adequately accounted for by the regional dummy variables may thus remain unidentified. Notwithstanding, the fact that the association is resilient to the inclusion of four important potential sources of bias is noteworthy.

None of these alternative interpretations, in my view, provides a compelling alternative explanation for the associations reported in Tables 2 and 3. Rather, the leading candidate is the evidence we have analyzed. That evidence supports the interpretation that one consequence of higher rates of firearm prevalence in a state is a greater frequency of police encountering individuals who are *armed or suspected to be armed*, which in turn results in a greater frequency of police using fatal force.

Policy Implications

What are the policy implications of this conclusion? One is to take steps to reduce the availability of firearms to active offenders or individuals at high risk of offending. Policies that are intended to have this effect are universal background checks and barriers to straw purchases (Cook 2018; Zimring 2017). Sherman (2018) also makes numerous policy recommendations related to the governance and training of local police. Keeping weapons out of the hands of the mentally ill may also be effective.

Although not the principal focus of the analysis, the analysis also found a pronounced negative association between the fatal shootings rate and proximity to trauma care—not a surprising finding. Promptly administered emergency care to traumatic injuries such as gunshot wounds can often make the difference between life and death. Thus, the analysis also serves to reinforce the policy recommendations on trauma care made in Jacoby, Reeping, and Branas (this volume), Zimring (2017), and Sherman (2018).

Notes

1. The state rather than city was chosen as the unit of observation because, as Sherman (2018) emphasizes, a sizable fraction of fatal police shootings occur in nonurban settings.

2. For reasons of economy, Table 3 does not include the specification including only the gun prevalence and trauma access measures. The coefficient estimates for these variables are highly significant in the regressions for individuals with and without firearms.

References

American College of Emergency Physicians. 2014. America's emergency care environment, A state-by-state report card 2014 Edition. *Annals of Emergency Medicine* 63 (2):100–242.

Barber, Catherine, Deborah Azrael, Amy Cohen, Matthew Miller, Deonza Thymes, David Enze Wang, and David Hemenway. 2016. National violent death reporting system, vital statistics, and supplementary homicide reports. *American Journal of Public Health* 106:922–27.

Cook, Philip J. 2018. Gun markets. *Annual Review of Criminology* 1:359–77.

Cook, Philip J., and Jens Ludwig. 2006. The social cost of gun ownership. *Journal of Public Economic* 90:379–91.

Ferdik, Frank, Robert Kaminski, Mikaela Cooney, and Eric Sevigny. 2014. The influence of agency policies on conducted energy device use and fatal police shootings. *Police Quarterly* 17:328–58.

Goldkamp, John S. 1976. Minorities as victims of police shootings: Interpretations of racial disproportionality and police use of deadly force. *Justice System Journal* 2:169–83.

Harmon, Rachael. 2008. When is police violence justified? *Northwestern University Law Review* 102:1119–88.

Hemenway, Daivid, Deborah Azrael, Andrew Connor, and Matthew Miller. 2018. Variation in rates of fatal police shootings across US states: The role of firearm availability. *Journal of Urban Health* 96 (1): 63–73.

Jacoby, Sara F., Paul M. Reeping, and Charles C. Branas. 2020. Effectiveness and scalability of rapid hospital transport by police for victims of violence. *The ANNALS of the American Academy of Political and Social Science* (this volume).

Klinger, David, Richard Rosenfeld, Daniel Isom, and Michael Deckard. 2016. Race, crime, and the microecology of deadly force. *Criminology & Public Policy* 15:193–222.

Miller, Mathew, Catherince Barber, Richard A. White, and Deborah Azrael. 2013. Firearms and suicide in the United States: Is risk independent of underlying suicidal behavior. *American Journal of Epidemiology* 178 (6):946–55.

Reiss, Albert. 1971. *The police and the public*. New Haven, CT: Yale University Press.

Sherman, Lawrence W. 2018. Reducing fatal police shootings as systems crashes: Research, theory, and practice. *Annual Review of Criminology* 1:421–49.

Takagi, Paul. 1974. A garrison state in a "democratic" society. *Crime and Social Justice* 1:27–33.

Tate, Julie, Jennifer Jenkins, Steven Rich, John Muyskens, Kennedy Elliott, Ted Mellnik, and Aaron Williams. 7 July 2016. How the *Washington Post* is examining police shootings in the United States. *Washington Post*.

Zimring, Franklin. 2017. *When police kill*. Cambridge, MA: Harvard University Press.

The Role of Individual Officer Characteristics in Police Shootings

By
GREG RIDGEWAY

Assessing whether individual characteristics of police officers such as age, race, and prior performance influence police behavior has been a long-standing topic of social science research. The effect of officer characteristics on their risk of shooting people is confounded by police assignments and by the environmental factors associated with those assignments. This article provides a method to separate out the influence of individual officer characteristics from environmental factors. Using data from the New York City Police Department (NYPD) and the Major Cities' Chiefs Association (MCCA), the analysis finds that police officers who join the NYPD later in their careers have a lower shooting risk: for each additional year of their recruitment age, the odds of being shooters declines by 10 percent. Both officer race and prior problem behavior (e.g., losing a firearm, crashing a department vehicle) predict up to three times greater odds of shooting, yet officers who made numerous misdemeanor arrests were four times less likely to shoot.

Keywords: police use of force; lethal force; conditional likelihood

D uring the October 20, 2014, fatal police shooting of Laquan McDonald, Chicago Police Officer Jason Van Dyke fired sixteen rounds. Officer Joseph Walsh stood a few feet to Van Dyke's right and fired no rounds. On November 25, 2006, Sean Bell, unarmed on the morning before his wedding, was fatally shot in his car by five New York City police officers who discharged a total of fifty rounds. Detective Isnora, who is black, fired first, ultimately discharging eleven rounds. Detective Headley, also black but seven years older, fired

Greg Ridgeway is an associate professor of criminology and statistics at the University of Pennsylvania. His research focuses on the development and use of statistical methods for improving understanding of crime and the justice system. He is an elected fellow of the American Statistical Association.

Correspondence: gridge@upenn.edu

DOI: 10.1177/0002716219896553

a single round. Detective Oliver, the same age as Detective Headley but white, fired thirty-one rounds.

These two fatal police shootings illustrate an important issue in police behavior: the extent to which overall killings of citizens are driven by individual officer factors, rather than larger systems and environmental factors. This article analyzes extensive data from both the New York City Police Department (NYPD) and other large U.S. cities to present a framework for analysis that can be employed in any large population of officers, one that could help police managers to predict and manage the small fraction of officers with elevated risk of fatal shootings.

Background

Sherman (1980) classifies the approaches to studying police behavior, including police use of force, into five levels of analysis: individual, situational, organizational, community, and legal. An individual analysis aims to link individual officer characteristics to an officer's pattern of decisions, including the risk of shooting his or her gun in the line of duty. The individual-level analysis of shooting decisions cannot ignore the other four levels that also influence police behavior. The situational level includes the time and place of an encounter; information given by a dispatcher or caller about the perceived danger of a call for service; the observed features of a subject, like their expressions of belligerence or mental health at the time of the incident; and numerous other factors in a given situation that influence the risk of a police shooting. The organizational level includes department policy and training on the use of deadly force, as well as the cultural norms regarding police shootings that may also affect the likelihood that these events occur. A community-level analysis examines links between police shootings and neighborhood factors, such as the demographic composition, the amount of crime, and the amount of personal risk officers perceive in that area. Last, the legal level of analysis examines how the formal legal system, court decisions, and legal constraints on the police influence police shootings.

All these levels can potentially alter the risk that officers shoot, the number of rounds they fire, and other aspects of a police shooting incident. Complicating analysis, these levels are often related to one another. For example, because officer characteristics influence officer assignments, certain officer characteristics may be more common in incidents with certain situational and community characteristics.

The individual level of analysis is of particular interest for police management and policy. A clear understanding of the relationship between officer characteristics and police shootings can generate policies that could effectively mitigate the occurrence of shootings. A discovered link, for example, between shooting and age at recruitment could lead to changes in recruiting strategy. A link between an officer's firearm type and number of rounds fired could lead to changes in equipment procurement. Links between decision-making and exposure to special training would help police agencies to refine their training curriculum. Showing that shooting risk increases as an officer accumulates more use-of-force complaints, is exposed to traumatic incidents, or has previous involvement in shootings might help to craft policies that assign certain police officers to reduced-risk environments. As opposed to situational, community, and legal factors, police departments can perhaps more directly manage or respond to officer characteristics in an effort to mitigate shooting risk.

The frequent challenge to discovering the role of officer characteristics is the risk of confounding one factor with another. If a particular officer characteristic is associated with more shootings, does that officer characteristic itself increase the risk, or are officers with that characteristic more likely to be assigned to higher-risk situations and communities? Numerous studies over decades find correlations between officer characteristics and some measure of officer performance, but then immediately question whether the observed relationship is the result of confounding. Fyfe (1981, 367), for example, wrote that in the NYPD in the 1970s, "the overrepresentation of minority officers among police shooters [was] closely associated with racially varying pattern of assignment, socialization, and residence." Fyfe (1988, 196) noted that "blacks were posted to high-risk assignments far more often than whites." In other departments the opposite relationship can be found, with Geller and Karales (1981, 1858) noting that in Chicago, "black officers are not prominent in the units of the Police Department which see the most shooting action," again noting that assignment is a confounding factor.

Using more complete data on the situations and communities in which shootings occur is a possible avenue to address confounding. Paoline, Gau, and Terrill (2018, 67–68) comment that "it is possible, then, that the significant result for white officers' force against black suspects would disappear if neighbourhood controls were added."

Yet officer assignment may confound more than just the relationship between race and shooting risk. Fyfe (1988, 197) wrote that an observed relationship between age and shooting risk is "an artifact of age-related variations in assignment and in exposure to potential shooting situations." Paoline and Terrill (2007, 189) speculated that "it is quite possible that other factors, such as the extent to which college-educated officers versus non-college-educated officers encounter resistant suspects, may account for why education appears to matter." McElvain and Kposowa (2008, 518) summarized the problem this way: almost every officer characteristic may be correlated with assignments that expose an officer to, or protect an officer from, shooting risk, "based on an officer's rank, time on the job, age, and gender, he or she may have been less active, assigned to areas with lower crime rates, or working in a position that did not have frequent contact with citizens." Since just about every research effort to study the link between officer characteristics and shooting risk wrestles with confounding, progress in this line of research depends on a methodology capable of untangling the confounding effect of assignment and the situational, organizational, community, and legal factors that come from those assignments. Confounding is present whenever unmeasured factors are associated with both officer characteristics and shooting risk. Confounding inadequately addressed with an experimental design or statistical adjustment can produce inaccurate conclusions, signal null effects even when an officer characteristic is predictive of a police shooting, make an officer characteristic appear to exacerbate risk when in fact it has no effect, or make an officer characteristic seem protective when in truth it elevates the risk. The scholars previously quoted all understood this and expressed concerns that their observed findings were the result of unmeasured or inadequately modeled potentially confounding factors.

In this article, I describe an approach for learning about the relationship between officer characteristics and (1) the decision to shoot, as well as (2) the number of rounds discharged. This approach is designed to mitigate the risk of confounding. I present a statistical argument to show that information about officer characteristics comes from two sources. The first source is the "collective group information." This is the data on the total number of officers at a particular time and place who shoot and the total number of rounds that they discharge. The second source of information is the "individual officer information." This is information about the specific individual officers who shoot and the specific number of rounds each individual officer discharges at a shooting scene. Ideally, we would use information from both sources. However, I show that analysis of the collective group information (the number of shooters or the total number of rounds fired) is at high risk of confounding, that some unobserved factor associated with officer characteristics is the true cause of elevated shooting risk. Furthermore, I show that analysis of the individual officer information, the individual officer actions, has no risk of confounding from situational, organizational, community, and legal factors. I argue that scholars studying police shootings should focus exclusively on the individual officer information to reduce the risk of confounding. In the appendix to this article, which is available online,[1] I lay out the methodology and statistical model for assessing whether individual officer characteristics affect the risk of police shootings. The following sections attempt to report the results of analyses using those methods and models, as well as some of the technical terms. For definitions of those terms, see the online appendix.

Empirical Demonstrations

Risk of shooting and shooting rate in New York City

In Ridgeway (2016), I explored whether officer characteristics influenced the risk of shooting among NYPD officers. From all 106 multi-officer police shooting investigations that were adjudicated between 2004 and 2006, I extracted officer identifiers for all officers who were at the scene at the time of the shooting. The first panel in Table 1 shows the results for the decision to shoot. While police officers and detectives have similar odds of shooting, the odds of shooting decreases greatly for those in higher ranks, as expected. Police officers who join the NYPD later in their careers also have a lower shooting risk. For each additional year of their recruitment age, the odds of being a shooter declines by 10

TABLE 1
Conditional Likelihood Analysis of Police Shootings, New York City,
Cases Adjudicated between 2004 and 2006

	Decision to Shoot			Number of Rounds Fired		
Officer Characteristic	Odds Ratio	95% CI	p-Value	Rate Ratio	95% CI	p-Value
Rank						
Police officer (reference)						
Detective	1.30	(0.34, 5.03)	.70	0.95	(0.28, 3.25)	.93
Sergeant	0.29	(0.10, 0.80)	°.01	0.40	(0.19, 0.86)	°.02
Lieutenant or above	0.04	(0.01, 0.30)	°.001	0.11	(0.03, 0.45)	°.002
Years at NYPD	0.98	(0.90, 1.07)	.68	0.99	(0.94, 1.05)	.83
Age when recruited	0.90	(0.81, 0.99)	°.03	0.94	(0.88, 1.01)	.09
Race						
White (reference)						
Black	2.96	(1.17, 7.46)	°.02	2.30	(1.09, 4.86)	°.03
Other	1.09	(0.45, 2.65)	.85	1.24	(0.71, 2.16)	.44
Male	2.19	(0.50, 9.63)	.29	1.64	(0.43, 6.27)	.46
Education						
High school (reference)						
High school+some college	1.30	(0.54, 3.16)	.55	0.75	(0.35, 1.59)	.44
College	1.98	(0.61, 6.40)	.24	0.69	(0.33, 1.47)	.33
College+some graduate	2.06	(0.08, 56.18)	.66	0.78	(0.20, 3.05)	.72
Precinct officer	0.29	(0.07, 1.14)	.07	1.17	(0.47, 2.94)	.73
Average annual						
Evaluation score < 3.5	0.60	(0.25, 1.46)	.25	0.62	(0.33, 1.16)	.13
Range score < 86	1.71	(0.70, 4.19)	.23	1.42	(0.83, 2.43)	.19
Complaints > 0.6	1.99	(0.71, 5.57)	.18	1.40	(0.77, 2.56)	.26
Medal count/year > 3.8	2.12	(0.62, 7.20)	.22	1.63	(0.80, 3.33)	.17
CPI points > 3.1	3.09	(1.11, 8.56)	°.03	1.44	(0.74, 2.81)	.28
Gun arrests > 2.4	0.83	(0.25, 2.79)	.76	0.94	(0.45, 1.95)	.87
Felony arrests > 9.3	1.38	(0.44, 4.38)	.57	0.73	(0.36, 1.48)	.37
Misdemeanor arrests > 10.0	0.26	(0.09, 0.74)	°.01	0.89	(0.41, 1.95)	.77
Days of leave						
Not line of duty injury > 8.4	1.11	(0.49, 2.52)	.80	1.23	(0.70, 2.16)	.47
Line of duty injury > 5.6	1.13	(0.45, 2.86)	.79	1.38	(0.64, 2.96)	.40

NOTE: All odds ratios and rate ratios computed as $\exp(\hat{\beta})$. Ninety-five percent confidence intervals (CI) and p-values computed using a permutation test and do not rely on independence assumptions or traditional asymptotic variance calculations. The cutoffs selected under the "average annual" heading flag those officers who are in the extreme 15th percentile of the officers. CPI is a point system documenting problematic police performance. Some figures from the decision to shoot analysis differ slightly from Ridgeway (2016) due to slight recoding in the data and simulation variation in the permutation tests.
°p-value < 0.05.

percent. Black officers had three times greater odds of shooting than white officers. The NYPD's Central Personnel Index (CPI) assigns points to problematic
police behavior (e.g., losing a firearm, crashing a department vehicle). Officers
accumulating more than 3.1 CPI points per year have three times greater odds
of shooting. Officers who made numerous misdemeanor arrests were four times
less likely to shoot.

A new analysis of the number of rounds fired that uses the same data is presented in the right panel of Table 1. The coefficients are generally in the same
direction, but only the race of the officer remains significant. On average, black
NYPD officers fire 2.3 times the number of rounds as white NYPD officers present at the same shooting incident. Officers in higher ranks also fire fewer rounds
on average.

Aside from the NYPD, I have searched for other data sources and other
departments with enough multi-officer shootings to determine whether these
findings persist across other departments. However, many departments do not
readily collect or report information on nonshooting officers at the scene of the
shooting. I argue here that police shootings involving multiple officers at the
scene contain a disproportionate amount of what statisticians call "Fisher information," which is enormously helpful in understanding officer risks of shooting
because data on both shooters and nonshooters are collected. Therefore, the
nationally widespread lack of data on nonshooting officers at the scene (outside
of the NYPD) is an unfortunate loss of information, one that should be remedied
going forward. The new consent decree for the Chicago Police Department represents an excellent model in this regard, which requires the documentation of
all "CPD units identified in the incident report as being on the scene of the use
of force incident" (*State of Illinois v. City of Chicago*, Consent Decree, 2018,
¶571f).

While data on nonshooting officers can be difficult to find, we can always find
data on officers who discharge a round. Conditional likelihood analysis of the
number of rounds is possible, even if data on the zero-round officers are
unavailable.

Shooting rate in major cities using only officer discharges

In 2015, the Major Cities Chiefs Association (MCCA) and the Police
Foundation established a partnership to help agencies understand descriptive
information about the police shooting incidents occurring within their agencies,
as well as whether certain factors lead to differing outcomes of these incidents.
Fifty-six agencies from the MCCA in the United States and Canada contributed
to this data collection effort. The collection resulted in 317 shootings involving
multiple officers, 849 officers in total, discharging 5,026 rounds.

This data collection included only data on officers who fired at least one
round. As a result, the analysis needs to account for the nonshooters using what
is technically called a "truncated Poisson distribution." This introduces substantial computational complexity. For one shooting involving 11 officers discharging
88 rounds, one component of the conditional likelihood involves more than 4

TABLE 2
Estimates of Risk Ratios Associated with Each Officer Characteristic

Officer Characteristics	Rate Ratio	Permutation 95% CI	Permutation p-Value
Age at recruitment	1.01	(0.99, 1.02)	.31
Years of experience	1.00	(0.98, 1.01)	.58
Female	0.86	(0.64, 1.14)	.27
Race (relative to white)			
Black	1.05	(0.86, 1.28)	.64
Hispanic	1.09	(0.89, 1.32)	.39
Other	0.76	(0.57, 1.01)	.05
Prior OIS (relative to 0)			
1 or more	1.02	(0.84, 1.24)	.85
2 or more	1.23	(0.88, 1.72)	.21
Prior force complaint	1.25	(0.92, 1.69)	.14
Role			
Detective	1.09	(0.78, 1.52)	.61
Sergeant or more senior	1.03	(0.87, 1.22)	.75
Other	0.66	(0.32, 1.37)	.26
Special assignment	1.28	(0.97, 1.68)	.07
Long gun (relative to pistol)	1.01	(0.78, 1.30)	.97

NOTE: All odds ratios and rate ratios computed as $\exp(\hat{\beta})$. Ninety-five percent confidence intervals (CI) and p-values computed using a permutation test and do not rely on independence assumptions or traditional asymptotic variance calculations. OIS stands for "officer-involved shooting."

trillion terms. Computing such terms efficiently requires what is called a "specialized recursive algorithm and Monte Carlo integration." Ridgeway, Cave, and Grieco (n.d.) derive this conditional likelihood and describe computational tools needed to estimate the effect of officer characteristics on the shooting rate from such truncated data.

The findings from the NYPD study did not persist when examining the number of rounds fired in the MCCA data. Table 2 shows results from that analysis. These results provide no evidence that any officer characteristic strongly influences the number of rounds fired. Officers with prior complaints, with two or more prior shootings, and officers with a special assignment appear to have elevated risk. Yet the model does not offer sufficiently precise shooting rate ratios to conclude that there is an effect of individual characteristics.

The NYPD and MCCA findings used only the individual officer contribution to the likelihood of shooting. They used data that are readily available at police departments and required no measurement or modeling of the shootings' environments. Any finding or lack of finding from these analyses cannot be due to confounding because of correlations between the officer's characteristics and the officer's assignment. It is possible that the NYPD officers with the highest CPI points charge through the door first or get within twenty-one feet of a knife-wielding individual and in this way differ from other officers on the scene. But this is the mechanism through which high-CPI-point officers elevate their shooting risk and exactly the reason we wish to detect the effect of CPI points and other officer characteristics that affect the risk of a shooting.

Discussion and Conclusion

This article began with partial descriptions of the moments in which the tragic shootings of Mr. McDonald (Chicago) and Mr. Bell (New York) occurred. As is the case with all fatal encounters with police, those moments are rich with information about the characteristics of the officers who made decisions to shoot—as well as the decision to not shoot and stop shooting. Confounding by assignment in the Laquan McDonald shooting is not possible: both officers are on the same scene, facing the same subject, and operating in the same organization and environment, but made different decisions on whether to shoot. The only differences were their own characteristics and chance variation in space and positioning. Similarly, confounding by assignment is not possible in the Sean Bell shooting in New York: the detectives on the scene of the Bell shooting were surrounding the same vehicle, in the same neighborhood, at the same time, and working the same operation, but made different decisions on how many rounds to fire. With Officer Headley firing fewer rounds than Officer Isnora, we may think that older officers fire less. However, with Officer Oliver emptying two magazines, we may be led to believe that the race of the officer matters most. Naturally we cannot infer much from a single shooting, but by compiling numerous shootings like this, we can extract patterns about which officers are more likely to shoot.

The framework presented in this article is a formal statistical process for extracting knowledge about the role of officer characteristics in such incidents. Focusing only on multi-officer shooting incidents and using the conditional likelihood does not use all the information about the role of officer characteristics, but it provides two critical advantages: (1) data collection needs to focus only on shooting incidents, a process that is already a regular part of police practice; and (2) the conditional likelihood does not depend on the shared environmental factors, eliminating the risk of confounding due to situational, organizational, community, or legal factors.

Fortunately, police shootings are rare events among the 80 million police-citizen encounters occurring annually. Even rarer are those police shootings that provide unconfounded information on officer characteristics. The conditional likelihood requires data on multi-officer shooting incidents, and the officers involved in those incidents need to have variation on their characteristics.

In the MCCA dataset, only 4 percent of the incidents provided information on the effect of having a special assignment. Since officers with a special assignment tend to cluster together, few incidents had a mixture of patrol officers and special assignment officers. Police departments should be collecting and recording information on all nonshooting officers at the scene.

In the MCCA dataset, it is possible that in many scenes that had both patrol and special assignment officers, only the special assignment officers discharged a round. In such cases, the data only report information on the special assignment officers. This means that any analyst will lose statistical power to detect the role of special assignment. Any police department with genuine interest in learning about the role of officer characteristics should record information on all non-shooting officers on the scene of police shootings.

Ridgeway (2016) showed that the conditional likelihood approach can assess whether officer characteristics are linked to an officer's decision to shoot. Ridgeway, Cave, and Grieco (n.d.) demonstrated that the conditional likelihood framework can also address how many rounds they fire. This article shows precisely how data from shooting incidents provide information on the role of officer and environmental factors in shooting risk and shooting rate. Conditional likelihood offers a rigorous approach to avoid confounding due to the situational, organizational, community, and legal factors that have been a challenge in the past. With improved data collection and methodological refinements, we can work to untangle the relationship between officer characteristics and their effect on shooting risk.

Note

1. See the online version of this paper for the appendix.

References

Fyfe, James. 1981. Who shoots? A look at officer race and police shooting. *Journal of Police Science and Administration* 9 (4): 367–82.

Fyfe, James. 1988. Police use of deadly force: Research and reform. *Justice Quarterly* 5 (2): 165–205.

Geller, William A., and Kevin J. Karales. 1981. Shootings of and by Chicago police: Uncommon crises— Part I: Shootings by Chicago police. *Journal of Criminal Law and Criminology* 72 (4): 1813–66.

McElvain, James P., and Augustine J. Kposowa. 2008. Police officer characteristics and the likelihood of using deadly force. *Criminal Justice and Behavior* 35 (4): 505–21.

Paoline, Eugene A., Jacinta M. Gau, and William Terrill. 2018. Race and the police use of force encounter in the United States. *British Journal of Criminology* 58 (1): 54–74.

Paoline, Eugene A., and William Terrill. 2007. Police education, experience, and the use of force. *Criminal Justice and Behavior* 34 (2): 179–96.

Ridgeway, Greg. 2016. Officer risk factors associated with police shootings: A matched case–control study. *Statistics and Public Policy* 3 (1): 1–6.

Ridgeway, Greg, Breanne Cave, and Julie Grieco. n.d. A conditional likelihood model of the relationship between officer features and rounds discharged in police shootings. Manuscript under review.

Sherman, Lawrence W. 1980. Causes of police behavior: The current state of quantitative research. *Journal of Research in Crime and Delinquency* 17 (1): 69–100.

State of Illinois v. City of Chicago, Consent Decree, 17-cv-6260 (United State District Court for the Northern District of Illinois, September 13, 2018). Available from http://chicagopoliceconsentdecree .org/wp-content/uploads/2018/09/Illinois-v.-Chicago-Final-Consent-Decree-with-signatures.pdf.

Predicting Bad Policing: Theorizing Burdensome and Racially Disparate Policing through the Lenses of Social Psychology and Routine Activities

By
PHILLIP ATIBA GOFF
and
HILARY RAU

Despite an increase in research relating to racial disparities in policing—particularly in the area of deadly force—there have been comparatively few attempts to theorize which factors predict disparate policing. We fill this gap by combining routine activity theory from criminology with situationist approaches to discrimination from social psychology. We propose that disparate policing is most likely to occur when officers who are vulnerable to situational risk factors for bias encounter citizens who are members of vulnerable out-groups. We argue that situational risk factors for bias and aggression among police provoke feelings of threat and motivate self-protection and/or feelings of disgust and out-group derogation. We present social psychological laboratory research and, where available, field research specific to policing as a way of exploring and bolstering the proposed framework. This work supports an agenda for future scientific research that may assist practitioners in identifying likely opportunities for reform even as we await further field research that tests these hypothesized parameters.

Keywords: routine activities theory; policing; racial bias; social psychology

Nearly everyone with access to a television or social media has seen cell phone videos of black people dying at the hands of police officers over the past five years. Walter Scott. Tamir Rice. Philando Castille. Gut-wrenching videos have brought new attention to old problems of race in policing. Yet despite the resultant national appetite to understand issues of

Phillip Atiba Goff is the inaugural Franklin A. Thomas Professor in Policing Equity at John Jay College of Criminal Justice and the cofounder and president of the Center for Policing Equity. His work focuses on the predictors of discrimination, particularly in policing.

Hilary Rau is a legal research scholar at the Center for Policing Equity, where her work focuses on police policy and regulation.

Correspondence: goff@policingequity.org

DOI: 10.1177/0002716220901349

race and policing—and the increase in research findings around police miscon-duct and racial disparities in police behaviors (Braga and Weisburd 2015; Fagan et al. 2010)—there have been few attempts to provide a theoretical framework for predicting policing that is racially disparate or that unnecessarily infringes on human dignity and autonomy (see Worden 2015).

According to a recent consensus report from the National Academy of Sciences, factors that predict aggressive, intrusive, and biased policing are among the least studied issues in the field of policing, despite being among the most urgent (National Academies of Sciences Engineering and Medicine 2018). In the absence of coherent academic explanations, two theories have come to dominate popular culture and most academic research on the topic: that police are driven by bigotry or that statistical discrimination may account for a disproportionate amount of these disparities. There are reasons to suspect, however, that these theories are insufficient to explain the patterns of disparities observed in policing outcomes. Even a casual review of both the literature on race in policing and the social science literatures on what causes discrimination suggests that a more nuanced theoretical framing is necessary to predict the situations in which dispa-rate outcomes proliferate.

The purpose of this article is to articulate a more robust theoretical framework for burdensome and disparate policing. We do this by combining existing crimi-nological and social psychological literatures: specifically, we exploit the existing literatures on routine activity theory (RAT) in criminology (Cohen and Felson 1979) and situationist approaches to discrimination in social psychology (Dovidio 2001; Ross and Nisbett 2011) to frame predictions about when the risk of bur-densome and racially disparate policing is likely to be greatest. Our goal is to articulate a theoretical framing that sets forth an agenda for future scientific research. This agenda may also be useful to practitioners seeking to identify likely opportunities for reform while that research is in progress.

Theorizing Burdensome and Disparate Police Behavior

While there have been few attempts to theorize what predicts burdensome and racially disparate police behavior, criminologists have theorized extensively about what predicts civilian criminal behavior. RAT, one of the most cited theories in criminology, holds that crimes are most likely to occur when a likely offender and a suitable target converge in time and space in the absence of a capable guardian (Cohen and Felson 1979). The absence of any of these three conditions is typi-cally sufficient to deter crime (Felson 1987; Cohen and Felson 1979). For instance, RAT would predict that an assault is more likely to occur in a dark alley than in the middle of a crowded grocery store, that homes are more likely to be burglarized when no one is home, and that a computer is more likely to be hacked if it lacks a firewall.

Although RAT has been cited in thousands of articles over the last 40 years, it has rarely (if ever) been used to provide a theoretical frame for burdensome or racially disparate policing. RAT is commonly used to predict when and where robberies will take place, but it has rarely if ever been used to predict when and where racial profiling and excessive force incidents will take place.

Two challenges immediately arise to the use of RAT in theorizing burdensome and disparate policing. First, using a theory of criminal behavior to predict what is often lawful policing may seem jarring. While excessive force, sexual abuse, and other police misconduct certainly can violate criminal law, burdensome and disparate policing practices are frequently understood to be "lawful but awful" (Wogan 2016). RAT has, however, been applied to other noncriminal violations of community norms, such as bullying (Peguero 2008), academic fraud (N. Walker and Holtfreter 2015), and prosecutorial misconduct (Schoenfeld 2005). Because burdensome and racially disparate policing represents a violation of community norms in a plurality of communities (Weitzer and Tuch 2004), we believe that RAT provides an appropriate frame to predict when burdensome and disparate policing is most likely to occur. In addition, at least one research article we know of has used a routine activity approach to model police behavior, though it focuses on lawful proactive enforcement, arguing that "for a motivated officer to exercise their search powers requires them to converge in time and space with a suitable 'searchable' person in circumstances that allow the officer to identify the offender and take action" (Ashby and Tompson 2017, 112).

The second obvious objection to applying RAT to burdensome and disparate policing is that RAT remains agnostic regarding what makes someone likely to violate norms—and is mute on its implications regarding bias (Clarke 1997). As a result, RAT is not designed to predict when disparities are most likely to arise. We therefore turn to social psychology literature, which has examined this question extensively. A social psychological framework would predict that racial bias and aggression will occur most often when individuals vulnerable to situational risk factors encounter members of vulnerable out-groups in the absence of sufficient social regulation. Situational risk factors for bias and aggression are those situations that strongly promote in-group or self-protection or out-group derogation. Put differently, these are situations that provoke personal, or group-level, threat or disgust. There is significant psychological research suggesting that these situations are particularly likely to produce aggression toward out-group members (Cuddy, Fiske, and Glick 2007; Bosson et al. 2009; Maass et al. 2003; Hitlan et al. 2009; Trinkner and Goff 2018), increase reliance on stereotypes (Bodenhausen 1990; Govorun and Payne 2006; Macrae, Milne, and Bodenhausen 1994; Payne 2006; Correll et al. 2002; Correll, Urland, and Ito 2006), and increase stereotype-consistent behaviors (Devine 1989; Najdowski, Bottoms, and Goff 2015; Trinkner and Goff 2018).

The presence of formal or informal regulation can mitigate the risk that threat or disgust will lead to discriminatory or aggressive conduct (Pryor, Giedd, and Williams 1995; Dovidio 2001; Dovidio et al. 2008; Dovidio and Gaertner 1998; Gaertner and Dovidio 1986; Rogers and Prentice-Dunn 1981). While individuals may vary in their responses to situational risk factors, the past century of social psychological research suggests that immediate situations and norms are far more powerful predictors of behavior than are attitudes (Mischel 1968; Wicker 1969; LaPiere 1934; Ross and Nisbett 2011; Dovidio 2001).

The parallels between the criminological and psychological frames are striking: both predict that the modeled behaviors will occur most often when (1) individuals who are most likely to engage in those behaviors (2) engage individuals who are suitable targets, (3) in the absence of a capable guardian or regulation. This suggests a synergy between criminological and social psychological literatures and a reasonable theoretical framing for future research on both burdensome and disparate police behaviors. By integrating these approaches, we can create a framework for predicting when burdensome and disparate policing is most likely to occur. As an added benefit, this framework addresses a common critique by qualitative scholars of race in policing, namely, that criminology tends to undertheorize dominant groups—especially police—in regard to their bad behaviors (Jones 2004, 2014; Gau et al. 2012; Brunson and Gau 2015).

This article begins with a theoretical roadmap describing the overlap between RAT and a situationist social psychological approach as applied to the problem of burdensome and disparate policing. Based on our integration of criminological and social psychological theory, we propose that *burdensome and disparate policing is most likely to occur in situations that promote feelings of threat or disgust in police officers in the absence of sufficient regulation*. We explore this framework from the perspective of social psychology lab research and, where available, criminological field research specific to policing. First, we discuss the emotional and behavioral consequences of threat, which encompass both physical threat assessments and psychological threats to self-concept or group value, such as masculinity threat and stereotype threat. Second, we discuss disgust, a common affective response to prevalent cultural stereotypes that is correlated with dehumanization and aggression toward specific outgroups. Third, we discuss the crucial role of regulation in determining whether situational vulnerabilities will result in racially disparate or aggressive behavior in a given situation. This article is not intended to be a review but, rather, a theoretical roadmap for future research on the causes of and potential remedies to burdensome and disparate policing—up to and including police use of deadly force. In addition, we propose ways that this theoretical frame might inform practitioners' strategies for reducing burdensome and disparate policing until better evidence is available to support specific interventions.

Why Burdensome and Disparate Policing?

It is not obvious that policing viewed as burdensome (e.g., infringing on individual liberty and dignity; Worden 2015) and policing viewed as disparate (based on race, gender, or other social identities) would share common causes. However, aside from a context where an explicit directive can account for patrol officers' actions, behavioral science is instructive in trying to predict deviations from shared norms—even when that deviation itself eventually becomes a norm. And this is particularly true in the context of aggression.

Aggression and violence are socially prohibited across social contexts and require social justification if one is to avoid sanction (Bandura 1973; Lorenz 2005). Psychologists who study aggression have long agreed that the necessary formula is that a person is made ripe for aggression by either a chronic or immediate situation (Berkowitz 1993), an appropriate target, and the lack of sufficient social regulation (e.g., a referee, police officer, or physically dominant opponent; N. Miller et al. 2003). For instance, a classic domestic violence trope involves a man chronically frustrated at work who returns to a woman who criticizes his inability to get a better job. This man may turn violent in the absence of someone else in the home capable of preventing it. Similarly, the social psychology of bias finds that individuals who are made to feel threatened or disgusted by appropriate out-group targets will act negatively toward those targets in the absence of shared norms of appropriate behavior (Dovidio 2001; Gaertner and Dovidio 1977; Fein and Spencer 1997). For instance, in Gaertner and Dovidio's classic study on helping behavior (1977), participants helped someone in distress just as quickly if they were black or white as long as the participant was alone. When participants were in a group, however, and no one else moved to help the individual in distress, the norms for what the participant should do were no longer clear. Here, participants were much faster to help a white person in distress than a black person in distress. These formulations of aggression and bias have in common an actor (more or less vulnerable to situations); an appropriate target; and the presence of a guardian in the form of either an individual, rules, or strong social norms. In this way, the parallels between both of these theoretical models for undesirable behavior and RAT are clear: actors + targets – guardians = trouble.

Having established the overlaps between these literatures, we next introduce the social psychological literatures predicting police burdens and biases in a way that mirrors this RAT formulation. Again, from this literature, actors that are dispositionally or situationally vulnerable to experience threat or disgust are the most likely actors to engage in aggressive or discriminatory behaviors (Cuddy, Fiske, and Glick 2007; Dovidio 2001; Fein and Spencer 1997). Because situational vulnerability to threat and disgust also overdetermines the "appropriate target" in this formulation of RAT, we focus on what the literature tells us about vulnerability to threat and disgust broadly, and then move to the role of formal and social regulation.

Factors That Predict Discriminatory or Aggressive Policing

Here, we review the psychological science regarding situational factors that may contribute to racially disparate and aggressive behavior in the general population and, more specifically, within policing. First, we discuss the emotional and behavioral consequences of *threat*, which encompasses both physical threat assessments and psychological threats to self-concept or group-value, such as masculinity threat and stereotype threat. Second, we discuss *disgust*, a common affective response to prevalent cultural stereotypes that is correlated with dehumanization and aggression toward specific outgroups. Finally, we discuss the crucial role of *regulation* in determining whether situational vulnerabilities will result in racially disparate or aggressive behavior in a given situation.

For social psychologists, the concept of situational factors influencing behavior is broader than it is for criminologists. For instance, consistent with the field, Sherman defines situational factors that influence police behaviors as limited to the unique features of a single interaction (Sherman 1980). These situational factors, in concert with individual, organizational, community, and legal factors, make up the social ecology that shapes police behavior. In contrast, social psychologists would define all these factors save for individual differences as *kinds* of situations (Sommers 2012)—and would add a sociocultural layer to the ones listed by Sherman (Fiske et al. 1998; Markus and Kitayama 1991). This difference in terminology does not substantively change our framing. However, it may be useful to clarify that we use the social psychological definition of *situations* throughout this article.

Psychological and physical threat assessments

Officer safety is a central theme in police training. Officers are frequently trained that their highest and most important duty is that of self-preservation. One commonly repeated law enforcement adage holds that the overriding duty of a police officer is to go home to his or her family at the end of the shift (Stoughton 2014b). A fundamental tenet of police tactical training is that officers must maintain physical and psychological control of a situation to protect their personal safety and the safety of their fellow officers (Alpert and Dunham 2004; Swencionis et al., n.d.). In short, threat assessments are a routine job duty for many patrol officers.

According to psychological research, however, both physical threat assessments and threats to identity or self-concept can increase the risk that people will engage in racially disparate or aggressive behavior. Routine policing practices may, therefore, place officers in situations that chronically increase the risk of highly disparate or burdensome policing in a department.

Physical threat assessment. Officers are trained to consider a wide variety of seemingly objective factors in assessing physical threat during civilian encounters, including the suspect's behavior, speed of movement, size, strength, and access to weapons; the distance between the officer and the subject; the availability of cover; and the feasibility of retreat (Stoughton 2017; Garrett and Stoughton 2017). Each of these factors seems, at face value, to be objective and susceptible to impartial evaluation. Unfortunately, psychological science reveals that the way individuals perceive physical threat can be influenced by racial stereotypes—even in the absence of individual-level prejudice.

Strong cultural stereotypes in the United States link black people to criminality, aggressiveness, hostility, and danger (Devine 1989; Devine and Elliot 1995; Eberhardt et al. 2004). These stereotypes can affect the way that individuals perceive even objectively measurable aspects of interracial encounters. Racial biases can cause individuals to interpret identical facial expressions as more hostile on black faces than on white faces (Hugenberg and Bodenhausen 2003), cause individuals to perceive identical behaviors as more aggressive or threatening when engaged in by black people as opposed to white people (Duncan 1976; Kenrick et al. 2016), and affect perception of speed and motion during interracial encounters (Kenrick et al. 2016).

Multiple laboratory studies have found that racial bias can negatively influence accuracy and speed of weapon identification. Research by Payne and colleagues has shown that subjects are significantly more likely to mistake a tool for a gun when the item is paired with a black man's face rather than a white man's face (Payne 2001, 2006). In addition, multiple studies have found racial bias in both reaction times and error rates in shoot/don't shoot simulations. Subjects are more likely to "shoot" unarmed black targets than unarmed white targets and are more likely to choose "don't shoot" in response to armed white targets than in response to armed black targets. Subjects also took less time to decide to "shoot" armed targets who were black rather than white (Plant and Peruche 2005; Plant, Peruche, and Butz 2005; Swencionis and Goff 2017; Correll et al. 2002, 2007).

The effects of racial bias in time pressured shoot/don't shoot scenarios are particularly pronounced when the subject is a novice at the shooting task. Laboratory experiments on both college students and police officers have shown that repeated practice decreases the effects of racial bias on shooting errors and reaction times in shoot/don't shoot simulations (Plant and Peruche 2005; Plant, Peruche, and Butz 2005; Correll et al. 2002, 2007). Little is currently known about the effects of different types of police training on racial disparities in use of force in the field, making this an important area for future research (Swencionis and Goff 2017).

Police decisions about whether to fire a weapon in the field may be complicated by situational factors that make accurate, unbiased decision-making more difficult. Officers may be fatigued, hungry, or afraid (Correll et al. 2014; Govorun and Payne 2006; Danziger, Levav, and Avnaim-Pesso 2011). They may face time pressure or be required to divide their attention between multiple tasks or threat assessments at the same time. Human beings have limited capacity for processing information simultaneously or when subjected to time pressure (Broadbent 1958; Navon and Gopher 1979; Pashler 1994). Cognitively demanding situations reduce available cognitive processing resources and increase the likelihood of performance errors (E. K. Miller 2000; Robinson, Schmeichel, and Inzlicht 2010; Macrae, Milne, and Bodenhausen 1994). When cognitive demand is high, individuals are more likely to rely on cognitive "shortcuts" like stereotypes when making decisions (Macrae, Milne, and Bodenhausen 1994). At the same time, high cognitive demand reduces the number of cognitive resources available to control prejudiced responses (Bodenhausen 1990; Govorun and Payne 2006; Macrae, Milne, and Bodenhausen 1994).

Law enforcement agencies may be able to reduce racial disparities in policing outcomes by enacting policy changes to reduce unnecessary time pressure and cognitive demand. Researchers have found, for example, that internal scheduling and shift length policies can increase or decrease officer fatigue (Amendola et al. 2011; James, James, and Vila 2018). Law enforcement agencies might also see benefit from policies designed to reduce unnecessary time pressure in encounters with civilians. A central goal of modern police tactics is to create additional decision time during encounters, precisely because time constraints negatively affect the accuracy of officer perceptions and the quality of officer decision-making (Garrett and Stoughton 2017).

While popular media and Supreme Court briefs alike often highlight the need for officers to make time-pressured decisions with life-and-death consequences, the "split-second" decision is not a typical or unavoidable feature of most police-civilian encounters. Most police-civilian encounters do not involve any use of force. Use of force encounters typically involve proactive use of force by an officer to establish control over a suspect engaging in low-level, nonviolent resistance like going limp, pulling away, or running away. Situations in which officers use defensive use of force to protect themselves or others from imminent harm are comparatively rare (Garrett and Stoughton 2017; Stoughton 2014a). As a result, there are many situations in which officers have the ability to slow or de-escalate the pace of an encounter, providing additional time for decision-making. Policies that restrict officer discretion to engage in pursuits or that require officers to use de-escalation tactics prior to using force may, therefore, be reasonable strategies to reduce the risk of bias in police decision-making.

Psychological/identity threat. Threats to physical safety are not the only type of threats that can increase the risk of disparate and burdensome policing. Threats to self-concept or identity threats can also have powerful effects on individual behavior and performance. Within the context of policing, certain identity threats increase the risk that officers will handle encounters with vulnerable civilians in aggressive, violent, or coercive ways. In this article, we focus on two specific types of identity threat: masculinity threat and stereotype threat.

Masculinity. Threats to masculinity are one form of identity threat that can increase the risk that individuals will engage in aggressive or abusive behavior. Under some circumstances, men may engage in acts of violence, aggression, or domination to restore their threatened masculinity.

Being deemed sufficiently masculine is socially important for most men. Masculinities theorists argue that the attributes, behaviors, and roles associated with gender are not inherent or biological in nature. Masculinity is, rather, "the socially generated consensus of what it means to be a man, to be 'manly' or to display such behaviour at any one time" (Kerfoot and Knights 1996, 86). Masculinity is a status that must be earned through repeated active demonstrations and that can be lost relatively easily. Consequently, men experience chronic anxiety that they will be judged by other men to be insufficiently masculine (Vandello et al. 2008).

While being deemed sufficiently normatively masculine is important to most men, it is particularly important within the culture of policing. Policing has long been a male-dominated profession. Approximately seven out of every eight local U.S. police officers and nine out of every ten first line supervisors are men (Reaves 2015), and researchers have repeatedly found that aggressive masculinity plays a central role in police culture (Herbert 2001; Shelley, Morabito, and Tobin-Gurley 2011; Prokos and Padavic 2002). Although dangerous pursuits, use of force, and displays of physical prowess make up a very small fraction of a typical police officer's work (Stoughton 2014a), these more aggressive aspects of policing are frequently glorified among rank-and-file officers as the epitome of "real" police work. Administrative duties, on the other hand, are often denigrated as feminine: one researcher reported that Los Angeles Police Department (LAPD) officers who preferred administrative duties to dangerous street encounters were derisively referred to by their peers as "station queens" (Herbert 2001). In some departments, hypermasculinity is endorsed by police leaders and trainers, as well. One study of a police academy training program observed a "hidden curriculum" teaching recruits that extreme, aggressive, and misogynist forms of masculinity were lauded and expected within police culture (Prokos and Padavic 2002).

Because challenges to masculine identity can provoke anxiety for men, they often prompt men to engage in compensatory behaviors to demonstrate their manhood and alleviate the anxiety associated with the masculinity threat (Goff et al. 2012; Vandello et al. 2008; Bosson and Vandello 2011). In some cases, threats to masculinity can prompt men to engage in violent or aggressive behavior. In one laboratory study, researchers threatened some men's masculinity by asking them to perform a stereotypically feminine hair-braiding task. The researchers also asked another group of men to complete a more gender-neutral rope-braiding task. After completing the initial tasks, all men were asked to choose between hitting a punching target or solving a puzzle. Men assigned to the stereotypically feminine hair-braiding task selected the punching task more frequently than the men assigned to the more gender-neutral rope-braiding task. In a related study, the same researchers found that men who experienced masculinity threat punched a punching pad more forcefully than men whose masculinity was not threatened (Bosson et al. 2009).

Subordination, harassment, and abuse of outgroups can also serve as means for men to reassert threatened masculinity. Hegemonic masculinity is tied to hierarchy: a man proves his masculinity by dominating both individuals further down in the social hierarchies and anyone who challenges his masculinity (Cooper 2009). Authority, control, aggression, repudiation of femininity, and the capacity for violence are all central to this type of masculinity (Prokos and Padavic 2002). Researchers have found that men who experience masculinity threats are more likely to engage in sexual harassment (Maass et al. 2003; Hitlan et al. 2009) and place greater blame on female rape victims for the assaults committed against them (Munsch and Willer 2012). For a subset of men, sexual assault can serve as a means of demonstrating and restoring threatened masculinity (Messersschmidt 2000). Men who experience masculinity threat are also more likely to endorse and justify hegemonic racial violence (Richardson and Goff 2014).

Within the hypermasculine culture of policing, violence, aggression, and harassment of vulnerable groups can be a particularly effective means of restoring an officer's threatened masculinity. Harassment and abuse of women are extremely common within police departments. Multiple studies have found that the majority of female police officers report having been sexually harassed by colleagues (Bartol et al. 1992; Chaiyavej and Morash 2009; Shelley, Morabito, and Tobin-Gurley 2011). While police sexual harassment and abuse of civilians is underreported and poorly tracked, a 2010 report by the Cato Institute found that sexual misconduct was the second most commonly reported form of police misconduct, exceeded only by use of excessive force (Cato Institute 2010). Gay men are also frequent targets of harassment and abuse by police officers. Gay male police officers are one of the lowest status groups in police departments and frequently face harassment, denigration, and exclusion by their fellow officers. Gay civilians also frequently experience violence at the hands of police officers (Richardson and Goff 2014).

Police experiences of masculinity threat can also prompt officers to engage in and excuse hegemonic racial violence. Because black men are stereotyped as so hypermasculine as to be bestial and subhuman (Goff, Steele, and Davies 2008; Goff et al. 2014), officers may be more likely to experience masculinity threat when interacting with black civilians than when interacting with white civilians. Moreover, because black men are stereotyped as hypermasculine, bestial, and dangerous, dominating black men provides a particularly powerful way for officers to reestablish threatened masculinity (Kimmel 2003; Cooper 2009). In her foundational article "Gender Violence, Race, and Criminal Justice," legal scholar Angela Harris argues that police brutality is a form of gender violence because it is a means for police officers to perform masculinity (A. P. Harris 2000). Research from the Center for Policing Equity has found that police officers' level of masculinity threat predicts their use of force against black men (Goff, Martin, and Gamson-Smiedt 2012). While hegemonic masculinity and racism are closely connected, the correlation between masculinity threat and racially disparate policing is not dependent on conscious racial bigotry on the part of police officers. An officer who consciously endorses racial equality may nonetheless be more likely to experience the anxiety of masculinity threat and to act aggressively in interactions with black men than in comparable interactions with white men.

Stereotype. Police officers may also be more likely to engage in disparate and burdensome policing when they are, or fear being, evaluated in terms of a negative stereotype about police officers. Within social psychology, the concern with conforming to or being evaluated in terms of a negative stereotype about one's group is referred to as "stereotype threat" (Steele 1997; Steele and Aronson 1995). Stereotype threat typically arises in situations in which a person perceives that he or she is being evaluated in an area that he or she cares about deeply. A person need not agree with the negative stereotype in question to be anxious that others will evaluate him or her in accordance with that stereotype. For example, a black university student who cares about her academic performance may experience stereotype threat when taking a math test based on concerns that her performance will be judged in accordance with racial and gender stereotypes about math ability. In the context of policing, an officer may experience stereotype threat if she fears that she will be stereotyped as racist when conducting a traffic stop, just because she is an officer.

Stereotype threats provoke anxiety: they challenge a person's individual social identity and self-worth while simultaneously challenging the standing of one's social groups (Goff, Steele, and Davies 2008; Trinkner and Goff 2018). And while the anxiety resulting from stereotype threat is consciously accessible, the physical and mental reactions to it often are not. Documented effects of stereotype threat include sweating, increased heart rate, cognitive depletion, and performance decrements in important domains (Steele, Spencer, and Aronson 2002). Ultimately, stereotype threat often leads to underperformance in the very area in which a person feared being evaluated negatively. In other words, experiencing stereotype threat can, ironically, increase the likelihood that a person will engage in stereotype-confirming behavior (Bosson, Haymovitz, and Pinel 2004; O'Brien and Crandall 2003; Beilock et al. 2006; Mendes et al. 2002; Schmader and Johns 2003).

While stereotype threat was originally identified and studied as a phenomenon that suppressed the performance of women and nonwhite students in academic settings (Steele and Aronson 1995), the phenomenon can occur in a wide variety of contexts. Stereotype threat affects members of majority and dominant groups as well as members of nonwhite or other stigmatized groups (Goff, Steele, and Davies 2008; Richeson and Shelton 2003; Vorauer, Main, and Connell 1998). One subtype of stereotype threat that can affect white people is racist stereotype threat: the fear of being stereotyped as racist (Goff, Steele, and Davies 2008). In the context of interracial interactions, white people who care about being seen as egalitarian but fear being stereotyped as racist may experience the classic anxiety symptoms associated with stereotype threat. Ironically, anxiety about being stereotyped as racist can produce stereotype-confirming behaviors—such as avoidance, physical distancing, avoiding eye contact, cognitive depletion, and nervous mannerisms—that foster negative interracial interactions (Goff, Steele, and Davies 2008; Najdowski, Bottoms, and Goff 2015).

The handful of studies on the effect of racist stereotype threat on police use of force are consistent with the general literature on stereotype threat: officers who are *concerned about* appearing racist are *more likely to use force* in racially disparate ways (Trinkner and Goff 2018). In one 2012 study of officers from a large urban police department, the Center for Policing Equity found a correlation between stereotype threat and greater use of force against black civilians (Goff, Martin, and Gamson-Smiedt 2012). In a second Center for Policing Equity study of an even larger department, stereotype threat was not correlated with disparities in frequency of use of force. It was, however, associated with more severe use of force against black civilians as compared to white and Latinx civilians (Goff and Martin 2012).

The correlation between racist stereotype threat and racially disparate use of force by police officers is counterintuitive. Yet it is consistent with the well-established general principle that stereotype threat increases the likelihood of stereotype-confirming behavior. It is easy to understand how explicit or implicit allegations that an officer has engaged in racially biased policing can cause a police-civilian encounter to escalate. In July 2009, for example, prominent Harvard professor Henry Louis Gates Jr. was arrested on the front porch of his own home by Cambridge police officer Sgt. James Crowley for alleged disorderly conduct after Professor Gates accused Sgt. Crowley of racial profiling.

Richardson and Goff (2014) argue that concern about being perceived as racist lowers officers' confidence in their own moral authority to address situations in noncoercive ways, thereby increasing the likelihood that officers will resort to physical force (or more serious force) to maintain control of a situation. In a study of 786 line officers and sergeants from the patrol division of a large urban police force, Trinkner and Goff (2018) found that officers who experienced greater stereotype threat had less confidence in their own legitimacy and moral authority as officers. Officers with less confidence in their own moral authority as police officers were more likely to approve of excessive force, less likely to accept their departments' use of force policy, and less likely to endorse procedurally fair policing.

Disgust

Cultural stereotypes that promote strong derogation of outgroups also increase the risk that individuals will engage in aggressive and harmful behavior. As a result, members of extreme social outgroups who are commonly dehumanized and viewed with disgust are likely to be particularly vulnerable to police aggression and misconduct.

Social psychology research indicates emotional reactions to outgroups are strongly influenced by exposure to cultural stereotypes, even if individuals do not personally endorse those stereotypes (Cuddy, Fiske, and Glick 2007; Gaertner and Dovidio 1986). According to the stereotype content model (SCM) proposed by social psychologist Susan Fiske and colleagues (2002), cultural stereotypes form along two dimensions: warmth and competence. Extreme outgroups stereotyped as both hostile and incompetent are subject to the worst kind of prejudice: disgust (Cuddy, Fiske, and Glick 2007; Fiske 2013; Harris and Fiske 2006). "Disgust is unique among the emotions predicted by the SCM because it can target either humans or nonhumans, making people functionally equivalent to objects" (Harris and Fiske 2006, 848). One neuroimaging study found that the portion of people's brains responsible for social decision-making, the medial prefrontal cortex, fails to activate in the presence of extreme outgroups, such as homeless people (Harris and Fiske 2006).

Emotions predict behavior more strongly than stereotypes, often mediating links between stereotypes and behavior (Cuddy, Fiske, and Glick 2007). Contempt and disgust elicited by low-warmth/low-competence stereotypes predict both active harm, such as physical violence and harassment; and passive harm, such as exclusion and neglect (Cuddy et al. 2009; Harris and Fiske 2006).

Within the context of policing, disgust and dehumanization may lead to members of vulnerable communities being overpoliced and overcriminalized yet underserved. Some of the extreme outgroups most vulnerable to disgust and dehumanization include homeless people, people with serious mental illness, people with substance abuse disorders, sex workers, welfare recipients, undocumented immigrants, Arab people, and low-income black people (Cuddy, Fiske, and Glick 2007; Harris and Fiske 2006; Lee and Fiske 2006; Fiske and Dupree 2014; Cuddy et al. 2009; Fiske 2012). Because these social outgroups are often among the groups most likely to have contact with police, disgust has the potential to contribute to widespread patterns of burdensome and disparate policing.

In some cases, disgust can lead to passive harm, such as failure to seriously investigate crimes against members of vulnerable outgroups. In the early 1990s, for example, LAPD officers commonly referred to assaults and murders of black and Latinx residents—especially low-status residents such as sex workers, individuals with substance abuse disorders, and gang members—by the disturbing and dehumanizing acronym "N.H.I.": no humans involved (*LA Times* 2010; Wigon 2014; Wells 2017; Leovy 2015).

Disgust can also lead to active harm, such as increased use of force against members of vulnerable outgroups. Individuals with serious mental illness, for example, are more likely to experience police use of force even after controlling for other confounding factors such as crime and poverty (Laniyonu and Goff, n.d.). Because disgust leads to dehumanization, police officers and police policy-makers may not always perceive police violence against members of extreme outgroups to be a problem. On July 28, 2017, for example, President Donald Trump referred to Latinx gang members as "animals" four times during a speech to a group of Long Island law enforcement officers, encouraging officers to be physically rougher with arrestees. While the hosting law enforcement agency swiftly distanced itself from the president's remarks on social media, the listening crowd of law enforcement officers seemed to react to this unconstitutional suggestion with laughter and applause (Bump 2017).

Based on the social psychological research, we would predict that police departments can reduce disparate and burdensome policing by taking steps to reduce unnecessary police contact with members of social outgroups vulnerable to disgust and dehumanization. The Minneapolis Police Department, for example, reduced its use of force by 46 percent the year that it began partnering with local social service agencies to reduce police enforcement contacts with homeless residents (Jany 2018).

Inadequate regulation

Regulation plays a key role in determining whether and when situations that prompt self-protection or outgroup derogation will lead to actual discriminatory or aggressive behavior. As a result, police policy-makers may be able to reduce disparate and burdensome policing by regulating situations that chronically produce undesirable outcomes.

In 2013, a federal district court ruled in *Floyd v. City of New York* that the New York Police Department's (NYPD) use of stop and frisk was unconstitutional as practiced, requiring the NYPD to implement changes to its policies, training, auditing, performance evaluation procedures, and handling of civilian complaints. One of the changes implemented as a result of the *Floyd* litigation was a new requirement that officers provide their supervisors with narratives for the justifications for each of their stops, frisks, and searches on a daily basis (Mummolo 2018). Beginning in the latter stages of the litigation, and continuing through at least 2015, the number of stops and frisks by NYPD officers decreased dramatically. Racial disparities in stop and frisk outcomes for black and Latinx individuals diminished over the same time period (MacDonald and Braga 2018). This was not the first time that the NYPD had found success in reducing problematic police outcomes through new regulation: in 1972, the NYPD saw a notable reduction in police shootings after adopting new administrative shooting guidelines that included multiple specific restrictions on officer discretion with respect to use of deadly force, including a prohibition on firing at moving vehicles except when the occupants of the vehicle were using deadly force against the officer by means other than the vehicle itself (Fyfe 1979).

The experience of the NYPD is consistent with a significant body of social psychology research indicating that people are far more likely to engage in discriminatory or aggressive behavior in situations that lack clear rules or norms mandating appropriate behavior or that allow for the exercise of discretion (Pryor, Giedd, and Williams 1995; Dovidio 2001; Dovidio et al. 2008; Dovidio and Gaertner 1998; Gaertner and Dovidio 1986; Rogers and Prentice-Dunn 1981).

Social science laboratory research has repeatedly found that social regulation plays a key role in determining whether individuals will rely on conscious or unconscious racial biases when making decisions. When people are placed in situations with clear norms and restricted discretion, they are more likely to behave in an equitable, egalitarian manner. When people are placed in situations in which rules and norms are unclear or allow for the exercise of discretion, they are more likely to rely on implicit biases in making decisions (Dovidio and Gaertner 2000; Gaertner, Dovidio, and Johnson 1982; Dovidio 2001). In a study on hiring recommendations, for example, Dovidio and Gaertner (2000) found that when candidate qualifications were ambiguous or debatable, white study participants recommended black candidates significantly less often than white candidates with exactly the same credentials. By contrast, white study participants did not discriminate against black candidates who were clearly and obviously qualified for the position. In other words, discrimination was more likely to occur when social norms dictating appropriate behavior were weak or ambiguous. Discrimination was less likely to occur when the socially expected course of action was clear.

Laboratory research also suggests that regulation or the lack thereof can influence whether people engage in aggressive behavior. Racial violence is more likely within social contexts that encourage or permit aggression. Biased aggression is less likely to occur when individuals fear censure from others, but it is disinhibited in situations in which people feel anonymous, deindividuated, or justified in their actions (Dovidio et al. 2008; Rogers and Prentice-Dunn 1981). Sexual harassment and sexual assault are also more likely to occur in situations in which perpetrators have neutral excuses for touching their victims or have reason to believe that their actions will be condoned by individuals in positions of authority (Pryor, LaVite, and Stoller 1993; Dekker and Barling 1998; Pryor, Giedd, and Williams 1995).

Based on this psychological research, we would predict that law enforcement policy-makers can reduce burdensome and disparate policing by increasing regulation to clarify expected behavior and limit officer discretion in situations that chronically produce disparate or burdensome outcomes. Regulation may take the form of either increased front-end restrictions on officer discretion or increased back-end accountability.

Front-end restrictions on officer discretion may include prohibitions on specific conduct, such as NYPD's 1972 administrative shooting guidelines prohibiting officers from firing at moving vehicles in most circumstances (Fyfe 1979). Front-end restrictions on officer discretion might also include clearer rules and policies addressing the criteria that should guide officer decision-making or requirements that officers obtain supervisor approval before engaging in specific types of enforcement action. In the early 2000s, for example, the U.S. Customs Service (now U.S. Customs and Border Protection) adopted more restrictive guidelines governing searches, setting specific criteria for when searches could be conducted and requiring prior supervisor approval for certain types of searches. The number of individuals searched declined by 47 percent while the hit rate rose by 65 percent. Racial disparities in search rates also declined (S. Walker and Katz 2008).

Successful regulation may also take the form of back end accountability. Written polices alone cannot restrict officer discretion or create clear expectations of officer behavior if those policies are not enforced. Unsurprisingly, law enforcement agencies that have observed improvements in policing outcomes following new policy restrictions on officer discretion often coupled new written restrictions on discretion with interventions designed to bolster back-end accountability. The 1972 changes to NYPD shooting guidelines were coupled with the establishment of a Firearms Discharge Review Board that was empowered to investigate and adjudicate incidents in which officers discharged their service weapons (Fyfe 1979). The post-*Floyd* reforms in New York City included not only written policy changes, but also the appointment of a federal monitor and changes to internal procedures for routine supervision, auditing, performance evaluation, and handling of civilian complaints (MacDonald and Braga 2018). Changes in policy required by reform agreements between the U.S. Department of Justice and local law enforcement agencies have always been coupled with oversight by the federal court system and an appointed independent monitoring team (U.S. Department of Justice 2017). In the absence of that regulatory framework, some departments have struggled to sustain organizational changes after the termination of formal external oversight (Chanin 2015).

Some law enforcement agencies have also found early intervention systems to be a useful tool for clarifying expected standards of officer behavior and reducing negative outcomes. Early intervention systems are "data-driven programs designed to identify officers whose behavior appears to be problematic and to subject those officers to some kind of intervention, usually in the form of counseling or training designed to correct the problematic behavior" (S. Walker, Alpert, and Kenney 2000, 132). Initial evidence also suggests that well-functioning early intervention systems can help to reduce the frequency of citizen complaints and officer misconduct (Macintyre, Prenzler, and Chapman 2008; S. Walker, Alpert, and Kenney 2000).

Because law enforcement agencies are unlikely to discover many types of misconduct unless members of the public report them, community trust, legitimacy, and communication are likely to be crucial to effective back-end accountability. Members of vulnerable populations like low-income nonwhite people, undocumented immigrants, people with substance use disorders, sex workers, and individuals on parole or probation may fear arrest or deportation if they report law enforcement misconduct or cooperate with a law enforcement investigation. As a result, law enforcement agencies seeking to improve officer accountability may benefit from interventions designed to improve public legitimacy and community trust, thereby encouraging community reporting of law enforcement misconduct. Ensuring that complaint procedures are accessible to people with disabilities or limited English proficiency may also be important if law enforcement agencies are to learn of officer misconduct against vulnerable populations.

Conclusion

This article shows how social psychology research and theory can provide significant insight into why the conditions of policing can elicit unfortunate behaviors from police officers. Specifically, we argue that both physical threat and perceived threats to officers' group and self-concept can provoke aggressive and/or biased responses toward civilians. Additionally, some situations that are likely to provoke those threats—from physical threats, to cognitive depletion, a motivation to perform normative masculinity, and concerns with appearing racist—are all prevalent in the daily experiences of patrol officers. Taken together, this suggests specific individuals with whom and situations about where burdensome and disparate policing is most likely for future research.

Additionally, because patrol officers are so frequently in contact with the segments of society that broadly elicit disgust (e.g., individuals who are homeless, have drug abuse problems, perform sex work, and/or struggle with serious mental illness), those officers are chronically at risk for the consequences of that exposure. This includes actively negative behaviors targeting those populations. This is a critical risk given the prevalence of police use of force targeted at individuals struggling with serious mental illness (Laniyonu and Goff, n.d.), many of which encounters could be prevented by policies promoting minimal police engagement (Jany 2018).

There is, however, more to research than which situations social psychology (in our modified version of RAT) says provoke burdensome and disparate policing. There are opportunities for both front- and back-end regulation to interrupt these risk factors and prevent these types of behavior. While we wait for scientists to produce the research that tests the validity of these hypotheses, identifying the risk factors for values-misaligned policing may provide a shorthand to police executives—and the communities they serve—who cannot wait for science to complete the task.

We do not suggest that the framework we outline in this article take the place of rigorous evidence-informed practice. For instance, in a forthcoming article, Goff and Buchanan argue that using analyses of police behavioral data can provide a feedback loop akin to COMPSTAT, but with the measurable outcome being racial disparities (that police can influence) rather than crime (Goff and Buchanan, forthcoming). However, we do believe that using theory to inform how police address urgent issues is a potentially underappreciated resource for practitioners when the field has not supplied any such rigorous evidence. In other words, we see no reason that practitioners should not be given the same hypotheses available to scientists, especially when their attempts to find solutions are far more consequential. By identifying the officers and situations most likely to produce behaviors that damage the public trust of law enforcement, we expand the community of concerned citizens capable of observing successful interventions against such behaviors.

References

Alpert, Geoffrey P., and Roger G. Dunham. 2004. *Understanding police use of force: Officers, suspects, and reciprocity*. Cambridge Studies in Criminology. Cambridge: Cambridge University Press.

Amendola, Karen L., David Weisburd, Edwin E. Hamilton, Greg Jones, and Meghan Slipka. 2011. *The impact of shift length in policing on performance, health, quality of life, sleep, fatigue, and extra-duty employment*. Washington, DC: National Institute of Justice.

Ashby, Matthew P. J., and Lisa Tompson. 2017. Routine activities and proactive police activity: A macro-scale analysis of police searches in London and New York City. *Justice Quarterly* 34 (1): 109–35.

Bandura, Albert. 1973. *Aggression: A social learning analysis*. Upper Saddle River, NJ: Prentice-Hall.

Bartol, Curt, George T. Bergen, Julie Seager Volckens, and Kathleen M. Knoras. 1992. Women in small-town policing: Job performance and stress. *Criminal Justice and Behavior* 19 (3): 240–59.

Beilock, Sian L., William A. Jellison, Robert J. Rydell, Allen R. McConnell, and Thomas H. Carr. 2006. On the causal mechanisms of stereotype threat: Can skills that don't rely heavily on working memory still be threatened? *Personality and Social Psychology Bulletin* 32 (8): 1059–71.

Berkowitz, Leonard. 1993. *Aggression: Its causes, consequences, and control*. New York, NY: McGraw-Hill Book Company.

Bodenhausen, Galen V. 1990. Stereotypes as judgmental heuristics: Evidence of circadian variations in discrimination. *Psychological Science* 1 (5): 319–22.

Bosson, Jennifer K., Ethan L. Haymovitz, and Elizabeth C. Pinel. 2004. When saying and doing diverge: The effects of stereotype threat on self-reported versus non-verbal anxiety. *Journal of Experimental Social Psychology* 40 (2): 247–55.

Bosson, Jennifer K., and Joseph A. Vandello. 2011. Precarious manhood and its links to action and aggression. *Current Directions in Psychological Science* 20 (2): 82–86.

Bosson, Jennifer K., Joseph A. Vandello, Rochelle M. Burnaford, Jonathan R. Weaver, and S. Arzu Wasti. 2009. Precarious manhood and displays of physical aggression. *Personality and Social Psychology Bulletin* 35 (5): 623–34.

Braga, Anthony A., and David L. Weisburd. 2015. Focused deterrence and the prevention of violent gun injuries: Practice, theoretical principles, and scientific evidence. *Annual Review of Public Health* 36:55–68.

Broadbent, D. E., ed. 1958. The effects of noise on behaviour. In *Perception and communication*, 81–107. Elmsford, NY: Pergamon Press.

Brunson, Rod K., and Jacinta M. Gau. 2015. Officer race versus macro-level context: A test of competing hypotheses about black citizens' experiences with and perceptions of black police officers. *Crime and Delinquency*. Available from https://doi.org/10.1177/0011128711398027.

Bump, Philip. 28 July 2017. Trump's speech encouraging police to be "rough," annotated. *Washington Post*.

Cato Institute. 2010. *National Police Misconduct Reporting Project, 2010 annual report*. Washington, DC: Cato Institute.

Chaiyavej, Somvadee, and Merry Morash. 2009. Reasons for policewomen's assertive and passive reactions to sexual harassment. *Police Quarterly* 12 (1): 63–85.

Chanin, Joshua M. 2015. Examining the sustainability of pattern or practice police misconduct reform. *Police Quarterly* 18 (2): 163–92.

Clarke, Ronald V. 1997. *Situational crime prevention: Successful case studies*. Guilderland, NY: Harrow and Heston.

Cohen, Lawrence E., and Marcus Felson. 1979. Social change and crime rate trends: A routine activity approach. *American Sociological Review* 44 (August): 588–608.

Cooper, Frank Rudy. 2009. "Who's the man?" Masculinities studies, Terry stops, and police training. *Columbia Journal of Gender and Law* 18:671–742.

Correll, Joshua, Sean M. Hudson, Steffanie Guillermo, and Debbie S. Ma. 2014. The police officer's dilemma: A decade of research on racial bias in the decision to shoot. *Social and Personality Psychology Compass* 5 (5): 201–13.

Correll, Joshua, Bernadette Park, Charles M. Judd, and Bernd Wittenbrink. 2002. The police officer's dilemma: Using ethnicity to disambiguate potentially threatening individuals. *Journal of Personality and Social Psychology* 83 (6): 1314–29.

Correll, Joshua, Bernadette Park, Charles M. Judd, Bernd Wittenbrink, Melody S. Sadler, and Tracie Keesee. 2007. Across the thin blue line: Police officers and racial bias in the decision to shoot. *Journal of Personality and Social Psychology* 92 (6): 1006–23.

Correll, Joshua, Geoffrey R. Urland, and Tiffany A. Ito. 2006. Event-related potentials and the decision to shoot: The role of threat perception and cognitive control. *Journal of Experimental Social Psychology* 42 (1): 120–28.

Cuddy, Amy J. C., Susan T. Fiske, and Peter Glick. 2007. The BIAS map: Behaviors from intergroup affect and stereotypes. *Journal of Personality and Social Psychology* 92 (4): 631–48.

Cuddy, Amy J. C., Susan T. Fiske, Virginia S. Y. Kwan, Peter Glick, Stéphanie Demoulin, Jacques-Philippe Leyens, Michael Harris Bond, Jean-Claude Croizet, Naomi Ellemers, and Ed Sleebos, et al. 2009. Stereotype content model across cultures: Towards universal similarities and some differences. *British Journal of Social Psychology / The British Psychological Society* 48 (1): 1–33.

Danziger, Shai, Jonathan Levav, and Liora Avnaim-Pesso. 2011. Extraneous factors in judicial decisions. *Proceedings of the National Academy of Sciences of the United States of America* 108 (17): 6889–92.

Dekker, Inez, and Julian Barling. 1998. Personal and organizational predictors of workplace sexual harassment of women by men. *Journal of Occupational Health Psychology* 3 (1): 7–18.

Devine, Patricia G. 1989. Stereotypes and prejudice: Their automatic and controlled components. *Journal of Personality and Social Psychology* 56 (1): 5–18.

Devine, Patricia G., and Andrew J. Elliot. 1995. Are racial stereotypes really fading? The Princeton trilogy revisited. *Personality and Social Psychology Bulletin* 21 (11): 1139–50.

Dovidio, John F. 2001. On the nature of contemporary prejudice: The third wave. *Journal of Social Issues* 57 (4): 829–49.

Dovidio, John F., and Samuel L. Gaertner. 1998. On the nature of contemporary prejudice: The causes, consequences, and challenges of aversive racism. In *Confronting racism: The problem and the response*, 3–32. Thousand Oaks, CA: Sage Publications.

Dovidio, John F., and Samuel L. Gaertner. 2000. Aversive racism and selection decisions: 1989 and 1999. *Psychological Science* 11 (4): 315–19.

Dovidio, John F., Adam R. Pearson, Samuel L. Gaertner, and Gordon Hodson. 2008. On the nature of contemporary prejudice: From subtle bias to severe consequences. In *Explaining the breakdown of ethnic relations: Why neighbors kill*, eds. Victoria M. Esses and Richard A. Vernon, 41–60. Hoboken, NJ: Blackwell Publishing Ltd.

Duncan, Birt L. 1976. Differential social perception and attribution of intergroup violence: Testing the lower limits of stereotyping of blacks. *Journal of Personality and Social Psychology* 34 (4): 590–98.

Eberhardt, Jennifer L., Phillip Atiba Goff, Valerie J. Purdie, and Paul G. Davies. 2004. Seeing black: Race, crime, and visual processing. *Journal of Personality and Social Psychology* 87 (6): 876–93.

Fagan, Jeffrey A., Amanda Geller, Garth Davies, and Valerie West. 2010. Street stops and broken windows revisited. In *Race, ethnicity, and policing: New and essential readings*, eds. Stephen K. Rice and Michael D. White, 309–48. New York, NY: NYU Press.

Fein, Steven, and Steven J. Spencer. 1997. Prejudice as self-image maintenance: Affirming the self through derogating others. *Journal of Personality and Social Psychology* 73 (1): 31–44.

Felson, Marcus. 1987. Routine activities and crime prevention in the developing metropolis. *Criminology* 25 (4): 911–32.

Fiske, Susan T. 2012. Warmth and competence: Stereotype content issues for clinicians and researchers. *Canadian Psychology* 53 (1): 14–20.

Fiske, Susan T. 2013. Objectification and (de)humanization. Nebraska Symposium on Motivation 60:53–71.

Fiske, Susan T., Amy J. C. Cuddy, Peter Glick, and Jun Xu. 2002. A model of (often mixed) stereotype content: Competence and warmth respectively follow from perceived status and competition. *Journal of Personality and Social Psychology* 82 (6): 878–902.

Fiske, Susan T., and Cydney Dupree. 2014. Gaining trust as well as respect in communicating to motivated audiences about science topics. *Proceedings of the National Academy of Sciences* 111 (Suppl. 4): 13593–97.

Fiske, Susan, Alan Page, Shinobu Kitayama, Hazel R. Markus, and Richard E. Nisbett. 1998. The cultural matrix of social psychology. In *The handbook of social psychology*, eds. D. T. Gilbert, S. T. Fiske, and G. Lindze, 915–81. New York, NY: McGraw-Hill.

Fyfe, James J. 1979. Administrative interventions on police shooting discretion: An empirical examination. *Journal of Criminal Justice* 7 (4): 309–23.

Gaertner, Samuel L., and John F. Dovidio. 1977. The subtlety of white racism, arousal, and helping behavior. *Journal of Personality and Social Psychology* 35 (10): 691–707.

Gaertner, Samuel L., and John F. Dovidio. 1986. *The aversive form of racism*. Cambridge, MA: Academic Press.

Gaertner, Samuel L., John F. Dovidio, and G. Johnson. 1982. Race of victim, nonresponsive bystanders, and helping behavior. *Journal of Social Psychology* 117 (1): 69–77.

Garrett, Brandon L., and Seth W. Stoughton. 2017. A tactical fourth amendment. *Virginia Law Review* 103:211–304.

Gau, Jacinta M., Nicholas Corsaro, Eric A. Stewart, and Rod K. Brunson. 2012. Examining macro-level impacts on procedural justice and police legitimacy. *Journal of Criminal Justice* 40 (4): 333–43.

Goff, Phillip Atiba, Brooke Allison, Lewis Di Leone, and Kimberly Barsamian Kahn. 2012. Racism leads to pushups: How racial discrimination threatens subordinate men's masculinity. *Journal of Experimental Social Psychology* 48 (5): 1111–16.

Goff, Phillip Atiba, and Kim Shayo Buchanan. Forthcoming. A data-driven remedy for racial disparities: COMPSTAT for justice. *New York University Annual Survey of American Law*.

Goff, Phillip Atiba, Matthew Christian Jackson, Di Leone, Brooke Allison Lewis, Carmen Marie Culotta, and Natalie Ann DiTomasso. 2014. The essence of innocence: Consequences of dehumanizing black children. *Journal of Personality and Social Psychology* 106 (4): 526–45.

Goff, Phillip Atiba, and Karin D. Martin. 2012. *Unity breeds fairness: The consortium for police leadership in equity report on the Las Vegas Metropolitan Police Department.* Los Angeles, CA: University of California, Los Angeles.

Goff, Phillip Atiba, Karin D. Martin, and Meredith Gamson-Smiedt. 2012. *Protecting equity: The consortium for police leadership in equity report on the San Jose Police Department.* Los Angeles, CA: University of California, Los Angeles.

Goff, Phillip Atiba, Claude M. Steele, and Paul G. Davies. 2008. The space between us: Stereotype threat and distance in interracial contexts. *Journal of Personality and Social Psychology* 94 (1): 91–107.

Govorun, Olesya, and B. Keith Payne. 2006. Ego-depletion and prejudice: Separating automatic and controlled components. *Social Cognition* 24 (2): 111–36.

Harris, Angela P. 2000. Gender, violence, race, and criminal justice. *Stanford Law Review* 52 (4): 777–807.

Harris, Lasana T., and Susan T. Fiske. 2006. Dehumanizing the lowest of the low: Neuroimaging responses to extreme out-groups. *Psychological Science* 17 (10): 847–53.

Herbert, S. 2001. "Hard charger" or "station queen?" Policing and the masculinist state. *Gender, Place and Culture* 8 (1): 55–71.

Hitlan, Robert T., John B. Pryor, Matthew S. Hesson-McInnis, and Michael Olson. 2009. Antecedents of gender harassment: An analysis of person and situation factors. *Sex Roles* 61 (11–12): 794–807.

Hugenberg, Kurt, and Galen V. Bodenhausen. 2003. Facing prejudice implicit prejudice and perception. *Psychological Science* 14 (6): 640–43.

James, Lois, Stephen James, and Bryan Vila. 2018. The impact of work shift and fatigue on police officer response in simulated interactions with citizens. *Journal of Experimental Criminology* 14 (1): 111–20.

Jany, Libor. 9 August 2018. Minneapolis police taking a different approach to homelessness. *Star Tribune.*

Jones, Nikki. 2004. "It's not where you live, it's how you live": How young women negotiate conflict and violence in the inner city. *The ANNALS of the American Academy of Political and Social Science* 595:49–62.

Jones, Nikki. 2014. "The regular routine": Proactive policing and adolescent development among young, poor black men. *New Directions for Child and Adolescent Development* 2014 (143): 33–54.

Kenrick, Andreana C., Stacey Sinclair, Jennifer Richeson, Sara C. Verosky, and Janetta Lun. 2016. Moving while black: Intergroup attitudes influence judgments of speed. *Journal of Experimental Psychology: General* 145 (2): 147–54.

Kerfoot, Deborah, and David Knights. 1996. "The best is yet to come?" The quest for embodiment in managerial work. In *Men as managers, managers as men*, eds. David Collinson and Jeff Hearn, 78–98. Thousand Oaks, CA: Sage Publications.

Kimmel, Michael S. 2003. Masculinity as homophobia: Fear, shame, and silence in the construction of gender identity. In *Privilege: A reader*, eds. Abby Ferber and Michael S. Kimmel. Boulder, CO: Westview Press.

Laniyonu, Ayobami, and Phillip Atiba Goff. n.d. Policing the most vulnerable: Measuring disparities in police use of force and injury among persons with serious mental illness. Manuscript under review.

LaPiere, R. T. 1934. Attitudes vs. actions. *Social Forces* 13 (2): 230–37.

LA Times. 16 November 2010. Shades of the "old" LAPD.

Lee, Tiane L., and Susan T. Fiske. 2006. Not an outgroup, not yet an ingroup: Immigrants in the stereotype content model. *International Journal of Intercultural Relations* 30 (6): 751–68.

Leovy, Jill. 19 February 2015. What you think about dangerous inner-city neighborhoods is wrong. *Washington Post.*

Lorenz, Konrad. 2005. *On aggression.* New York, NY: Routledge.

Maass, Anne, Mara Cadinu, Gaia Guarnieri, and Annalisa Grasselli. 2003. Sexual harassment under social identity threat: The computer harassment paradigm. *Journal of Personality and Social Psychology* 85 (5): 853–70.

MacDonald, John, and Anthony A. Braga. 2018. Did Post-Floyd et al. reforms reduce racial disparities in NYPD stop, question, and frisk practices? An exploratory analysis using external and internal benchmarks. *Justice Quarterly* 8825:1–30.

Macintyre, Stuart, Tim Prenzler, and Jackie Chapman. 2008. Early intervention to reduce complaints: An Australian Victoria police initiative. *International Journal of Police Science & Management* 10 (2): 238–50.

Macrae, C. Neil, Alan B. Milne, and Galen V. Bodenhausen. 1994. Stereotypes as energy-saving devices: A peek inside the cognitive toolbox. *Journal of Personality & Social Psychology* 66 (1): 37–47.

Markus, Hazel R., and Shinobu Kitayama. 1991. Culture and the self: Implications for cognition, emotion, and motivation. *Psychological Review* 98 (2): 224–53.

Mendes, W. B., J. Blascovich, B. Lickel, and S. Hunter. 2002. Challenge and threat during social interactions with white and black men. *Personality and Social Psychology Bulletin* 28 (7): 939–52.

Messersschmidt, James. 2000. Becoming "real men": Adolescent masculinity challenges and sexual violence. *Men and Masculinities* 2 (3): 286–307.

Miller, E. K. 2000. The prefrontal cortex and cognitive control. *Nature Reviews Neuroscience* 1 (1): 59–65.

Miller, Norman, William C. Pedersen, Mitchell Earleywine, and Vicki E. Pollock. 2003. A theoretical model of triggered displaced aggression. *Personality and Social Psychology Review* 7 (1): 75–97.

Mischel, Walter. 1968. *Personality and assessment*. New York, NY: Wiley.

Mummolo, Jonathan. 2018. Modern police tactics, police-citizen interactions, and the prospects for reform. *Journal of Politics* 80 (1): 1–15.

Munsch, Christin L., and Robb Willer. 2012. The role of gender identity threat in perceptions of date rape and sexual coercion. *Violence against Women* 18 (10): 1125–46.

Najdowski, Cynthia J., Bette L. Bottoms, and Phillip Atiba Goff. 2015. Stereotype threat and racial differences in citizens' experiences of police encounters. *Law and Human Behavior* 39 (5): 463–77.

National Academies of Sciences Engineering and Medicine. 2018. *Proactive policing: Effects on crime and communities*. Washington DC: The National Academies Press.

Navon, David, and Daniel Gopher. 1979. On the economy of the human-processing system. *Psychological Review* 86 (3): 214–55.

O'Brien, Laurie T., and Christian S. Crandall. 2003. Stereotype threat and arousal: Effects on women's math performance. *Personality and Social Psychology Bulletin* 29 (6): 782–89.

Pashler, Harold. 1994. Dual-task interference in simple tasks: Data and theory. *Psychological Bulletin* 116 (2): 220–44.

Payne, B. Keith. 2001. Prejudice and perception: The role of automatic and controlled processes in misperceiving a weapon. *Journal of Personality and Social Psychology* 81 (2): 181–92.

Payne, B. Keith. 2006. Weapon bias: Split-second decisions and unintended stereotyping. *Current Directions in Psychological Science* 15 (6): 287–91.

Peguero, Anthony A. 2008. Bullying victimization and extracurricular activity. *Journal of School Violence* 7 (3): 71–85.

Plant, E. Ashby, and B. Michelle Peruche. 2005. The consequences of race for police officers' responses to criminal suspects. *Psychological Science* 16 (3): 180–84.

Plant, E. Ashby, B. Michelle Peruche, and David A. Butz. 2005. Eliminating automatic racial bias: Making race non-diagnostic for responses to criminal suspects. *Journal of Experimental Social Psychology* 41 (2): 141–56.

Prokos, A., and I. Padavic. 2002. "There oughtta be a law against bitches": Masculinity lessons in police academy training. *Gender, Work & Organization* 9 (4): 439–59.

Pryor, John B., Janet L. Giedd, and Karen B. Williams. 1995. A social psychological model for predicting sexual harassment. *Journal of Social Issues* 51 (1): 69–84.

Pryor, John B., Christine M. LaVite, and Lynnette M. Stoller. 1993. A social psychological analysis of sexual harassment: The person/situation interaction. *Journal of Vocational Behavior* 42:68–83.

Reaves, Brian A. 2015. Local police departments, 2013: Personnel, policies, and practices. U.S. Department of Justice Bulletin. Washington, DC: U.S. Department of Justice.

Richardson, L. Song, and Phillip Atiba Goff. 2014. Interrogating racial violence. *Ohio State Journal of Criminal Law* 12 (1): 115–52.

Richeson, Jennifer A., and J. Nicole Shelton. 2003. When prejudice does not pay: Effects of interracial contact on executive function. *Psychological Science* 14 (3): 287–90.

Robinson, Michael D., Brandon J. Schmeichel, and Michael Inzlicht. 2010. A cognitive control perspective of self-control strength and its depletion. *Social and Personality Psychology Compass* 4 (3): 189–200.

Rogers, Ronald W., and Steven Prentice-Dunn. 1981. Deindividuation and anger-mediated interracial aggression: Unmasking regressive racism *Journal of Personality and Social Psychology* 41 (1): 63–73.

Ross, Lee, and Richard E. Nisbett. 2011. *The person and the situation: Perspectives of social psychology*. London: Pinter & Martin Publishers.

Schmader, T., and M. Johns. 2003. Converging evidence that stereotype threat reduces working memory capacity. *Journal of Personality and Social Psychology* 85 (3): 440–52.

Schoenfeld, Heather. 2005. Violated trust: Conceptualizing prosecutorial misconduct. *Journal of Contemporary Criminal Justice* 21 (3): 250–71.

Shelley, Tara O. Connor, Melissa Schaefer Morabito, and Jennifer Tobin-Gurley. 2011. Gendered institutions and gender roles: Understanding the experiences of women in policing. *Criminal Justice Studies* 24 (4): 351–67.

Sherman, Lawrence W. 1980. Causes of police behavior: The current state of quantitative research. *Journal of Research in Crime and Delinquency* 17 (1): 69–100.

Sommers, Sam. 2012. *Situations matter: Understanding how context transforms your world.* New York, NY: Riverhead Books.

Steele, Claude M. 1997. A threat in the air: How stereotypes shape intellectual identity and performance. *American Psychologist* 52 (6): 613–29.

Steele, Claude M., and Joshua Aronson. 1995. Stereotype threat and the intellectual test performance of African Americans. *Journal of Personality and Social Psychology* 69 (5): 797–811.

Steele, Claude M., Steven J. Spencer, and Joshua Aronson. 2002. Contending with group image: The psychology of stereotype and social identity threat. *Advances in Experimental Social Psychology* 34:379–440.

Stoughton, Seth W. 2014a. Policing facts. *Tulane Law Review* 88 (5): 847–98.

Stoughton, Seth W. December 2014 (2014b). How police training contributes to avoidable deaths. *The Atlantic.*

Stoughton, Seth W. 2017. Terry v . Ohio and the (un)forgettable frisk. *Ohio State Journal of Criminal Law* 15 (19): 19–33.

Swencionis, Jillian K., and Phillip Atiba Goff. 2017. The psychological science of racial bias and policing. *Psychology, Public Policy, and Law* 23 (4): 398–409.

Swencionis, Jillian K., Enrique R. Pouget, Susan A. Bandes, and Phillip Atiba Goff. n.d. From order maintenance to hierarchy maintenance: Social dominance and police use of force.

Trinkner, Rick, and Phillip Atiba Goff. 2018. The force of fear: Police stereotype threat, self- legitimacy, and support for the use of force. Available from https://www.law.nyu.edu/sites/default/files/upload_documents/Stereotype%20Threat%20Paper.pdf.

U.S. Department of Justice, Civil Rights Division. 2017. *The Civil Rights Division's pattern and practice police reform work: 1994-present.* Washington, DC: U.S. Department of Justice.

Vandello, Joseph A., Jennifer K. Bosson, Dov Cohen, Rochelle M. Burnaford, and Jonathan R. Weaver. 2008. Precarious manhood. *Journal of Personality and Social Psychology* 95 (6): 1325–39.

Vorauer, Jacquie D., Kelley J. Main, and Gordon B. O. Connell. 1998. How do individuals expect to be viewed by members of lower status groups? Content and implications of meta-stereotypes. *Journal of Personality and Social Psychology* 75 (4): 917–37.

Walker, Nicholas, and Kristy Holtfreter. 2015. Applying criminological theory to academic fraud. *Journal of Financial Crime* 2:48–62.

Walker, Samuel, Geoffrey P. Alpert, and Dennis J. Kenney. 2000. Early warning systems for police: Concept, history, and issues. *Police Quarterly* 3 (2): 132–52.

Walker, Samuel, and Charles M. Katz. 2008. *The police in America: An introduction.* 6th ed. New York, NY: McGraw-Hill.

Weitzer, Ronald, and Steven A. Tuch. 2004. Race and perceptions of police misconduct. *Social Problems* 51 (3): 305–25.

Wells, Rachel. 1 May 2017. Lessons from the LA riots : How a consent decree helped a troubled police department change. *CNN.*

Wicker, Allan W. 1969. Attitudes versus actions: The relationship of verbal and overt behavioral responses to attitude objects. *Journal of Social Issues* 25 (4): 41–78.

Wigon, Cachary. 18 December 2014. Tales of the grim sleeper: How the L.A.P.D. didn't catch an alleged serial killer for 30 years. *Vanity Fair.*

Wogan, J. B. 2016. How police chiefs plan to avoid "lawful but awful" shootings. Governing.com.

Worden, Robert E. 2015. The "causes" of police brutality: Theory and evidence on police use of force. *Criminal Justice Theory: Explaining the Nature and Behavior of Criminal Justice* 2:149–204.

Network Position and Police Who Shoot

This study applies the growing field of network science to explore whether police violence is associated with characteristics of an officer's social networks and his or her placement within those networks. To do this, we re-create the network of police misconduct for the Chicago Police Department using more than 38,442 complaints filed against police officers between 2000 and 2003. Our statistical models reveal that officers who shoot at civilians are often "brokers" within the social networks of policing, occupying important positions between other actors in the network and often connecting otherwise disconnected parts of the social structure between other officers within larger networks of misconduct. This finding holds, even net measures of officer activity, career movement, and sociodemographic background. Our finding suggest that policies and interventions aimed at curbing police shootings should include not only individual assessments of risk but also an understanding of officers' positions within larger social networks.

Keywords: police; police misconduct; social networks; brokerage; betweenness

By
LINDA ZHAO
and
ANDREW V. PAPACHRISTOS

The most common explanations for acts of police violence tend to focus on the *individual* attributes of officers who use excessive or lethal force as compared to those who do not, such as officer age (Chappell and Piquero 2004; Terrill and Mastrofski 2002), race (Fyfe 1981;

Linda Zhao is a PhD candidate in the Department of Sociology at Harvard University. She studies how population configurations of attributes such as ethnicity and socioeconomic class come together to shape various forms of social integration. Her research also investigates how interpersonal networks predict social outcomes and diffusion.

Andrew V. Papachristos is a professor of sociology and faculty fellow at the Institute for Policy Research at Northwestern University. He is also a fellow at the Institute for Policy Research. His research applies network science to the study of neighborhood and police violence, neighborhood change, and violence prevention efforts.

Correspondence: lzhao@fas.harvard.edu

DOI: 10.1177/0002716219901171

Ridgeway 2016; Worden 1996), gender (Bloch and Anderson 1974; Novak, Brown, and Frank 2011), experience (M. White and Kane 2013), and psychological background (Brandl, Stroshine, and Frank 2001; Wolfe and Piquero 2011). Much of this prior work, however, often takes for granted the inherent *networked* nature of policing. Simply put, police work is group work.

Police organizations, by design, create teams and groups of varying—and often nested or interconnected—levels. Officers are part of districts, units, or teams; and they are almost always assigned partners. Furthermore, from their time in the academy to their everyday lives in squad cars and on the beat, police officers rely on the formal and informal ties with fellow officers not only to carry out their required tasks but also for formal and informal learning. In much the same way, police deviance and violence—just like deviance more generally—might be associated with the contours of officers' social networks. Several recent studies have begun to show that the structure of a police officer's network is also correlated with misconduct, including the use of force (Oullet et al. 2019; Quispe-Torreblanca and Stewart 2019).

This study expands this growing body of network-oriented research by asking whether police officers who shoot their guns occupy a unique position within networks of alleged police misconduct. If networks influence police shootings and other types of use of force, then it might be that officers who shoot are exposed to different sorts of situations, fellow officers, information, beliefs, norms, and so on within their networks. They may also occupy different sorts of positions within networks that increase their probability of shooting.

Our study examines police violence using a structural approach that also accounts for some individual and district-level officer characteristics. We use a unique set of data on one of the largest police agencies in the United States: the Chicago Police Department (CPD). Using publicly available data on all reports of alleged police misconduct over a span of four years, we are able to track officers who are associated with each other through joint activity that resulted in a report of misconduct. We investigate whether network position within these networks predict increased risk of subsequent shooting.

Specifically, we investigate whether a position as a *broker* within misconduct networks, where an officer is on the shortest path of associations that connect other pairs of officers, marks higher risk of shooting net of differences in officer activity (such as policing in certain districts, or involvement in activities that are more likely to receive complaints) and career movement (related to officers' salaries or unit assignment over time). These sorts of network insights offer potentially new points of intervention aimed at reducing police shootings that consider the impact of individual, organizational, and network factors.

A Networked Approach to Police Violence

A long history of research documents the group nature of crime and delinquency (Warr 2002). Recent developments in network science have ushered in ways to determine how the structure of one's social network—and their placement within such structures—impacts criminal and delinquent outcomes (Haynie and Kreager 2013; Papachristos 2011). Recent extensions of such a "networked criminology" find evidence of contagion in violence, broadly defined, where violent behaviors are related to exposure to violence in one's local network and, moreover, that such networks contribute to the spread or diffusion of violence among network associates (Fagan, Wilkinson, and Davies 2007; Green, Horel, and Papachristos 2017; Loeffler and Flaxman 2018; Papachristos, Wildeman, and Roberto 2015; Short et al. 2014; Towers et al. 2015; G. White, Ruggeri, and Porter 2016). For example, a recent Chicago study found exposure to gunshot victimization in one's social network—that is, having an associate who was a gunshot victim—dramatically increases one's odds of subsequently being a gunshot victim (Papachristos, Wildeman, and Roberto 2015).

Our study aims to extend such network thinking to the study of police violence. We consider how a police officer's position in a larger network is associated with his or her propensity to use violence and even fire his or her weapon at a civilian.[1] Such a network approach resides between individual-level perspectives, which offer a bottom-up explanation of police violence, and organizational/cultural-level explanations; the latter offer a top-down explanation by focusing on those meso-level structures where officers spend the majority of their time "on the job" (Wood, Roithmayr, and Papachristos 2019). Consistent with social learning theories of deviance—as well as research on social and peer influence more broadly—police officers are most strongly socialized into their roles *as* police officer through informal and on-the-job interactions (Chappell and Piquero 2004; Roithmayr 2016). Ethnographic research demonstrates that the informal mentoring relationships and an officer's peers exert a strong influence on an officer's perception of misconduct and deviant behavior (Moskos 2008; Savitz 1970). For example, field training officers (FTOs), who help acclimate new recruits during their first months on the job, exert tremendous influence (Savitz 1970). Getty, Worrall, and Morris (2016) found that roughly one-quarter of the variation in new police officers' allegations of misconduct were attributable to FTOs.

Our aim is to use network structure to determine which individual officers are more at risk of shooting their firearms. This analysis differs from both purely individual-level accounts of police violence that understand the propensity for violence as a risk factor inherent to individual officers. It also differs from purely structural accounts that understand the propensity for violence as a feature of broader organizations. Network analyses can help point to ways in which broader social connections indicate differential risk based on both individual attributes (such as age, race, and gender) and the social structures of networks.

Studies of network effects in police behavior are relatively new (Oullet et al. 2019; Quispe-Torreblanca and Stewart 2019; Wood, Roithmayr, and Papachristos 2019). They largely characterize differential risk in terms of the number and behavior of immediate and direct associates. To date, most studies on police networks have focused only on *local structure*, that is, an officer's immediate social connections. We build upon this emerging research by underscoring how officers' network positions matter. Our study differs from existing studies because we aim to understand differential risk as a function of position relative to *global structure* of networks, above and beyond first degree (one person to one person) network connections.

Conceptually, focusing on potentially deviant peers implies that an officer is most likely to engage in police violence with only a subset of his or her peers. Risk is not randomly distributed within networks. This approach is consistent with other network studies that consider a foundational source of risk to be co-engagement in risky *behaviors* (e.g., needle sharing, gun violence, and disease transmission) as opposed to networks more broadly (e.g., friendship or kinship).

Network "Brokers"

Our study focuses on one particularly important network position: that of a network *broker*. In short, brokers occupy important positions "in between" other actors in a network (Freeman 1977; Gould and Fernandez 1989) and oftentimes connect otherwise disconnected parts of a structure (Burt 1992). For example, an officer who is transferred from one police district to a detail in a different unit or district would have network connections to two different possible pools of officers—those in the previous district and those in the new district. The transferred officer might, thus, occupy a position as a "broker" between officers in these two districts. This "in-between" position can bestow both risks and benefits associated with access to different pools of ideas, information, assets, and resources. For example, empirical studies often find that "brokers do better" on a range of behaviors such as job referrals, peer assessments, and promotions as a result of their access to valuable information (Burt 1992, 2004; Stovel and Shaw 2012). Conversely, however, brokers are also exposed to more risks, such as different types of conflicts or diseases, thus increasing certain negative outcomes (Faris and Felmlee 2011; Stovel and Shaw 2012). While there are many important forms of brokerage, in the current study we are specifically interested in betweenness, which refers to the extent to which actors stand on the *shortest paths*[2] of ties between other actors in a network—that is, the structural potential for individual police officers to both influence (and be influenced by) the broader network.

In the current context, we focus on "deviant" police networks—that is, networks of police collaborations that resulted in an alleged incident of misconduct. These networks can be understood as a combination of chance, organizational assignment (related to career movement), officer activity, and individual choice.[3]

Betweenness

Our primary interest is what *betweenness* in these deviant networks can tell us about subsequent officer behavior. Officers with higher betweenness, again, are defined as having more people linked through them as the shortest path between two people. Such officers are more exposed to information or beliefs (accurate or not) that flow from different officers. We aim to determine first, whether officers who are brokers are more likely to shoot and, second, whether this can be explained by (or is independent of) officer activity and career movement. This leads to two hypotheses:

1. We hypothesize that *officer activity and career movement are likely to both predict shooting and correlate with betweenness.*
2. We also hypothesize that *officers who inhabit high-betweenness network positions will be at greater risk of subsequent shooting* after accounting for other risk factors (activity, movement, demographic background, local network position, etc.).

Data and Methods

Study design

We construct misconduct allegation networks of police officers using data from all complaints collected by the CPD between 2000 and 2003. The datasets used in this study are made accessible by the ongoing effort of the Invisible Institute.[4] We are interested in officers who received at least one complaint between 2000 and 2003 ($n = 9,210$ unique officers who are collectively the subjects of $n = 38,442$ complaints).[5] Officers listed in complaints were identified using personnel records on all Chicago police officers. These personnel records, which also contain information on demographic background, are used to identify and link complaints records with several additional datasets that are sourced originally from the CPD and released in response to Freedom of Information Act (FOIA) requests. Data on police shootings and other use of force are available from Tactical Response Reports (TRR) between the years 2004 and 2016. Using TRR data, we identify officers who shot a firearm ($n = 338$ officers), who used some other form of force ($n = 5,364$), and who did not use any form of force ($n = 3,508$).[6]

Our primary goal is to investigate whether officers' brokerage roles in networks of cocomplainants between 2000 and 2003 are associated with subsequent shooting behavior between 2004 and 2016, net of officer demographic background.[7] We also consider whether any association between shooting and betweenness centrality could be explained by differences in officer activity, career movement, or degree centrality (the number of officers to which a given officer is directly linked through a cocomplaint). We use total complaints as a proxy for volume of activity and fixed effects for district assignments as a proxy for type and place of activity. Frequent transfers to different police units and salary change indicate career movement. Degree centrality can reflect both activity and career movement. Data on unit and district activity are derived from unit and district assignments observed on complaint records. Data on officer careers come from a record of salaries received by Chicago Police employees in 2002 and 2003 that are kept by the City of Chicago's Human Resources Department.

Complaints in our dataset included a range of allegation types (most frequent categories are search of premise or vehicle without warrant, neglect of duty, wrongful arrest, and failure to provide adequate services). We differentiate between department complaints and civilian allegations and complaints, where the latter is filed by a citizen against a police officer and the former is filed by a fellow police officer or other police personnel against an officer.[8] Each unique complaint involved anywhere between a single officer and sixty-four officers. The average complaint involved 2.3 officers (2.68 and 1.48 in civilian complaints and department complaints, respectively). In the resulting networks, each "node" (or point) is an officer. The presence of a tie (i.e., a link between two officers or "nodes") indicates involvement at some point between 2000 and 2003 in the same complaint (i.e., cocomplaint). Officers are connected with anywhere between 0 and 81 (but on average with 4.66) other officers in networks based on department complaints. Similarly, officers are connected with anywhere between 0 and 63 (but on average with 3.42) other officers in the civilian complaints network over the same time interval.

Betweenness centrality

We measure brokerage as *betweenness centrality*. Broadly defined, betweenness refers to the number of times a node falls upon the shortest paths (geodesic distance) between all other possible network pairs (dyads of two officers with a tie) in a network.[9] Note that since betweenness is only defined within connected graphs, we define a node's betweenness centrality to be relative to its connected component.[10]

Figure 1 illustrates two hypothetical networks to illustrate the defining characteristics of high-betweenness nodes. The highest betweenness node in each network is labeled node A. The nodes labeled B have high centrality, but not high betweenness centrality. The nodes labeled C have the lowest possible betweenness centrality (B[V] = 0) because they are entirely peripheral.

Figure 1A depicts two "star" shapes radiating from the nodes labeled A, which are connected by the node B. In this network structure, the highest betweenness nodes are labeled A. While B also has high betweenness and is a type of broker in terms of disconnecting the graph, it is on fewer shortest paths than nodes labeled A. Every shortest path between the left star and the right start as well as between the two stars necessarily runs through node A. Figure 1B presents a "kite"-shaped network (Krackhardt 1990), which is useful for understanding how betweenness relates to clustering and other forms of centrality. Node B, which is at the center of a large cluster, has the highest degree centrality (largest number of immediate ties). Although it also lies between many paths, these paths are all relatively redundant. In contrast, node A, which is again the highest betweenness node, is a critical connector between the nodes on the left outside of the cluster and the nodes within the cluster.

A common feature of network centrality measures, including betweenness, is that they tend to be heavily skewed to the right. The smallest possible value of betweenness (zero betweenness) is not uncommon, and it corresponds with officers who either have too few ties to connect other officers or have many ties but

FIGURE 1
Hypothetical Examples of Betweenness

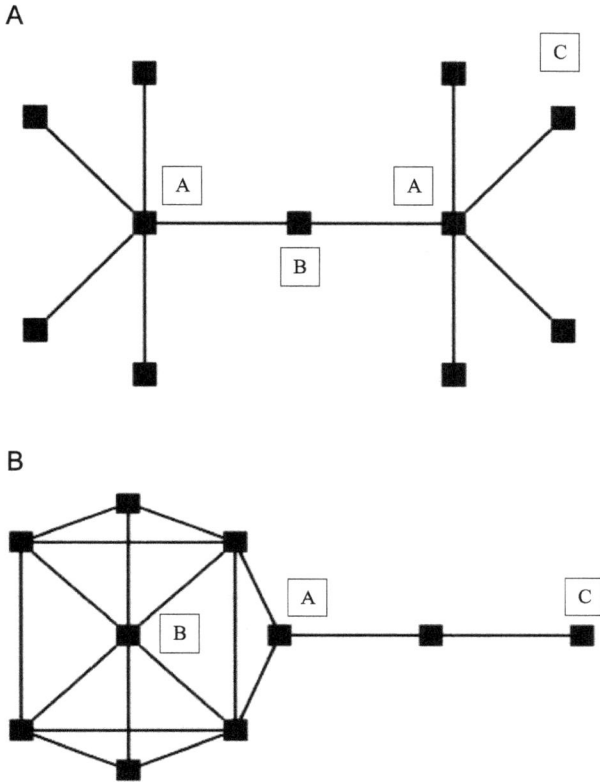

are never on the shortest path between other officers. There are only a handful of officers who have large betweenness centrality scores.[11]

Outcome measure

The outcome of interest is whether officers fired their weapon at a civilian between 2004 and 2016. A total of 388 officers fired their weapons at some point in this interval (defined as firing a gun at least once in any TRR incident); these include 46 officers who fired their weapons on multiple occasions. Main analyses do not distinguish between shooters and multiple shooters[12] nor between the number of times officers use force in this time interval.[13] Separate analyses compare (1) officers who shoot to officers who did not shoot but *did* use some other form of force (such as emergency handcuffing, use of a chemical weapon, or take downs) and also compare (2) officers who shoot to officers who did not use any force.

Covariates

Officer background. To assess the possibility of organizational, structural, or interpersonal implications of being a network "broker," we estimate associations between the odds of shooting and betweenness centrality net of several key covariates. All analyses control for officer background, including age and age at hire, gender, and ethnoracial category. Gender is coded with males as the reference category. Ethnoracial categories include Asian/Pacific Islander, black, Hispanic, Native American/Alaskan, and white, and are coded as a factor variable with white as the reference category.

An additional measure of officer background that may relate to the odds of shooting versus other use of force (and may also relate to betweenness) is the number of years in which a particular officer has the opportunity to shoot or use force while in the line of duty. All our models control for the number of years an officer is observed after 2004, where the maximum number of years is 13. Officers who remain at risk are by definition further from the end of their careers. The modal officers (62 percent of all officers) are observed for all 13 years, but the mean officer remains in the data for 10.44 years due to retirement. We account for these differences because officers who do not remain in the dataset are closer to the end of their careers and may thus have different relative inclinations or susceptibilities to shoot.

Officer activity. Brokerage (high betweenness) could reflect differences in officer activity and behavior. For instance, officers who are involved in more activities, who are involved in activities in which complaints are more likely, or who engage in more complaint-warranting behavior may also be on a larger number of shortest paths connecting other officers. In other words, cops may have high betweenness by nature of the volume or type of activities involved in their work. This possibility is accounted for in part by controlling for the total number of complaints (separately by department complaints and civilian complaints) received between 2000 and 2003, and in part by including fixed effects by modal district. Modal district is defined as the district in which officers spend the most time as observed in complaints data. Fixed effects by modal district help to account for differences in the propensity to shoot and the propensity for becoming subject to complaints, which may be due to such district-specific differences as level of crime, types of crime, and police relations with the local community.

Two additional concepts are central to our analyses. The first is what we call officer *complaints degree* (separately by department complaints and civilian complaints networks). Officers with a high network degree of complaints—relative to other officers—can still have low betweenness if their cosubjects of complaints are not well connected (e.g., node B in Figure 1B), and thus the two are different concepts. The second concept is the number of complaints, which is a different concept from complaints degree. Some officers receive multiple complaints but are network isolates; other officers receive only one complaint but are connected to many other officers through that complaint.

Taken together, the three measures of officer activity (number of complaints, modal district, and network degree) help to determine whether officer activity may explain some of the connection between likelihood to shoot and betweenness centrality.[14]

Career movement. In addition to differences in officer activity, the level of betweenness found for brokers could be driven by organizational patterns that yield greater centrality and involve career movement. Career movements may relate to the activity of specific officers but are also shaped by broader organizational decisions and protocols (such as promotions or the creation of special units). The nature of policing creates a network by design: most basic police work is dyadic (Chicago police generally work in pairs), and police organizations themselves are hierarchies that create particular types of network structures. For example, if officers are in specialized units, they may be assigned to work collaboratively or in more than one geographic area. In contrast, standard patrol officers are generally assigned to very precise geographic areas—and usually with one (or more) partner—and rarely have the opportunity to work outside that area except for a promotion or change in work assignment. Officers might also move between units, assignments, and geographic districts if they are promoted to a new rank.

For reasons such as these, we control for three measures of career movement. First, while degree centrality (especially for degree centrality in networks that are based on civilian complaints) in part reflects "activity" related to collaborative work *within* a given assignment, it also reflects "movement" because it in part reflects work with distinct individuals *between* separate assignments. Second, we control for the raise in each officer's salaries between 2002 and 2003. Although officer salary data are available in later years, we limit all predictor variables to be prior to the outcome measure. Missing salary data in 2002 and 2003 are rare. Results are not sensitive to the choice of whether to omit these observations, flag them, or code them to the mean.

Note that in the CPD, officers work in twenty-five police districts[15] and a number of special units, which can include assignment to a specific district or to cross-district units (i.e., narcotics or gang units). Officers are initially assigned districts and units but also move or change assignments throughout their career. At any given time, officers are mostly working with partners who share the same unit assignment.

Our last control for officer career movement, therefore, is *shuffling*. This concept is defined as dispersion in unit assignments noted in complaints against them over the years 2000 to 2003. We call this movement through different police units "shuffling," and we define it mathematically.[16] The average officer is observed in only two units over this time interval (with a unit variance measure of roughly 0.5). While we account for shuffling in terms of dispersion in unit assignments, dispersion in district assignments is not included because district assignment is a subset of unit assignment.[17] The most direct interpretation of shuffling in the current context is the probability that two randomly selected assignments (on which an officer received a complaint) are within different units. For a given officer, a value of 1 indicates that a complaint was never observed in the same unit twice, whereas a value of 0 indicates that complaints were always within the same unit.

Statistical analyses

In preliminary analyses, we use linear regressions to predict betweenness centrality to better understand the extent to which differences in betweenness correspond with officer activity and career movement. In the main analyses, we use logistic regressions[18] to predict which officers will shoot and which will not in the years 2004 and 2016. Our goal is to determine whether the two measures of betweenness centrality predict the propensity to shoot, net the demographic variables and the measures for career movement and activity (including the fixed effects on modal district). All continuous variables are mean centered and scaled in regressions such that coefficients are easily interpretable as the implications of an increase of one standard deviation net the other covariates. If betweenness predicts higher propensity to shoot, this may be explained in part by officer activity or career movements that increase betweenness (especially if the preliminary analyses indicate that betweenness is related to activity or movement). To consider this possibility, we incrementally add the measures for activity and movement in the main regressions that predict shooting. If betweenness continues to predict higher propensity to shoot after accounting for these measures, this would suggest that higher betweenness, produced by variation in the underlying organizational structure of officer collaborations, could contribute to differences in officer behaviors.

Results

During the observation period between 2004 and 2016, a total of 338 officers fired their weapon at a civilian,[19] 5,364 officers used some other form of force but did not shoot anyone, and 3,508 officers used no force at all. Thus, only a small percentage of officers in the sample fired their weapon. A much larger percentage used other sorts of force such as the discharge of Tasers, other types of physical force, or the use of an impact weapon (such as a police baton). Table 1 summarizes the covariates by all possible outcome measures[20] to investigate simple bivariate differences in the groups.

Based on bivariate comparisons, officers who shoot are younger at the time of event and younger at hire. Net of current age, being younger at hire could reflect either joining the CPD at a younger age or being with the CPD for a longer amount of time. There do not appear to be racial or gender differences between shooters and officers who use other force at the bivariate level. Based solely on bivariate relationships, shooters are more often shuffled through different police units and receive bigger raises in comparison to nonshooters. Bivariate comparisons of complaints by shooting also show that officers who shoot receive more of both types of complaints, receive more complaints together with other officers (i.e., they have higher network degree), and are higher in betweenness centrality. Network metrics are separate for civilian complaints and department complaints networks.

TABLE 1
Sample Characteristics by No Use of Force, Other Use of Force, or Shooting

	Shooters ($n = 338$)				Other Use of Force ($n = 5,364$)				No Use of Force ($n = 3,508$)			
	Mean	SD	Min	Max	Mean	SD	Min	Max	Mean	SD	Min	Max
Event background												
Year of random event	2008	3.20	2004	2016	2008	3.50	2004	2016	—	—	—	—
Age at random event	39.19	5.75	25	60	42.56	8.03	24	63	—	—	—	—
Officer background												
Years at risk	12.47	1.73	4	13	11.79	2.71	0	13	8.20	4.88	0	13
Age	34.81	6.54	24	58	45.00	7.61	24	62	45.98	8.80	25	63
Age at hire	27.42	4.38	21	45	28.76	5.19	14	55	29.63	5.91	11	58
Female	0.12	0.60	0	1	0.13	0.52	0	1	0.12	0.54	0	1
Race												
Asian / Pacific Islander	0.01	0.12	0	1	0.02	0.15	0	1	0.01	0.10	0	1
Black	0.21	0.41	0	1	0.24	0.43	0	1	0.30	0.46	0	1
Hispanic	0.20	0.40	0	1	0.18	0.38	0	1	0.12	0.32	0	1
Native Am. / Alaskan	0.01	0.10	0	1	0.00	0.05	0	1	0.00	0.05	0	1
White	0.57	0.50	0	1	0.56	0.40	0	1	0.57	0.50	0	1
Career												
Shuffling	0.62	0.22	0.00	0.96	0.55	0.27	0.00	0.96	0.42	0.32	0.00	0.96
Raise (thousands)	3.50	3.18	1.15	13.55	2.75	2.64	-3.76	20.09	2.04	1.70	-2.12	15.69
Complaints												
Total number (civ.)	4.97	6.02	0	42	3.22	3.88	0	46	1.62	2.60	0	52
Total number (dpt.)	1.85	1.73	0	9	1.59	1.58	0	15	1.28	1.37	0	16
Degree (civ.)	7.68	8.40	0	51	5.20	6.33	0	63	3.27	4.53	0	44
Degree (dpt.)	4.08	6.92	0	76	3.62	6.52	0	81	3.03	6.72	0	68
Betweenness (civ.)	6.18	4.75	0	13.37	4.35	4.74	0	13.27	2.29	3.98	0	12.49
Betweenness (dpt.)	4.22	4.85	0	13.25	2.97	4.44	0	12.95	1.62	3.56	0	12.82

NOTE: Betweenness and degree (civ.) are summarized for officers whose total number of civilian complaints are nonzero. Betweenness and degree (dpt.) are summarized for officers whose total number of department complaints are nonzero.

Correlates of betweenness centrality

To demonstrate the utility of including separate civilian complaints and department complaints network measures, we provide information on

FIGURE 2
Correlations between Features of Complaint Networks

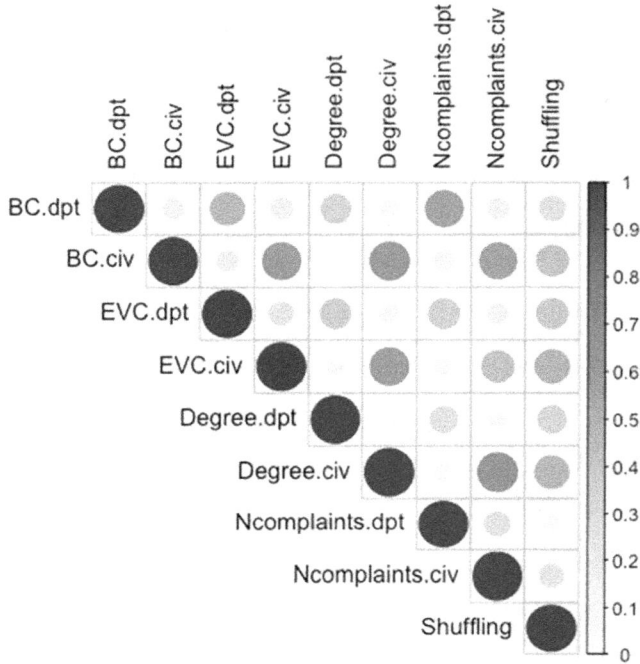

NOTE: (1) BC denotes betweenness centrality and EVC denotes eigenvector centrality; dpt = department; civ = civilian. (2) Larger circles are larger correlations. (3) For the subset of the analytic sample (51.2 percent of the sample) that are in both civilian complaints and department complaints networks.

correlations between network measures in Figure 2 for the subset of officers who are in *both* civilian and department complaints networks.

Betweenness centrality is not highly correlated between civilian complaints and department complaints networks—that is, high centrality in one network does not imply high centrality in the other network. In addition, in the online appendix (Figure A1), we show that more than half of officers are in only civilian complaints or department complaints networks, rather than both. Thus, we present separate analyses of department complaints and civilian complaints network measures.[21]

Figure 2 shows that each betweenness measure is strongly but not completely correlated with the total number of complaints of their own type, which suggests a strong betweenness-activity link. Betweenness is only moderately correlated with degree centrality since, by definition, officers cannot be on the shortest path between other pairs of officers without some direct connections. Direct connections are no guarantee, however, that officers are on the shortest path between other pairs of officers (e.g., in Figure 1B, node B is highest in degree, but node

FIGURE 3
Predictors of Betweenness Centrality

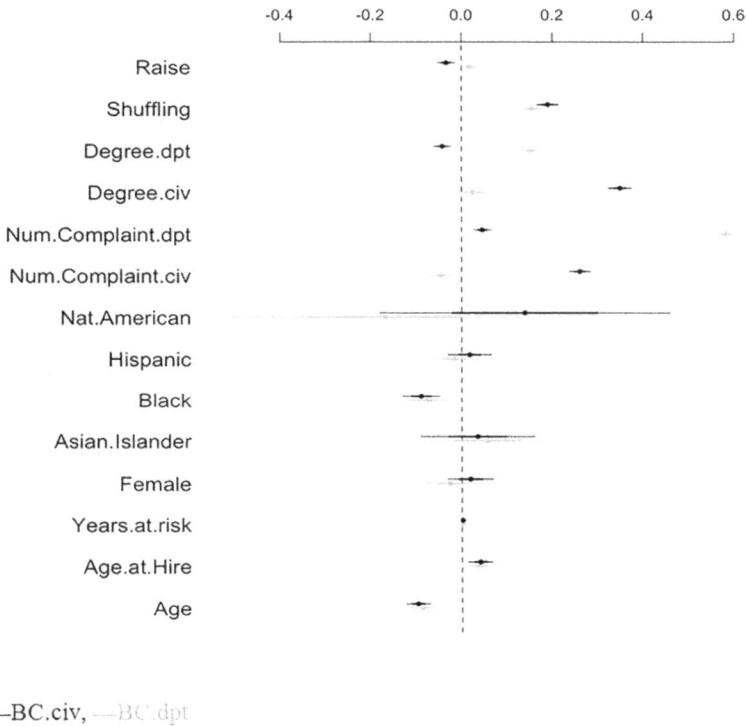

—BC.civ, —BC.dpt

NOTE: BC denotes betweenness centrality; dpt = department; civ = civilian.

A is highest in betweenness). Finally, betweenness is moderately correlated with network movement as captured by shuffling through different police units.

To determine whether the bivariate correlations observed in Figure 2 persist in multivariate analyses, we predict department complaints and civilian complaints betweenness centrality (in separate linear regressions) using the covariates on officer background, activity, and movement. We report the estimated coefficients and associated 95 percent confidence interval in Figure 3. Note that continuous variables, including measures of betweenness, are mean centered and standardized.

Figure 3 indicates that older officers are lower in betweenness but officers who are older when hired are higher in betweenness. Black officers are lower in betweenness.[22] The total number of department and civilian complaints predict higher betweenness in the respective networks. Network degree for the department and civilian complaints networks also correspond with higher betweenness in the respective networks. This suggests that officers with more complaints and who have more first-order collaborators in the complaints network are likely to be on a greater number of shortest paths between other officers. Finally, shuffling predicts higher betweenness in both network types, whereas a larger raise predicts slightly, but significantly, lower civilian complaints betweenness but is not significantly related to department complaints betweenness.

The coefficients in Figure 3 support the idea that higher betweenness might reflect career movement—officers become brokers as they advance in their career. We consider movement in in three ways: (1) observed shuffling through different police units; (2) smaller raises or being new to the job (which could reflect less career mobility as one's career just began); and (3) being a problem to the department (more department complaints), with more coparties named in collaboration in the same complaints (especially for civilian complaints networks, where this might mean they were temporarily pulled from another unit or district for a big assignment). Shuffling and civilian complaints degree are consistently related to network betweenness because they relate to higher betweenness in both networks. The coefficients in Figure 3 also support the idea that officer activity, especially as reflected by the total number of civilian complaints, can produce high betweenness. Civilian complaints are consistently related to betweenness in both civilian and department networks. Note that the importance of officer activity for network betweenness is also reflected by the significant coefficients on the fixed effects for modal district.[23]

Predicting shootings

The bivariate association between officer actions (shooting, other use of force, or no use of force) and betweenness centrality is presented in the kernel density plots in Figure 4.

For betweenness in the civilian complaints network (panel A), officers who used no force (broken dashes) are predominantly officers who are never on the shortest path between two other officers. While this is also the case for those who used some form of force (dotted lines) and those who shot (solid lines), officers who used some form of force or who shot are increasingly represented at higher levels of betweenness, with the largest contrasts being between those who shot and those who did not use any force. Similar but slightly smaller associations can be seen for the bivariate association between officer actions and department complaints betweenness centrality (panel B).

Table 2 presents logistic regressions predicting the probability of shooting relative to using other forms of force. The sample used in this table includes the full analytic sample of officers who received at least one of *any* kind of complaint (regressions also include a dummy variable to flag officers who are not represented in one of the two networks and who are thus missing values for one set of network measures).

We first control only for betweenness and officer background, then incrementally introduce the measures of activity and movement. Younger age, being male, getting a larger raise, and having faced many civilian complaints all help to predict officers who shoot rather than use another form of force (model 0). Race is not reported in any of the models because it was not significant in any of the

FIGURE 4
Distribution of Betweenness Centrality by No Use of Force, Other Use
of Force, or Shooting

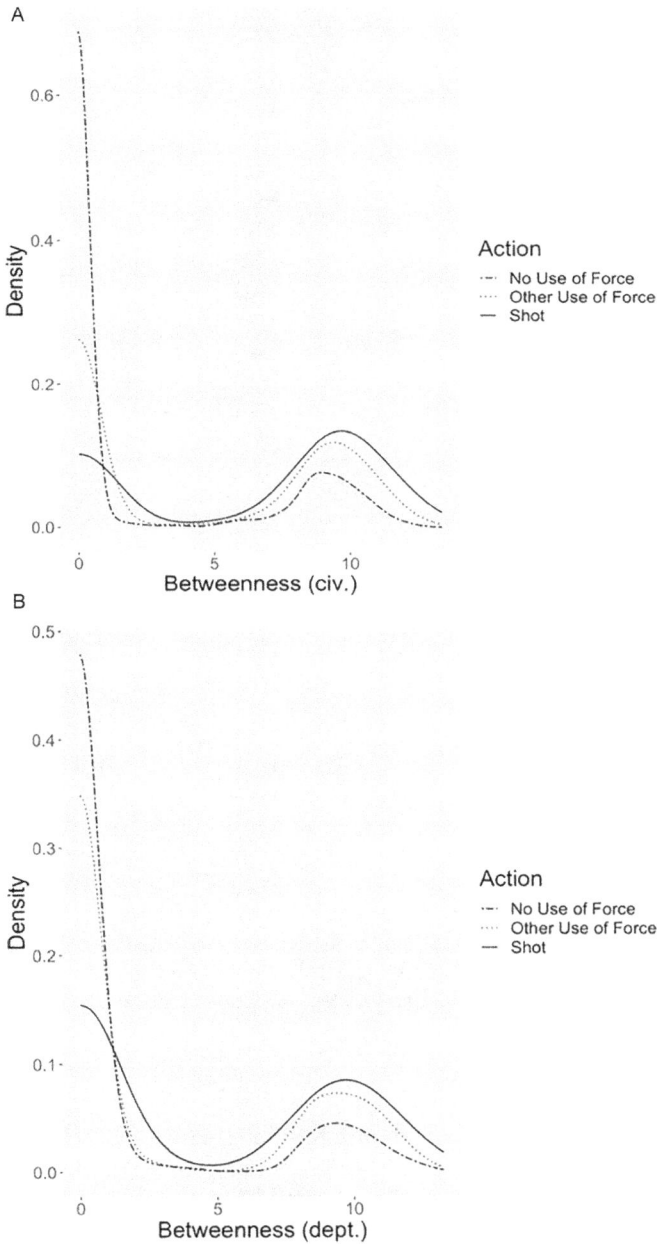

NOTE: civ. = civilian; dept. = department.

TABLE 2
Logistic Regression of Shooting versus Other Use of Force

	Model 0	Model 1	Model 2
Officer background			
Age	−0.62°°°	−0.64°°°	−0.51°°°
	(0.12)	(0.12)	(0.13)
Age at hire	0.17	0.20	0.14
	(0.15)	(0.15)	(0.15)
Years at risk	0.23	0.24	0.27°
	(0.13)	(0.13)	(0.13)
Female	−0.52°	−0.51°	−0.43°
	(0.21)	(0.21)	(0.21)
Officer activity			
Number of civilian complaints	—	0.20°°°	0.23°°°
		(0.07)	(0.07)
Number of department complaints	—	−0.07	−0.06
		(0.09)	(0.11)
Degree of civilian complaints network	—	0.02	0.00
		(0.07)	(0.08)
Degree of department complaints network	—	−0.02	−0.04
		(0.07)	(0.08)
Career movement			
Raise	—	—	0.12°
			(0.10)
Shuffling	—	—	0.22
			(0.09)
Betweenness centrality			
Civilian complaints	0.32°°°	0.16°	0.15
	(0.06)	(0.08)	(0.08)
Department complaints	0.17°°	0.20°	0.19°
	(0.06)	(0.08)	(0.08)
Akaike's Information Criteria (AIC)	2,523	2,483	2,480

NOTE: (1) All models also control for modal district, race, and the flag for missing salary data or missing network measures. (2) Models 1 and 2 also control for fixed effects by modal district. (3) Continuous variables are centered and scaled. (4) Coefficients are log-odds, *SE* in parentheses. (5) $N = 5{,}702$.
°$p < .05$. °°$p < .01$. °°°$p < .001$.

models. Without taking into consideration officer activity and career movement, a one standard deviation increase in betweenness corresponds with a 0.32 and 0.16 higher log-odds (1.38 and 1.17 higher odds) of shooting.

The remaining models in Table 2 consider the extent to which these patterns hold vis-à-vis officer activity and career movement. After introducing measures of officer activity, including fixed effects on modal district, total number of complaints, and network degree (model 1), the magnitude of the coefficient on betweenness is dramatically reduced in the case of civilian complaints betweenness. The strength of association is slightly larger in the case of department complaints betweenness and shooting. Coefficients on civilian complaints and department complaints betweenness are still both statistically significant. Officer activity, especially as it relates to the number of civilian complaints, strongly predicts the propensity for officers to shoot rather than use another form of force, net the other covariates. However, officer activity explains only some but not all of the betweenness-shooting link.

In the next analyses, we also introduce measures of career movement, salary raises, and shuffling (model 2). Here, we observe that officers who receive larger raises are more likely to shoot net the other covariates. Officers who are shuffled through many different police units are more likely to shoot net the other covariates,[24] but not net betweenness centrality. On the other hand, betweenness centrality predicts shooting, net shuffling. This could reflect that some types of betweenness are unrelated to shuffling, but that shuffling is usually related to higher betweenness. Such an interpretation would be consistent with a *within* police district broker—that is, officers who are brokers within smaller parts of the network as opposed to brokers across the larger network (this interpretation might correspond with node A rather than node B in Figure 1A).

Finally, it is important to note that civilian complaints and department complaints centrality relate to shooting in distinct ways, after considering shuffling. While Figure 3 showed that shuffling is significantly and positively associated with higher betweenness in both civilian and department complaints networks, it renders the betweenness-shooting link on the cusp of statistical insignificance (p-value = .06) *only* for civilian complaints and not for department complaints networks. While shuffling relates equally strongly to both forms of betweenness, department complaints betweenness may be slightly better at independently explaining shooting.

Table 3 repeats the analyses in Table 2 but compares officers who shoot with officers who use no form of force. The implications of betweenness centrality are similar but a bit more dramatic when distinguishing between officers who shoot and officers who do not use force at all.

The main differences between the analyses in Table 3 and the analyses in Table 2 are that officers who shoot are further from retirement (the coefficient on years at risk is positive) compared to officers who do not use force. In addition, the coefficient on age at hire is also significant in this comparison. Since the analyses control for age, the coefficient on age at hire could either indicate higher rates of shooting among officers who joined the CPD at an older age or among officers who have been with the CPD for less time. Taking stock of the evidence in Table 2 and Table 3, it appears that officers with high betweenness are more likely to shoot. While our analyses cannot make a strong causal argument, we also show that some of this association appears to be mediated by officer activity in terms of civilian complaints and career movement in terms of shuffling.

TABLE 3
Logistic Regression of Shooting versus No Use of Force

	Model 0	Model 1	Model 2
Officer background			
Age	−1.80°°°	−1.78°°°	−1.58°°°
	(0.15)	(0.15)	(0.16)
Age at hire	1.00°°°	0.99°°°	0.85°°°
	(0.18)	(0.18)	(0.18)
Years at risk	0.74°°°	0.81°°°	0.83°°°
	(0.12)	(0.13)	(0.13)
Female	−0.52°	−0.40	−0.35
	(0.23)	(0.24)	(0.24)
Officer activity			
Number of civilian complaints	—	0.36°°°	0.36°°°
		(0.09)	(0.09)
Number of department complaints	—	−0.07	−0.06
		(0.12)	(0.12)
Degree of civilian complaints network	—	−0.01	−0.02
		(0.10)	(0.10)
Degree of department complaints network	—	−0.11	−0.12
		(0.10)	(0.09)
Career movement			
Raise	—	—	0.22°°°
			(0.06)
Shuffling	—	—	−0.01
			(0.11)
Betweenness centrality			
Civilian complaints	0.52°°°	0.28°°	0.31°°
	(0.07)	(0.10)	(0.10)
Department complaints	0.21°°	0.24°	0.24°
	(0.07)	(0.10)	(0.10)
Akaike's Information Criteria (AIC)	1,563	1,572	1,566

NOTE: (1) All models also control for modal district, race, and the flag for missing salary data or missing network measures. (2) Models 1 and 2 also control for fixed effects by modal district. (3) Continuous variables are centered and scaled. (4) Coefficients are log-odds, SE in parentheses. (5) $N = 3,846$.
°$p < .05$. °°$p < .01$. °°°$p < .001$.

Sensitivity analysis

The main results suggest that high betweenness in the complaints networks increases probability of shooting over a relatively long period of time.[25] In those analyses, we use logistic regressions to predict the probability that an officer ever shoots. As a robustness check, we consider time to first shooting as the dependent variable to determine whether betweenness indicates likeliness of shooting irrespective of timing, or whether betweenness indicates a shorter amount of time to shooting. We predict time to shooting and account for censoring by assuming that the true time to shooting is latent if unobserved, using a tobit model (see online appendix Table A2). The models in the online appendix (Table A2) are estimated for the subset of officers in the analytic sample who are observed until the end of follow-up, such that censoring occurs at the same point in time.

The results of these sensitivity analyses show that both measures of betweenness centrality are significant predictors of faster time to first shooting. The raw association between each standard deviation increase in the civilian complaints and department complaints betweenness measures corresponds with a reduction of 2.97 (civilian) and 1.41 (department) years in time to first shooting, without accounting for officer activity and career movement. While the coefficient on civilian complaints betweenness is less negative after accounting for officer activity and career movement, there remains a significant negative coefficient on both measures of betweenness.

In our final set of sensitivity analyses, we do not find that being embedded in or hanging onto a dense network predicts higher rates of shooting. Instead, officers who are positioned along nonredundant paths between their colleagues are more likely to shoot. The latter is consistent with the idea that wide-scope, indirect, and diffuse connections could inform officer actions.[26]

Conclusion

Our findings show that although only a small percentage of all CPD officers shoot, those officers who do shoot appear to occupy a unique structural position, that of a network broker. This finding appears to hold even when considering *individual-level factors*, such as age, race, gender, and activity.[27] Our estimates suggest that each standard deviation increase in betweenness centrality predicts roughly 1.17 higher odds of shooting net individual factors. The remaining association is strongly related to *organizational-level factors* such as shuffling but may not be completely explained by shuffling.

Brokerage in the misconduct networks discussed here is correlated with both shuffling and activity. This indicates at least that (1) certain levels or types of activities or shuffling put officers at higher risk of shooting, and (2) activities and shuffling generate greater opportunities for the nonredundant connections. Brokerage positions, thus, put officers at higher risk of shooting. Activity—here measured as modal police district and total number of complaints—correlates quite strongly with brokerage and risk of shooting. This suggests that officers involved in activities that garner them more allegations of misconduct are also more likely to be along short paths to many other officers. Further research is necessary to understand whether it is activity that generates brokerage or vice versa, but our analyses suggest that brokerage and activity are at least partially independent predictors of subsequent shooting. It is also the case that shuffling—here measured as the movement of officers across districts—correlates quite strongly with brokerage and risk of shooting.

These correlations offer insight in that brokerage may, in part, be a function for how police organizations handle assignments. It suggests transfer policies may inadvertently contribute to the diffusion of misconduct. Future research might consider whether this is generated by "problem" officers being moved from one unit or district to the next, which may inadvertently make problem officers brokers and, in essence, "spread" aggressive behavior.[28] Finally, the fact that there may be at least some independent association between brokerage and shooting (net activity and shuffling) suggests that brokerage itself may be relevant even when unrelated to other factors. While we cannot make a causal claim using our data, our association is consistent with the structural definition of brokers: they are in a position both to reach and be reached most efficiently by other nodes.

Limitations

Several limitations in the current data and analyses are worth noting. First, we lack data on nonmisconduct networks, such as patrol assignments or informal peer networks, that might offer a richer picture of the other types of social ties that influence officer behavior. Such network data might very well offer insights into additional paths of influence as well as possible network structures that help to *prevent* misconduct. Second, it is also likely that we are underestimating the scope of misconduct networks, because misconduct itself is likely underreported by both civilians and fellow police officers. Finally, we have analyzed data for only a single city; thus, caution should be warranted when attempting to generalize.

Limitations notwithstanding, our findings on brokerage within networks of alleged police misconduct provide some useful insights for potentially addressing police use of violence. Perhaps the most important insight is that networks likely play an important role in police shootings of civilians—a finding consistent with similar recent network studies of policing (Oullet et al. 2019; Quispe-Torreblanca and Stewart 2019).

If this is true, then it stands to reason that *efforts at reducing police shootings might also leverage police networks for intervention or prevention purposes.* In the case of brokerage, for example, policies related to officer assignments or the "shuffling" of officers with problematic behaviors might benefit from a better understanding of the networks into which and from which officers are moved. Future research should examine the impact of shuffling "bad apples" to understand if such movement has an impact on both the focal officer of concern as well as the new network in which he or she might be inserted. Many such policies focusing on networks can be adopted by police leaders who exert considerable control over assignments and movements of officers. At the same time, however, changing entire networks—let alone cultures that support behavior in such networks—will require larger organizational and cultural shifts.

Notes

1. While not every instance of force or police shootings constitute the use of excessive force, police violence is thought to be unnecessarily high; furthermore, many high-profile shootings have drawn

attention to the severity and possible legality of cases that are later deemed to be justified. Note also that while our study does not explicitly distinguish between legitimate and nonlegitimate instances of police violence, we focus on police shootings where an officer fired the first shot.

2. Two nodes are adjacent when they share a tie. A path P between two nonadjacent nodes (v_1 and v_n) refers to a sequences of adjacent nodes P = (v_1, v_2, . . ., v_n) such that v_i is adjacent to v_{i+1} . Such a path P is called a path of length n – 1 from v_1 to v_n. Often, many path lengths are possible between two nodes. Note that node numbering here relates to their position in the sequence and does not relate to any canonical labeling of the vertices.

3. The use of complaint data is not without limitations. Complaints suffer from potential underreporting problems, since people who believe they were mistreated by police do not always file a complaint due to the intimidating and complicated process. In addition, not all alleged misconduct corresponds with problematic behavior (e.g., breaking laws, or rule of regulations). Allegations of misconduct are to some extent a factor of a civilian's perspective on police behavior as well as police activity. We account for the activity hypothesis using several strategies.

4. The Invisible Institute is a journalism production company whose mission is to enhance the capacity of citizens to hold public institutions accountable (http://invisible.institute). The Invisible Institute obtained these data by filing independent FOIA requests.

5. All officers with potential for network ties as defined here (receipt of at least one complaint between 2000 and 2003) are represented in the sample. Officers with the potential for network ties account for 71 percent of all officers who are active at some point between 2000 and 2003 (roughly 12,900 officers). Note that more than 85 percent of shootings in the TRR data are captured by the analytic sample. Online appendix Table A3 shows the demographic background of officers who were excluded from the analysis.

6. Specifically, we identify officers who fired the *first* shot in a TRR report to ensure that this officer did in fact fire at a civilian. TRR reports contain information on "use" of a firearm; but in a substantial proportion of cases, use is indicated when no shots were reported to be fired by either party. Thus, we only consider instances in which officers rather than civilians fired the *first* shot in the main analyses. Sensitivity analyses that ignore this potential issue (and include an additional 101 officers who "used" a firearm in a situation where at least one shot was fired) show that results regarding civilian complaints betweenness and the propensity to shoot are highly robust, but results on department complaints betweenness are less robust.

7. In sensitivity analyses, we predict the timing of shooting instead of ever-shooting to consider whether betweenness indicates likeliness of eventually shooting irrespective of timing, or whether betweenness predicts a shorter amount of time to shooting over the window of observation.

8. We model these networks as separate because over half of officers are in either one network or the other (see appendix Table A1 in the online appendix). Thus, officer betweenness within one network does not necessarily spill over to betweenness into the other. When an officer is not present in either department complaints or civilian complaints networks, they are flagged as not present in that type of network, and this is accounted for (but not significant) in all models.

9. The betweenness B(v) of a vertex v in a graph G with a set of vertices V is defined as

$$\left| B(v) = \sum_{s \neq v \neq t \in V} \frac{\sigma_{st}(v)}{\sigma_{st}} \right., \text{ where } \left| \sigma_{st} \text{ is the total number of shortest paths from node } s \text{ to node } t \text{ and } \overline{|\sigma_{st}(v)}$$

is the number of those paths that pass through v (Freeman 1977). This metric allows us to quantify the extent to which nodes are essential to connecting other nodes and captures brokerage via path lengths. While some consider brokerage to be higher when it completely disconnects graphs rather than shortening the shortest paths, these concepts are highly related, and both are forms of brokerage (Everett and Valente 2016). We consider path length because it is an intuitive (Freeman 1977, 1979; Gould and Fernandez 1989) and broad definition of brokerage.

10. Roughly 64 percent and 42 percent of officers are in the largest connected component in the civilian complaints and department complaints networks, respectively. Analyses that are restricted to the largest connected component resulted in similar signs and magnitudes on coefficients. Unsurprisingly, findings became insignificant after removing nearly half the sample.

11. In our analyses, betweenness centrality in the two networks (department complaints and civilian complaints networks) are log transformed to satisfy assumptions of normality and to avoid giving undue influence by observations with very large betweenness. Given the debate on whether centralities are

informative throughout the distribution or just at the high end of the distribution (Borgatti and Everett 2006), we also include robustness checks to determine sensitivity of our models to alternate specifications on betweenness, and alternate centrality measures. Main results are robust to the use of a continuous transformation versus using quantile binning (i.e., assigning betweenness to equally sized categories of "low," "moderate," and "high").

12. There are thirty-nine, five, and two officers, respectively, who shot in two, three, and four separate incidents during the window of observation. There are not key differences between officers who shot once and officers who shot in multiple incidents. These require further research.

13. Sensitivity analyses predict time to shooting as an alternative outcome.

14. Network degree is a distinct concept from total number of complaints (see Figure 2 for correlation). Some officers receive multiple complaints but are network isolates, while other officers receive only one complaint but are connected to many other officers through that complaint. Both network degree and number of complaints are somewhat related with modal district because officers who are sent to high-volume areas, for instance on proactive patrol duties, are involved in distinct encounters and activities.

15. During this observation period, the number of police districts went from twenty-five to twenty-two due to collapsing of three districts.

16. We define this concept to be calculated as one minus the Herfindahl Index of concentration calculated over all units in which an officer is observed in a given time interval.

17. Dispersion in district assignments is also collinear with fixed effects for modal district, which are included in all regressions.

18. All analyses are performed using R version 3.5.1.

19. Of the officers in the TRR database, 52 percent are present in our analytic sample. We restrict our analyses to officers for whom we can recover data on movement and activity, which is not possible for the remaining 48 percent of the data.

20. We define our analytic sample to be the population of officers with a registered complaint between years 2000 and 2003. For a summary of officer behavior and officer demographics among those who are not part of this sample, please refer to appendix Table A3.

21. Results of sensitivity analyses that do not differentiate between complaint-type still indicate that betweenness centrality is associated with shooting. Sensitivity analyses that merge and do not differentiate between the two networks are available upon request.

22. In supplementary analyses, we find that black officers are also lower in shuffling. But this does not necessarily explain why black officers have lower betweenness in Figure 3, which accounts for shuffling. In other words, black officers are less frequently moved through different police units, but also have lower betweenness for both networks even net shuffling.

23. Not shown in Figure 3 for the sake of parsimony.

24. Separate analyses, available upon request, indicate that shuffling is related to shooting, when not accounting for the betweenness covariates.

25. The main results use log-transformed betweenness to normalize the right-skewed distribution. Model selection on models using full sets of covariates, pointed to this specification as the best choice. We use the AIC (Akaike's Information Criteria) for model selection because it considers the tradeoff between model fit and parsimony and it is useful for model selection in the case of nonnested models. Results using other specifications are reported in online appendix Table A1. AIC scores are similar across models in Table A1 but were larger (worse) for other functional forms that we evaluated, but they are not reported in Table A1. Crucially, the interpretation of the coefficients is substantively similar across models, showing lack of sensitivity to functional form. There is one minor exception, which is that in the models that use categorical betweenness centrality (where betweenness measures are each discretized or "binned" on a four-point scale), the model that includes the full set of covariates (model 6 in Table A1) differs less from the baseline model (model 5 in Table A1) than expected for moderate levels of civilian complaints betweenness. This could be the case if only the highest values of betweenness are heavily correlated with officer activity and career movement, but moderate values are not.

26. We consider eigenvector centrality (EVC) as a measure of centrality instead of betweenness. EVC is an indicator of global network importance that recursively captures the notion that a node's well-connectedness depends on the well-connectedness of its connections. Broadly defined, EVC refers to the extent to which a node is influential or popular. In the current context, EVC would equate to involvement through complaints with officers who are themselves involved with other officers. Our main analyses

consider betweenness instead of EVC because we do not want to give a boost to "hanger-ons." EVC can still be high for disconnected officers hanging on to the overall network by just one other officer *if* that one connection is well connected (in contrast, betweenness would assign centrality for that nearly disconnected officer as 0). The results of the sensitivity analyses (appendix Table A4) indicate that betweenness centrality and EVC are far from interchangeable (this intuition is also supported by Figure 2). In comparison to the main results, analyses that use EVC indicate a more tenuous and less robust relationship with the propensity to shoot, especially after accounting for activity and movement. One potential explanation for this is that networks of collaborators are a conduit for information, behaviors, or norms that might shape officer actions.

27. Our results are in line with the studies that show minority officers are not more likely to use excessive force (Riksheim and Chermak 1993; Worden 1996), contradicting the idea that black officers are more likely to shoot (Ridgeway 2016) or that there are racial differences in policing due to activity (Fyfe 1978). Our study is also consistent with the idea that job performance for police officers is similar by gender (Novak, Brown, and Frank 2011) with the exception of possible gender differences in activity (Bloch and Anderson 1974).

28. Such an interpretation would be consistent with Roithmayr's (2016) theory as well as recent empirical findings about social influence and use of force (Oullet et al. 2019).

References

Bloch, Peter B., and Deborah Anderson. 1974. *Policewomen on patrol: Final report*. Washington, DC: Urban Institute/Police Foundation.

Borgatti, Stephen P., and Martin G. Everett. 2006. A graph-theoretic perspective on centrality. *Social Networks* 28 (4): 466–84.

Brandl, Steven G., Meghan S. Stroshine, and James Frank. 2001. Who are the complaint-prone officers? An examination of the relationship between police officers' attributes, arrest activity, assignment, and citizens' complaints about excessive force. *Journal of Criminal Justice* 29 (6): 521–29.

Burt, R. S. 1992. *Structural holes*. Cambridge, MA: Harvard University Press.

Burt, Ronald S. 2004. Structural holes and good ideas. *American Journal of Sociology* 110 (2): 349–99.

Chappell, Allison, and Alex Piquero. 2004. Applying social learning theory to police misconduct. *Journal of Deviant Behavior* 25:89–108.

Everett, Martin G., and Thomas W. Valente. 2016. Bridging, brokerage and betweenness. *Social Networks* 44:202–8.

Fagan, Jeffrey, Deanna L. Wilkinson, and Garth Davies. 2007. Social contagion of violence. In *The Cambridge handbook of violent behavior and aggression*, eds. D. Flannery, A. Vazsonyi, and I. Waldman. Cambridge: Cambridge University Press.

Faris, Robert, and Diane Felmlee. 2011. Status struggles. *American Sociological Review* 76 (1): 48–73.

Freeman, Linton C. 1977. A set of measures of centrality based on betweenness. *Sociometry* 40:35–41.

Freeman, Linton C. 1979. Centrality in social networks: Conceptual clarification. *Social Networks* 1:215–39.

Fyfe, James J. 1978. *Shots fired: An examination of New York City police firearms discharges*. Albany, NY: State University of New York at Albany.

Fyfe, James J. 1981. Who shoots? A look at officer race and police shooting. *Journal of Police Science and Administration* 9 (4): 367–82.

Getty, Ryan M., John L. Worrall, and Robert G. Morris. 2016. How far from the tree does the apple fall? Field training officers, their trainees, and allegations of misconduct. *Crime and Delinquency* 62 (6): 821–39.

Gould, Roger V., and Roberto M. Fernandez. 1989. Structures of mediation: A formal approach to brokerage in transaction networks. *Sociological Methodology* 19:89–126.

Green, Ben, Thibaut Horel, and Andrew V. Papachristos. 2017. The social contagion of gunshot violence in co-offending networks. *Journal of American Medical Association Internal Medicine* 177 (3): 326–33.

Haynie, Dana L., and Derek A. Kreager. 2013. Peer networks and crime. In *The Oxford handbook of criminological theory*, eds. F. T. Cullen and P. Wilcox, 257–73. New York, NY: Oxford University Press.

Krackhardt, David. 1990. Assessing the political landscape: Structure, cognition, and power in organizations. *Administrative Science Quarterly* 35 (2): 342–69.

Loeffler, Charles, and Seth Flaxman. 2018. Is gun violence contagious? A spatiotemporal test. *Journal of Quantitative Criminology* 34 (4): 999–1017.

Moskos, Peter. 2008. *Cop in the hood.* STU-Stud. Princeton, NJ: Princeton University Press.

Novak, Kenneth, Robert Brown, and James Frank. 2011. Women on patrol: An analysis of differences in officer arrest behavior. *Policing: An International Journal of Police Strategies and Management* 34 (4): 566–87.

Oullet, Marie, Sadaf Hashimi, Jason Gravel, and Andrew V. Papachristos. 2019. Social transmission of police misconduct. *Criminology and Public Policy* 18 (3): 675–704.

Papachristos, Andrew V. 2011. The coming of a networked criminology? *Advances in Criminological Theory* 17:101–40.

Papachristos, Andrew V., Christopher Wildeman, and Elizabeth Roberto. 2015. Tragic, but not random: The social contagion of nonfatal gunshot injuries. *Social Science & Medicine* 125:139–50.

Quispe-Torreblanca, Edika G., and Neil Stewart. 2019. Causal peer effects in police misconduct. *Nature Human Behaviour* 3:797–807.

Ridgeway, Greg. 2016. Officer risk factors associated with police shootings: A matched case–control study. *Statistics and Public Policy* 3 (1): 1–6.

Riksheim, Eric C., and Steven M. Chermak. 1993. Causes of police behavior revisited. *Journal of Criminal Justice* 21 (4): 353–82.

Roithmayr, Daria. 2016. The dynamics of excessive force. *University of Chicago Legal Forum* 2016 (10).

Savitz, Leonard. 1970. The dimensions of police loyalty. *American Behavioral Scientist* 13 (5–6): 693–704.

Short, M. B., G. O. Mohler, P. J. Brantingham, and G. E. Tita. 2014. Gang rivalry dynamics via coupled point process networks. *Discrete and Continuous Dynamical Systems - Series B* 19 (5): 1459–77.

Stovel, Katherine, and Lynette Shaw. 2012. Brokerage. *Annual Review of Sociology* 38:139–58.

Terrill, William, and Stephen D. Mastrofski. 2002. Situational, and officer-based determinants of police coercion. *Justice Quarterly* 19 (2): 215–48.

Towers, Sherry, Andres Gomez-Lievano, Maryam Khan, Anuj Mubayi, and Carlos Castillo-Chavez. 2015. Contagion in mass killings and school shootings. *PLoS ONE* 10(7).

Warr, Mark. 2002. *Companions in crime: The social aspects of criminal conduct.* Cambridge: Cambridge University Press.

White, Gentry, Fabrizio Ruggeri, and Michael Porter. 2016. *Endogenous and exogenous effects in contagion and diffusion models of terrorist activity.* Available from https://www.researchgate.net/publication/311514633_Endogenous_and_Exogenous_Effects_in_Contagion_and_Diffusion_Models_of_Terrorist_Activity.

White, Michael D., and Robert J. Kane. 2013. Pathways to career-ending police misconduct. *Criminal Justice and Behavior* 40 (11): 1301–25.

Wolfe, Scott E., and Alex R. Piquero. 2011. Organizational justice and police misconduct. *Criminal Justice and Behavior* 38 (4): 332–53.

Wood, George, Daria Roithmayr, and Andrew Papachristos. 2019. The network structure of police misconduct. *Socius: Sociological Research for a Dynamic World* 5:1–18.

Worden, Robert E. 1996. The causes of police brutality: Theory and evidence on police use of force. In *Police violence: Understanding and controlling police abuse of force*, eds. A. W. Geller and H. Toch, 23–29. Washington, DC: Police Foundation.

Policy-Making and Fatal Police Shootings

Police Killings as a Problem of Governance

By
FRANKLIN E. ZIMRING

Police kill more than a thousand civilians each year in the United States, a much higher death rate than occurs in any other developed nation. One important cause of the epidemic of civilian deaths is the larger risk that the police who patrol American communities face from civilian assaults with firearms, widely owned and often not visible. Yet many hundreds of killings each year of civilians in the United States are not necessary to protect either police or others from life-threatening attacks. Governments in the United States have failed to collect reliable data, investigate the causes of high death rates, or develop administrative standards to reduce unnecessary killings. The power and expertise vacuums that govern the current ignorance and overkill in the police use of deadly force are the direct, if unintended, consequences of state and federal government failures to assert authority over the many thousands of local police forces that are progeny of the American federal system.

Keywords: unnecessary deaths; accidental governmental incapacities; administrative rules

The unnecessary killings of civilians by police is both a singular and a serious problem in the United States. Police shoot and kill about a thousand civilians each year, and other types of conflict and custodial force add more than one hundred other lives lost to the annual total death toll. This is a death toll far in excess of any other fully developed nation, and the existing empirical evidence suggests that at

Franklin E. Zimring is the William G. Simon Professor of Law at the University of California, Berkeley. His special interests are the empirical study of violence and efforts to control it. He is the author of When Police Kill *(Harvard University Press 2017), a statistical and policy analysis of police use of fatal force.*

NOTE: I thank Charles Wellford, Lawrence Sherman, and the participants in *The ANNALS* conference held February 7 and 8, 2019, for comments on an earlier draft of this article.

Correspondence: fzimring@law.berkeley.edu

DOI: 10.1177/0002716219888627

least half and perhaps as many as 80 percent of these killings are not necessary to safeguard police or protect other citizens from life-threatening force. Three killings a day, every day, and at least half of these unnecessary to protect life (Zimring 2017, 228–35).

One reason why U.S. police kill so many civilians is that U.S. police themselves are vastly more likely than police in other rich nations to die from violent civilian attacks. In Great Britain or Germany, the number of police deaths from civilian attack most years is either one or zero. In the United States—four or five times larger—the death toll from civilian assaults is fifty times larger. And the reason for the larger danger to police is the proliferation of concealable handguns throughout the social spectrum. When police officers die from assault in Germany or England, the cause is usually a firearm (Zimring 2017, 79, 83), but firearms ownership is low, and concealed firearms are rare. There are, however, at least 60 million concealable handguns in the United States and the firearm is the cause of an officer's death in 97.5 percent of intentional fatal assaults (Zimring 2017, 96), an effective monopoly of life-threatening force even though more than 95 percent of all assaults against police and an even higher fraction of those said to cause injury are not gun related (Zimring 2017, 93, Table 5.2).

Even though guns are the only serious threat to police safety, other forms of assault still provoke more than four hundred civilian deaths every year from police lethal force, and this group of non-life-threatening incidents is the core of currently known civilian deaths that are not necessary to save lives. But it is also likely that there are a large number of gun cases that do not involve shots fired by civilians and that need not provoke police gunfire, and there are also a large number of cases where the death rate from police shootings doubles and triples because officers keep shooting after any danger to them has passed (Zimring 2017, 68–69).

But the peculiarities of the distribution of power in the U.S. federal system and the problematic focus of reformers on criminal prosecution of police officers rather than administrative restrictions on police shooting have made the always difficult task of effective reforms of police shootings impossibly complicated. For most of the 35 years after 1976, when the risk of a fatal attack of a police officer declined by two-thirds, the much higher death toll of civilians stayed remarkably stable (Zimring and Arsiniega 2015). In the complex labyrinth of the levels and branches of federal and state governmental authority in the United States during this period, research and policy analysis on police use of lethal force was nobody's responsibility. After the firestorm of concern struck in the wake of Ferguson, Missouri, in 2014, the only modest national resource that could provide any support to reform was the program in the Civil Rights Division of the federal Department of Justice that had been created in reaction to Rodney King's death in the 1990s (see Rushin 2017).

This article briefly describes some of the procedural and jurisdictional problems that are limiting the effectiveness of government efforts to save civilian lives from lethal force by police. I first discuss the error of reliance on expanding criminal prosecution almost exclusively to reduce unnecessary killings when administrative controls within police agencies are also an important vehicle for effective reform. The second part of the article focuses on the particular problems of current governmental organization in the United States. A brief concluding section discusses one model for creating a statistical and research branch in the national government to generate better data and to create incentives for administrative reforms in the thousands of operating law enforcement agencies that must become the main arena for the protection of civilian lives in the United States.

The Limits of Criminal Law in the Reform of Police Use of Lethal Force

One important problem in the governmental control of unnecessary police use of deadly force is the fact that police officers have been operating with near impunity when efforts are made by citizens or law enforcement to prosecute police officers for criminal misuse of their lethal weapons. The thousand or so killings of civilians by police officers in the United States each year have in recent history produced about one felony conviction of a uniformed officer per year. According to research by Philip Stinson of Bowling Green University, there were in the years 2000 to 2014 an average of 4.4 cases per year in the United States where police killings resulted in murder or manslaughter *charges* against one or more officers, and the prospects for obtaining felony *conviction* in these cases were low. The odds of a death producing a felony conviction were close to one in one thousand (see Zimring 2017, 174–75). There is also empirical evidence that this tiny conviction hazard is much lower than it should be. Even though there is no evidence of any camera record in 80 percent of the fatal cases in the first six months of 2015 reported in the *Guardian* newspaper study, Professor Stinson reports that "video evidence was available in at least 11 of the (18) cases" where he confirmed there was a felony charge (Zimring 2017, 189). If the rate of criminal charges is actually six times as high in camera record cases, the odds of prosecution would probably increase if more of these unfilmed cases had been filmed, that suggests that the rate of charges in cases without film of the event is much lower than it would be if better evidence were available.

The much higher rate of prosecution with camera evidence also suggests that as camera records increase, so too will the proportion of cases that result in criminal charges. But how many of these charges will also result in convictions? When measured against the five hundred to eight hundred unnecessary deaths per year in current American experience, the reach of criminal convictions to reduce shooting deaths will be far short of the hundreds of unnecessary civilian deaths we need to prevent. Why is this? What other approach would be superior to only criminal prosecution for saving lives?

The extraordinary limits on the reach of criminal liability for prevention of unnecessary police killings is closely related to the circumstances of police shooting incidents in the United States. While there is of course wide variation in the events that provoke police to kill in the United States, most of the provoking circumstances that produce gunfire by the police were not part of an intentional attack by police. Police are on patrol, or responding to a service call reporting a disturbance, when they encounter what they regard as the threat of attack, usually an assault against the officer. In about 88 percent of these cases, the officer reports the presence of a weapon in possession of the adversary (Zimring 2017, 57, Figure 3.6). In this important sense, the police officer is usually not the author of the conflict that generates his or her fatal force. This is significant because the criminal law is about personal fault and is much more comfortable making judgments about personal fault for harms that were wrongfully intended by individual actors.

The unpremeditated character of fatal force in the United States is similar in character to the circumstances that produce civilian shootings by police in other developed nations, but of course the rate of fatal force in these other nations is much lower than in the United States. By contrast, however, it appears that many nations outside the United States that experience very high volumes of lethal force by police also involve much more intended and premeditated killing by police. While precise statistical data on what legal analysts call "extrajudicial killings" is not available in the United States, such killings are frequently reported in India (Johnson and Zimring 2009, 434–35), in Brazilian urban favela areas (Sinhoretto, Schlittler, and Silvestre 2016), and in recent years as part of a "war on drugs" encouraged by current Philippine President Rodrigo Duterte.

When premeditated murder becomes a tool of law enforcement policy, the criminal law should become the weapon of choice in the control of violence by police, but the distinctive American pattern is far from any model of extrajudicial execution. Police may and often do overreact to the emergencies they encounter, but police themselves are rarely the cause of the emergencies. If the high death rates generated by police activity in the United States were for the most part the result of blameworthy activity by a few bad cops, then criminal law would make sense as a primary control strategy. But the problems are a mix of ineffective administrative controls, vague regulations, and the absence of administrative policy analyses and incentives for reducing death rates. It is hard to pin 100 percent of the blame for this mess on one or two officers.

The impediments to effective prosecution of extreme cases of police killings is of course a very serious problem. The worst of fatal force episodes in the United States tiptoe very close to intentional murder. The failure to criminally punish in circumstances like those of Oscar Grant in Oakland or Laquan McDonald in Chicago does tremendous damage to feelings of safety and personal integrity in the neighborhoods where intentional police killings happen. If extreme personal fault of police officers is in fact a rare event in the mass of fatal force episodes, that is all the more reason why it is necessary to isolate and condemn it when it does happen.

But simply because much more effective enforcement of the criminal law is a necessary reform in the governance of police use of force does not mean that is a sufficient reform for a nation that averages three citizen funerals a day from the conduct of its law enforcement. Public morale and effective police discipline both require better criminal law enforcement of grossly excessive fatal force and corrupt falsification of the facts of police violence during the investigation of incidents. But these reforms in extreme cases will not save the hundreds of lives now lost to unnecessary shootings every year.

The critical problem with reform priorities in the first years after Ferguson, Missouri, was the exclusive emphasis on criminal prosecutions and criminal prosecutors. Ineffective police administrators—and the vague and permissive non-specificity of their deadly force standards—have been unjustly spared in the reexamination of why the epidemic of civilian deaths is a chronic part of our national experience. The shortest distance between three killings a day and cutting the death toll from police force in half is sustained administrative priority for reducing civilian death tolls by means of evidence-based rules of engagement for treating the inevitability dangerous interaction of police with armed civilians. This would be a difficult and complex agenda in any political democracy, but as I argue in the next section, the uniquely American distribution of power, resources, and responsibility in our federal system has produced a critical shortage in research, in policy analysis, and in expertise in evaluating police deadly force problems and responses.

The Hazards of Federalism in the Management of Police Deadly Force

The American federal system is both unique in its structure and division of responsibilities and noncomprehensive in its design. The three basic levels of government—federal, state, and local—have parallels in other nations. But there are no exact equivalents to the United States when it comes to both the allocation of functions and power between the levels of government and the distribution of authority and responsibilities within the various branches at each level of government. The federal government is what has been called the supreme law in the federal system in the United States in the sense that if a particular topic is within the legislative prerogative of the national government, the federal regulation controls in conflicts with state and local laws. This is what could be called a "conditional supremacy" depending on the legitimacy of the national government's claim to subject matter power, a matter for the national courts to decide when federal versus state or federal versus local conflicts arise. But there is also a second sense in which the federal responsibility for particular topics is conditional. That condition is that the national government must choose to exercise its authority, for it only has as much authority as it takes on.

By traditional and current circumstance, the role of the federal government in the establishment and enforcement of criminal law is limited in the United States. The national government has its own penal code as well as both prosecutors and courts to adjudicate criminal charges and prisons to hold convicted offenders. But each of the fifty states in the federal union also has its own penal code and institutions to adjudicate and punish criminal offenders, and the collective impact of state criminal law enforcement dwarfs that of the national. State government traditionally imprisoned the vast majority of all persons behind bars and now accounts for 85 percent of state prisoners and more than 90 percent of all persons in secure confinement (Zimring, forthcoming). The federal government has an even smaller share of nonmilitary police, excluding specialized security personnel at airports and borders. The Federal Bureau of Investigation (FBI) employs thirty thousand or so of the nation's six hundred thousand police, and the Drug Enforcement Administration (DEA) has about four thousand agents.

If most criminal law and criminal punishment is a creature of the state level of government, police functions are dominated by two much smaller levels of local government, municipalities for police agencies and county-level government— typically with larger areas and populations—for sheriffs' offices and local jails.

Which of these levels of government are responsible for regulating the police use of deadly force? The prosecution of police conduct in criminal courts is usually the responsibility of local prosecutors, county government officials who also depend on local police to provide suspects and evidence. Criminal charges are rare, as noted above. The training, promotion, discipline over, and discharge of police officers is the responsibility of municipal police departments (for police) and county sheriffs (for sheriffs).

But what levels of government and agencies are responsible for evaluating the impact and legitimacy of a police agency's standards governing use of deadly force? What agencies analyze the impact and necessity of different deadly force policies on police safety and citizen risks? Often, the answer is nobody. And one reason for this gap is the singular architecture of police organization and authority in the federal system.

The national government has one police agency with a wide variety of investigative and arrest functions limited to federal law—the FBI—and a series of special function police or administrative security agencies. The FBI has a modest program of statistical reporting on crime and on police activity, which uses reports the agency collects from local police agencies to construct aggregate national profiles. The FBI does not audit any of the data that local agencies submit except for reported crime numbers, where the self-interests of local agencies to underreport crime generated some efforts of FBI quality control starting in the 1950s. For assaults against police officers or for the "justified killings by police of felons" reports that the agency collects and reports, there is no program of quality control.

The other branch of the national government with four modest programs that concern the activities of police functions is the U.S. Department of Justice, which has (1) a research institute to support some police programs—the National Institute of Justice; (2) a statistical reporting branch—the Bureau of Justice Statistics (BJS); and (3) two programs that are concerned with police behavior that puts citizens at risk. The Civil Rights Division of the department has an office that investigates and negotiates with local police departments, often generating consent decrees that subject reform efforts to the regulatory concern of federal district courts (Rushin 2017). The "COPS" program, an even smaller office in the Department of Justice, sends consultants to local police departments to help chiefs who request technical assistance. Both of these modest programs were involved in efforts to reduce police use of lethal force in the months following the Ferguson emergency in 2014. Both programs have been substantially limited by the Trump/ Sessions administration of the U.S. Department of Justice since 2017.

While state government is the most powerful level of government for criminal laws and criminal punishments, it is the least important level of government in policing. Putting aside only state highway patrol agencies, no level of government in the United States has less administrative or operational presence in policing than states.

The limited authority of state governments in police matters rather naturally leads to this level of government having little expertise about or influence on the conduct of local law enforcement. This has in one case led to serious problems of quality control in a program of the BJS in the U.S. Department of Justice. That bureau created and administered a well-functioning program of reporting deaths in custody in prisons and jails, the Deaths in Custody reports that were established by Congress in 2000. The best level of government for reporting deaths in prisons and jails was the state governments in the United States because the majority of persons are locked up in state custody, the administrative center for prisons (Zimring 2017, 29–30). But when the federal BJS program added an analysis of police data on "arrest related deaths" in 2003, it centered responsibility for these data in the same office in fifty state capitals that was collecting information on deaths in custodial confinement. Fully 61 percent of the "arrest related deaths" that the program reported were law enforcement homicides, almost always the result of local police and sheriffs in cities and towns not closely linked to agencies of state administration. The state agency collecting these data could only request accounts from local enforcement agencies and add up the numbers and descriptions and pass them on to Washington, D.C. (Zimring 2017, 29–32). The program was thus destined to be problematic.

The larger problems generated by the incapacity of state government in police regulation are sins of complete omission, rather than mere weaknesses in well-intended efforts at reporting influence and control. Every state in the federal system has an attorney general with some claim to statewide leadership in the administration of criminal law. But no state government has either the authority or the desire to regulate or evaluate the mission or behavior of municipal police or county sheriffs. With about eighteen thousand different police agencies operating independently, there are also very few departments with the size and specialized personnel to conduct research on the impact of various police activities. Most police administrators came up through the ranks and often from within the same organizations where they started their careers on the street. With the possible exception of criminal investigation, the operational departments provide very little scientific or technical training of officers. The ubiquitous police academy "weapons instructors" teach recruits how to service, store, aim, and shoot their weapons. The lore that many weapons instructors provide on use of deadly force in conflict with civilians is never research-based and often preposterous, as in the fanciful theory that any citizen brandishing a bladed weapon within twenty-one feet of an officer is a threat to kill the officer (Martinelli 2014).

Police departments lack experts and therefore they also lack expertise. The responsibility by default to create and evaluate deadly force policy that falls on unspecialized county and municipal police agencies is in no sense a thoughtful or deliberate decision about governance. It just exists as an artifact of the United States' particular brand federalism. Any real success in going beyond the current police self-interested self-government in matters of lethal force policy must involve giving some funding and authority to other branches and levels of government.

Let me make my central point explicit. The power and expertise vacuums that govern the current ignorance and overkill in police use of deadly force are the direct, if unintended, consequence of state and federal government failures to assert authority over the use of lethal force by law enforcement. The unit of government that maintains authority in many other criminal justice operations—the state level—usually has no concern with and little statutory authority about policing.

This point was illustrated in my earlier study by comparing the great success of the national government's Kevlar evaluations and promotion as standard equipment for police in communities with the failure to test the unproven theories that provide cover for hundreds of unnecessary killings of civilians by police:

> In contrast to the systemic application of empirical evidence in developing national standards that surrounded the introduction of soft body armor to police forces nationwide, the lack of evaluation for a number of life-threatening law enforcement tactics—the 21-foot rule, the firing of multiple shots and infliction of multiple wounds in response to perceived threats—indicates the inherent anarchy and lack of accountability we find in the animating principles of police use of deadly force. (Zimring 2017, 100–101)

What causes this "inherent anarchy" is an accidental allocation of responsibility for fact-finding and policy evaluation about police use of deadly force. In the current federal system, a critical approach to research, fact-finding, and policy evaluation on lethal policing is the current responsibility of no branch of government. Because local police forces are small, unspecialized, and susceptible to conflicts of interest, they would be nobody's first choice to test policies and recommend strategies to reduce the risks for citizens and police. Local police forces do not have either the concern or the capacity to protect citizen lives without outside pressure. But local police have become the decision-makers by default. This probably costs the nation hundreds of civilian deaths each year—the deadly shame of the missing links in the American federal system.

Filling in the Governance Gaps

My earlier book on police killing presented an outline of some of the vital missing tasks of government that were necessary to create effective control of police use of lethal force. One chapter titled "The Missing Links" emphasized a few of the important tasks that no level of American government has been performing, including collecting reliable data on the volume, circumstances, and necessity of use of lethal force incidents; reliable data on the volume and circumstances of life-threatening assaults against police officers; assessments of the cases where lethal force is necessary to police officer or citizen safety; the identification of strategies other than deadly force that can be safely used in conflict with civilians; the evaluation of limitations on shots fired and the effectiveness of "stop shoot- ing" rules; and the financial support for such programs of research and analysis (Zimring 2017, 143–65). If we had national or state police forces as the main arena for deadly force policy, they could do much more by themselves to create appropriate policy. But eighteen thousand separate police agencies require standards and support they do not now receive.

I want to pay special attention in this brief conclusion to one procedural ques- tion about the places in American government that are best suited to funding and administering such programs of research and evaluation. What level of govern- ment is best suited to these vital support functions?

The best method of assessing the competence of various levels of government in these critical tasks is a process of elimination. The vast majority of all policing agencies of government are in units of local government, either municipalities or counties. But individual police departments lack the resources, the motivation, and the competence to conduct empirical research and to evaluate police pro- grams. The police chief can and should become a sophisticated consumer of research and evaluation. Police chiefs must also be the agents who transform policy findings into the operational rules that keep both their officers and their citizens safe. Some police forces can also serve as the hosts for the field research and policy evaluations that outside experts will conduct. But city and county gov- ernments are too small to run and finance their own laboratories of police experi- mentation. This means that the institutions of government that will fund and administer fact-finding and policy analysis should be separate from those that manage police services. This separation of functions would make sense in any event, but it is compelling in the administrative reality of the American federal system.

The units of government that control most criminal justice policy in the United States—state government—are less involved with police and policing than with most other aspects of crime. There are, however, a few areas of govern- mental responsibility where the distance between state government and policing administration may be an advantage, such as taking responsibility out of the hands of local prosecutors when police use of lethal force becomes an issue of potential criminal liability.

There is one other consideration, however, that points away from state govern- ment, and toward national governmental institutions, as the primary focus of responsibility for policy research and standards. Police use of fatal force and police vulnerability to life-threatening assault are both national problems. There are some regional variations in the rate at which police kill and are killed in the United States, but it is a fifty-state problem. The national government has the most to gain from relevant and well-designed research and should therefore have the largest incentive to support it.

There are modest historical precedents that also provide indications of which branches of the national government (and which institutions within them) are best suited to filling the research, information, and policy analysis gaps in contemporary police lethal force policy. The National Institute of Justice has funded both research and policy innovation that has saved thousands of police officer lives (McMullen 2008). Ten million federal dollars a year in the Institute's budget in 2020 could transform policy research in police use of lethal force. The Civil Rights Division in the Department of Justice has been administering a consent degree program for police departments with chronic problems that turned its attention to lethal force issues after Ferguson. The small "COPS" program in the Department of Justice provides management consulting and expert advisors to police chiefs who request help, and this can pay substantial dividends (Zimring 2017, 235–38). Both programs are tiny now and could be tripled in scale and impact for very few millions per year.

There is also one important foreign model of a national fact-gathering institution that could also be incorporated into the U.S. government's Department of Justice, perhaps in the civil rights division. Police departments in England and Wales have decentralized administrations, not unlike the United States. But the United Kingdom also created an Independent Office for Police Conduct (formerly known as the Independent Police Complaints Commission) that has become a statistical and analysis resource that is worthy of emulation on this side of the Atlantic (Zimring 2017, 80–85).

The Bright Side of Historical Neglect

The complete lack of data and research across the landscape of American police lethal force questions does provide one cheerful budgetary prospect. Ten to 20 million dollars a year invested wisely can produce life-saving results of a scale that is almost impossible to imagine in many other areas of national public health concern. Saving citizens lives from unnecessary police use of lethal force is a bargain—all the more reason why we had best be starting soon.

References

Johnson, David T., and Franklin E. Zimring. 2009. *The next frontier: National development, political change, and the death penalty in Asia*. New York, NY: Oxford University Press.

Martinelli, Ron. 18 September 2014. Revisiting the "21-foot rule." *Police Magazine*. Available from http://www.policemag.com/channel/weapons/articles/2014/09/revisiting-the-21-foot-rule.aspx.

McMullen, M. Jo. 2008. Injuries to law enforcement officers shot wearing personal body armor: A 30-year review. *The Police Chief* 2(8).

Rushin, Stephen. 2017. *Federal intervention in American police departments*. New York, NY: Cambridge University Press.

Sinhoretto, J., M. Schlittler, and G. Silvestre. 2016. Juventude e Violencia Policial No Municipio de São Paulo. *Rev. Bras. Segur. Publica* 10 (1): 10–35.

Zimring, Franklin E. 2017. *When police kill*. Cambridge, MA: Harvard University Press.

Zimring, Franklin. Forthcoming. *The insidious momentum of mass incarceration*. New York, NY: Oxford University Press.

Zimring, Franklin E., and Brittany Arsiniega. 2015. Trends in killings of and by police: A preliminary analysis. *Ohio State Journal of Criminal Law* 13 (1): 247–64.

Social Interaction Training to Reduce Police Use of Force

By
SCOTT WOLFE,
JEFF ROJEK,
KYLE McLEAN,
and
GEOFFREY ALPERT

Controversial incidents involving uses of force by police in recent years have led to calls for improving officers' de-escalation skills. A more fruitful approach to police training reform may be a broader focus on improving officers' social interaction skills. By viewing all police-citizen encounters as social interactions that can either escalate toward or de-escalate away from the use of force, police training can develop what other fields call a "deliberate, repetitive practice" framework. This article describes the implementation of a randomized trial that brought such training to two U.S. police agencies and yielded encouraging results. We conclude that the conceptual framework was generally well received but that results depended heavily on the selection and performance of each agency's own trainers.

Keywords: police; use of force; social interaction; training; de-escalation

M ichael Brown's shooting death by a Ferguson (MO) officer in August 2014, as well as other shootings of unarmed African Americans across the United States, has provoked widespread criticism of police use of force. Controversy surrounding Brown's death had a significant impact on officers and citizens alike. Research from agencies around the

Scott Wolfe is an associate professor in the School of Criminal Justice at Michigan State University. His research focuses on police, organizational justice, legitimacy, and criminological theory. His work has appeared in Justice Quarterly, Journal of Research in Crime and Delinquency, *and* Law and Human Behavior.

Jeff Rojek is an associate professor in the School of Criminal Justice and director of the Center for Anti-Counterfeiting and Product Protection at Michigan State University. His research focuses on policing and examines topics that include police practitioner-researcher partnerships, intelligence led policing, violent crime, law enforcement response to disasters, officer decision-making, officer safety, and police training.

Correspondence: wolfesc1@msu.edu

DOI: 10.1177/0002716219887366

country demonstrates that police officers feel less motivated to work in law enforcement, perceive their job to be more dangerous, and are less willing to work with the community to solve problems (MacDonald 2017; Nix and Wolfe 2017, 2018; Nix, Wolfe, and Campbell 2018; Pyrooz et al. 2016; Shjarback et al. 2017; Wolfe and Nix 2016). Other evidence suggests that some segments of the public are more critical of the police and less likely to report crime post-Ferguson (Culhane and Schweitzer 2018; Culhane, Boman, and Schweitzer 2016; see also Desmond, Papachristos, and Kirk 2016). President Obama's Task Force on 21st Century Policing (President's Task Force on 21st Century Policing 2015) called for policing strategies to increase citizens' trust in the police, including training designed to help officers de-escalate encounters with citizens. The report suggests that with improved de-escalation skills, officers will be better prepared to minimize the likelihood of using force, including deadly force.

Such well-intentioned calls for improved de-escalation training are concerning for two reasons. First, we have an extremely small evidence base concerning what works in police training (Hansson and Markström 2014; Rosenbaum and Lawrence 2017). There are only a handful of studies that have evaluated training that includes components of de-escalation (see Engel, McManus, and Isaza, this volume; Krameddine et al. 2013). Second, as Engel, McManus, and Isaza (this volume) maintain, there are significant challenges when defining de-escalation and determining what constitutes de-escalation training. In this article, we present a detailed account of what may be a more fruitful approach to police training: using de-escalation interventions based on theoretical work grounded in general social interactions and the social interactions of police officers specifically.

Viewing problematic use of force encounters as primarily a symptom of poor de-escalation skills among officers makes what we suggest is a mistaken assumption: that many or most fatal police shootings begin in an escalated emotional or threatening environment. That assumption is falsified by substantial evidence that social interactions with the police are dynamic in nature.

Kyle McLean is an assistant professor in the College of Criminology and Criminal Justice at Florida State University. His research interests are in policing, criminological theory, and social psychology. His recent work has been published in Justice Quarterly, Journal of Research in Crime and Delinquency, *and the* British Journal of Criminology.

Geoffrey Alpert is a professor of criminology and criminal justice at the University of South Carolina and holds an appointment at Griffith Criminology Institute, Griffith University, Brisbane, Australia. He is also a chief research advisor for the United States Department of Justice, National Institute of Justice, and has taught at the FBI National Academy.

NOTE: The authors contributed equally to this article. This research was supported by the National Institute of Justice under Grant 2016-IJ-CX-0018. Points of view and opinions provided are those of the authors and do not represent the official position of the U.S. Department of Justice. We thank Sergeant Andy Carlstead and Major James Nollette from the Fayetteville Police Department and Chief Chris Magnus and Captain Chris Dennison from the Tucson Police Department for their partnership on this project. We also thank the many officers from both agencies that participated in the training and provided their candid feedback. Finally, we thank Larry Sherman for organizing this volume and providing helpful comments on the article. We also thank John MacDonald for his constructive feedback on an earlier version of this article.

The training we report on here views police-citizen encounters as social inter-actions that can either escalate toward, or de-escalate away from, the use of force. That assumption allowed the implementation of skills training that police can use to improve the outcome of such interactions, and to account for variation in citi-zens' responses to police actions and communications. Specifically, we examine an effort to apply the idea that *social interaction training should be the focus of efforts to reduce the likelihood of officer-involved shootings* and other uses of force.

The first section of this article summarizes a body of the theoretical work on police social interactions and use of force (Alpert and Dunham 2004; Sykes and Clark 1975). The second section critiques traditional approaches to police train-ing, using empirical evidence concerning deliberate, repetitive training as a mechanism for improving skills and advancing expertise. The third section pre-sents the design and implementation of a social interaction training program for patrol police officers called "Tact, Tactics, and Trust." This program is an example of police social interaction training that integrates deliberate, repetitive practice in a way that is logistically and financially feasible for many agencies. The fourth section distils key lessons from the challenges of implementation of this training in two different regions of the United States.

We do not present substantive results of the training evaluation in this article. We have reported those results elsewhere (Wolfe et al. 2019), but we summarize them here: two randomized trials of a nearly identical training program were conducted in two separate police agencies (Tucson, AZ, and Fayetteville, NC). The trials found that officers who participated in the training program placed higher priorities on procedurally fair communication with citizens and lower priorities on physical control during hypothetical officer-citizen encounters than officers who did not participate in the training program. No effect of the training was found for officers' stated prioritization of maintaining self-control. Overall, the findings of the study demonstrate support for social interaction training pro-grams in police departments.

Our focus is on the key question of how to implement this kind of training, in a context in which many officers may be opposed to the very idea of de-escalation (Engel, McManus, and Isaza, this volume). Further, we discuss evidence regard-ing the methods of training delivery and how it meshed (or not) with receptivity to social interaction training by both the officers being trained and the in-house officers who trained them. Our goal is to provide a view from the front lines of innovations in training, as an important context and possible guidance for both policy-makers and police leaders considering the implementation of this type of social interaction training in their own agencies.

A Theory of Police Encounters with Citizens: Social Interaction and the Use of Force

The evolving body of research on police use of force has provided valuable insights. One limitation of most of these efforts, however, is that police use of force is treated as a static event (Alpert and Dunham 2004). Few studies have captured the dynamic process within police-citizen encounters that leads to the escalation of force being used or de-escalation away from force. The exception has been the work of a handful of scholars working from a social interactionist perspective.

Sykes and Clark's (1975) theory on deference exchange in police-citizen encounters represents the foundation of this approach. Their framework is grounded in Goffman's (1956, 1961) perspective that encounters between individuals are governed by a set of exchange rituals that create order during interactions. There is a mutual expectation among individuals in an encounter that they will show respect for one another. Sykes and Clark demonstrate that the rules for showing respect and deference during police-citizen encounters are asymmetrical because officers have legal authority to enforce the law and maintain order. This causes officers to expect deference *from* citizens, yet not to expect they must reciprocate the same level of respect *to* citizens. Scholars have observed that officers seek to maintain authority through this asymmetry because it allows them to control a situation—including the ability to question, command, and even physically coerce if necessary (Bittner 1970; Collins 2004; Muir 1977; Van Maanen 1978). Officers will attempt to reassert their authority when citizens do not abide by this asymmetrical deference expectation.

Alpert and Dunham (2004) subsequently refined Sykes and Clark's work into a theory that explains better how police-citizen interactions turn into use of force events—referred to as Authority Maintenance Theory. Their framework is distinct because it places more emphasis on the importance of citizens' roles during interactions. They acknowledge that officers enter interactions with the goals of maintaining their authority and controlling the situation, but citizens also have expectations that may range from being treated fairly to avoiding apprehension. Both parties will become more aggressive or coercive when their goals are blocked. Officers are more likely to use force, and citizens are more likely to resist officers' commands or physical control efforts, when either believes the other party will not allow them to achieve their goal. Alpert and Dunham argue that goal blockage creates an action-reaction chain that can escalate toward or de-escalate away from the use of force by the citizen or officer.

Alpert and Dunham's theory is useful because it frames encounters leading to the use of force by either party as an escalating exchange of coercion and resistance. This perspective highlights the potential for turning points in the exchange cycle where officers can take actions that lead to de-escalation. This does not suggest that all use of force events can be avoided through some action on the part of officers. There are cases where officers must react immediately to being attacked without the opportunity to de-escalate. Similarly, officers become involved in encounters in which citizens are not receptive to de-escalation efforts. Moreover, even with cases that do not immediately start with an attack on an officer, it may be a reasonable course of action for an officer to escalate his or her level of coercive efforts. Officers may have a duty, for example, to overcome resistance to a lawful arrest or prevent escape, albeit by using only a level of force appropriate to the situation.

An appreciation of these interaction dynamics and shifting trajectories of escalation and de-escalation in a given encounter is critical to current calls for de-escalation training. However, training that *only* focuses on de-escalation fails to capture the complex nature of police-citizen encounters. A total focus on de-escalation does not improve officers' ability to determine when de-escalation, or even escalation, of force is the most appropriate course of action. Training based on this lack of appreciation is unlikely to build the appropriate skill sets for accomplishing these goals.

This is not to suggest that improving the capacity of officers to de-escalate encounters is an undesirable goal. Rather, we suggest the path to building this capacity may be found in improving officer social interaction skills in general. Further, traditional use of force training often focuses squarely on overcoming resistance and threats, which avoids an appreciation for the dynamic nature of police-citizen interactions that presents paths for escalation and de-escalation. A more effective approach may be found in improving the ability of officers to read situational cues, effectively communicate, and make decisions to be more effective in choosing the best course of action, whether it is escalation or de-escalation. In short, we need to improve officers' abilities to interpret and respond to social cues to improve the outcomes of police-citizen social interactions.

A critique and theory of police training

The importance of officers having effective social interaction skills has long been recognized in policing scholarship. For example, Bittner's (1970) classic work on policing skid row articulated the importance of officer social interaction skills. For police officers to become what he called a "careful craftsman," he argued that they needed an ability to read the people they encounter. That capacity enabled them to communicate effectively and to make good decisions on whether to employ coercive actions—to become experts at social interaction skills. Bittner also argued that there are two critical mechanisms for becoming an expert: experience and training. Although the nature of police work demands that both experienced and novice officers engage in citizen interactions, the latter are unlikely to be as skilled as more tenured colleagues. Bittner's theory was that the development of interaction expertise increases with experience, but experience alone is insufficient to produce that expertise.

Bittner's (1970) limits on the likely value of police experience is consistent with the more recent body of empirical literature on expertise development. Early research measured expertise through simple length of experience in a given field and an individual's reputation (Simon and Chase 1973). Subsequent research has shown that experts defined by these measures often perform only a little or no better at representative tasks than their less experienced peers (Doane, Pellegrino, and Klatzky 1990; Camerer and Johnson 1991; Ericsson 1998; Ericsson and Ward 2007; Ericsson, Krampe, and Tesch-Römer 1993). These findings identified the specific mechanisms that create expert performance across a wide set of domains, including medicine, sports, chess, firefighting, and aviation.

Ericsson noted that when individuals initially attempt to develop new skills, they display heightened concentration to avoid committing errors in a given task. With limited training or experience, individuals engaging in the same task achieve acceptable performance—performance that is functional but not error free. Consistent with Bittner's arguments, Ericsson observed that experience alone provided little additional performance improvement. Alternatively, continued improvement in performance results when experience is coupled with what he calls "deliberate practice" (Ericson 2004; Ericsson and Ward 2007; Ericsson, Krampe, and Tesch-Römer 1993; Ward, Suss, and Basevitch 2009). According to Ericsson (2004), "deliberate practice" requires three elements: (1) instruction to improve performance on a defined task, (2) immediate feedback on performance, and (3) ample opportunity for task repetition to refine performance.

This framing of experience, "deliberate practice," and expertise has relevance to police training, and especially to social interaction skill development. Traditionally, officers get some level of training related to social interaction in police academy instruction of new recruits. Officers will typically engage in training scenarios and presumably receive feedback from trainers on their performance (Reaves 2016). In addition, officers may have the opportunity to receive training and feedback in work settings from their field training officer (FTO). It is unknown whether this initial police academy or FTO instruction translates into effective social interaction skills, but it reflects at least an initial effort at developing expertise. Thus, following Ericsson's (2004) skill acquisition framework, officers will develop a functional level of performance in the ability to engage in social interactions and make determinations on force escalation, nonescalation, and de-escalation through a combination of academy training, FTO supervision, and individual experience. Like Bittner, however, Ericsson thought that performance will improve little if an individual relies solely on experience.

What police call "in-service" training in the years after the initial recruits' police academy is intended to provide additional training to officers throughout their career. While research on the nature, structure, and effectiveness of in-service training is mostly nonexistent (Heuy 2018), officers are often required by their agencies, in some cases based on state certification requirements, to engage in a prescribed number of training hours on an annual or biannual basis. A good portion of this training is dedicated to classroom instruction on issues such as legal updates or new policy initiatives. Other components may include use of force tactics, firearm instruction, and driving training. While important, this training framework does not allow for deliberate practice or ample opportunity for task repetition to refine performance. It should be recognized, however, that while these are perishable skills, the demand to cover state-mandated topics limits the opportunity for multiple repetitions of the applied components of in-service training. Moreover, the need to keep personnel on the street to meet organizational demands generally prevents officers from being taken out of service to attend training several times a year. A deliberate practice, repetitive approach to training—one that is best at increasing expertise (Ericsson 2004)—is not the norm in policing for logistical reasons that, historically, have prevented such a philosophy from becoming part of a police training culture.

Thus, if agencies wish to develop their officers' social interaction expertise framed in a deliberate practice framework, alternatives to the traditional in-service structure are necessary. Any training conceptualized in the deliberate practice model also must be modified to fit the reality of policing operations. It is not possible to have officers engage in hours of deliberate practice like military personnel or competitive athletes. In other words, a successful deliberate practice program must find a way to increase the repetition of exercises on social interactions without unduly burdening the operational demands of a department.

Given this conclusion, effective training must now compete with other organizational demands to create a repetitive social interaction training program that provides necessary skills. Critically important questions must be answered, such as,

- How can an agency work out the logistics of delivering such training given personnel and resource limitations?
- Will officers be receptive to this focus on building social interaction skills? and
- Will officers be receptive to a repetition training model that differs from their traditional in-service experience?

The remainder of this article addresses these questions with a report from a training experiment in social interaction skills for policing. The training succeeded in delivery of multiple exercises with substantial fidelity to the plan over a defined time period, in two different police agencies. In the process, it generated further questions for considering how best to use training to reduce the frequency of fatal police shootings and other use of force events.

Implementing a Social Interaction Training Program

The training program that we evaluated was Polis Solutions' "Tact, Tactics, and Trust" (hereafter, T3) training—a proprietary program based on U.S. Department of Defense work called the "Good Stranger" program (Klein et al. 2014). This program was developed by the Defense Advanced Research Programs Agency (DARPA) for improving the social interaction skills of U.S. soldiers in Iraq and Afghanistan. The adaptation of that program by Polis Solutions, a Seattle-based training, consulting, and research company, as "T3" focuses on developing the knowledge, skills, and attitudes of police personnel concerning social interactions with members of the public. Based on our research team's observations, the training focuses on improving the use of procedurally fair communication skills (e.g., being empathetic, building rapport, being honest), the need to maintain self-control, and de-escalation skills, through repetitive exposure to real-life officer-citizen social interactions. T3 is an example of social interaction training that goes beyond focusing only on de-escalation.

Research context

Evaluation of T3 involved a partnership with Fayetteville (NC) Police Department (FPD) and Tucson (AZ) Police Department (TPD). FPD serves a racially diverse population of approximately 205,000. About 46 percent of Fayetteville residents are white, while 42 percent are African American. The department had 164 patrol officers at the time of the study and reported about 750 violent crimes per 100,000 citizens. TPD, by contrast, serves a larger jurisdiction, but also with two major social groups: 530,000 citizens reside in Tucson, with about 42 percent of the population being Hispanic and 47 percent non-Hispanic white. TPD had 320 patrol officers at the time of the study and experienced about 795 violent crimes per 100,000 residents.[1]

Research design

While our evaluation was primarily focused on determining whether T3 influenced officers' attitudes and behaviors regarding social interactions, we were also interested in whether the amount of training influenced these outcomes. Accordingly, we developed a protocol in collaboration with each police agency in which a high-dose group of officers would receive six months of T3 training, and a low-dose group would receive three months of training. We also worked with departmental contacts to randomly assign all patrol officers to either the experimental training or control conditions using rosters within each agency. Accordingly, a randomized-controlled trial was used to evaluate T3.[2]

Program description

The T3 program consisted of several components. First, Polis Solutions' instructors (a team of current and former law enforcement and military personnel, hereafter referred to as "Polis trainers") provided train-the-trainer sessions to groups of officers selected by command staff at each of our partner agencies (hereafter referred to as "department trainers"). This session provided information to the department trainers regarding the principles of T3 and how to provide the training to patrol officers over the course of the program. One month prior to starting the delivery of training to patrol officers, Polis Solutions delivered a "refresher" training to the department trainers. In addition to reviewing the core principles, this session provided detail on the delivery of the training and the implementation plan. Fayetteville assigned nineteen officers to attend this training and perform as the designated trainers, and Tucson assigned twenty officers for these responsibilities.

The second component of T3 involved department trainers providing a two-hour introductory course to all officer trainees. This course focused on teaching officers the core principles of T3 (communication skills, maintaining self-control, and de-escalation) and "GIRing-in" (Goal, Identity, and Relation)—a term used by Polis Solutions to refer to concepts focused on rapport building. The third, and most important, component of T3 involved officers taking part in department trainer–facilitated video-based decision-making exercises. These exercises were conducted just before uniformed patrol officers went out on patrol (or just after patrol for those ending their shifts on overlap days), at roll calls, and were limited to officers who had been assigned to the experimental groups.

These video sessions were referred to as tactical decision exercises (TDEs) by Polis Solutions. They involved officers watching real police-citizen interactions (recorded by body camera, dash cam, or cell phone). The videos were programmed to pause at various points, and officers were responsible for completing worksheets that asked them to identify major areas of concern in the video and their priorities moving forward if they were involved in the interaction. Rapid thoughts were encouraged by only giving officers a brief period to provide written responses (2.5 minutes for each video stop point, with about 30 seconds allowed to answer each question, and three stop points per video). Each stop point and worksheet completion were followed by a five-minute group discussion of the previously viewed video segment. Agency instructors guided these discussions to focus on the importance of being respectful to suspects, allowing citizens opportunity to voice their concerns, rapport building, maintaining self-control, and using force only as a last resort when social interaction strategies fail. Each TDE exercise lasted about 45 to 60 minutes. Officers completed a TDE every two weeks for either three or six months depending on their dosage assignment. Thus, the high-dose officers completed thirteen TDEs, and the low-dose officers completed seven TDEs.

Polis Solutions developed this TDE format for several reasons. First, roll calls were used to deliver the training because they avoided the need to train in an academy setting. Roll calls provided the opportunity to train large groups of officers repeatedly over time, consistent with the principles of deliberate, repetitive practice. Second, the video-based TDEs allowed officers to critically analyze the actions of real police and learn from real situations. A critique of traditional reality-based scenario training is that, while it allows officers live practice, it is inherently artificial because officers know what types of behaviors are expected and the most likely responses from role players (e.g., shoot/don't shoot scenarios). Third, keeping the TDEs under an hour allowed for repeated training sessions that minimally impacted patrol coverage and officer training fatigue.

The fourth component of the T3 training involved midpoint and conclusion/capstone refresher courses led by Polis trainers. The midpoint refresher course lasted four hours, focused primarily on rapport building with suspects, and occurred at the end of the low-dose period. Both high- and low-dose officers attended this training. The capstone lasted eight hours and was administered at the end of the high-dose training period. Therefore, only the high-dose officers attended this training. Each course was designed to allow Polis trainers to have direct contact with officer trainees and reinforce the lessons delivered from department trainers.

Challenges to Implementing Social Interaction Training

The key challenges we anticipated, as noted above, were (1) the logistics of delivering such training given personnel and resource limitations, (2) officers' receptivity to this focus on building social interaction skills, and (3) officers' receptivity to a repetition training model that differs from their traditional in-service experience. It was largely to address those concerns that the design of T3 required unusual flexibility on the part of the police departments involved in the training, in three ways:

- the program utilized both in-house and outside experts to deliver training,
- it required repetitive training sessions, and
- it took place over an extended period.

All these features posed challenges. The discussion that follows draws on our formal interviews with officers and trainers, observations of the training, and findings from surveys of the trainees to highlight some of the key lessons learned from the training implementation.

Training staff

The balance of training with department and Polis trainers provided some interesting perspectives. Some of the trainers expressed to us during informal conversations that line-level officers often loathe training that involves a hired "outside expert." At times, these experts are seen to have little understanding of the nuances of policing if they do not have a law enforcement background. Furthermore, individuals outside the agency, even those with a law enforcement background (as nearly all the outside trainers in this program had), do not know the department's culture and do not have earned respect among the officers. As part of the TDE process, officers and department trainers would engage in some level of critique of officers in the videos. The department trainers leading the TDE sessions walked officers through the discussion of the videos, raising critiques of the actions and offering alternatives, as well as soliciting feedback from trainees. Some trainees were resistant to the idea of critiquing another officer in hindsight, arguing that it was a bad idea to "Monday morning quarterback" their decisions. In response, department trainers framed the exercise not as an effort to judge the officers in the video but as a tool for learning from the experiences of others. As officers critiqued the video, trainers would provide feedback and question officers on why they made particular assessments. We did not hear any criticism of this effort, and, in fact, many officers responded positively to hearing another officer's point of view on an interaction. In contrast, some officers expressed irritation when they, or fellow officers, were questioned by the Polis trainers about their assessments, with one officer referring to it as "insulting." Mentioning this perspective is not intended to validate this viewpoint; rather, it highlights that some officers may be uncomfortable when individuals from outside their agency review their policing decisions.

However, simply having training delivered by a cadre of officers within the department is not a guarantee for success. At one of the sites there had been a change in the training leadership during the early stages of the project. The new training commander contacted the research staff about a month before the second train-the-trainer session and noted that he was making changes to the department trainers attending the second course. He made the point that more thought had to be given to who should be the department trainers administering the TDEs. One of the key limitations he observed was that some of the trainers selected by the previous commander had little policing experience. He noted this was not meant to question the quality of these officers, but that more seasoned officers may not respond well to training delivered by officers with little experience. In other words, using trainers with little experience may result in a lack of buy-in because of a lower level of respect for such trainers.

The relevance of having trainers with enough experience and respect became evident early in the training sessions. At the beginning of the program, some officers had concerns that the training would make officers more hesitant to use force at the expense of officer safety. To combat this perspective, trainers would commonly note that T3 was not "hug-a-thug" and that no one expected them not to use force when it was necessary. Trainers also fielded concerns from officers about the content of the training. For example, in one exchange, a corporal commented,

> You need a caveat to this, some of these younger guys are going to think you have to do this every time. This doesn't fit every situation. Yes, for the general public, and 90 percent of the bad guys, but with some assholes they should not be doing this. It's not how you handle [some situations].

The trainer, who had more years of experience, replied,

> Even if you use force, it does not mean you did anything wrong. You are never going to get rid of force in policing. The goal is to employ this as much as you can. The goal of this is to hone the tactics in our bag . . . to reduce the chance of using force in a situation. There are times when we force the situation, and we want to reduce that.

The corporal accepted the trainer's response and the session continued. It is hard to imagine the corporal would have accepted or trusted this response coming from a junior or less-experienced officer delivering the training.

Complexity in scheduling

To achieve the repetition required by the deliberative practice model, commanders from both Fayetteville and Tucson agreed that conducting training at patrol districts/divisions rather than at the academy would be necessary. However, even conducting the training at roll call created operational concerns because officers needed to be off the road for approximately an hour to complete the training. Thus, the training schedule had to accommodate the structure of the patrol schedules in each district to achieve an efficient schedule for training delivery. The level of complexity in doing this was substantial, but the complexity depended entirely on the unique features of patrol schedules in each of the two police agencies.[3]

A persistent scheduling challenge was the use of a training cadre consisting of officers who have primary duty responsibilities other than training (e.g., patrol, investigations, specialized unit). As noted above, it was critical to the success of the training program that the officers delivering the training had policing experience and trainees' respect. However, officers with these credentials are typically promoted and given duties other than patrol. Many of the trainers were not patrol officers and had schedules that did not mesh well with the efficient schedules developed for the trainees. As a result, these officers were commonly pulled off their primary duty to conduct T3 training, which caused continual depletion in their primary units to support the repetition of training.

The extended duration of training: Fatigue and fidelity

The extended duration of training for T3 posed another unique challenge: fatigue and fidelity to the training design. While getting officers to a central location for training sessions poses a greater logistic constraint to normal operations, it is in some ways easier for training staff because officers must attend only one time. For a repetitive training program that takes place over several months, officers, by design, must show up and participate multiple times. At one level this raises the question, If officers are supposed to get a specific number of training hours or sessions, does falling short of this prescribed number limit the impact of the training?

Officers within our study missed sessions for sick days, vacations, court, and other mandatory training. Within our research context, these absences were critical given our empirical interest in dosage; however, once you move away from research and empirical assessment concerns these issues may be less relevant. Missing a few of the twelve sessions is not likely a serious problem. However, the more sessions that are missed, the greater the impact on training effectiveness. That said, missing many sessions will not likely be tolerated by training staff when the program is implemented as part of mandated training rather than as a research project.

Relatedly, fatigue for both officers and trainers toward the end of the training program resulted in increased absences and less engagement with the training material. In our discussions with trainees, high-dose officers were more likely to voice concerns over the number of TDEs than low-dose officers. Similarly, in observations of the training, some trainers began to move through the material related to the TDEs faster, giving less time for discussion among the officers toward the end of the training period. Relatedly, the officers were contributing less to the discussions. The material and format were technically carried out, but with less engagement. These observations suggest fatigue is important to any training endeavor attempting to follow a deliberate practice approach. Thus, practice should be repetitive but not excessive.

It should be noted, however, that even in the beginning of the training, we observed variation in the degree to which trainers took ownership of the material and how much commitment they displayed while delivering it. Some trainers would use personal and local examples to illustrate the T3 concepts and present the material as if it were coming from their perspective. Other trainers would dissociate themselves from the training by presenting the material with the prefix "they said," referring to Polis Solutions. While at times these trainers were stating what Polis Solutions had written on their trainer guide for the TDE, the difference between personal stories on the subject and quoting the trainer guide likely gives officers cues on the trainer's commitment or belief in the material. This is not to suggest that trainers did not deliver the training as prescribed but, rather, that there was variation in the level of "ownership" of the training.

This variation has two relevant impacts on the previously discussed issues of trainers and scheduling. First, picking trainers who believe in the training and relate it to their own work may generate better results. As one of the officers who went through the training noted about selecting trainers, "I think just making sure that the instructors are in line with the type of training that they're trying to implement to us, that maybe they have a passion for it. . . ." Second, these findings are especially critical for scheduling given the varying approaches to assigning trainers. On one hand, in Fayetteville, where trainers were responsible for specific training sessions rather than a group of officers, if some trainers did not "own" the training, it may have diluted the training effects, but officers were still exposed to other passionate trainers. On the other hand, in Tucson, where trainers were assigned a group of officers rather than a specific training session, if a trainer did not "own" the training, the effects may have been completely erased, as officers were never exposed to a different trainer.

Officer Receptivity

We now turn attention toward examining officers' receptivity to T3. Here our aim is to determine whether officers in our experiment were receptive to social interaction training of this type and the methods of training delivery. The overarching purpose is to pinpoint areas of the training that officers reacted well to and those they believed needed improvement.

Data

Members of the T3 evaluation research team administered posttraining questionnaires during roll calls at each agency over a one-week period that provided the best opportunity for officers on all shifts and across all districts/divisions to participate. The survey collected data from officers on their reactions to both the content of the training and the design of the program. The survey was anonymous and did not collect personally identifying information. Only one officer present during the roll calls did not complete the survey, and one participant did not respond to any of the questions. This resulted in a sample of 128 officers who received T3 training. Fifteen officers in the sample were T3 trainers. Accordingly, 77 percent of officers originally randomly assigned to the training completed a posttest survey.[4]

Results

Receptivity to social interaction training. Table 1 presents descriptive statistics for a series of survey questions that gauged officers' receptivity to

TABLE 1
Receptivity to T3 as a Social Interaction-Based Training Program

Question	Mean	1 = No Value %	2 = Little Value %	3 = Moderate Value %	4 = High Value %
How would you rate the overall value of the T3 training?	2.81	3.2%	25.4%	58.7%	12.7%
How would you rate the value of the seven T3 principles and the GIRing in concepts?	2.84	4.7%	25.0%	51.6%	18.8%

Question	Mean	1 = Strongly Disagree %	2 = Disagree %	3 = Neutral %	4 = Agree %	5 = Strongly Agree %
Participation in T3 has increased my appreciation for the dynamics of police interactions with community members.	2.88	10.2%	22.7%	40.6%	21.9%	4.7%
Participation in T3 has increased my understanding of how my decisions and actions impact an interaction with a community member.	2.98	8.6%	25.0%	32.8%	27.3%	6.3%
Participation in T3 has improved my skills of interacting with community members in general.	2.75	11.7%	28.9%	36.7%	18.0%	4.7%
Participation in T3 has improved my ability to de-escalate potential conflicts with community members.	2.80	11.7%	23.4%	42.2%	18.0%	4.7%
Officers in my agency who did not participate in the T3 program would benefit from going through the T3 program.	3.19	7.8%	13.3%	40.6%	28.9%	9.4%

(continued)

TABLE 1 (CONTINUED)

Question	Mean	1 = Strongly Disagree %	2 = Disagree %	3 = Neutral %	4 = Agree %	5 = Strongly Agree %
The average law enforcement officer in the United States would benefit from going through the T3 program.	3.44	5.5%	10.2%	30.5%	43.0%	10.9%

T3 as a social interaction training program. About 71 percent of T3 officers believed the T3 program was of "high" or "moderate" value. About 28 percent of participants indicated T3 had "little" or "no" value. A similar pattern of receptivity emerged with respect to officers' views of T3's main social interaction-based principles. Slightly more than 70 percent of T3 officers indicated the T3 principles and GIRing-in concepts had "moderate" or "high" value, whereas about 30 percent believed they had "little" or "no value."

Slightly more negative findings emerged when we asked officers to reflect on the skills they acquired during the T3 training. About 27 percent of T3 officers agreed/strongly agreed that the training increased their appreciation for the dynamics of interactions with community members. Forty percent were neutral regarding this issue, and about one-third of participants disagreed/strongly disagreed. One-third of officers believed that participation in T3 increased their understanding of how their decisions impact interactions with community members. Yet two-thirds of participants were neutral or disagreed/strongly disagreed that they have a better understanding of how their decisions impact citizens. Likewise, more than 40 percent of T3 participants disagreed/strongly disagreed that the training improved their skills of interacting with community members. About 23 percent of officers believed their interaction skills had improved as a result of T3. Thirty-five percent of respondents disagreed/strongly disagreed that T3 improved their ability to de-escalate potential conflicts with community members. About 23 percent of officers indicated that T3 improved their de-escalation skills.

These results suggest that while many officers perceived the social interaction training to be somewhat valuable, fewer believed the program improved their own skills. From a practical standpoint, this suggests that agencies pursuing social interaction training may find that many of their officers believe they are already skilled at communication and de-escalation. The trick will be to find ways to obtain officer buy-in to such training despite these attitudes.

We also asked officers two questions about whether they believed other officers would benefit from the T3 training. About 38 percent of respondents agreed/ strongly agreed that officers in their agency who were not assigned to the training would benefit from the T3 program. About 21 percent disagreed/strongly disagreed that other officers in their agency would benefit from participating in T3. A different view emerged when considering officers across the United States. Fifty-four percent of participants agreed/strongly agreed that the average U.S. law enforcement officer would benefit from the program. Only 16 percent of T3 officers disagreed/strongly disagreed with this sentiment.

This is an interesting finding because it suggests that officers were lukewarm on their receptivity toward T3 but tended to believe the training would be more valuable for other officers. This may be what psychological research refers to as the "third-person effect." For example, traffic collision research has shown that warning drivers about the potential outcomes of dangerous driving (e.g., speeding) causes survey respondents to indicate that their own driving behaviors will not necessarily be changed, but the messages are likely to change other drivers' behaviors (Lewis, Watson, and Tay 2007). Police executives pursuing a training program of this type can expect to experience a similar effect among their own officers. Again, the key to success may lie in finding strategies that cause officers to view the training as beneficial to themselves. Messaging and marketing of the training prior to the start of the program may prove useful in this effort.

Receptivity to methods of training delivery. Table 2 presents the results from a series of questions we used to assess officers' receptivity to T3's training delivery methods. The department trainers received positive evaluations from their trainee colleagues. While only 58 percent of participants believed the introductory course had value, a vast majority—80 percent—believed the department trainers did a good job facilitating the training.

With respect to the four-hour refresher training that was offered at the end of the low-dose training and at the halfway point of the high-dose training, 59 percent of officers believed it was valuable. Nearly 72 percent of trainees agreed/strongly agreed that the Polis trainers did a good job facilitating this course. Seventy-eight percent of the high-dose officers believed the 8-hour capstone training was valuable, and 77 percent agreed/strongly agreed that Polis did a good job facilitating this course.

With respect to the core of the T3 program, 68 percent of officers viewed the TDEs as either of moderate or high value, and 41 percent of participants agreed/strongly agreed that the video-based TDEs were an effective way to train on social interactions with community members. We also asked officers to compare the T3 video sessions to reality-based scenario training because both agencies used such training prior to T3. About 40 percent of respondents agreed/strongly agreed that the T3 video sessions were a valuable alternative to reality-based scenario training. Yet 34 percent of respondents selected "neutral" for this item, and 26 percent disagreed/strongly disagreed. These results suggest that T3 trained officers did not believe the video-based scenario training should supplant reality-based training. Qualitative interviews with officers echoed this finding. Officers found value in T3 as a social

TABLE 2
Receptivity to T3 Methods of Training Delivery

Question	Mean	1 = No Value %	2 = Little Value %	3 = Moderate Value %	4 = High Value %
How would you rate the value of the introductory overview of the T3 program?	2.66	6.3%	35.2%	45.3%	13.3%
How would you rate the value of the GIRing in training session?	2.70	11.5%	29.5%	36.9%	22.1%
How would you rate the value of the Capstone training session? (N = 59)	3.08	6.8%	15.3%	40.7%	37.3%
How would you rate the value of the Tactical Decision Exercises?	2.82	5.6%	26.4%	48.8%	19.2%

Question	Mean	1 = Strongly Disagree %	2 = Disagree %	3 = Neutral %	4 = Agree %	5 = Strongly Agree %
The department trainers that led my training sessions did a good job of facilitating the training.	4.00	2.4%	0%	17.5%	55.6%	24.6%
The trainers from Polis Solutions that conducted the 4-hour course at the academy did a good job facilitating the training.	3.90	2.4%	4.8%	21.0%	44.4%	27.4%
The trainers from Polis Solutions that conducted the 8-hour course at the academy did a good job facilitating the training.	4.00	3.3%	5.0%	15.0%	41.7%	35.0%
The video-based tactical decision exercises were an effective way to train on social interactions with community members.	3.20	7.8%	14.8%	35.9%	32.8%	8.6%

(continued)

TABLE 2 (CONTINUED)

Question	Mean	1 = Strongly Disagree %	2 = Disagree %	3 = Neutral %	4 = Agree %	5 = Strongly Agree %
The T3 video sessions are a valuable alternative to reality-based scenario training.	3.16	6.3%	19.5%	34.4%	31.3%	8.6%
It was useful to have multiple T3 training sessions over the past several months.	3.19	7.8%	16.4%	32.8%	35.2%	7.8%
There were too many tactical decision exercises to attend.	3.02	3.1%	28.1%	38.3%	24.2%	6.3%
There needed to be more tactical decision exercises to attend for the training to be effective.	2.46	13.3%	35.9%	43.8%	5.5%	1.6%
The T3 training was worth the amount of time I put into attending the tactical decision exercises every other week.	3.05	8.6%	20.3%	34.4%	30.5%	6.3%

interaction training program, but many suggested that it would work better if paired with reality-based scenarios.

The final set of questions gauged officers' opinions about the quantity of the T3 training. About 43 percent of officers agreed/strongly agreed that "It was useful to have multiple T3 training sessions over the past several months." But nearly one-third of officers selected "neutral" for this statement, and 24 percent disagreed/strongly disagreed. Thirty percent of officers believed there were too many TDEs to attend, and only 7 percent believed there needed to be more TDEs. When considering the amount of time they spent attending the TDEs, 37 percent agreed/strongly agreed that it was worth their time. More than one-third neither agreed or disagreed that the TDEs were worth their time, and 29 percent did not believe it was worth their time.

Conclusion

Improving social interaction skills for police-citizen encounters requires an innovative approach, not just to policing, but to entire systems of police training. Polis Solutions' T3 program attempted to achieve these goals by implementing a high-repetition, "deliberate practice" training regime that focused on improving officers' communication and de-escalation skills. To the extent that we can evaluate the program without posttraining data on police use of force in field settings, T3 succeeded in modifying trainees' attitudes toward certain practices of procedural justice. That finding would be a necessary, if not sufficient, cause for promoting more skilled interaction that can avoid unnecessary escalation. But for many police agencies, the complexity of delivering the T3 program, in this way, could well be insurmountable if they do not prepare for the major barriers to implementation.

The main barrier to implementation may be that social interaction skills are "nothing new." Throughout our training observations and interviews, police officers often expressed the opinion that these skills, and their use, were not new to them or officers in their agency. This general sentiment parallels Todak and James's (2018) observation that officers assert they engage in de-escalation daily (and without specific training). While officers are receptive to social interaction training, they feel it is something they already do, and the training would be more valuable for less-skilled officers.

It is also important to consider the possibility that asking officers to self-reflect on whether they are experts at social interaction may be a sensitive issue because it calls into question their core personal abilities. This sentiment was expressed by one of the trainers in our project. He noted that telling officers they need to improve their shooting is less sensitive than telling them they need to improve their ability to interact with others. In his mind, the latter was a more sensitive critique of an officer's personal character and ability.

Police agencies adopting T3 should also appreciate that a deliberate practice approach with repetitive training, like that used in the T3 program, is new for policing. The initial DARPA program that was the foundation of T3 was founded in a military context where repetitive training is a cultural norm. The constant balance between operational demand and constrained personnel resources limits the amount of training police officers receive. Repeated training is not an organizational practice or cultural norm of policing, at least relative to the military, professional athletics, firefighting, and other professions. While deliberate practice may be the best method for improving officer expertise for any skill set, it may take a shift in cultural norms and practice for officers to become more receptive to it. In short, policing needs to develop a stronger training culture mentality.

Agencies that decide to improve officer performance through this kind of training repetition will benefit from several key lessons learned during our implementation. First, selecting the right trainers is critical. Trainers should believe in the content of the training if they are to maximize engagement with the trainees. This includes not only having a passion for the content, but also "owning" the training in a way that does not project the content as coming from an outside source.

Second, training should be repetitive, but not excessively so—if that line can be drawn. While there did not appear to be much fatigue among officers receiving the low-dose training, there were several indicators of fatigue among the officers in the high-dose group. This included trainers appearing to "go through the motions," officers engaging in less discussion, and survey responses that there were "too many" training sessions.

Finally, flexible and efficient scheduling is difficult, but not impossible. Aligning officers' and trainers' schedules created substantial strain on personnel resources. These challenges would likely expand if an agency attempted to deliver similar social interaction training to all their officers, or if they wanted to use this training repetition approach to develop other officer skills.

A move toward training repetition may require agencies to adopt alternative training platforms where possible. In line with this recognition, the Bureau of Justice Assistance's VALOR program has provided funding to Polis Solutions to move their TDEs to a web-based delivery platform. Thus, instead of officers attending TDE sessions in person, they can participate in essentially the same video-based scenarios at a convenient time without a trainer (Bureau of Justice Assistance 2018). At the same time, we found that officers appreciated being able to discuss the TDEs with departmental colleagues. Moving to an online format may compromise this advantage, while providing the benefit of scheduling flexibility.

In any case, there is no evidence about the effectiveness of an online version of social interaction training for police. Such a vital matter should, in our view, only be made on the basis of good evidence. It will be critical for agencies to conduct independent evaluations to determine not only their officers' receptivity to in-person or web-based training formats but also whether an online version has the same attitudinal or behavioral effects.

In the end, our hope is that this article will motivate more discussion, implementation, and evaluation of deliberate, repetitive police training in social interaction skills. Our nation will see positive impacts on officer and citizen safety if we move beyond simple calls for de-escalation training and reliance on traditional police training frameworks that lack repetition.

Notes

1. While it was not possible to obtain a representative sample of U.S. officers for our evaluation, we believe data from these two agencies help to improve the generalizability of the findings because they are situated in different regions of the United States and serve diverse populations of citizens.

2. A total of 166 officers were randomly assigned to the experimental group and 228 to the control group. There was not an equal number of officers assigned to each group because we conducted the random assignment about one month prior to the start of the training program. This was done for logistical reasons but created a situation where some officers who were not on the patrol roster during randomization ended up being placed on patrol assignment after the experiment was under way. For example, officers freshly out of the academy or on military or maternity leave during randomization were not on the roster. Any officers that were added to the patrol roster after randomization were simply included in the control group.

3. Anyone who requires full details on scheduling is welcome to contact the first author for a description of the plans and the problems they faced.

4. A training evaluation of this scale will experience attrition. We were unable to capture responses from all officers originally assigned to the experimental training condition (23 percent attrition rate). Some officers were not present during survey administration (e.g., sick or at court), but others had left the agency, were on leave (e.g., military, maternity, or investigation), or were reassigned off patrol. Ideally, we

could have been able to track these individuals if we had collected their names. However, the virtues of survey anonymity and importance of truthful questionnaire responses outweighed the need for identifiable data. Yet we observed no differences in officer gender, age, years of service, or race among officers in the pretest ($N = 166$) and posttest surveys ($N = 128$). This increases the confidence we have in our evaluation results despite meaningful attrition.

References

Alpert, Geoffrey P., and Roger G. Dunham. 2004. *Understanding police use of force: Officers, suspects, and reciprocity*. New York, NY: Cambridge University Press.

Bittner, Egon. 1970. *The functions of the police in modern society*, vol. 88. Chevy Chase, MD: National Institute of Mental Health.

Bureau of Justice Assistance. June 2018. VALOR Officer Safety Initiative quarterly providers meeting. Washington, DC: Bureau of Justice Assistance.

Camerer, C. F. J., and E. Johnson. 1991. The process-performance paradox in expert judgment: How can experts know so much and predict so badly? In *Towards a general theory of expertise*, eds. K. A. Ericsson and J. Smith, 195–217. New York, NY: Cambridge University Press.

Collins, Randall. 2004. *Interaction ritual chains*. Princeton, NJ: Princeton University Press.

Culhane, Scott E., John H. Boman IV, and Kimberly Schweitzer. 2016. Public perceptions of the justifiability of police shootings: The role of body cameras in a pre-and post-Ferguson experiment. *Police Quarterly* 19:251–74.

Culhane, Scott E., and Kimberly Schweitzer. 2018. Police shootings and body cameras one year post-Ferguson. *Policing and Society* 28:1038–49.

Desmond, Matthew, Andrew V. Papachristos, and David S. Kirk. 2016. Police violence and citizen crime reporting in the black community. *American Sociological Review* 81:857–76.

Doane, Stephanie M., James W. Pellegrino, and Roberta L. Klatzky. 1990. Expertise in a computer operating system: Conceptualization and performance. *Human-Computer Interaction* 5:267–304.

Engle, Robin, Hannah McManus, and Gabrielle Isaza. 2020. Moving beyond "best practice": The need for evidence to reduce officer-involved shootings. *The ANNALS of the American Academy of Political and Social Science* (this volume).

Ericsson, K. Anders. 1998. The scientific study of expert levels of performance: General implications for optimal learning and creativity. *High Ability Studies* 9:75–100.

Ericsson, K. Anders. 2004. Deliberate practice and the acquisition and maintenance of expert performance in medicine and related domains. *Academic Medicine* 79:S70–S81.

Ericsson, K. Anders, Ralf T. Krampe, and Clemens Tesch-Römer. 1993. The role of deliberate practice in the acquisition of expert performance. *Psychological Review* 100:363–406.

Ericsson, K. Anders, and Paul Ward. 2007. Capturing the naturally occurring superior performance of experts in the laboratory: Toward a science of expert and exceptional performance. *Current Directions in Psychological Science* 16:346–50.

Goffman, Erving. 1956. The nature of deference and demeanor. *American Anthropologist* 58:473–502.

Goffman, Erving. 1961. *Encounters: Two studies in the sociology of interaction*. Oxford: Bobbs-Merrill.

Hansson, Lars, and Urban Markström. 2014. The effectiveness of an anti-stigma intervention in a basic police officer training programme: A controlled study. *BMC Psychiatry* 14:55–63.

Huey, Laura. 2018. What do we know about in-service police training? Results of a failed systematic review. *Sociology Publications* 40. Available from https://ir.lib.uwo.ca/cgi/viewcontent.cgi?article=1043&context=sociologypub.

Klein, Gary, Helen Altman Klein, Brian Lande, Joseph Borders, and James C. Whitaker. 2014. The good stranger frame for police and military activities. In *Proceedings of the Human Factors and Ergonomics Society Annual Meeting* 58 (1): 275–79.

Krameddine, Yasmeen, David DeMarco, Robert Hassel, and Peter H. Silverstone. 2013. A novel training program for police officers that improves interactions with mentally ill individuals and is cost-effective. *Frontiers in Psychiatry* 4:1–10.

Lewis, Ioni, Barry Watson, and Richard Tay. 2007. Examining the effectiveness of physical threats in road safety advertising: The role of the third-person effect, gender, and age. *Transportation Research Part F: Traffic Psychology and Behaviour* 10:48–60.

MacDonald, Heather. 2017. *The war on cops: How the new attack on law and order makes everyone less safe*. New York, NY: Encounter Books.

Muir, William K. 1977. *Police: Streetcorner politicians*. Chicago, IL: University of Chicago Press.

Nix, Justin, and Scott E. Wolfe. 2017. The impact of negative publicity on police self-legitimacy. *Justice Quarterly* 34:84–108.

Nix, Justin, and Scott E. Wolfe. 2018. Management-level officers' experiences with the Ferguson effect. *Policing: An International Journal* 41:262–75.

Nix, Justin, Scott E. Wolfe, and Bradley A. Campbell. 2018. Command-level police officers' perceptions of the "war on cops" and de-policing. *Justice Quarterly* 35:33–54.

President's Task Force on 21st Century Policing. 2015. *Final report of the President's Task Force on 21st Century Policing*. Washington, DC: Office of Community Oriented Policing Services.

Pyrooz, David C., Scott H. Decker, Scott E. Wolfe, and John A. Shjarback. 2016. Was there a Ferguson effect on crime rates in large US cities? *Journal of Criminal Justice* 46:1–8.

Reaves, Brian A. 2016. State and local law enforcement training academies, 2013. Washington, DC: Bureau of Justice Statistics. Available from https://www.bjs.gov/content/pub/pdf/slleta13.pdf.

Rosenbaum, Dennis P., and Daniel S. Lawrence. 2017. Teaching procedural justice and communication skills during police-community encounters: Results of a randomized control trial with police recruits. *Journal of Experimental Criminology* 13:293–319.

Shjarback, John A., David C. Pyrooz, Scott E. Wolfe, and Scott H. Decker. 2017. De-policing and crime in the wake of Ferguson: Racialized changes in the quantity and quality of policing among Missouri police departments. *Journal of Criminal Justice* 50:42–52.

Simon, Herbert A., and William G. Chase. 1973. Skill in chess. *American Scientist* 61:394–403.

Sykes, Richard E., and John P. Clark. 1975. A theory of deference exchange in police-civilian encounters. *American Journal of Sociology* 81:584–600.

Todak, Natalie, and Lois James. 2018. A systematic social observation study of police de-escalation tactics. *Police Quarterly* 21:509–43.

Van Maanen, John. 1978. The asshole. In *Policing: A view from the street*, eds. Peter K. Manning and John Van Maanen, 221–38. Santa Monica, CA: Goodyear Publishing Company.

Ward, Paul, Joel Suss, and Itay Basevitch. 2009. Expertise and expert performance-based training (ExPerT) in complex domains. *Technology, Instruction, Cognition and Learning* 7:121–45.

Wolfe, Scott, Kyle McLean, Jeff Rojek, and Geoff Alpert. 2019. Evaluating a long-term social interaction police training program: A randomized-controlled trial in the real world. Presentation at the ANNALS of the AAPSS Fatal Police Shootings Conference, February 7, The Annenberg Public Policy Center, University of Pennsylvania, Philadelphia, PA.

Wolfe, Scott E., and Justin Nix. 2016. The alleged "Ferguson effect" and police willingness to engage in community partnership. *Law and Human Behavior* 40:1–10.

Moving beyond "Best Practice": Experiences in Police Reform and a Call for Evidence to Reduce Officer-Involved Shootings

By
ROBIN S. ENGEL,
HANNAH D. McMANUS,
and
GABRIELLE T. ISAZA

In post-Ferguson America, police departments are being challenged to implement evidence-based changes in policies and training to reduce fatal police-citizen encounters. Of the litany of recommendations believed to reduce police shootings, five have garnered widespread support: body-worn cameras, de-escalation training, implicit bias training, early intervention systems, and civilian oversight. These highly endorsed interventions, however, are not supported by a strong body of empirical evidence that demonstrates their effectiveness. Guided by the available research on evidence-based policing and informed by the firsthand experience of one of the authors in implementing departmental reforms that followed the fatal shooting of a civilian by an officer, this article highlights promising reform strategies and opportunities to build the evidence base for effective use-of-force reforms. We call upon police executives to engage in evidence-based policing by scientifically testing interventions, and we call on academics to engage in rapid research responses for critical issues in policing.

Keywords: evidence-based policing; police shootings; use of force; police reform

On July 19, 2015, Samuel DuBose was stopped by University of Cincinnati Police Division (UCPD) Officer Raymond Tensing approximately 0.5 mile south of the University of Cincinnati (UC) campus for a minor equipment violation (missing front license plate, a traffic violation in the State of Ohio). After a brief exchange, DuBose, an unarmed 43-year-old black male, was shot and killed by Officer

Robin S. Engel is director of the IACP/UC Center for Police Research and Policy and a professor of criminal justice at the University of Cincinnati. She recently served as vice president for safety and reform at the University of Cincinnati. Her work includes establishing academic-practitioner partnerships and promoting evidence-based practices in policing, with empirical assessments of police behavior and evaluations of crime reduction strategies.

Correspondence: robin.engel@uc.edu

DOI: 10.1177/0002716219889328

Tensing, a 25-year-old white male. The incident was captured on Tensing's department-issued body-worn camera (BWC), but still the circumstances surrounding the shooting were widely debated within the Cincinnati community, sparking protests, independent investigations, civil litigation, and criminal trials. An independent consulting firm commissioned by the university to perform an external review of the incident found that the shooting was "entirely preventable" and concluded it was the officer's "critical errors in judgment that created an elevated risk of a serious or fatal bodily injury" (Kroll 2015, 46). Ten days after the incident, Tensing was indicted by the Hamilton County Prosecutor's Office for murder. His first criminal trial concluded in November 2015, resulting in a hung jury, while a second trial in June 2017 garnered the same outcome. Concerns regarding racial bias overshadowed the criminal proceedings and flowed into the public discourse. In July 2017, the county prosecutor announced a third trial would not be conducted, and the charges against the defendant were dropped.[1]

This tragic incident and its aftermath sent shockwaves through the Cincinnati community, a city with a troubled history of racial tension and damaged police-community relations (Eck and Rothman 2006); however, it is far from a unique story in American policing. The fatal DuBose-Tensing encounter in summer 2015 occurred amid a spate of other police-involved deaths of unarmed black males.[2] Described by Sherman (2018) as the "Second Great Awakening," the reaction to these high-profile incidents involving the killing of unarmed citizens by American police has included public protests, civil unrest, widespread media attention, and heightened public scrutiny of police.

Notably, the growth in public angst regarding police bias and use of force has been accompanied by rising concerns regarding police officers' safety. Violent incidents, including the murder of five police officers and wounding of nine others in Dallas, Texas, in July 2016, followed by an ambush attack killing three officers and wounding three more in Baton Rouge, Louisiana, led to national reflection and discussions regarding officer safety. Although overall assaults, injuries, and death of officers in the line of duty have continually decreased over the

Hannah D. McManus is a research associate for the IACP/UC Center for Police Research and Policy and a doctoral candidate in the School of Criminal Justice at the University of Cincinnati. Her recent work includes the evaluation of police training, the study of public perceptions of police, and the promotion of evidence-based practice to enhance police officer safety and wellness.

Gabrielle T. Isaza is a research associate for the IACP/UC Center for Police Research and Policy and a doctoral candidate in the School of Criminal Justice at the University of Cincinnati. Her areas of research include police effectiveness; survey design; and evaluations of police training programs, including de-escalation and implicit bias.

NOTE: Ideas and concepts presented within this article were generated in coordination with other research conducted for the IACP / UC Center for Police Research and Policy, funded by Arnold Ventures. The information and commentary within this article, however, are from the authors and do not necessarily represent the official positions or policies of Arnold Ventures or the International Association of Chiefs of Police.

last two decades, the number of officers injured or killed through ambush-style attacks has increased in the last 10 years, reaching a peak in 2016 (Federal Bureau of Investigation [FBI] 2019).

Acknowledging the dangers to both citizens and officers embedded in this police-community relations crisis, efforts have intensified to identify "solutions" to reduce the frequency and severity of violent encounters between police and the public. Expert panels, such as the President's Task Force on 21st Century Policing, have convened to explore best practices in policing that "can promote effective crime reduction while building public trust" (2015, 1). Simultaneously, American citizens have organized to demand police reform, including changes regarding officer use of force. These demands have emerged during a time when the application of evidence-based policy and practice by law enforcement is increasingly expected yet infrequently followed. Indeed, most "best practices" for police reform are not based on a strong body of empirical evidence (see Lum et al. 2016).

In an effort to better inform the discussion regarding "what works" to reduce the frequency and severity of potentially violent police-citizen encounters, this article considers the evidence regarding the effectiveness of routinely recommended police reforms, including (1) deployment of BWCs; (2) changes to use-of-force policies and training that emphasize de-escalation; (3) implicit bias training for officers; (4) early intervention (warning) systems; and (5) citizen oversight (review) boards. Although each of these interventions has been recommended by the President's Task Force or other policing experts, careful consideration of the evidence available demonstrates a patchwork of studies that collectively provide little confidence that these reforms will directly impact police shootings. Guided by the available research on police use of force and evidence-based practices and informed by the experience of one of the authors (Engel) in implementing reforms within the UCPD, this article highlights promising strategies, along with the remaining gaps in knowledge and opportunities to build the evidence base for effective use-of-force reform.

We recognize that in the absence of evidence, police executives must still move forward with recommended best practices. However, we further contend that it is an ethical duty of police officials to combine the implementation of innovative approaches with continuous review and testing to identify ineffective practices and unintended consequences. We articulate the urgent need for researchers to work collaboratively with police executives to generate and disseminate knowledge regarding these and other police reform efforts, generating a *rapid research response* (also see Engel, McManus, and Herold, forthcoming). Lacking this research, it cannot be stated with confidence that the proposed use-of-force reforms can prevent future fatal police-citizen encounters. As such, it is of the utmost importance that our academic and practitioner colleagues, along with local, state, and federal agencies and organizations and the philanthropic community, prioritize research designed to advance rigorous scientific testing of police reform efforts at the local level, including the reduction of fatal police shootings. The safety of our nation's police officers, and members of the public they serve, hinges on this collective work.

Police Use of Force

More than four decades ago, policing scholar Egon Bittner (1974) argued that police are defined by their ability—and duty—to use force. It is the public's expectation that police use force when necessary that separates policing from all other occupations. It is this ability to use force that shapes all other aspects of police practice. Given this distinction, it is surprising that we still know relatively little about how, when, and under what circumstances police officers use force (Engel and Serpas 2017; Garner et al. 2018). As of this writing, the best available national databases capturing fatal police-citizen encounters are not compiled by government officials, but by reporters from *The Guardian* and the *Washington Post* (Sherman 2018; Zimring 2017). Most notable of the findings from these data sources are as follows:

1) Over half of all fatal police shootings occur in small jurisdictions with fewer than 50,000 residents, and only one-third occur in cities with populations greater than 250,000 residents (Sherman 2018).
2) There was no firearm present in 44 percent of fatal police shootings (Zimring 2017).
3) When compared to the national population, African Americans are 2.3 times more likely to be killed by police than whites (Zimring 2017).

Combined, these quantitative findings support the narratives generated through the sharing and resharing of individual images and videos of police-citizen encounters that have resulted in tragedy. What these figures do not provide, however, is an understanding of the details regarding the individual, situational, environmental, and organizational factors likely to impact officer's decision-making during encounters with citizens. Despite this lack of information, Zimring (2017) boldly predicts that fatal interactions with police could be cut in half without compromising officer safety. He bases this prediction, in part, on the large estimated percentage of fatal encounters with police where the suspect does not have a firearm. Referring to these fatal encounters as "unnecessary killings," Zimring and others argue that systematic changes in policing, implemented at the national level, could reduce citizen injury and death (Sherman 2018).

Within a nation that claims approximately eighteen thousand distinct police organizations with little consistency in training, policies, and practices (Reaves 2011), the prospect of implementing significant police reform systematically is daunting. For police shootings specifically, it is even more challenging to impact individual officer decision-making during potentially violent encounters. Sherman (2018) argues for employing a system-accident framework to drive appropriate policies and research necessary to reduce fatal encounters with police. Similarly, David Klinger (2005, this volume) has renewed his proposal to use Perrow's (1984) normal accidents framework to guide understanding of violent police-citizen encounters. Further, Zimring (this volume) argues that creating a statistical and research branch within the federal government is likely the only way to implement needed police reforms designed to reduce police killings.

In contrast to the apparent logic of these recommendations, our premise is that the decentralized nature of policing in the United States will make many efforts to reduce officer shootings at the federal and state levels ineffective. Even when mandated or otherwise influenced by oversight at the state or federal levels, meaningful changes in police practice must be implemented and embraced at the local level. Citizens intuitively recognize this. Although there is often pressure placed on state and federal officials to "do something" about police use of force, the majority of citizen demands involve changes directly targeted at individual police agencies. Therefore, much of the movement in police reform is occurring at the local level, agency by agency. In this context, this article considers the role of evidence-based policing (EBP) in reducing officer shootings at the local level by presenting the most common calls for change, reviewing the evidence-base supporting these recommendations, and considering the experience of the University of Cincinnati Police Division in the implementation of evidence-based police use-of-force reform.

The Role of Evidence-Based Policing in Reform

At its core, EBP is a movement encouraging the use of research to guide practice and evaluate practitioners (Sherman 1998). Seeking to progress beyond the use of anecdotal or experiential evidence alone, EBP suggests that police decision-making on "what works" to address specific problems should be guided by objective facts produced from scientific research. Further, EBP encourages police to embed science within their respective agencies through the evaluation of current policies and practices (Sherman 1998, 2013). Police agencies that use and generate research to guide strategic and tactical decision-making should experience greater success in identifying cost-effective approaches (Weisburd and Neyroud 2011).

The movement toward EBP has been a gradual one, gaining significant traction in the last 20 years due to the increased availability and application of research and innovative technologies in policing (Lum, Koper, and Telep 2011; Sherman 2013). Many scholars, practitioners, and policy-makers now adopt the view that EBP is critical for successful reform across a number of outcomes, including reducing police use of lethal force (Telep 2016). However, our review of existing evidence on five commonly recommended police reforms provides a limited picture on "what works" in addressing police use of force, particularly lethal force, at the local level (also see Lum et al. 2016).

Regardless of the availability of scientific evidence to support critical decisions, police administrators are responsible for crisis management. Furthermore, police administrators are often pressed through public and political demands to make significant changes to policies and training immediately following critical incidents, leading to the perception that police accountability is best measured by the speed of response. Police executives are acutely aware that their jobs often hinge on how they respond to community pressure within the first few days following a critical incident. Within this time constraint, the careful planning of an evidence-based response is often unrealistic. Therefore, although the clamor for police reform has been pervasive, it also appears that these reform efforts are largely divorced from the expectation that these interventions be evidence-based.

Reform within the University of Cincinnati Police Division

The UCPD is a fully empowered law enforcement agency with a complement of seventy-two sworn officers that provides all public safety services for the UC community (seventy thousand students and employees), including primary jurisdiction on all university-owned and operated buildings. Based on a Memorandum of Understanding with the City of Cincinnati, UCPD also patrols and conducts police activities in city neighborhoods in the one-mile corridor surrounding the UC uptown campus. The UCPD has approximately five hundred or fewer Part I crime incidents reported on campus each year, which are largely driven by reports of theft/larceny (Isaza et al. 2017).[3] In general, the UCPD does not record many instances of police use of force in any given year. Between January 2017 and December 2018, for example, the agency reported only four use-of-force incidents, one of which included a display of force only (Exiger 2019). Overall, the UCPD is representative of many midsize police agencies that have few critical incidents. However, the UCPD's experience with the fatal DuBose-Tensing encounter demonstrates the magnitude of a single police-citizen interaction gone terribly wrong.

In the aftermath of the shooting, immediate changes in police executive leadership were made at the university. The lead author of this article (Engel) was appointed to the newly created position of vice president for safety and reform to develop and implement an immediate police reform effort. Two weeks later, she added executive leadership positions to her team, including a director of public safety (with operational oversight of the UCPD) and director of police community relations. She led her team in the design and implementation of over three years of systematic reforms, including top-to-bottom organizational changes in policies, procedures, training, and accountability systems, along with the completion of voluntary external monitorship.[4] Although the reform efforts implemented by this team were intended to be evidence-based, the immediacy of implementation, as well as the general lack of evidence available to inform organizational change (as articulated below), characterizes these efforts more appropriately as "best practices." The selection and implementation of reform strategies and the evidence-base surrounding the effectiveness of these efforts is discussed in greater detail below.

The Evidence Base for Agency-Level Solutions to Reduce Police Shootings

Following the shooting of Samuel DuBose, the political and public demands for change in Cincinnati were highly predictable, echoing the approaches being requested and implemented across the country to reduce fatal police encounters and rebuild community trust. First, although UCPD officers were already equipped with BWCs, calls for more transparency within the police department reverberated. Second, UCPD's use-of-force policy and training were heavily scrutinized and, ultimately, dramatically changed to incorporate de-escalation tactics. Third, direct calls for implicit bias training for officers were made and answered with the rapid delivery of the leading curriculum in the field. Additionally, an early intervention system—designed to identify potentially problematic officers prior to a critical incident—was hastily implemented. Finally, the long and challenging task of rebuilding public trust through increased community engagement and citizen oversight began. Each of these approaches—(1) BWCs, (2) de-escalation training, (3) implicit bias training, (4) early intervention systems, and (5) civilian oversight—are the most typical and frequently called for reform efforts after a controversial shooting. As such, many might be surprised to learn that the body of evidence supporting the effectiveness of most of these initiatives is generally thin and, in some cases, nearly nonexistent. The remaining sections of this article outline the research evidence for each of the five initiatives outlined above, highlighting the UCPD's experience in the implementation of use-of-force reforms. Implications for evidence-based use-of-force reform are discussed, and critical next steps for effective change are highlighted.

•

Body-worn cameras

Calls for police to adopt BWCs have proliferated in recent years across the United States. A recent study using a nationally representative sample of police agencies estimated that one-third of American law enforcement agencies currently deploy BWCs to some or all of their officers, and an additional 50 percent of agencies have immediate plans to deploy them (Police Executive Research Forum 2018). These devices are theorized to impact officer behavior through their deterrent effect on unconstitutional interactions with the public, particularly for excessive use of force (Ariel, Farrar, and Sutherland 2015). There is an abundance of research suggesting that when people know they are being observed, they alter their behavior to better adhere to social norms (Diener and Wallbom 1976). Theory follows, then, that when officers know they are being recorded, they will be more likely to behave in a constitutional manner. Despite this assumption, a majority (over 90 percent) of surveyed police agencies indicate that the primary reason for their adoption of BWCs is to improve community trust by promoting accountability, transparency, and legitimacy (Police Executive Research Forum 2018), not necessarily to change police behavior.

Research on BWCs has increased exponentially in recent years, spurred on, in part, by significant interest and funding from the philanthropic community. This research has examined multiple outcomes with varying units of analysis, including the attitudes and behavior of officers and citizens, police investigations, and organizational effects (Lum et al. 2019). A recent comprehensive review of research on BWCs, conducted by Lum and colleagues (2019), identified seventy studies, sixteen of which specifically measured officers' reported use of force as a dependent variable. These studies report inconsistent findings concerning the impact of BWCs on officers' use of force. Specifically, multiple experimental studies indicate that officers wearing cameras used significantly less force compared to those who did not wear cameras. Yet several other studies using experimental and quasi-experimental designs found no statistical differences among officers wearing cameras and those who do not.

One particular study provides important insight regarding these mixed findings. Ariel and colleagues (2016) conducted a subgroup analysis of ten randomized control trials examining BWCs to better understand why BWCs did not statistically impact officers' use of force in a single direction. They conclude that officers are more likely to use higher levels of force when turning BWCs on during a citizen encounter is left to their discretion. While this finding offers an interesting nuance related to the impact of BWCs on use of force, few research studies have tracked the activation of cameras. Therefore, it is unclear whether these findings would be replicated elsewhere (Lum et al. 2019).

Collectively, this research suggests that simply outfitting officers with BWCs is insufficient to significantly reduce police use of force. Rather, it is likely that deployment of the cameras needs to be coupled with strong policies and supervisory oversight to achieve maximum benefits in reducing use of force. It also remains unclear what impact, if any, BWCs could expect to have on reducing fatal police encounters, which are significantly less likely than other uses of force. Indeed, in the case of the UCPD, the introduction of BWCs did not decrease officers' use of force or the likelihood of a fatal police-citizen encounter. It did, however, capture video of the fatal police-citizen encounter (Noble 2015). Rather than bring clarity to that incident, the video footage demonstrated that citizens (and competing experts) could watch the same images yet have significantly different interpretations regarding the legitimacy and legality of the use of force. Indeed, Tensing's two separate murder trials resulted in hung jury decisions where the primary piece of evidence was the body camera footage (Grasha 2017).

Use-of-force/de-escalation policies and training

A primary recommendation for police reform has been the incorporation of use-of-force/de-escalation policies and training within law enforcement. Many law enforcement leaders supporting the adoption of de-escalation training espouse that these techniques can help to resolve police-citizen encounters with less frequent and severe uses of force and, thereby, also increase officer safety. Notably, de-escalation tactics and training received an endorsement from the President's Task Force; and more recently, the National Consensus Policy on Use of Force (International Association of Chiefs of Police 2017, 3) encouraged officers to use de-escalation techniques "whenever possible or appropriate before resorting to force."

De-escalation policies and training are not without critics, however, with a growing number voicing serious concerns about perceived risks to officer safety (Blake 2017; Landers 2017; Williams 2015). Several tactics common in de-escalation training run counter to more traditional operational responses in policing. Critics argue that changes in the traditional approach could increase the risk of officer injury. In the absence of evidence to the contrary, Landers (2017) argues that "by sending officers to de-escalation training courses, chiefs and sheriffs have risked these men and women becoming hesitant about using force"; and furthermore that "while [de-escalation] concepts are practical and effective in some situations, they are useless and even dangerous in others." Concerns regarding officer safety run deep within police organizational cultures, and some trainers have resorted to avoiding the use of the word *de-escalation* altogether in training sessions, rather describing these techniques as opportunities to defuse situations.

In many ways, these concerns are amplified by the ambiguity of de-escalation policies and training. Specifically, there is no uniformly accepted definition of de-escalation within the policing field. Most recommendations, including from the President's Task Force, neglect to provide a specific definition, or even a general description, of de-escalation. As such, de-escalation has become a catchall of sorts, symbolizing a different but perhaps more progressive policing approach for handling potential use-of-force encounters. A systematic review of literature across disciplines finds *de-escalation* to typically refer to a process or tactics used to prevent, reduce, or manage behaviors associated with conflict—including verbal or physical agitation, aggression, violence, or similar behaviors—during an interaction between two or more individuals (for review, see Engel, McManus, and Herold, forthcoming).

Similar to most other police training curricula, de-escalation training has not been subjected to rigorous scientific testing (National Research Council 2004; Lum at el. 2016; Skogan, Van Craen, and Hennessy 2015). As a result, little is known about the development, delivery, and impact of police de-escalation training. To assess this gap in knowledge, Engel, McManus, and Herold (forthcoming) conducted a multidisciplinary systematic review, identifying only a limited number of de-escalation training evaluations appearing across professions ($n = 64$), and no evaluations within the realm of policing or criminal justice were identified. The findings from studies outside of policing provide some insight on the attitudinal (i.e., self-reported) and behavioral effects that de-escalation training could have on officer use-of-force outcomes. Specifically, studies examining self-reported outcomes suggest that de-escalation training in other professions has led to favorable effects on the attitudes, perceptions, and self-reported experiences and behaviors of trained individuals. The impact of de-escalation training on behavioral outcomes, however, has not been established. Although the majority of the studies report favorable effects of de-escalation training (e.g., reduction in number and severity of violent incidents, increased application in use of de-escalation techniques), there were also findings that suggest de-escalation training has no effect and, in some cases, unfavorable effects on use-of-force outcomes.

Confidence in the validity and generalizability of these findings is threatened by several factors, including the (1) substantial variation across de-escalation training programs under examination; (2) reliance on pretest/posttest research designs with no comparison groups; (3) heavy focus on self-reported, rather than behavioral, outcomes; and (4) emphasis on short-term outcomes

(Engel et al., forthcoming). As a result, recommendations for de-escalation, as well as larger conversations on the safety and well-being of police officers and the individuals they encounter, rely heavily on anecdotal evidence and untested propositions about best practice. Nevertheless, a majority of police agencies in large cities across the country are currently training officers in de-escalation techniques, as this is one of the most common demands from community activists and political officials (CBS News 2019). Although more rigorous research studies of de-escalation training curriculums for police are under way (e.g., Engel et al. 2019; McLean et al., this volume; White and Pooley 2018), the current state of evidence leaves many questions related to the effectiveness of de-escalation policies and training unanswered.

Based on the limited evidence from other disciplines, anecdotal accounts, reviews of practice in other agencies, experts' advice, and our best judgments, the UCPD executive team engaged in a comprehensive and innovative overhaul of all use-of-force policies, procedures, and training. The underlying principle of the *sanctity of life*—respecting the value of every human life—along with the implementation of a robust training and accountability structure necessary to support the use of de-escalation tactics were the primary focus of the UCPD team (Police Executive Research Forum 2016). While the scientific evidence regarding the likelihood of reducing use of force based on these changes was quite limited, a robust accountability structure was embedded, and several evaluation opportunities to build our own body of evidence were undertaken. For example, when officers were trained in use of force and de-escalation, a series of surveys (pre, post, and follow-up) were created and administered to officers to identify changes in officers' attitudes, knowledge, and self-reported behaviors. These survey instruments are now being used by other agencies looking to examine the impact of similar de-escalation trainings (see Engel et al. 2019). Coupled with strong research designs (e.g., randomized controlled trials) for training delivery, this evidence base will quickly grow, and soon critical information regarding the impact of de-escalation training on officer use of force will be available.

Implicit bias training

Racial and ethnic disparities in policing practices—including vehicle and pedestrian stops, citations, searches, arrests, and use of force—have been noted for decades. The reasons for these disparities, however, are multifaceted, and researchers have traditionally struggled to disentangle critical factors to determine if disparities are the result of discrimination (Engel and Swartz 2014). Nevertheless, based on the supposition that differences in policing outcomes are the result of individual police bias or discrimination, the operational response to reduce racial disparities has consistently involved the provision of additional training for officers. For example, racial sensitivity training was adopted in the 1980s and 1990s, followed by antiracial profiling training in the 2000s, and bias-free policing in the early 2010s. The most recent training proposed to address the

problems associated with racial/ethnic disparities in policing—including disparities in use of force—is implicit bias training (Fridell 2017; Nix et al. 2017).

Implicit bias refers to an unconscious prejudice that people may develop due to
differential life experiences (Devine 1989). In contrast to explicit bias, which is akin
to traditional "racism," all humans are subject to some form of unconscious bias
that may impact perceptions and behaviors, resulting in discriminatory decision-
making (Dovidio, Kawakami, and Gaertner 2002). Due to the high rates of minority citizen contact with police, the impact of implicit bias in policing could be
especially profound. Indeed, the existence of implicit bias has been demonstrated
in research using police as subjects (Payne 2001).

The President's Task Force (2015) specifically acknowledged implicit bias and
its role in producing disparities in outcomes, calling for police training to reduce
the impact of such biases. Based upon a large body of psychological research
demonstrating that biases can be managed (see Monteith, Arthur, and Flynn
2010; Pettigrew and Tropp 2005), interventions typically begin by educating individuals regarding the existence of implicit bias and, subsequently, teaching various skills to reduce and manage these biases (Fridell 2017). A meta-analysis of
nearly five hundred studies identified that implicit bias is malleable (albeit with
relatively weak effects). However, changes in implicit bias measures may not
necessarily translate into changes to explicit bias or in behavior (Forscher et al.
2018; also see Atewologun, Cornish, and Tresh 2018). Specifically, Forscher and
colleagues (2018) conclude that although interventions to change implicit bias
may not consistently change behavior, some procedures for change are more
effective than others. Others conclude that an important key is to not only raise
awareness of implicit biases but to complement trainings with strategies to
reduce and manage biases (Atewologun, Cornish, and Tresh 2018).

Of concern, some research has suggested that there may be unintended consequences of implicit bias training, including increases in the expression of bias.
For example, research has identified a "rebound effect," which occurs when
individuals attempt to suppress stereotypical thoughts. The act of suppression
may cause the stereotypical thoughts to later reappear with even greater insist-
ence had they not been suppressed (Macrae et al. 1994). Other research has
suggested that trainings to increase awareness of stereotypes may also normalize
stereotyping, thereby undermining the desired effect of the training (Duguid and
Thomas-Hunt 2015). It is unknown how these potential negative consequences
may impact implicit bias training for law enforcement.

Collectively, this research presents a mixed picture regarding the impact of
implicit bias training on changes in behavior. And despite the accumulating evidence from other disciplines, there remains a critical need to examine implicit
bias training for police, as reviews have found no experimental evaluations of
implicit bias training for police officers that have been completed (Mitchell and
James 2018). In short, agencies across the country are training officers in implicit
bias without evidence that this training is effective. For most police executives,
however, the cost-benefit analysis for providing implicit bias training may hinge
on whether they perceive that their agency will receive a boost in community
trust and improve police-community relations, rather than any expected changes

in police officers' attitudes and behaviors due to the training. For example, despite being unaware of its likely impact or effectiveness, within three months of the UCPD officer-involved shooting, all UCPD officers were trained in implicit bias, and a special session was conducted with community members in an attempt to both educate and rebuild trust (Jones 2015). The impact of this training was never formally assessed within the UCPD. However, recognizing the lack of evidence regarding the impact of implicit bias training, the lead author of this article secured funding and is overseeing a larger research team conducting a randomized control trial evaluation of implicit bias training with the New York City Police Department. Findings are scheduled for release in spring 2020. Given the popularity of implicit bias training within police agencies across the United States, replication studies could and should be generated.

Early intervention systems

Another frequently mentioned opportunity for changing officer behavior is the implementation of early intervention systems (EIS), also referred to as early warning systems. EIS are data-driven administrative systems used to detect officer misconduct. The goal of EIS is to identify officers whose performance includes a pattern of undesirable behavior and to implement corrective interventions quickly. By monitoring indicators of problematic behavior (e.g., citizen complaints, use of force, high-speed pursuits), police administrators may be able to identify officers at risk of future misconduct and intervene before that misconduct occurs (Worden et al. 2013). EIS generally consist of four components: performance indicators, procedures for officer identification, intervention, and postintervention monitoring. Typically framed as a nonpunitive approach, these systems often operate external to a law enforcement agency's disciplinary processes, providing the opportunity for officer retraining, counseling, or other interventions (Worden et al. 2018).

The use of EIS spread rapidly across the landscape of American law enforcement in the 1990s and 2000s. The proliferation of these systems was supported, in particular, by the inclusion of recommendations for EIS in consent decrees developed by the U.S. Department of Justice as part of their investigations of the "pattern or practice" of citizen rights violations within police agencies (Walker 2003). By 2007, 40 percent of agencies serving populations of fifty thousand or more reported having implemented an EIS within their agency (Worden et al. 2018). Among many, EIS are now considered a "best practice" for police accountability, particularly regarding officer use of force (Harmon 2009; Walker 2003). The use of EIS is not without criticism, however. The ability of systems to accurately identify problematic officers is a primary concern. Though law enforcement agencies have begun to incorporate secondary screening measures (e.g., supervisory review) to bolster the review and selection of "problem" officers, the process for identification remains an imperfect science (Worden et al. 2018).

Furthermore, despite the "best practice" label, EIS have not been a common subject of evaluation. A recent review of EIS evaluations (Worden et al. 2018) identified only six evaluations appearing in four research studies examining the impact of agencies' EIS interventions on citizen complaints against officers, officer use of force, and officer arrest activity. Due to agency specificity in the structure of EIS components, including the types of indicators used and the nature of interventions, it has been suggested that each evaluation is best defined as a case study (Worden et al. 2013). As a whole, these six case studies report positive findings, suggesting that EIS interventions may reduce the likelihood of future complaints against officers and subsequent uses of force. However, our confidence in the accuracy and generalization of these findings is limited by the considerable threats to internal validity within each study (Worden et al. 2018). Further doubt is cast on the effectiveness of EIS interventions because the most rigorous evaluation provides the least favorable results (see Worden et al. 2013). Overall, the evidence supporting the use of EIS as a mechanism to decrease officer use of force, and in particular officer-involved shootings, is not strong. The limited number of evaluations, combined with weak research designs, and the limited scope of the outcomes examined leaves many questions surrounding the positive effects, as well as the potential unintended consequences, of EIS interventions.

The UCPD was already in the process of implementing an EIS when the officer-involved shooting occurred. The purchased software was quickly integrated into the records management system, and the use of the EIS was publicly announced. However, inherent issues within the tracking system (e.g., setting appropriate thresholds to identify outliers within a small agency) presented continuous challenges for effectiveness. Likewise, integrating the EIS into a more comprehensive accountability and oversight strategy within the UCPD became an overarching goal. The impact of this specific reform, however, has not been adequately studied, as the small number of UCPD officers assigned to similar shifts and tasks creates a challenge for identifying outliers and determining impact based on statistical significance. What is measured and tracked, however, is the use of the system by supervisors to identify subordinate behavior that is potentially problematic.

Civilian oversight

A final popular call to reduce officer killings includes multiple forms of community engagement, including citizen oversight of the police. For example, the President's Task Force (2015) highlights the use of civilian oversight mechanisms and specifically recommends that incidents involving suspect death or officer-involved shootings be subject to external oversight, including external review boards and serious incident review boards. The President's Task Force suggests that the purpose of these boards is to "identify any administrative, supervisory, training, tactical, or policy issues that need to be addressed" (2015, 88). From a broader perspective, these oversight mechanisms are viewed to provide an important alternative to "police investigating complaints against police" and are typically recommended to increase police transparency and accountability, as well as help to build trust and perceptions of police legitimacy within the community (Briggs 2017, 146).

Research on the prevalence of civilian oversight, particularly in the form of civilian review boards, suggests oversight is fairly common among large police agencies, with approximately 80 percent of the fifty largest U.S. police agencies incorporating such oversight mechanisms (Lum et al. 2016), but much less common in mid- to small-size agencies, with estimates of fewer than 150 departments nationwide that incorporate these oversight mechanisms (De Angelis, Rosenthal, and Buchner 2016). Furthermore, significant variation in the composition and role in oversight processes are observed among the civilian review boards that exist. In many cases, this variation is a function of factors both internal and external to specific law enforcement agencies (De Angelis, Rosenthal, and Buchner 2016; Ferdik, Rojek, and Alpert 2013).

Despite calls for research (National Research Council 2004; Walker 2001), the evidence for civilian oversight of police agencies remains limited (Lum et al. 2016). The extreme variability across civilian review boards has proven a difficult hurdle in the examination of the prevalence, effects, and best models for oversight. Additionally, the question remains of how best to measure the effectiveness of civilian oversight within law enforcement agencies (De Angelis, Rosenthal, and Buchner 2016), although available research studies typically opt to examine rates of sustained complaints. Collectively, this research provides mixed findings regarding the sustained rates of citizen complaints when civilian oversight is present, with some noting fewer sustained complaints in agencies with some form of civilian oversight (Hickman 2006), while others observe higher rates of sustained complaints when oversight is present (Terrill and Ingram 2015).

In the immediate weeks following the officer-involved shooting in Cincinnati, the UC executive team established the Community Advisory Council (CAC) to provide community input and guidance regarding reform efforts of the UCPD. Modeled after the Cincinnati City Manager's Advisory Group (MAG), which has been identified as a model for a successful citizen oversight organization (Eck and Rothman 2006; Wasserman 2014), the CAC became a primary mechanism for community input and collaboration. Representatives include UC students, faculty, staff, and alumni; neighborhood community groups; city civic, faith, and business leaders; and law enforcement officials. The varied membership of the CAC was designed to reflect the diverse makeup of the larger Cincinnati community and to promote diversity of thought, ideas, and information exchange. Although the effectiveness of this council was not quantitatively evaluated, qualitative assessments suggest a profound enhancement of police community relations. The CAC (renamed the Community Compliance Council) is now beginning a new phase of work, including review of the processes followed for all complaints against UCPD officers and use-of-force incidents.

Discussion

In response to the recent national crisis in police-community relations sparked by controversial police-involved shootings, police executives in the United States are routinely encouraged (and in some cases, mandated) to implement reforms, including deploying BWCs, de-escalation training, implicit bias training, early intervention systems, and civilian oversight. Similar to other recent reviews (e.g., Lum et al. 2016), our examination of the available policing research exposes vast gaps in the collective knowledge regarding the effectiveness of reforms most commonly recommended to reduce officer use of force. As police executives seek to answer calls for reform while meeting expectations of evidence-based practice, there is limited scientific research to support them. Yet the pressure is intensifying for police executives to rapidly implement changes designed to reduce use-of-force incidents, as the public is eager to move "beyond what is legal and start focusing on what is preventable" (Kindy 2015). These recommended reforms, however, likely do more in the way of "damage control" after a critical incident than actually preventing future fatal police-citizen encounters.

In the immediate aftermath of the fatal shooting of Samuel DuBose, the UC executive team focused on crisis management, while still seeking to implement evidence-based strategies for long-term reform and sustainability. As protesters gathered and politicians demanded action, we searched for evidence-based solutions. What we found, instead, was a collection of best practices—that is, interventions that were supported by anecdotal accounts and experts' endorsements, but not scientifically validated. While the effectiveness and unintended consequences of many of our reform efforts were largely unknown, the immediate nature of police work did not allow time for years of study and debate. Ultimately, we selected and implemented interventions based on the limited science available, along with our best judgments and intuition. Our experience reflects a reality in American policing: changes in policing practice are happening now, and police executives cannot wait for the research field to keep pace. This experience also highlights a reality in policing research: we often fail to adequately test innovations in policing practices, and we rarely examine the impact of police training. Even more concerning is the lack of scholarly interest (or perhaps opportunity or ability) to test the effects of interventions designed to directly impact what many have identified as the crucial issue underlying the current policing crisis—officer use of force.

What can be done? To facilitate the implementation of evidence-based approaches in reducing officer-involved shootings and other police reforms, law enforcement agencies must (1) consider findings from available research; and (2) where evidence is lacking, engage in opportunities to fill that void. Our review demonstrates that much of the evidence base surrounding the most popular reform initiatives to reduce officer shootings is limited in scope or nonexistent. Therefore, to advance EBP principles for reform, agencies must monitor the application and impact of training, policies, and procedures designed to reduce police use of force. That is, law enforcement must take responsibility in collecting data to generate evidence on the delivery and effects of their practices (Sherman 2013), moving beyond being consumers of research and instead engaging in the production of knowledge.

This is the approach we used to facilitate the reform efforts within the UCPD. Our first step was to redesign data collection systems to include the data necessary to evaluate the impact of our work. Our executive team modified existing data collection processes and also mandated the collection of new data. Changes in data collection instruments and practices resulted in new data generated during traffic and pedestrian stops, during the citizen complaint process, through the review and cataloging of BWC footage, during potential use-of-force encounters (e.g., when officers draw their Tasers or firearms but do not deploy them), along with multiple citizen and officer surveys. Each of these data collection changes required an accompanying change in policy, training, and supervisory oversight to ensure that the data were being properly collected and used. The UCPD is now in a better position to test specific propositions about the effectiveness of our own reform efforts. Based on these experiences, we believe that our best chance to reduce officer-involved shootings is working at the local (agency) level by building and sharing capacity for EBP and testing to determine what works.

Given the realities of policing, as new policies are introduced and officer training advances, police executives must take it upon themselves to consider how they might evaluate these practices to understand the effects on their agency, including partnering with researchers when their expertise is needed. Unfortunately, with the exception of a handful of progressive police agencies, this type of testing is rare. Nevertheless, as the EBP movement continues to gain acceptance, a tipping point in the profession is likely to occur. Similar to the impact in medicine and other disciplines, the acceptance of evidence-based practices should ultimately propel the proliferation and dissemination of research in policing.

For this change to come to light, however, policing researchers, as a profession, must also do better. We must develop the infrastructure to provide a rapid research response to the most pressing issues in policing. Currently, our approaches to research are too slow, and the topics selected for examination are too limited. The scientific evaluation of training and technical assistance within law enforcement must be recognized as a worthwhile area of research, deserving dedication of time and resources. A faster and more relevant research response will require the establishment of fully collaborative police-academic partnerships (Engel and Henderson 2013; Engel and Whalen 2010). Academics must step away from the ivory tower to take a seat at the table with police agencies and, simultaneously, police agencies must be gracious hosts. In sum, we must work together to build the evidence base necessary to better guide police agencies in their reform efforts. In the specific case of police use of force, facilitating the transition from "best practice" to evidence-based practice through research has the potential to reduce officer and citizen injuries and fatalities. In the collective, such research will fill a tremendous gap in knowledge, informing the field on successful models and overall effectiveness to better direct the national conversations surrounding policing and police reform.

Notes

1. Prior to the criminal trials, the university settled a civil rights and wrongful death claim with DuBose's family valued at $5.3 million. Tensing ultimately settled a union grievance with the university for

wrongful termination and was awarded approximately $345,000 for back pay and legal fees but was not reinstated within the UCPD.

2. During this time period, other high-profile deaths of unarmed black males by police included Michael Brown (Ferguson, MO, 2014), Tamir Rice (Cleveland, OH, 2014), Eric Garner (New York, NY, 2014), Walter Scott (North Charleston, SC, 2015), Freddie Gray (Baltimore, MD, 2015), and Terence Crutcher (Tulsa, OK, 2016), among others.

3. The Uniform Crime Report (UCR) produced by the FBI identifies Part I crime incidents to include eight types of offenses: criminal homicide, rape, robbery, aggravated assault, burglary, larceny-theft, motor vehicle theft, and arson (see UCR Offense Definitions at https://www.ucrdatatool.gov/offenses.cfm).

4. A comprehensive independent review of all UCPD policies, procedures, practices, and training resulted in a hefty report containing 129 findings and 276 specific recommendations to meet best practices (Exiger 2016). In the final stages of the planned reforms, all but one of these recommendations were deemed as meeting substantial compliance by the external monitor. The lone recommendation not meeting substantial compliance was found in partial compliance awaiting an additional assessment period (Exiger 2019).

References

Ariel, Barak, William A. Farrar, and Alex Sutherland. 2015. The effect of police body-worn cameras on use of force and citizens' complaints against the police: A randomized controlled trial. *Journal of Quantitative Criminology* 31 (3): 509–35.

Ariel, Barak, Alex Sutherland, Darren Henstock, Josh Young, Paul Drover, Jayne Sykes, Simon Megicks, and Ryan Henderson. 2016. Report: Increases in police use of force in the presence of body worn cameras are driven by officer discretion: A protocol based subgroup analysis of ten randomized experiments. *Journal of Experimental Criminology* 12 (3): 453–63.

Atewologun, Doyin, Tinu Cornish, and Fatima Tresh. 2018. *Unconscious bias training: An assessment of the evidence for effectiveness.* Manchester: Equality and Human Rights Commission. Available from www.equalityhumanrights.com.

Bittner, Egon. 1974. Florence Nightingale in pursuit of Willie Sutton: A theory of the police. *The Potential for Reform of Criminal Justice* 3:17–44.

Blake, David. 3 November 2017. Does de-escalation endanger police officers or save lives? *PoliceOne*.

Briggs, William. 2017. Police oversight: Civilian oversight boards and lessons learned from our neighbors to the north. *Suffolk Transnational Law Review* 40 (1): 139–64.

CBS News. 7 August 2019. We asked 155 police departments about their racial bias training. Here's what they told us. *CBS News*.

De Angelis, Joseph, Richard Rosenthal, and Brian Buchner. 2016. *Civilian oversight of law enforcement: Assessing the evidence.* Tucson, AZ: National Association for Civilian Oversight of Law Enforcement. Available from www.ncjrs.gov.

Devine, Patricia G. 1989. Stereotypes and prejudice: Their automatic and controlled components. *Journal of Personality and Social Psychology* 56 (1): 5–18.

Diener, Edward, and Mark Wallbom. 1976. Effects of self-awareness on antinormative behavior. *Journal of Research in Personality* 10 (1): 107–11.

Dovidio, John F., Kerry Kawakami, and Samuel L. Gaertner. 2002. Implicit and explicit prejudice and interracial interaction. *Journal of Personality and Social Psychology* 82 (1): 62–68.

Duguid, Michelle M., and Melissa C. Thomas-Hunt. 2015. Condoning stereotypes? How awareness of stereotyping prevalence impacts expression of stereotypes. *Journal of Applied Psychology* 100 (2): 343–59.

Eck, John E., and Jay Rothman. 2006. Police-community conflict and crime prevention in Cincinnati, Ohio. In *Public security and police reform in the Americas*, eds. John Bailey and Lucia Dammert, 225–44. Pittsburgh, PA: University of Pittsburgh Press.

Engel, Robin S., Nicholas Corsaro, Gabrielle T. Isaza, and Hannah D. McManus. 2019. *Proposal for the evaluation of ICAT training for the Louisville Metro Police Department.* Submitted to the Louisville Metro Police Department, Louisville, KY.

Engel, Robin S., and Samantha Henderson. 2013. Beyond rhetoric: Establishing police-academic partnerships that work. In *The future of policing*, ed. Jennifer M. Brown, 247–66. London: Routledge.

Engel, Robin S., Hannah D. McManus, and Tamara D. Herold. Forthcoming. Does de-escalation training work? A systematic review and call for evidence in police use of force reform. *Criminology and Public Policy*.

Engel, Robin S., and Ronal Serpas. 2017. Evidence-based use-of-force policy: How research could improve development and training. *Police Chief*, April: 28–36.

Engel, Robin S., and Kristin Swartz. 2014. Race, crime, and policing. In *The Oxford handbook of ethnicity, crime, and immigration*, eds. Sandra M. Bucerius and Michael Tonry, 135–65. New York, NY: Oxford University Press.

Engel, Robin S., and James L. Whalen. 2010. Police–academic partnerships: Ending the dialogue of the deaf, the Cincinnati experience. *Police Practice and Research: An International Journal* 11 (2): 105–16.

Engel, Robin S., Robert E. Worden, Nicholas Corsaro, Hannah D. McManus, Danielle Reynolds, Hannah Cochran, Gabrielle T. Isaza, and Jennifer Calnon Cherkauskas. 2019. *The power to arrest: Lessons from research*. New York, NY: Springer.

Exiger. 2016. *Final report for the comprehensive review of the University of Cincinnati Police Department*. Submitted to University of Cincinnati Office of Safety and Reform, Cincinnati, OH. Available from www.uc.edu.

Exiger. 2019. *Final report of the independent monitor for the University of Cincinnati Police Division*. Submitted to University of Cincinnati Board of Trustees Audit Committee, Cincinnati, OH. Available from www.uc.edu.

Federal Bureau of Investigation (FBI). 2019. *Law enforcement officers killed and assaulted*. Available from www.fbi.gov/leoka.

Ferdik, Frank V., Jeff Rojek, and Geoffrey P. Alpert. 2013. Citizen oversight in the United States and Canada: An overview. *Police Practice and Research* 14 (2): 104–16.

Forscher, Patrick S., Calvin K. Lai, Jordan R. Axt, Charles R. Ebersole, Michelle Herman, Patricia G. Devine, and Brian A. Nosek. 2018. A meta-analysis of procedures to change implicit bias measures. Pre-Print.

Fridell, Lorie A. 2017. *Producing bias-free policing: A science-based approach*. New York, NY: Springer.

Garner, Joel H., Matthew J. Hickman, Ronald W. Malega, and Christopher D. Maxwell. 2018. Progress toward national estimates of police use of force. *PLos ONE* 13 (2): 1–23.

Grasha, Kevin. 18 July 2017. No third trial for ex-UC cop Ray Tensing in shooting death of unarmed motorist Sam DuBose. *Cincinnati Enquirer*.

Harmon, Rachel A. 2009. Promoting civil rights through proactive policing reform. *Stanford Law Review* 62 (1): 1–68.

Hickman, Matthew J. 2006. *Citizen complaints about police use of force*. Washington, DC: Bureau of Justice Statistics. Available from www.bjs.gov.

International Association of Chiefs of Police. 2017. *National consensus policy on use of force*. Alexandria, VA: International Association of Chiefs of Police. Available from www.theiacp.org.

Isaza, Gabrielle, Murat Yildirim, Jillian Shafer, and Murat Ozer. 2017. *2016 campus crime report*. Submitted to the University of Cincinnati Campus Crime Reduction Committee, Cincinnati, OH. Available from www.uc.edu.

Jones, Hannah G. 12 October 2015. The science of bias policing. *Local 12 News*.

Kindy, Kimberly. 30 May 2015. Fatal police shootings in 2015 approaching 400 nationwide. *Washington Post*.

Klinger, David. 2005. *Social theory and the street cop: The case of deadly force*. Washington, DC: Police Foundation. Available from www.policefoundation.org.

Klinger, David. 2020. Organizational accidents and deadly police-involved violence: Theory, research, public policy, and police practice. *The ANNALS of the American Academy of Political and Social Science* (this volume).

Kroll. 2015. *Review and investigation of Officer Raymond M. Tensing's use of deadly force on July 19, 2015: University of Cincinnati Police Department*. Submitted to the University of Cincinnati Office of General Counsel, Cincinnati, OH. Available from www.uc.edu.

Landers, Brian. 14 October 2017. Are de-escalation policies dangerous? *Police Magazine*. Available from https://www.policemag.com/342333/are-de-escalation-policies-dangerous.

Lum, Cynthia, Christopher S. Koper, Charlotte Gill, Julie Hibdon, Cody Telep, and Laurie Robinson. 2016. *An evidence-assessment of the recommendations of the President's Task Force on 21st Century Policing – Implementation and research priorities*. Fairfax, VA: Center for Evidence-Based Crime Policy, George Mason University. Available from www.cebcp.org.

Lum, Cynthia, Christopher S. Koper, and Cody W. Telep. 2011. The evidence-based policing matrix. *Journal of Experimental Criminology* 7 (1): 3–26.

Lum, Cynthia, Megan Stoltz, Christopher S. Koper, and J. Amber Scherer. 2019. Research on body-worn cameras: What we know, what we need to know. *Criminology and Public Policy* 18 (1): 1–26.

Macrae, C. Neil, Galen V. Bodenhasuen, Alan B. Milne, and Jolanda Jetten. 1994. Out of mind but back in sight: Stereotypes on the rebound. *Journal of Personality and Social Psychology* 67 (5): 808–17.

McLean, Kyle, Scott E. Wolfe, Jeff Rojek, Geoffrey P. Alpert, and Michael R. Smith. 2020. Evaluating a long-term social interaction police training program: A randomized controlled trial in the real world. *The ANNALS of the American Academy of Political and Social Science* (this volume).

Mitchell, Renee J. and Lois James. 2018. Addressing the elephant in the room: The need to evaluate implicit bias training effectiveness for improving fairness in police officer decision-making. *Police Chief Magazine*. Available from https://www.policechiefmagazine.org/addressing-the-elephant-in-the-room.

Monteith, Margo J., Steven A. Arthur, and Sara M. Flynn. 2010. Self-regulation and bias. In *The SAGE handbook of prejudice, stereotyping and discrimination*, eds. John F. Dovidio, M. Hewstone, P. Glick, and V. M. Esses, 493–507. Thousand Oaks, CA: Sage Publications.

National Research Council. 2004. *Fairness and effectiveness in policing: The evidence*. Washington, DC: National Academies Press.

Nix, Justin, Bradley A. Campbell, Edward H. Byers, and Geoffrey P. Alpert. 2017. A bird's eye view of civilians killed by police in 2015: Further evidence of implicit bias. *Criminology & Public Policy* 16 (1): 309–40.

Noble, Greg. 29 July 2015. Watch: Body cam video released in Sam DuBose shooting. *WCPO Cincinnati*.

Payne, B. Keith. 2001. Prejudice and perception: The role of automatic and controlled processes in mis-perceiving a weapon. *Journal of Personality and Social Psychology* 81 (2): 181–92.

Perrow, Charles. 1984. *Normal accidents: Living with high risk technologies*. New York, NY: Basic Books.

Pettigrew, Thomas F., and Linda R. Tropp. 2005. Allport's intergroup contact hypothesis: Its history and influence. In *On the nature of prejudice: Fifty years after Allport*, eds. John F. Dovidio, Peter Glick, and Laurie A. Rudman, 262–77. Malden, MA: Blackwell Publishing.

Police Executive Research Forum. 2016. *Critical issues in policing series: Guiding principles on use of force*. Washington, DC: Police Executive Research Forum.

Police Executive Research Forum. 2018. *Cost and benefits of body-worn camera deployments: Final report*. Washington, DC. Available from www.policeforum.org.

President's Task Force on 21st Century Policing. 2015. *Final report of the President's Task Force on 21st Century Policing*. Washington, DC: Office of Community Oriented Policing Services.

Reaves, Brian A. 2011. *Census of state and local law enforcement agencies, 2008*. Washington, DC: U.S. Department of Justice, Bureau of Justice Statistics. Available from www.bjs.gov.

Sherman, Lawrence W. 1998. *Evidence-based policing*. Ideas in American Policing Series. Washington, DC: Police Foundation. Available from www.policefoundation.org.

Sherman, Lawrence W. 2013. The rise of evidence-based policing: Targeting, testing, and tracking. *Crime and Justice* 42 (1): 377–451.

Sherman, Lawrence W. 2018. Reducing fatal police shootings as system crashes: Research, theory, and practice. *Annual Review of Criminology* 1:421–49.

Skogan, Wesley G., Martin Van Craen, and C. Hennessy. 2015. Training police for procedural justice. *Journal of Experimental Criminology* 11 (3): 319–34.

Telep, Cody W. 2016. Expanding the scope of evidence-based policing. *Criminology & Public Policy* 15 (1): 243–52.

Terrill, William, and Jason R. Ingram. 2015. Citizen complaints against the police: An eight city examination. *Police Quarterly* 19 (2): 150–79.

Walker, Samuel. 2001. *Police accountability: The role of citizen oversight*. Belmont, CA: Wadsworth.

Walker, Samuel. 2003. The new paradigm of police accountability: The U.S. Justice Department "pattern or practice" suits in context. *St. Louis University Public Law Review* 22 (3): 3–52.

Wasserman, R. 2014. *Building relationships of trust: Recommended steps for chief executives.* Tallahassee, FL: Institute for Intergovernmental Research.

Weisburd, David, and Peter Neyroud. 2011. *Police science: Toward a new paradigm.* Washington, DC: Office of Justice Programs, National Institute of Justice. Available from www.ncjrs.gov.

White, Michael D., and Michael Pooley. 2018. *Testing the impact of de-escalation training on officer behavior: The Tempe, Arizona SPI.* Presented to Tempe Police Department, Tempe, AZ.

Williams, Timothy. 27 June 2015. Long taught to use force, police warily learn to de-escalate. *New York Times.*

Worden, Robert E., Moonsun Kim, Christopher J. Harris, Mary Anne Pratte, Shelagh E. Dorn, and Shelley S. Hyland. 2013. Intervention with problem officers: An outcome evaluation of an EIS intervention. *Criminal Justice Behavior* 40 (4): 409–37.

Worden, Robert E., Sarah J. McLean, Kelly J. Becker, Eugene A. Paoline III, Hannah Cochran, and Chris Harris. 2018. *Police early intervention systems: The state of the art.* Albany, NY: The John F. Finn Institute for Public Safety, Inc.

Zimring, Franklin E. 2017. *When police kill.* Cambridge, MA: Harvard University Press.

Zimring, Franklin E. 2020. Police killings as a problem of governance. *The ANNALS of the American Academy of Political and Social Science* (this volume).

Reducing Violent Incidents between Police Officers and People with Psychiatric or Substance Use Disorders

By
HAROLD A. POLLACK
and
KEITH HUMPHREYS

This article describes evidence-based strategies designed to reduce the prevalence of police encounters with people in behavioral crisis (PBCs) and to make such encounters less dangerous for all parties when they do occur. Some of these strategies are implemented by law enforcement, including gun violence restraining orders and the training of officers to provide time, distance, and cover during encounters with PBCs. Other strategies involve broader systems of community care, including assertive community treatment for people with serious psychiatric disorders, and critical time interventions for individuals leaving incarceration or inpatient psychiatric care. Broader adoption of such strategies should both reduce the risk of police shootings of PBCs as well as improve the effectiveness and well-being of police officers.

Keywords: behavioral crisis; police; psychiatric disorder; substance use; violence; crisis intervention

The *Chicago Reader* and other news sources recently ran stories about a man named Vincent Gaughan, who had participated in a confrontation with police 48 years before. The son of Irish immigrants, Gaughan grew up in Chicago and attended Catholic schools. In 1964, he joined the Army and served three tours in Vietnam as a forward artillery observer, earning a Bronze Star for combat heroism,

Harold A. Pollack is the Helen Ross Professor of Social Service Administration at the University of Chicago and faculty codirector of the University of Chicago Crime Lab and University of Chicago Health Lab. He researches strategies to improve services for individuals at the boundaries of behavioral health and criminal justice systems.

Keith Humphreys is the Esther Ting Memorial Professor at Stanford University and a senior research career scientist at the VA Health Services Research Center in Palo Alto, California. His research addresses the prevention and treatment of addictive disorders, the formation of public policy, and the generalizability of psychiatric clinical trials.

Correspondence: haroldp@uchicago.edu

DOI: 10.1177/0002716219897057

which included rescuing wounded comrades under heavy fire (St. Clair 2018; Bogira 2016).

Gaughan returned to Chicago and enrolled in DePaul Law School. But combat experience left its scars. He struggled with post-traumatic stress disorder (PTSD), and in April 1970 he became particularly agitated after a car accident. He locked himself in his room at his parents' home. Around 3 a.m., he fired two shots from an M1 rifle into a neighbor's bedroom. After police arrived, Gaughan fired two more shots, narrowly missing two officers.

Officers converged on the scene with their guns drawn, but they did not fire. And by then, Gaughan was done. He called down the stairs and asked to speak with a priest: "I want a policeman to come, too. An Irish sergeant." This being Chicago, both were quickly found. Gaughan surrendered without incident. The priest accompanied him in the police squad car to the police station. The Cook County Circuit Court has no record of any charges being filed or resolved. Three years later, Gaughan joined the public defender's office.

For those who identify Chicago policing with the Laquan McDonald case (see Ridgeway, this volume), the contrast could hardly be sharper. McDonald was a 17-year-old African American male who was behaving erratically; toxicology tests later revealed he was under the influence of the drug PCP. He damaged a police vehicle with a knife and did not obey an order to drop the knife, but he injured no one. He was at some distance from surrounding police officers. Police dashcam videos show several officers behaving in the same way, deploying time and distance principles as if in a police training film, waiting for further assistance. But then Officer Jason Van Dyke drove up. Six seconds later, he fired sixteen shots, killing Laquan McDonald.

Vincent Gaughan had nearly shot multiple police officers when police provided him time and space to regain his composure and negotiate a dignified surrender. Almost 50 years after Gaughan's mental health crisis ended without incident, Officer Van Dyke was charged with murder. The presiding judge in his case was a respected figure in Chicago's legal community: Vincent Gaughan.

Anyone who follows cases like these can supply a litany of examples in which confrontations between police and people with psychiatric and/or substance use disorders (whom we will refer to here as "people in behavioral crisis" or PBCs) resulted in tragedy. Robert Saylor, a man living with intellectual disabilities, died of asphyxiation when three deputies restrained him face-down after wresting him from a chair at a movie theater (Pollack 2016). Saheel Vassell was well known by the locals in his neighborhood for having psychiatric problems, but the police who responded to a call about a man "holding a gun" (which turned out to be a curved silver pipe) did not know this before they shot him to death (Mueller, Ransom, and Ferré-Sadurní 2018). Sonny Lam suffered from schizophrenia and had stopped taking his

---

NOTE: Dr. Pollack was supported by grants from the Robert Wood Johnson Foundation and the Arnold Foundation. Dr. Humphreys was supported by grants from the Veterans Health Administration and Wu Tsai Neurosciences Institute. Opinions in this article are the responsibility of the authors.

medication prior to his fatal confrontation with Officer Jairo Acosta, who had been called to the Lam home by family members. A jury later awarded the Lam family $2.75 million in damages, finding that the encounter had been grossly mishandled by Acosta, who himself was a combat veteran who suffered from chronic PTSD (Sullivan 2018).

The Gaughan and McDonald cases highlight the lifelong consequences that turn on whether police handle such incidents well or poorly. Sometimes, disastrous results are not so much a product of someone's decision to call the police as they are a product of who actually responds to the call.

This article seeks to summarize clinical and research evidence on how to reduce the prevalence of incidents with PBCs, and, when confrontations are unavoidable, how they can be handled in the best possible ways. We thus seek to address both law enforcement agencies that handle such incidents and the broader network of professional and nonprofessional resources that surround PBCs. We discuss police interaction in light of broader systemic realities that extend beyond law enforcement per se, exploring what can be done outside of the "heat of the moment" to reduce the occurrence of such incidents. Our concern is to assist police and other criminal justice professionals to help PBCs who have psychiatric or substance use disorders live happier, healthier, and safer lives.

Background

Ample research documents that PBCs are far more likely than other individuals to have contact with police. There are three primary routes to such contacts, all of which can bring a PBC into contact with law enforcement: violence by PBCs, victimization of PBCs, and homelessness among PBCs.

Violence by PBCs

Contrary to stereotype, very few people with serious mental illness go on violent rampages or perpetrate mass shootings. Data from the Epidemiologic Catchment Area (ECA) study in Baltimore, St. Louis, and Los Angeles in the 1980s indicate that serious mental illness (e.g., schizophrenia) accounts for an estimated 4 percent of reported violence within the general population (Swanson, McGinty, et al. 2015). Mental illness is not markedly more prevalent in the United States than in other wealthy democracies. Yet many of these other democracies experience far lower rates of deadly violence.

Steadman and colleagues examined the prevalence of violence by 951 patients after discharge from acute civil inpatient facilities using data from the MacArthur Violence Risk Assessment Study (Steadman et al. 2015). Only 2 percent (23/951) of patients available for follow-up committed a violent act involving a gun. Only 6 percent (55/951) committed a violent act involving a stranger, and only 1 percent (9/951) committed a violent act involving both a gun and a stranger.

However, substance use disorders are a significant driver of criminal behavior both among people with and without a co-occurring psychiatric disorder (Swanson, McGinty, et al. 2015; Steadman et al. 2015; Drake et al. 2001). In the same 1980s ECA data combining three cities, lifetime risk of violence was approximately 15 percent among people without mental illness, 33 percent among those with serious mental illness only, and 55 percent among the dual-diagnosis population (Swanson et al. 2015, 367–68). Substance use disorders, particularly alcohol disorders, are also of course major risk factors for violence among people without serious mental illness, being implicated in a plurality of murders, assaults, domestic violence, and suicides (Edwards 1997).

Absent a substance use disorder, neither mental illness nor intellectual disability shows a strong relationship to stranger-directed violence. Nonetheless, mental illness and intellectual disability are associated with aggression within families. In one study of individuals with fragile X syndrome, one-third of parental caregivers were injured by their sons. When such violence occurred at all, it was usually a regular occurrence (Bailey et al. 2012). The vast bulk of physical aggression by people with mental illnesses and related disorders is perpetrated against people they know, particularly family members.

The most common setting for behavioral crisis is the family home, often involving romantic partners, caregivers, or other family members. Such episodes pose cruel dilemmas for caregivers ambivalent about calling for emergency services. They also pose dilemmas for police officers as they must try to protect and serve at the same time. Police also know how dangerous family conflict calls can become.

PBCs as crime victims

Although the news media tend to focus on the role of mental illness in *committing* violence, psychiatric disorder is more strongly predictive of being a *victim of* violence. PBCs are also far more likely than the rest of the population to be criminally victimized (Wolff, Diamond, and Helminiak 1997), bringing them into more contact with police at a time when they are understandably distressed.

Homelessness among PBCs

Adverse economic shocks (e.g., the local plant closes and everyone is laid off, or rents soar due to massive migration to an area) can drive many people into homelessness. That said, many chronically homeless people are PBCs (Fazel et al. 2008). Police may encounter PBCs sleeping in a shop doorway, urinating on the sidewalk, panhandling aggressively, screaming strange or aggressive things, or otherwise being disruptive. When police try to get someone to "move along," these interactions can easily turn adversarial. Even a well-meaning effort by police officers to transport a street-dwelling person to a shelter on a cold night can result in a difficult interaction if that individual is frightened or intoxicated.

Summary

PBCs are a population with which the police interact frequently. This includes many situations where the person may be aggressive, upset, difficult to understand, intoxicated, or some combination thereof. All of these interactions carry a risk of escalation. We now turn to strategies that can make such risks less common and also help police to handle them better when they arise.

Evidence-Based Approaches to Police/PBC Interactions

We divide these strategies into three categories. The first is intended to prevent violent confrontations between law enforcement and PBCs. The second is "in the heat of the moment" strategies, that is, how should police handle potentially dangerous situations involving people who are impaired in some way? The third is long-term management strategies for PBCs who have been involved in the criminal justice system. The categories can overlap; for example, long-term assertive community treatment could prevent future incidents for PBCs who receive it. But we nonetheless discuss them separately for ease of presentation.

As readers will see, the quality of evidence differs across the three categories and across interventions. Quite a bit is now understood regarding forensic assertive community treatment and other long-term management strategies to assist PBCs. The strengths and weaknesses of particular police tactics in managing behavioral crises is also increasingly well understood. Far less is known about how to prevent behavioral crises from occurring (or reoccurring).

Preventive Strategies

Some preventive strategies are generic, meaning that they reduce incidents between police and people both with and without addictive and psychiatric disorders. These include policies such as raising alcohol taxes (Cook 2016) and reducing access to firearms. Such policies are important but beyond the scope of this article. We focus here on three preventive strategies specifically tailored to PBCs: risk-based gun removal measures, predictive individual and place-based interventions, and improved mental health services for police.

Risk-based gun removal

By both law and tradition, Americans are accorded broad legal access to firearms. This poses an inherent public safety challenge, given the central role firearms play in both suicide and homicide. The right to bear arms is not unlimited, however. Individuals may be barred from gun ownership or possession if they have been convicted of a felony or have been subject to a mental health adjudication. Grounds for the latter include a legal determination that they require guardianship due to mental incompetence, involuntary civil commitment, incompetence to stand trial in a criminal matter, or being found not guilty of a crime by reason of insanity. In the less than gracious phrasing of U.S. Code 18 922(d), individuals are prohibited from buying or possessing a firearm if they have been "adjudicated as a mental defective" or were committed to a mental institution.

These restrictions on gun access could be modernized and more effectively enforced. Although the role of law enforcement in preventing self-harm is less emphasized than the role of law enforcement in preventing crimes against others, police play a critical role in this arena as well. The most deadly and prevalent connection between mental illness and violence arises for suicide (Swanson 2018). Suicides among individuals with major depression and other psychiatric disorders pose many challenges, particularly for gun policy, given the ease and lethality of suicide through firearms (Swanson, McGinty, et al. 2015; McGinty, Webster, and Barry 2014). Efforts, such as the Brady Bill, that constrain gun access in the name of crime control may show more success preventing gun suicides than they do in preventing gun homicides (Crifasi et al. 2015; Ludwig and Cook 2000). One recent study found that Connecticut's permit-to-purchase laws were associated with a 15.4 percent reduction in firearm suicide rates, while Missouri's repeal of a similar law was associated with a 16.1 percent increase in firearm suicide rates (Crifasi et al. 2015).

Even among the group of individuals diagnosed with and in care for serious mental illness, current laws do surprisingly little to bar individuals who actually are dangerous from obtaining (or from keeping) deadly weapons. Swanson and colleagues (2017) matched and merged Connecticut mental health, court, and arrest records for more than twenty-three thousand people diagnosed with schizophrenia, bipolar disorder, or major depression who were actually receiving services in the state's public behavioral healthcare system. They found that improvements in Connecticut's reporting to the National Instant Criminal Background Check System (NICS) produced a 6 percent reduction in violent crime among individuals legally barred from possessing guns. Yet the policy's overall impact was "substantively trivial." It affected only 7 percent of the Connecticut population under care for serious mental illness. Fully 96 percent of the violent crimes recorded within this population were committed by persons who were not disqualified from gun ownership on the basis of their mental health adjudication history (Swanson et al. 2017).

American gun policy also conflates serious mental illness with dangerousness. Yet most dangerous people are not mentally ill, and most people with mental illness are not dangerous. Swanson and colleagues (2017) report that millions of Americans self-report patterns of impulsive angry behaviors *and* either possess firearms *at home* (8.9 percent) or carry guns *outside the home* (1.5 percent). Many of these individuals also report problematic patterns of alcohol use that are correlated with violent behavior, though less than 10 percent have ever been (1) involuntarily hospitalized (Swanson, McGinty, et al. 2015), (2) been convicted of a violent felony, or (3) otherwise satisfied criteria for prohibited gun possession (Swanson, Sampson, et al. 2015).

Conflating serious mental illness with dangerousness stigmatizes people with mental illness. Such stereotypes may lead police or others to overlook public safety threats posed by individuals who wish to harm others but who are not psychotic and do not satisfy classic symptoms of serious mental illness. Such stereotypes may also lead first responders to needlessly escalate encounters with individuals who experience serious mental illness, yet who pose no public safety threat (Swanson 2017).

Morabito and colleagues examined Portland, Oregon, policing data to explore other stereotypes, assumptions, and impressions that influence police use of force in encounters involving PBCs (Morabito et al. 2017). Subjects perceived as experiencing serious behavioral health disorders were more likely than those with no perceived disorders to have force used against them, or to be characterized as violently resisting police officers. At the same time, individuals who displayed stereotypical signs of mental illness were viewed as less blameworthy for their behaviors.

Subjects who officers perceived to have no behavioral health disorder were less likely to be perceived as resisting officers. Yet this group of PBCs was more likely to have guns pointed at them in police encounters and to be labeled "assholes" in police parlance (Miller 2015; Van Maanen 1978). This latter pattern is especially dangerous given the reality that individuals living with serious mental illness or related challenges do not always display stereotypical signs of that illness.

Gun violence restraining orders (GVRO)

One strategy to address such risks is to provide families, clinicians, and law enforcement a tool to temporarily restrict an individual's gun access in a crisis. GVROs are modeled after domestic violence procedures that have been under development for several years and have been in place in California since late 2014. Such mechanisms received bipartisan attention under the label "red flag laws" or "extreme risk protective orders" in the wake of mass shootings such as in Parkland (Anonymous, n.d.).

GVRO laws allow a court to temporarily bar an individual from purchasing or possessing a gun. Police, clinicians, and criminal justice authorities can cite behaviors that indicate risk to self or others as the basis for court petitions. Although the mechanics vary in accordance with specific state laws, GVROs might be issued on the basis of specific criteria such as being arrested for a violent crime, being under a domestic violence restraining order, repeated convictions for alcohol-impaired driving or other substance-associated crimes, or short-term involuntary hospitalization (not subject to formal civil commitment).

One GVRO model proceeds in two stages. In an initial hearing, a judge assesses whether an individual is at risk of harming self or others. The subject of that hearing is sometimes but not always informed that the hearing will occur. If the judge finds a likely risk, the subject is temporarily barred from gun possession or ownership. If she has a gun, she must surrender it. That initial period is usually a few weeks. Before that period expires, a subsequent hearing is held that would extend the protective order out to a year. At that second hearing, the subject may present evidence to show that she is not a danger to herself or others.

Connecticut and Indiana have implemented risk-based gun removal laws on the GVRO model. The Indiana model, crucially, allows police to seize a gun immediately, with the burden on the gun owner to go to court to get it back (Brooks 2019). Other states require police to go to court before they can seize the gun, which can create delays of several weeks. Nonetheless, since 1999, Connecticut courts have imposed fifty-one "risk warrants" per year since 1999, of which 41 percent were initiated by family members and 8 percent by employers or clinicians. The typical subject of gun removal was a middle-aged man with no criminal record and no exposure to Connecticut's public behavioral health system. In both Connecticut and Indiana, more than 60 percent of cases involved the risk of suicide. Swanson and colleagues estimate one averted death per ten to twenty gun removals (Swanson et al. 2017).

Predictive individual and place-based interventions

Police often have opportunities to intervene with PBCs before things get to a crisis point. However, such opportunities do not guarantee success. In one among many prominent cases, Elliot Rodger's parents as well as others who knew him had been sufficiently concerned about him to call the police. Four deputies; a University of California, Santa Barbara police officer; and a dispatcher in training interviewed Rodger at some point (Flores, Winton, and Mather 2014).

After a short conversation, each police officer determined that Rodger was lucid and posed no imminent threat to himself or others. The first of these assessments was likely accurate. The second was not. Police did not check the California's Dealer's Record of Sale database, which would have identified Rodger's pattern of handgun and ammunition purchases as a subject of concern. None of them viewed the YouTube videos that so concerned Rodger's parents. Rodger went on to commit mass homicide in Isla Vista, California. Although it was obvious to those around him that Rodger's mental health was worsening, nothing concrete in his record would have supported barring him from possessing a gun (Pollack 2014; Flores, Winton, and Mather 2014).

When it comes to preventive opportunities, the entire criminal justice and emergency response (e.g., 911 call staff) systems are inherently vulnerable to errors of omission and commission. The decision theorist would call these Type I and Type II errors. Within that lexicon, a Type I error occurs when an individual is labeled dangerous when she or he is not. A Type II error occurs when a truly high-risk person is not detected, such as when a violent or suicidal individual is permitted to buy a gun.

Fortunately, data-informed approaches can help to reduce the risk of Type I and Type II errors in such situations. Recent research explores additional strategies to improve emergency first response to behavioral crises (Tentner et al. 2019). Administrative data systems offer one important opportunity to identify *individuals* who are at risk; *locations* that are high volume, or high-risk locations where such crises are most likely to occur; and *events* in which information available to 911 call center staff or others can be used to identify immediate risk factors that merit a mental health response.

Event-based interventions include more effective allocation of crisis intervention teams or co-responding police and social service units and availability of nonlethal equipment such as Tasers. Several research groups are now attempting to use "natural language processing" to code calls to 911 systems and other methods to improve identification of behavioral crises. These methods might be considered secondary or tertiary prevention, because they seek to improve the quality of response before specific contact is made.

Person-based interventions rely on predictive analytics or other methods to identify individuals who may benefit from proactive outreach and interventions before a behavioral crisis occurs. A Chicago pilot intervention called MHEART (Mental Health Emergency Alternative Referrals to Treatment) recently used Chicago Fire Department and Police Department data to identify candidates for proactive interventions. This is one early effort to engage individuals with frequent contacts with first responders and link them to assertive community treatment (ACT) and related services provided by a local mental health agency.

Within Chicago data, more than 25 percent of individuals with frequent behavioral-health-involved encounters with first responders are indicated to be homeless (Tentner et al. 2019). These individuals are especially difficult to find. Others pose staff safety issues for outreach staff in ACT and related efforts. Yet when they present to care, case managers can be alerted and can intervene. Extensions of such models may incorporate health care data from local integrated care entities, using diagnostic and claims records.

As a final note on person-based prediction, we should not overlook its potential uses for predicting police officers at heightened risk of violence. Chicago police officer Jason Van Dyke, for example, had accumulated twenty prior complaints before he killed Laquan McDonald. Many of these complaints involved the use of excessive force. Attentive personnel procedures might have provided Officer Van Dyke with mental health resources or might have led him to be reassigned (Citizens Police Data Project 2018).

Predictive interventions can also be place-based, identifying *high-volume locations* where crises involving PBCs predictably occur (e.g., transportation hubs, hospitals, parks, and related public facilities). Once such locations are identified, place-based staff can be specifically trained in de-escalation strategies. Procedures can be refined regarding when police should (or just as importantly, should not) be called in the event of a mental health crisis. Police and ambulance personnel can coordinate with staff at these locations to improve a coordinated response.

The myriad of high-risk locations is more difficult to address. Families with a household member who is a PBC can enroll in services such as Smart911, which provides first responders with key information difficult to communicate in an emergency. Staff at group homes and other community-based facilities can similarly be trained in de-escalation, can participate in Smart911, and can coordinate with first responders.

When group home staff are confronted with PBCs, one important guideline concerns when not to call the police if a resident is disobedient or disruptive but is not endangering himself or others. First responders are not trained or equipped to manage such situations; nor is it their role to enforce a resident's behavioral management plan.

Improved mental health services for law enforcement personnel

When analyzing police shootings of PBCs, most observers correctly note that the shooting victim's behavior (e.g., saying or doing strange things, ignoring police commands, being aggressive, engaging in an impulsive and destructive action) was shaped by substance use and/or a psychiatric disorder. Far more rarely is it suggested that perhaps the behavior of a police officer involved in a shooting or other violent incident could be explained the same way.

Being a police officer is a difficult job. Exposure to tragedy and violence is inherent in the role, as is occupational stress. Because of shift changes and emergency calls to duty, police are also disproportionately likely to have disrupted sleep, which can cause higher blood cortisol, irritation, and symptoms of depression (Violanti et al. 2017, 2006). Police officers have high rates of substance use disorders, depression, and suicide (Stanley, Hom, and Joiner 2016; Ballenger et al. 2011; P. Smith 2019). Police are also at high risk for PTSD, either from on-the-job experiences or experiences prior to policing (a disproportionate number of police are military veterans).

Effectively responding to PBCs requires police to be in control of their emotions, to correctly judge—perhaps in a split-second—whether an ambiguous behavior is threatening, and not to respond disproportionately to verbal and physical aggression. All else equal, the odds of a police officer succeeding in these tasks are lower when the officer is sleep-deprived, depressed, traumatized, or hung over. As the Laquan McDonald case shows, it often only requires one of a number of responding officers to make the wrong judgment for a shooting to occur (Ridgeway, this volume).

We propose that enhanced prevention and treatment of psychiatric and substance use disorders among police officers could have positive spillovers by reducing the number of incidents that end in violence. Such programs benefit police, which is a good in itself (see Galovski et al. 2016). But their impact on how incidents with PBCs are handled deserves further evaluation. This claim may not have the level of evidence met by the strategies discussed earlier, yet it is important to explore.

Strategies for PBC-Police Encounters in the Heat of the Moment

As mentioned, PBCs encounter (and reencounter) police and other first responders at many points in their adult lives. These encounters pose classic dilemmas for police. Indeed, the basic contours of the challenge have been discussed for generations (Lamb, Weinberger, and DeCuir 2002).

Egon Bittner (1967) noted that police lack the training or information to draw granular judgments about individuals who appear to be experiencing psychiatric symptoms; that police are expected to fill gaps left by mental health and social service systems charged with assisting the mentally ill; and that police encounter many people who appear symptomatic yet pose no obvious danger to themselves or others, even as they interact with many others who appear far less ill but more dangerous or hostile. Bittner noted organizational obstacles to policing these encounters better. Assisting or apprehending individuals with mental illness is an important part of officers' everyday work. Yet such assistance brings little professional reward or prestige. Bittner noted officers' frustrations with the bureaucratic obstacles and logistical delays that arise when police seek to connect troubled individuals with mental health services. With some change in terminology, much of Bittner's account might be applied to community policing five decades later (Bittner 1967).

Such encounters with PBCs occur across diverse settings within the community, medical, and criminal justice systems and involve many organizations and service providers (e.g., Reuland and Yasuhara 2015, Table 3.1; pp. 44–45). Evidence-informed policy requires collaboration across public services and systems to meet people's basic needs and to minimize the risk of criminal offending. The profusion of such settings and the interactions among them create endless possibilities for missed opportunities and normal accidents that involve people who live with psychiatric and/or substance use disorders.

A short inventory of critical criminal justice organizations that may encounter PBCs includes police, parole, probation, jails, and prisons, not to mention private actors such as the security guards who encounter homeless individuals stealing socks or beer at a drugstore. Health and social care systems include mental health and addiction treatment programs; ambulance services; hospital emergency departments and clinics; public housing and community housing services, such as group homes; transportation hubs; libraries; and other facilities where homeless individuals congregate.

Crisis intervention teams (CITs)

There are some situations in which trained mental health experts can provide a wider range of options for de-escalating PBC behavior, and even save lives. The deaths of Quintonio LeGrier and Bettie Jones underscore the value of CITs as an alternative to police as first responders. These cases also suggest a need for improved training of police.

On December 26, 2015, Chicago police responded to a domestic disturbance call. LeGrier, who was experiencing mental health challenges, had previous confrontations with fellow college students and with police. He was staying with his father on Chicago's West Side. Apparently out of paranoia, LeGrier called 911 three times to request police protection in the hour before his death. Perhaps misinterpreting LeGrier's call as a prank, the first call-taker became audibly irritated. She hung up when LeGrier would only identify himself as "Q," despite his increasingly agitated claims that his life was in danger. The second call-taker also missed an opportunity to engage LeGrier. The third call-taker sent a patrol car. So did a separate call-taker after LeGrier's father Antonio called from his bedroom as his son attempted to break down the door with an aluminum bat.

Officer Robert Rialmo and a colleague were dispatched. Ms. Jones answered the front door and pointed toward an upstairs apartment. Hearing the officers, LeGrier apparently moved down the stairs to confront them with the bat. Officer Rialmo responded by firing eight shots. LeGrier was hit six times and fell across the threshold of Ms. Jones's open apartment door. Another of Rialmo's bullets killed Bettie Jones. Subsequent investigations revealed that Rialmo had limited training in de-escalating behavioral crises. The officers were not aware of LeGrier's prior incidents and mental health challenges.

Even if no formally organized CIT had been available that evening (or any time), CIT training might have helped Officer Rialmo to resolve the situation more peacefully. Such training (sometimes called the Memphis model) is the most widespread model of specialized police response. Thousands of police organizations seek to implement such methods. The Obama administration's Justice Department endorsed CIT, requiring several major departments to implement CIT training in consent decrees or settlement agreements following police misconduct (Watson, Compton, and Draine 2017). Smaller municipalities (which face statistically higher risks of officer-involved shootings and use of force) are increasingly adapting CIT, as well (Strassle 2019).

CIT emphasizes the importance of de-escalation, time, distance, and cover in police encounters with PBCs. *Time* allows the individual to regain his composure. It allows officers to summon other officers with greater expertise or nonlethal equipment if coercion is ultimately required. Time also allows the engagement of mental health professionals, or of someone with a direct personal connection with the individual in crisis to provide help. *Distance* matters because most confrontations can be peacefully resolved if an individual experiencing a behavioral crisis can be kept physically separate from officers and from others with whom there is a risk of violence. *Cover* is an important consideration for officer safety, particularly when an individual may be armed with a knife or blunt object.

CIT provides a welcome alternative to overly aggressive training that might lead officers to escalate ambiguous situations, for example, in applying the so-called 21-foot rule (M. Smith and Williams 2016). Relative to the 80 million annual police encounters with citizens in the United States, lethal violence is rarely directed against police officers. Police warrior training and similar approaches may lead officers to construe a wide range of noncompliant or dys-regulated behaviors as more dangerous than they generally are. That, in turn, may encourage tactical escalation when it is unwise. The de-escalation principles of CIT are a counterpoint to such training, offering an alternative framework for decision-making.

These de-escalation principles also have broad application when police encounter individuals who have no psychiatric disorders at all. As psychiatrist Harry Stack Sullivan liked to say, people with schizophrenia are a lot more like us than anything else (for more on Sullivan's perspective, see Elkind 1972). The most effective strategies to assist mentally ill people who are dangerous have much in common with the most effective strategies to assist other people who are dangerous yet have no psychiatric or substance use disorder. Understanding this principle often helps to reduce officers' anxiety about accurately diagnosing each individual encounter. Officers need tools that work across a broad range of situations.

It is therefore reassuring that CIT deemphasizes the need to make particular diagnoses. While officers receive training regarding common psychiatric, developmental, and communication disorders, CIT training does not seek to help officers to diagnose any particular disorder. Skilled mental health professionals cannot reliably diagnose such disorders in the midst of a crisis. Moreover, accurate diagnoses do not particularly alter the proper police response, which emphasizes time, distance, and cover principles across a range of challenges.

Ironically, the first minutes of the Laquan McDonald video provide an excellent example of CIT principles properly applied. Officers keep their distance, giving McDonald time to calm down as they wait for additional supports and a Taser-equipped officer. Had Jason Van Dyke driven up 10 minutes later, McDonald may have already been taken safely into custody and care.

Although many police agencies embrace CIT, there remains considerable scientific debate over CIT's true benefit in serving PBCs (Steadman and Morrissette 2016; Morabito et al. 2017). Existing pre-post studies suggest that CIT training improves officers' knowledge and attitudes regarding mental illness. Officers who undertook CIT training displayed greater knowledge of mental illness and were less likely to endorse the use of force serving individuals with mental illnesses (Watson and Compton 2019).

Such differences in knowledge and attitudes can translate into police behavior on the street. Studies of police officers in Chicago, Illinois, and Akron, Ohio, suggest that CIT-trained officers are more likely to refer or transport subjects to mental health services and were less likely to use force (Watson, Compton, and Draine 2017; Compton et al. 2014). Researchers have not found differences in arrests. Because officers typically self-select into CIT training, differences between CIT-trained and other officers at least partly reflect pre-existing differences. Officers who volunteer for CIT appear to display more favorable attitudes, skills, and behavior posttraining than do nonvolunteers assigned to the same instruction (Compton et al. 2017). Whether self-selected officers experienced greater pre-post improvement than assigned officers remains unknown. Some commentators have interpreted these findings as reason for caution, since many police departments are considering assigning all officers to CIT training. Such an approach may dilute average quality of the intervention. Depending on a department's overall needs, a smaller group of CIT volunteers may provide higher-quality services.

Psychiatrists note both the necessity and the limitations of improving police responses. Although CIT receives the greatest attention, it is one limited intervention at only one stage of the interactions individuals vulnerable to behavioral crises are likely to experience with mental health and criminal justice systems. CIT does not appear to improve downstream outcomes for individuals who come into contact with police. Even when CIT makes the immediate police encounter safer and less likely to end in arrest, long-term outcomes reflect the quality and accessibility of mental health services and other factors beyond the control of police (Gatens 2018).

Strategies for Long-Term Intervention with Criminal Justice–Involved PBCs

A large population of PBCs have extensive contact with the criminal justice system. Many of them have had negative interactions with police in the past. All carry that risk in the future. Fortunately, there are evidence-based strategies that reduce criminal justice involvement in the long term and benefit the individual's health and well-being at the same time. We highlight three effective models in this section: critical time interventions, ACT, and 24/7 Sobriety.

Critical time interventions

Critical time interventions form an evidence-based strategy to assist individuals transitioning from institutional settings such as inpatient psychiatric facilities and homeless shelters, often returning to the family home. Critical time intervention has shown to reduce psychiatric re-hospitalization and homelessness in randomized trials (Draine and Herman 2007).

A key phase of critical time interventions occurs while the patient remains institutionalized, when transition coaches work with him and with family or others to navigate predictable challenges and conflicts. They also develop a feasible transition plan. Staff then work postrelease to assist individuals with entitlements, resolve disputes with landlords or others, and provide employment and other supports.

More limited evidence suggests that critical time intervention might also be effective for people leaving jails and prisons, though the model requires modification to serve individuals leaving these settings. This is particularly true of jails, given the sporadic and unpredictable nature of entries and release.

Assertive community treatment (ACT)

ACT and its variants offer a related strategy to assist people at the margins of the criminal justice and mental health systems (Morrissey, Meyer, and Cuddeback 2007; Lamberti et al. 2017; Calsyn et al. 2005). This is a challenging assignment. Many individuals prone to behavioral crises are unable to consistently engage treatment providers without significant supports. Others face stressors and mental health risks that are best engaged within their own community and family settings rather than waiting for them to present to care within the confines of a mental professional's office.

ACT was developed and refined to provide team-based, intensive supports with low caseloads and frequent contacts, typically a few times per week, available any time, day or night within the patient's own community settings. Some of the most important ACT components address basic activities of daily living: assisting people with food shopping, transportation, cooking, care for clothing, managing bills, and family counseling. ACT can also include job coaching, assistance with budgeting and public benefits, negotiating landlord disputes, medication management, and connections with medical care.

ACT has been found helpful for individuals with serious mental illness, reducing psychiatric hospitalization and housing instability. ACT has not been found effective in reducing arrests or reoffending (Calsyn et al. 2005). Less intensive, and thus less costly, variants of ACT such as community support teams also provide community-based services for individuals experiencing serious mental illness or behavioral disorders.

Individuals who frequently interact with the criminal justice system typically require stronger supervision and some degree of legal leverage to address criminogenic risk-factors and to ensure continued compliance with psychiatric treatment. Forensic Assertive Community Treatment (FACT) provides this structure and has been found to significantly reduce reoffending in randomized trials (Lamberti et al. 2017).

FACT includes a high-fidelity implementation of the ACT model. But it also includes additional specific elements to improve outcomes among individuals at risk of criminal offending. It pays explicit attention to criminogenic risk factors (e.g., substance use, antisocial cognition and associates, family and marital stresses, and employment). Particularly important is judicial monitoring to ensure continued retention and engagement. FACT also includes close collaboration between mental health and criminal justice authorities, with judicious use of graduated sanctions to ensure continued engagement with required services and care (Lamberti et al. 2017; Wooditch, Tang, and Taxman 2014).

Diagnosis-based Medicaid reimbursement is one of many challenges facing such interventions. Many individuals who experience repeated challenges with first responders might potentially benefit from ACT and related interventions. Yet many of these individuals live with recalcitrant alcohol or other drug disorders rather than a specific serious mental illness (SMI) diagnosis recognized for Medicaid reimbursement.

24/7 Sobriety

Alcohol is far and away the drug that most contributes to arrests, violence, and incarceration. Referral of alcohol-involved criminal offenders to treatment instead of incarceration may have a modest effect on the likelihood of future offending, but "24/7 Sobriety" has more evidence of effectiveness. In this strategy, rather than being jailed for repeat alcohol-involved offending, individuals are under community supervision with an order not to drink any alcohol.

Unlike most such orders, in 24/7 Sobriety compliance is closely monitored, and response to breaches is swift and certain. Specifically, individuals either have to present themselves daily to authorities for morning and evening breathalyzers or wear a bracelet that monitors perspiration for ethanol metabolites. Every breach results in immediate arrest and an immediate but modest consequence, typically being held in jail overnight.

The RAND Corporation evaluations of 24/7 Sobriety have produced striking results, including showing a 12 percent reduction in DUI arrests, a 9 percent reduction in domestic violence arrests at the county level (Kilmer et al. 2013), and reduced recidivism by 49 percent at the individual level (Kilmer and Midgette 2018). As any of those averted arrests could have resulted in a dangerous encounter between police officers and an intoxicated individual, this strategy is highly relevant to the subject of this article.

Conclusion

Police frequently encounter people in crisis due to psychiatric and/or substance use disorders. Such people are more likely to commit crimes, more likely to be crime victims, more likely to be homeless, and more likely to otherwise attract attention under circumstances in which police may be called. Such encounters are often fraught because PBCs may be hard to understand, may engage in unusual or oppositional behavior, may be frightened and confused, and may be impaired by substance use. For their part, some police officers may have their own mental health concerns or stereotypes about people with mental illnesses that make these officers less effective at managing such encounters. Given all that, it is not surprising that some such encounters end in tragedy.

These risks can never be eliminated, but they can be systematically reduced and managed. This article has described preventive strategies that can reduce the frequency of such incidents, strategies that can be applied in the heat of the moment to promote positive resolutions, longer-term management strategies that can help the individuals to recover from their problem, and strategies that can reduce their involvement with the criminal justice system and their degree of potential harm to other people.

The strategies described in this article are valuable only to the extent that they are implemented. This will require improved organizational culture and—especially—careful attention to the mundane realities of policing (Morabito et al. 2017; Bittner 1967). It is easier to provide proper training at the Police Academy than it is to ensure that this training will be followed once recruits are on the street encountering PBCs and learning the ropes from more seasoned officers.

Officers are understandably attuned to sources of recognition and prestige within their local departments. Officers will respond to the obvious incentives if they are rewarded for their bravery in subduing a powerful suspect, yet they are ignored if they achieve that same arrest without physical force. Officers will join crisis response units that seek nonviolent resolution of behavioral crises when these postings provide valued paths to recognition and promotion. Officers will be far more reluctant if these postings are less prestigious and less upwardly mobile. Officers also notice the mechanisms of accountability within their own departments—whether incidents that involve shootings or physical force are properly investigated—and respond accordingly (Police Accountability Task Force [PATF] 2016).

Attention to mundane realities of police work also facilitates proper deployment of de-escalation principles. Adequate manpower and other supports are especially important. It is labor-intensive to apply compassionate policing through patient application of time and distance principles. A man shouting at passers-by is more likely to be compassionately engaged on Saturday at 2 p.m. in a low-crime neighborhood than in a rougher part of town 12 hours later, when police are scrambling to answer calls. He is also more likely to be compassionately treated if he is a 62-year-old veteran—or maybe a 28-year-old veteran—than if he is a 17-year-old experiencing a no less dangerous behavioral crisis. Attention also must be paid to the psychological well-being of police officers, who are subjected to compassion fatigue, PTSD, and moral injury that result from their street experiences.

We are not starry-eyed about how hard it will be to accomplish all this. But we would underscore the benefit of steady progress: fewer police shootings, more safety for PBCs and those around them, and quite possibly greater satisfaction and well-being for police officers as well.

References

Anonymous. n.d. Extreme risk protection orders. Available from http://efsgv.org/wp-content/uploads/2018/07/ERPO-One-Pager-7-23-18.pdf.

Bailey, Donald, Melissa Raspa, Ellen Bishop, Debanjali Mitra, Susan Martin, Anne Wheeler, and Pat Sacco. 2012. Health and economic consequences of fragile X syndrome for caregivers. *Journal of Developmental and Behavioral Pediatrics* 33 (9): 705–12.

Ballenger, James F., Suzanne R. Best, Thomas J. Metzler, David A. Wasserman, David C. Mohr, Akiva Liberman, Kevin Delucchi, Daniel S. Weiss, Jeffrey A. Fagan, Angela E. Waldrop, and Charles R. Marmar. 2011. Patterns and predictors of alcohol use in male and female urban police officers. *American Journal on Addictions* 20 (1): 21–29.

Bittner, Egon. 1967. Discretion in emergency apprehension of mentally ill persons. *Social Problems* 14 (3): 278–92.

Bogira, Stee. 18 January 2016. What the Van Dyke murder trial judge has in common with Laquan McDonald. *Chicago Reader*.

Brooks, Susan. 2019. Here's what a red flag law is and how it works in Indiana. Available from https://susanwbrooks.house.gov.

Calsyn, Robert J., Robert Yonker, Matthew R. Lemming, Gary A. Morse, and W. Dean Klinkenberg. 2005. Impact of assertive community treatment and client characteristics on criminal justice outcomes in dual disorder homeless individuals. *Criminal Behavior and Mental Health* 15 (4): 236–48.

Citizens Police Data Project. 2018. Disciplinary record lookup for Officer Jason Van Dyke. Available from https://cpdp.co/officer/29310/jason-van-dyke/.

Compton, Michael T., Roger Bakeman, Beth Broussard, Barbara D'Orio, and Amy C. Watson. 2017. Police officers' volunteering for (rather than being assigned to) Crisis Intervention Team (CIT) training: Evidence for a beneficial self-selection effect. *Behavioral Science & the Law* 35 (5–6): 470–79.

Compton, Michael T., Roger Bakeman, Beth Broussard, Dana Hankerson-Dyson, Letheshia Husbands, Shaily Krishan, Tarianna Stewart-Hutto, Barbara M. D'Orio, Janet R. Oliva, Nancy J. Thompson, and Amy C. Watson. 2014. The Police-Based Crisis Intervention Team (CIT) Model: II. Effects on level of force and resolution, referral, and arrest. *Psychiatric Services* 65 (4): 523–29.

Cook, Philip J. 2016. *Paying the tab: The costs and benefits of alcohol control*. Princeton, NJ: Princeton University Press.

Crifasi, Cassandra K., John Speed Meyers, Jon S. Vernick, and Daniel W. Webster. 2015. Effects of changes in permit-to-purchase handgun laws in Connecticut and Missouri on suicide rates. *Preventive Medicine* 79:43–49.

Draine, Jeffrey N., and Daniel B. Herman. 2007. Critical time intervention for reentry from prison for persons with mental illness. *Psychiatric Services* 58 (12): 1577–81.

Drake, Robert E., Susan M. Essock, Andrew Shaner, Kate B. Carey, Kenneth Minkoff, Lenore Kola, David Lynde, Fred C. Osher, Robin E. Clark, and Lawrence Rickards. 2001. Implementing dual diagnosis services for clients with severe mental illness. *Psychiatric Services* 52 (4): 469–76.

Elkind, David. 24 September 1972. "Good me" or "bad me"—The Sullivan approach to personality. *New York Times*.

Edwards, Griffith. 1997. Alcohol policy and the public good. *Addiction* 92 (S1): S73–79.

Fazel, Seena, Vivek Khosla, Helen Doll, and John Geddes. 2008. The prevalence of mental disorders among the homeless in Western countries: Systematic review and meta-regression analysis. *PLoS Medicine* 5 (12): e225.

Flores, Adolfo, Richard Winton, and Kate Mather. 30 May 2014. Deputies didn't know Elliot Rodger had firearms before deadly rampage. *Los Angeles Times*. Available from http://www.latimes.com.

Galovski, Tara E., Zoë D. Peterson, Marin C. Beagley, David R. Strasshofer, Philip Held, and Thomas D. Fletcher. 2016. Exposure to violence during Ferguson protests: Mental health effects for law enforcement and community members. *Journal of Traumatic Stress* 29:283–92.

Gatens, Alysson. 2018. *Responding to individuals experiencing mental health crises: Police-involved programs*. Chicago, IL: Center for Justice Research and Evaluation.

Kilmer, Beau, and Greg Midgette. 2018. *Using certainty and celerity to deter crime: Insights from an individual-level analysis of 24/7 Sobriety*. Santa Monica, CA: RAND Corporation.

Kilmer, Beau, Nancy Nicosia, Paul Heaton, and Greg Midgette. 2013. Efficacy of frequent monitoring with swift, certain, and modest sanctions for violations: Insights from South Dakota's 24/7 Sobriety Project. *American Journal of Public Health* 103 (1): e37–e43.

Lamb, H. Richard, Linda E. Weinberger, and Walter J. DeCuir Jr. 2002. The police and mental health. *Psychiatric Services* 53 (10): 1266–71.

Lamberti, J. Steven, Robert L. Weisman, Catherine Cerulli, Geoffrey C. Williams, David B. Jacobowitz, Kim T. Mueser, Patricia D. Marks, Robert L. Strawderman, Donald Harrington, Tara A. Lamberti, and Eric D. Caine. 2017. A randomized controlled trial of the Rochester Forensic Assertive Community Treatment Model. *Psychiatric Services* 68 (10): 1016–24.

Ludwig, Jens, and Philip J. Cook. 2000. Impact of the Brady Act on homicide and suicide rates. *JAMA* 284 (21): 2718–21.

McGinty, Elizabeth E., Daniel W. Webster, and Colleen L. Barry. 2014. Gun policy and serious mental illness: Priorities for future research and policy. *Psychiatric Services* 65 (1): 50–58.

Miller, Laurence. 2015. Why cops kill: The psychology of police deadly force encounters. *Aggression and Violent Behavior* 22:97–111.

Morabito, Melissa S., Kelly Socia, Amanda Wik, and William H. Fisher. 2017. The nature and extent of police use of force in encounters with people with behavioral health disorders. *International Journal of Law and Psychiatry* 50:31–37.

Morrissey, Joseph, Piper Meyer, and Gary Cuddeback. 2007. Extending Assertive Community Treatment to criminal justice settings: Origins, current evidence, and future directions. *Community Mental Health Journal* 43 (5): 527–44.

Mueller, Benjamin, Jan Ransom, and Luis Ferré-Sadurní. 5 April 2018. Locals knew he was mentally ill. The officers who shot him did not. *New York Times*. Available from https://www.nytimes.com.

Police Accountability Task Force (PATF). 2016. *Police Accountability Task Force: Recommendations for reform: Restoring trust between the Chicago Police and the communities they serve*. Chicago, IL: PATF.

Pollack, Harold A. 17 June 2014. Why law enforcement missed Elliot Rodger's warnings signs. *Washington Post*. Available from https://www.washingtonpost.com.

Pollack, Harold A. 2016. Better police training: Learning to interact with people living with intellectual or developmental disabilities. *Washington Monthly* (June/July/August).

Reuland, Melissa, and Kento Yasuhara. 2015. Law enforcement and emergency services. In *The sequential intercept model and criminal justice*, eds. Patricia A. Griffin, Kirk Heilbrun, Edward P. Mulvey, David DeMatteo, and Carol A. Schubert. New York, NY: Oxford University Press.

Ridgeway, Greg. 2020. The Role of Individual Officer Characteristics in Police Shootings. *The ANNALS of the American Academy of Political and Social Science* (this volume).

Smith, Mitch, and Timothy Williams. 15 July 2016. Minnesota police officer's "bulletproof warrior" training is questioned. *New York Times*. Available from https://www.nytimes.com.

Smith, Patrick. 26 February 2019. 5 Chicago police officers died by suicide since July. Is the department doing enough? *All Things Considered*. National Public Radio.

St. Clair, Stacy. 24 August 2018. Vincent Gaughan: The Van Dyke judge known for his smarts, sharp tongue and secretive style. *Chicago Tribune*. Available from https://www.chicagotribune.com.

Stanley, Ian H., Melanie A. Hom, and Thomas E. Joiner. 2016. A systematic review of suicidal thoughts and behaviors among police officers, firefighters, EMTs, and paramedics. *Clinical Psychology Review* 44:25–44.

Steadman, Henry J., John Monahan, Debra A. Pinals, Roumen Vesselinov, and Pamela Clark Robbins. 2015. Gun violence and victimization of strangers by persons with a mental illness: Data from the MacArthur Violence Risk Assessment Study. *Psychiatric Services* 66 (11): 1238–41.

Steadman, Henry J., and David Morrissette. 2016. Police responses to persons with mental illness: Going beyond CIT training. *Psychiatric Services* 67 (10): 1054–56.

Strassle, Carla G. 2019. CIT in small municipalities: Officer-level outcomes. *Behavioral Science & the Law*. doi:10.1002/bsl.2395.

Sullivan, Molly. 10 September 2018. An officer with PTSD fatally shot a mentally ill man. He's still on the force. *Sacramento Bee*.

Swanson, Jeffrey W. 2017. Alternative perspectives on police encounters and psychotic experiences. Invited Commentary on DeVylder et al. "Psychotic experiences in the context of police victimization." *Schizophrenia Bulletin* 43 (5): 946–48.

Swanson, Jeffrey W. 2018. Redirecting the mental health and gun violence conversation from mass shootings to suicide. *Psychiatric Services*. doi:10.1176/appi.ps.201800365.

Swanson, Jeffrey W., Elizabeth E. McGinty, Seena Fazel, and Vickie M. Mays. 2015. Mental illness and reduction of gun violence and suicide: Bringing epidemiologic research to policy. *Annals of Epidemiology* 25 (5): 366–76.

Swanson, Jeffrey W., Michael A. Norko, Hsiu-Ju Lin, Kelly Alanis-Hirsch, Linda K. Frisman, Madelon V. Baranoski, Michele M. Easter, Allison G. Robertson, Marvin S. Swartz, and Richard J. Bonnie. 2017. Implementation and effectiveness of Connecticut's risk-based gun removal law: Does it prevent suicides? *Law and Contemporary Problems* 80:179–208.

Swanson, Jeffrey W., Nancy A. Sampson, Maria V. Petukhova, Alan M. Zaslavsky, Paul S. Appelbaum, Marvin S. Swartz, and Ronald C. Kessler. 2015. Guns, impulsive angry behavior, and mental disorders: Results from the National Comorbidity Survey Replication (NCS-R). *Behavioral Sciences and the Law* 33 (2–3): 199–212.

Tentner, Andrea Ruth, Amy Spellman, Allison Stinson, Cameron Day, Tonie Sadler, Ruth Coffman, and Harold A. Pollack. 2019. Identifying Chicago's high users of police-involved emergency services. *American Journal of Public Health* 109 (4): 607–13.

Van Maanen, John. 1978. The "asshole." In *Policing: A view from the street*, eds. Peter K. Manning and John Van Maanen, 221–38. Santa Monica, CA: Goodyear Publishing.

Violanti, John, Cecil M. Burchfiel, Diane Miller, Michael Andrew, Joan Dorn, Jean Wactawski-Wende, Christopher M. Beighley, Kathleen Pierino, Parveen Nedra Joseph, John Vena, Dan S. Sharp, and Maurizio Trevisan. 2006. The Buffalo Cardio-Metabolic Occupational Police Stress (BCOPS) Pilot Study: Methods and participant characteristics. *Annals of Epidemiology* 16:148–56.

Violanti, John M., Desta Fekedulegn, Michael E. Andrew, Tara A. Hartley, Luenda E. Charles, Diane B. Miller, and Cecil M. Burchfiel. 2017. The impact of perceived intensity and frequency of police work occupational stressors on the cortisol awakening response (CAR): Findings from the BCOPS study. *Psychoneuroendocrinology* 75:124–31.

Watson, Amy C., and Michael T. Compton. 2019. What research on crisis intervention teams tells us and what we need to ask. *Journal of the American Academy of Psychiatry and the Law*. doi: 10.29158/JAAPL.003894-19.

Watson, Amy C., Michael T. Compton, and Jeffrey N. Draine. 2017. The crisis intervention team (CIT) model: An evidence-based policing practice? *Behavioral Science and the Law* 35:431–41.

Wolff, Nancy, Ronald J. Diamond, and Thomas W. Helminiak. 1997. A new look at an old issue: People with mental illness and the law enforcement system. *Journal of Mental Health Administration* 24 (2): 152–65.

Wooditch, Alese, Liansheng Tang, and Faye S. Taxman. 2014. Which criminogenic need changes are most important in promoting desistance from crime and substance use? *Criminal Justice Behavior* 41 (3): 276–99.

Preventing Avoidable Fatalities

Police-to-Hospital Transport for Violently Injured Individuals: A Way to Save Lives?

By
SARA F. JACOBY,
PAUL M. REEPING,
and
CHARLES C. BRANAS

Transportation of violently injured individuals to the hospital by police, also known as "scoop and run," may shorten the time between injury and hospital care when emergency medical services are delayed or unavailable. In this article, we explore the history and contemporary applications of this strategy and its broader impact on public safety systems. Current evidence suggests that when comparing police hospital transport and emergency medical services transport for violently injured individuals, survival rates are at least equivalent; in some studies, survival rates are better for violently injured individuals transported by police. Though understudied, police transport may improve survival for violently injured individuals as well as perceptions of police in communities where mistrust is common. Only a select few cities have codified this approach and police role. Geographic context, emergency response capacity, and the nature of encounters between law enforcement and victims of violence are important for other jurisdictions considering police-to-hospital transport.

Keywords: violence; prehospital medical care; traumatic injury; violence; police; first responders

In the aftermath of violence, nonmedical police personnel can and have acted in place of emergency medical service (EMS) providers by expeditiously extricating and transporting injured individuals to definitive medical care in otherwise dangerous situations. A modicum of evidence has emerged in past decades suggesting that prehospital transport by police for violently injured individuals, in lieu of EMS, may be a lifesaving municipal policy worthy of broader consideration. This policy may be especially applicable in situations where firearm

Sara F. Jacoby is an assistant professor in the Department of Family and Community Health at the University of Pennsylvania School of Nursing and a senior fellow of the Leonard Davis Institute of Health Economics.

Correspondence: c.branas@columbia.edu

DOI: 10.1177/0002716219891698

violence has occurred, advanced trauma care is accessible, and police and other security forces exceed the capacity of EMS.

Despite its potential, police transport for violently injured individuals is an infrequently used prehospital strategy. Only a small number of U.S. cities have formalized policies, permitted, or have otherwise explored using police transport to respond to injuries incurred during shootings or other violent events (Van Brocklin 2018a). Underutilization may reflect a host of implementation concerns, including the possibility of unintended harm by nonmedical police personnel, public perceptions of police and the role of police, and scope of work conflicts between police and EMS providers. In this article, we explore the history and potential of police-to-hospital transportation strategies and their broader social impact on public safety systems.

Cities That Permit and Employ Police Transport of Violently Injured Individuals

Immediately after a serious traumatic injury, the most urgent imperative is to transport a wounded individual safely from the scene of injury and into the care of medical providers equipped with lifesaving knowledge and resources (Sakran et al. 2018; Hashmi et al. 2019). In the civilian population, this responsibility routinely falls to EMS providers who have been trained in field-based first aid and best practices for moving injured people into ambulances or other kinds of transport vehicles. In some cases, EMS providers offer more advanced prehospital interventions, such as intravenous fluid resuscitation, or assisted breathing following endotracheal intubation. Yet as hospital trauma systems have improved, there is mounting evidence that on-scene interventions may be less effective than a "scoop-and-run" strategy, defined as minimal on-scene intervention and expedited hospital transport—at least for certain classes of traumatic injuries (Haas and Nathens 2008; Smith and Conn 2009). Specifically, penetrating injuries like gunshots or stab wounds can cause extensive and rapid hemorrhaging. For these cases, minimizing the "stay and play" time required for at-scene interventions in favor of prompt transport to hospitals may mean the difference between life and death (Harmsen et al. 2015). Moreover, many at-scene interventions for penetrating injuries have been shown to be of questionable value in achieving optimal patient outcomes (Bickell et al. 1994).

Police officers are often the first to respond to injuries caused by shootings and other acts of violence. (When police themselves have shot the individual, they are by definition always the first potential lifesavers at the scene.) Many municipal 911 systems will dispatch police to all violent situations prior to activating other

Paul M. Reeping is an epidemiology PhD student studying at the Columbia Mailman School of Public Health.

Charles C. Branas is the Gelman Endowed Professor and chair of the Department of Epidemiology at the Columbia Mailman School of Public Health.

first responders. This policy may be due to police having greater resources and more vehicles on patrol than other first responders. As first responders, police can also determine imminent public safety threats, secure the scene, manage bystanders, and facilitate EMS access to the wounded. Yet rather than waiting for EMS to arrive, some municipalities allow nonmedical police personnel to provide direct transport to hospitals for wounded individuals.

The practice of police hospital transport was first codified in Philadelphia, Pennsylvania. In the late twentieth century, the rate of gunshot injuries in Philadelphia outpaced the resources available for EMS, which is administered solely through the city's fire department. After police transport began informally in Philadelphia in the 1980s (Van Brocklin 2018b), official policy was instituted in 1996 instructing officers to transport "persons suffering from a serious penetrating wound, e.g. stab wound, and similar injuries of the head, neck, chest, abdomen, and groin to the nearest accredited trauma center." The policy explicitly stated that "transportation should not be delayed to await arrival of Fire Department paramedics" (Philadelphia Police Department 2010, 1). It further specified that when carrying out a transport, police are required to exercise health safety precautions (like wearing gloves), to use handcuffs for transporting potentially dangerous suspects, and to communicate the type of injury and hospital destination via police radio—to alert trauma centers of incoming patients and the Detective Division of a potential crime.

The new policy was probably reinforced by the context of an era in which select hospitals had been designated as "regional trauma centers." This designation often required municipal prehospital providers to bypass the nearest hospital and instead take seriously injured individuals to trauma centers. A decade later, this bypass clause was shown to significantly reduce mortality (MacKenzie et al. 2006). It also increased the value of police adopting a scoop-and-run policy for anyone wounded by a gunshot.

As a result of Philadelphia's policy, a substantial and growing proportion of patients with penetrating wounds arrive at Philadelphia trauma centers in police vehicles. In 1995, Philadelphia police transported 29 percent of assault victims, while EMS transported 44 percent (Branas, Sing, and Davidson 1995). A second study found that from 2003 to 2007, Philadelphia police transported 27 percent of assault victims, while EMS transported 73 percent (Band et al. 2011). From 2005 to 2016, an average of 30 percent of patients with penetrating injuries in Philadelphia were transported by police; by 2016, the proportion had exceeded 50 percent, in the context of a relatively stable incidence of penetrating injuries across the city in the prior decade (Kaufman et al. 2017).

A recent review of cases from the U.S. National Trauma Data Bank identified other municipalities—notably Detroit and Sacramento—that also recorded cases of police hospital transport. These three municipalities accounted for the majority (87.8 percent) of all national police hospital transports (Wandling et al. 2016). The use of police hospital transport across twelve major cities with the highest rates of gun violence in the United States is shown in Table 1 (Van Brocklin 2018a). Almost all of these twelve cities rarely use police transport, perhaps except in specific circumstances such as opioid overdoses. However, more than

TABLE 1
Use of Police-to-Hospital Transport across Various U.S. Cities

City	Written Policy Permitting Police Transport?	Occurrence
Baltimore, MD	No	Rare
Chicago, IL	Yes	Rare
Cincinnati, OH	No	Rare
Cleveland, OH	Yes	Rare
Detroit, MI	Yes	Rare, <1%
Kansas City, MO	No	Rare
Memphis, TN	No	Rare to never
Newark, NJ	No	Rare to never
New Orleans, LA	No	Never, except for opioid overdose
Philadelphia, PA	Yes	Approximately 30%
Sacramento, CA	Yes	Rare
St. Louis, MO	No	Rare

40 percent of the cities on our list of twelve have written policies permitting police transport. The majority of police transports occur in Philadelphia, making it an ideal case city from which to observationally evaluate the lifesaving potential and role for nonmedical law enforcement personnel when there is a victim with a penetrating wound.

Is Police Hospital Transport Effective?

The underlying rationale for police hospital transport is that for penetrating injuries, reducing the time required to reach a trauma center is the optimal prehospital medicine. This reflects what some refer to as the "golden hour" in trauma care or that limited time after injury in which definitive medical or surgical services must be rendered to save an individual's life (Rogers, Rittenhouse, and Gross 2015). The emphasis on expedient transport as a primary prehospital strategy is not new. The military medical experiences of the Korean and Vietnam Wars demonstrated that rapid evacuations of the combat wounded to definitive care resulted in major reductions in combat mortality (Fishman and Branas 2004). However, innovation in civilian prehospital approaches took a different direction.

In the late 1960s, advanced life support (ALS) was introduced in urban settings primarily to reduce mortality from cardiac emergencies. At the time of implementation, basic life support (BLS) included skills like noninvasive cardiopulmonary resuscitation, external hemorrhage control, spinal immobilization, and supplementary oxygen administration. ALS increased the capacity of BLS prehospital care to include advanced techniques like field intubation and the administration of intravenous fluids and resuscitative medication (Fishman and Branas 2004). When evaluation of ALS demonstrated improved outcomes following cardiac emergencies, the ALS approach was applied in response to traumatic injuries with the assumption that the improved outcomes would be mirrored in trauma patients. In theory, prehospital ALS should reduce injury mortality by increasing hemodynamic and cardiopulmonary stability in a bleeding patient, thus "buying time" to get a patient to the hospital. However, these techniques take time to administer; they may also delay transport. To date, there is no definitive evidence to support the benefit of ALS over BLS (Ryynänen et al. 2010). No randomized control trial has yet been published that compares ALS, BLS, and transport-only strategies for penetrating trauma.

Police scoop and run offers less medical intervention than BLS; police are not routinely trained in BLS techniques; nor do they have consistent access to the equipment required for BLS interventions. Yet in certain areas, immediate police transport to the hospital could potentially be faster than any other mode of transport. Whether that policy translates into reduced mortality can only be understood, so far, with evidence from observational retrospective cohort studies.

The first study of scoop-and-run outcomes was published more than 20 years ago: a retrospective analysis of 6 years of trauma registry data that compared survival rates of 1,692 gunshot or stabbing-injured patients who arrived at Philadelphia trauma centers via EMS to 1,107 such patients who arrived via police personnel (Branas, Sing, and Davidson 1995, Table 4). Mortality rates of patients with penetrating trauma (i.e., gunshot and stab wounds) transported by police were significantly lower (13.3 percent) than those transported by EMS (17.8 percent), a relative reduction of about 25 percent. These findings were the first empirical support for the effectiveness, or at least the lack of increased harm, of police transport for penetrating trauma. The authors noted that there was likely some sort of case negotiation occurring between police and EMS personnel, where police were likely able to implicitly triage (without formal criteria) those severe injuries that needed immediate transport. Thus, when scoop and run was performed properly (i.e., with appropriate triage), it could be a valuable tool to prevent death after survivable injuries. The authors noted that their study did not include select confounders of the relationship between transport type and outcomes. Police were also unable to stabilize spinal injuries that may have occurred coincidently or concurrently with a violent assault; but, notably, after the study was completed, Philadelphia police were trained in cervical spine immobilization techniques and the use of equipment for transfers.

Some 15 years later, Band et al. (2011, 2014) produced a pair of papers that reexplored the effectiveness of police scoop and run for penetrating traumatic injuries. Also using a retrospective cohort of Philadelphia trauma patients identified in registry data, the first study (Band et al. 2011) compared patients with a proximal penetrating trauma (excluding injuries to distal body parts like arms and legs) who arrived to a level I trauma center between 2003 and 2007 via police transport or EMS. They also found that nearly 30 percent of penetrating injury patients were being transported by police. In unadjusted analyses, patients transported by police were more likely to die in the hospital; however, after using a standard clinical metric for injury severity and probability of survival (the Trauma Injury Severity Score [TRISS]), they found no statistically significant difference between those transported by police and those transported by EMS. Higher mortality in police-transported patients likely reflected a higher severity of injury. There was also no difference in hospital length of stay between police and EMS transported patients, suggesting that once patients arrived at the hospital and survived initial resuscitation, the intensity of hospital care that both groups required was similar.

In their second study, Band et al. (2014) included all patients with a proximal penetrating trauma who arrived at a level I or II trauma center, which nearly doubled their sample size. As with previous research, and upon statistical adjustment, they found that patients with penetrating injuries transported by police were significantly more likely to survive than those transported via EMS. After adjusting for injury severity, age, sex, and some comorbid conditions, Band and colleagues identified evidence of a protective effect for police transport. This protective effect was highest in subgroups of patients who were shot, stabbed, or had severe injuries. At a minimum, this finding suggests that scoop and run is at least as safe as waiting for EMS and, beyond that, may even increase the survival of police-transported patients who experience violent and severe injuries.

Most recently, the safety and effectiveness of police hospital transport was studied at the national level (Wandling et al. 2016). Using data from the National Trauma Data Bank, which culls all trauma registry data from accredited trauma centers across the United States, researchers identified nearly ninety thousand adults who arrived at a level I or level II trauma center following a gunshot or stab wound between 2010 and 2012. Nationwide, a small percentage of patients (2.8 percent) are transported to the hospital by police, primarily in the cities of Philadelphia, Sacramento, and Detroit. In unadjusted analysis, patients transported by police were less likely to survive than those transported by EMS; however, after statistically adjusting for injury severity, there was no difference in survival between police and EMS transport.

Due to the observational nature of these four epidemiological studies, there are limitations to concluding that there is a cause-and-effect relationship between police hospital transport and survival rates for persons shot or stabbed. In each of the four studies, the investigators retrospectively collected the exposure, outcome, and confounding variables using registries that were not designed specifically for the purpose of these studies. That could mean that there was residual bias or misclassification error. For example, a record of the "mode of transport" was missing in 4.7 percent of the population in the Band et al. (2014) analysis, and all of the studies excluded patients transported by private vehicle to the hospital, resulting in selection bias (Band et al. 2014). Furthermore, due to lack of randomization, unmeasured confounders could be driving the associations across the studies.

These studies also face a problem of limited data. Data are limited on actual transport times, time from injury to care, prehospital care, or specific hospitals to which patients were taken. For example, if police transport was more likely to bring victims of penetrating trauma to a higher- (or lower-) performing hospital, this could lead to bias in the results of the studies. Finally, the biggest problem is whether facts drawn mostly from Philadelphia can be generalized to the rest of the nation. Since the majority of evidence is generated from this one urban EMS system, generalizability of these results might prove difficult. Due to these limitations, there is a need for future study using randomized control trials or quasi-experimental designs across diverse jurisdictions (although these methods will be difficult to employ to study this topic).

Other Evidence Relevant to "Scoop and Run"

Despite the limitations of the four observational studies, there is other evidence that scoop and run could be advantageous for injuries such as shootings and stabbings. Treatment, and the extended time that treatment takes, at the scene of an injury may be unhelpful or even harmful to patient outcomes. For example, after adjusting for severity of injury, receiving intravenous fluids at the scene of the injury had no effect on mortality (Bores et al. 2018). The administration of fluids can be dangerous in cases where it elevates blood pressure because doing so can dislodge blood clots and thereby increase the rate of blood loss en route to the hospital (Maher, Goldberg, and Katz 2016). Another study found that prehospital medical interventions for a class of severe penetrating trauma to the chest region increased the odds of death by more than 2.5 times (Seamon et al. 2007). And in a review of articles that examined whether ALS procedures in the field were beneficial for trauma patients, authors concluded that efficient transport to the trauma center should be prioritized over any other prehospital strategy (Haas and Nathens 2008).

The effectiveness of police hospital transport is further supported by the few studies that have compared EMS to private vehicle transport. After adjusting for severity of injury, trauma patients who arrive at trauma centers via private vehicles have been shown to have a lower rate of mortality than patients who arrived via EMS (Bores et al. 2018). In one study, those transported by EMS were actually twice as likely to die than those transported by a private vehicle (Zafar et al. 2014).

New evidence also shows that across all modes of transport to hospital, death during transport has been rising since 2007 (Sakran et al. 2018). This means that the time window for saving lives after these injuries is shrinking, leaving even less leeway for at-scene interventions that have little value. At the same time, more rapid death in transport could increase the benefit conferred through police-to-hospital transport. A recent study compared 2007–2010 to 2011–2014, demonstrating that between the earlier and later periods, there was a fourfold increase among gunshot wound patients in their risk of dying during transport to the hospital. For stab wounds, the rate of increase was ninefold (Sakran et al. 2018). This trend reinforces the need to optimize prehospital transport efficiency and rapidly transport patients with penetrating injuries to an equipped trauma center

(Sakran et al. 2018). When comparing EMS transport to police and private transport, the survival parity (or benefit seen in privately transported patients) is most likely a function of their time and expediency. Bystanders and police out on patrol may be able to move a patient from the scene of injury to a trauma center in minutes, which may be far less than for EMS units who are deployed following notification from 911 systems, or who are unable to access the scene of a violent injury until police declare it safe (Carr et al. 2006).

Trauma Treatment "Deserts" and "Oases": A Geographic Context for Police Transport

Because a majority of the evidence for the effectiveness and safety of police hospital transport is based on the experience of police and health systems in Philadelphia, we must consider the transferability of these findings from Philadelphia to other municipalities. A first consideration is trauma center accessibility. Philadelphia has eight well-distributed level 1 trauma centers (six adult and two pediatric).[1] Within other large U.S. metropolitan areas, however, including Chicago, Los Angeles, and New York, there have been notable "trauma deserts." In these locations, gun violence is high but transport times to equipped trauma centers are longer than in any other area of the city (Crandall et al. 2013; Tung et al. 2019). Research has demonstrated that within these cities trauma deserts are more likely in neighborhoods where the majority of residents are black, suggesting that disparities in access to trauma care reflect legacies of intracity disinvestment and inequality (Tung et al. 2019).

There is also tremendous variability in trauma care access from one state to the next—a variation that is correlated with the rates of fatal police shootings per 100,000, as another study in this volume reports (Nagin, this volume). State-level measures of access to trauma centers in average minutes of transport have been shown to have significantly different injury outcomes in general: states with lesser access to trauma centers have significantly higher overall trauma injury mortality (Hashmi et al. 2019). Pennsylvania, for example, has approximately 2.04 level I and II trauma centers per million people, and 99 percent of its population has access to a trauma center within an hour. In comparison, Arkansas has only recently received its first trauma center—just one in the entire state. In recent studies, Illinois had the most capacity (4.91 trauma centers per million people), and New Jersey had the highest access in terms of speed, with more than twenty trauma centers accessible to its residents on average within an hour (MacKenzie et al. 2013; Branas et al. 2005). Trauma center accessibility has also been shown to vary significantly by geographic and demographic categories, with higher levels of accessibility in more wealthy, nonwhite, urban, and suburban environments; and lower levels of accessibility in areas with higher rates of Medicaid- or Medicare-eligible or uninsured patients and greater rurality (Carr et al. 2017).

A second important consideration in generalizing from Philadelphia is how the 911 system is organized in a municipality. In Philadelphia, all calls made to 911 are centralized, arriving first to the Police Department, and then transferred to the Fire Department from which all EMS service in the city is deployed (there are no private ambulance services dispatched through Philadelphia 911). As a result, police are the first notified and likely first to arrive to the scene of a violent situation. But the 911 process in Philadelphia is not necessarily the norm across other cities and states. The services and process for contacting 911 can vary widely (Neely et al. 1990; Reed et al. 1998). The geographic service area recognized by EMS may also depend on the location of the call, ranging from a local response area, to a township or municipality or county (National Highway Traffic Safety Administration and U.S. Department of Transportation 2011). These differences can affect time to arrival on the scene of police or EMS and thus could alter the effectiveness of police transport compared to EMS transport.

Finally, some cities are launching improved at-scene medical care that may outweigh the advantages that are gained through a scoop-and-run strategy. At-scene care can vary greatly across municipalities and should be a major consideration for implementation of police transport services after trauma. For example, the San Antonio Police Department has launched a tactical medical program that borrows from military-style medical strategies to train police in field-based first aid and injury care. Most of the injuries that they treat are gunshot wounds or occur in motor vehicle crashes. For both classes of injuries, there appears to be improvement in patient outcomes (Smith, Manifold, and Wampler 2013).

Yet the benefits of at-scene care may be highly contingent on specific methods and the context. Earlier research comparing different approaches to injury first response in three cities in Canada demonstrated a somewhat contradictory impact of high-acuity on-site injury interventions. Even prehospital teams included physicians who provided at-scene ALS, such as in Toronto, Canada, the odds of injury mortality were more than 20 percent higher using at-scene treatment than when compared to the provision of BLS and expedited hospital transport (Liberman et al. 2003). Additional research is needed to determine if cities with similarly advanced at-scene medical treatment would demonstrate the same benefit from police transport as has been seen in Philadelphia (where little at-scene treatment has been used). More evidence, including new implementation science, is also needed to evaluate how many lives police transport programs are currently saving or could be saved in the future, and the extent to which these programs are replicable.

Broader Social and Systemic Impact

Beyond the potential for police scoop and run to enhance survival, there are opportunities for other beneficial outcomes to be yielded by police hospital transport. A majority of police-transported patients in the United States are young black men (Kaufman et al. 2017; Wandling et al. 2016). They are often injured in communities with historically strained police-citizen relationships (Johnson 2004; Brunson and Miller 2006; Isom 2016; Desmond, Papachristos, and Kirk 2016).

By comparison, EMS personnel have significantly greater public trust than is granted to police in such areas, perhaps because EMS has a solely medical mission (Zakrison, Hamel, and Hwang 2004). Yet police may also benefit from providing a highly visible, lifesaving role.

In a qualitative study of traumatically injured black patients in Philadelphia, some who had experienced police hospital transport offered their view of the police role. They interpreted the speed and reassurances that officers provided en route as evidence that police were acting in service of their well-being (Jacoby et al. 2017). Ongoing research in Philadelphia has similarly highlighted this perception. For some trauma patients, the experience of transport has changed their view of police and police capacity to be altruistic actors in the patients' communities. For similar reasons, the *National Consensus Policy and Discussion Paper on Use of Force* (International Association of Chiefs of Police 2017) concludes that transport of the victim is a general provision that should be upheld to reduce injury or deadly force. This report, which was developed through a collaborative effort of eleven law enforcement agencies including the International Association of Chiefs of Police, is "intended to serve as a template for law enforcement agencies to compare and enhance their existing policies" (International Association of Chiefs of Police 2017, 1) It states, "Once the scene is safe and as soon as practical, an officer shall provide appropriate medical care consistent with his or her training to any individual who has visible injuries, complains of being injured, or requests medical attention. This may include providing first aid, requesting emergency medical services, and/or arranging for transportation to an emergency medical facility" (International Association of Chiefs of Police 2017, 2).

For police, providing direct transport can be professionally fulfilling as well as a way to diminish the community unrest that can escalate at the scene of a shooting or similar act of violence (Van Brocklin 2018b). In neighborhoods with high rates of gun violence and precarious trust in police, police transport may help to de-escalate emotionally charged situations by allaying bystanders' demands for emergency help. Police transport also removes a victim from the scene of the shooting (Busch 2013). In appropriate scenarios, transport can give the police the opportunity to hear directly from the injured so that the crime and its precipitating circumstances can be better understood. Since these situations are often time-sensitive, this kind of information could be key in stopping future violence.

On the other hand, there are also potentially negative consequences of police hospital transport that have not been rigorously evaluated. Direct police-to-hospital transport may create interprofessional conflict between EMS and police, including union and bargaining concerns, when there is not a clear standard or protocol for responsibilities at the scene of a violent crime. There may also be concern that ceding EMS responsibilities to the police could signal the loss of EMS jobs or that police hospital transport policies delegitimize EMTs and paramedics and the scope of their practice.

Another potential is for "mission creep," when police transport patients who have types of injuries that are beyond the purview of what they should appropriately manage. Patients who could particularly benefit from EMS, for example, include blunt-force motor vehicle crash injuries, spinal cord injuries, and burns

(Holena, Jacoby, and Reilly 2017). An evaluation of nearly thirty thousand trauma patients in Philadelphia from 2006 to 2015 identified that a small minority (1.2 percent) of blunt injury patients arrived at trauma centers via police, but that of these, more than 60 percent may have benefited from prehospital procedures like supplemental oxygen and spine stabilization (Kaufman et al. 2017). Public controversy over whether police can appropriately implement triage for transport in Philadelphia was highlighted in the wake of an Amtrak train derailment in 2015, which caused more than two hundred injuries and eight deaths (Whelan 2016). Although the situation was a mass-casualty event and therefore distinct from the day-to-day injuries typically transported by police, nearly 80 percent of victims had primary blunt injuries and were taken to non-trauma-center hospitals by police. In addition, the distribution of patients to the city's trauma centers was not centrally coordinated or balanced with each center's capacity (Whelan 2016).

Scoop-and-run transports by police may also have unforeseen legal and ethical implications. It is possible that these transports disrupt or contaminate crime scenes that limit investigation and evidence collection after homicides. Unlike their EMS counterparts, nonmedical police personnel are unable to declare an individual dead at the scene of injury and are thus beholden to transport any injury victim to a trauma center regardless of the survivability of the patient. It is also possible that police transport will be seen as injurious by those transported. To our knowledge, there have been no civil or criminal cases in which police have been convicted of negligence or wrongful injury during a scoop-and-run transport (Van Brocklin 2018b). Nonetheless, transport in a police vehicle that is not outfitted for the transport of individuals with injuries could lead to additional injuries or deaths, especially for rare but dangerous conditions that can accompany a violent assault such as a cervical spine fracture.

The medical and legal implications of police hospital transport can also be complicated when the individual being transported is both a victim of injury and a suspect in a crime. The death of Freddie Gray during transport in a police van in Baltimore in 2015, and subsequent public condemnation of the officers' actions, epitomizes the potential for this kind of conflict (Waisbord, Saeed, and Tucker 2017). A 2003 U.S. Supreme Court ruling upholds the constitutionality of police seeking testimony from an injured and non-Mirandized individual for a criminal investigation during emergency medical transport (Hughes 2003). Nonetheless, the courtroom admissibility of the information elicited during transport remains questionable, and a police officer's negotiation of his or her concurrent priorities between law enforcement and emergency transport can conflict with a patient's civil rights and the bioethical imperatives of contemporary health care.

With more research, there is opportunity to better understand the range of collateral, and perhaps unwanted, impacts created in police hospital transport. The many opportunities to optimize current practice for its translation in other municipalities may create more research opportunities as well. To do so, innovations that increase police transport to hospital need to be studied for their short- and long-term ramifications for public health and safety. Much like police work during mental health emergencies, there are substantial "gray zones" in how police respond to the kinds of systemic and structural problems that are beyond the purview of law enforcement alone (social violence and underresourced emergency medical systems) (Wood, Watson, and Fulambarker 2017). For example, while some patients transported by police appreciate this practice, others have found police questioning in the immediate aftermath of an injury to be highly stressful and disruptive—at a time when they felt that their life was in the balance (Patton et al. 2016; Jacoby et al. 2017). These kinds of perceptions may worsen police-citizen relationships and diminish trust in the larger health system (Liebschutz et al. 2010).

Ongoing research has also identified potential health threats for police officers who carry out transports. They are exposed to blood and physical strains during these emergency transports and may not be outfitted to protect themselves appropriately. In addition, police arrivals offer limited notification to receiving hospitals. These surprises can disrupt the systematic care required for emergency trauma resuscitations. Those who save lives through scoop and run should be mindful of the potential for such disruption to offset some of the benefit gained through rapid transport.

Global Implications for Police-Citizen Encounters in Response to Violence

Research and policy implications for hospital transport by police have been overwhelmingly focused on U.S. cities. However, many, if not most, of the world's citizens outside the United States live without access to effective EMS and trauma systems. Moreover, the burden of violence and penetrating injury are particularly pervasive in underresourced regions of the world that regularly experience war and conflict. Almost three-quarters of the people in the world's poorest societies have recently lived through or are currently living through a civil war. Civil wars last five years on average, and even when concluded, they can lead to societal norms and forms of social organization in which violence and traumatic injuries are a hyperprevalent and pervasive reality (Bourgois 2001; Ghobarah, Huth, and Russett 2003; Collier 2007). The public in these especially challenged nations often develop widespread adaptations to contend with extended and seemingly unending cycles of violence, like personal safety precautions and informal police patrols (Puac-Polanco et al. 2015). However, these adaptations can sometimes generate additional violence and are often carried out with few, if any, supporting resources from formal institutions like health systems.

The World Health Organization (WHO) has advocated for the global advancement of prehospital trauma care systems that are simple, sustainable, practical, efficient, and flexible (WHO 2005). Especially in contexts with limited resources, a priority in prehospital trauma care should be integration with existent medical, public health, and transportation infrastructures (WHO 2005). Not only can these systems enhance survival after injury, but they may also be an essential foundation for the enhanced capacity of emergency medical care in general. With this in mind, police transport may be a promising strategy for nations and regions in which violence is highly prevalent yet EMS capacity and infrastructure for advanced trauma care services are lacking.

As one example, Guatemala City is one of the most violent urban centers in the world and has developed more police and private security personnel than active military. However, EMS staff in Guatemala remain highly underdeveloped relative to their police and private security forces. This is complicated by the fact that EMS is currently provided by rival fire departments (Bomberos Voluntarios and Bomberos Municipales) with no integrated and centralized call center, which has led to extensive wait times and unreliable response to calls for assistance. Connecting to the police, and retasking highly abundant law enforcement services to provide basic medical transport of violently injured civilians, might drastically reduce time to hospital care and therefore mortality in Guatemala City.

This same need for the retasking of police and security forces could also apply to many other countries with persistent and pervasive violence, like South Africa (Möller et al. 2018), Honduras, Brazil, and El Salvador, among others. In developing and developed nations with little to no EMS services and many, often underutilized or misutilized law enforcement personnel, hospital transport by police for victims of violence could serve as an essential missing link in saving lives on a broad scale.

Conclusion

Despite its demonstrated potential to save lives, police transport is a rarely instituted prehospital strategy. Across the United States, and in most other countries, rates of death from violence could be substantially reduced with faster transport to trauma centers. Current evidence suggests that this potential is highest in contexts where the burden of penetrating injuries and shootings is high; where emergency medical services are underdeveloped or underresourced; or where police and hospital systems offer the infrastructure, collaboration, and training required for wounded civilians to fully benefit from the course of care and outcomes. While more research is needed, the evidence is more than strong enough to justify far greater investment in such research.

Note

1. See http://ptsf.org/index.php/our-trauma-centers/trauma-centers.

References

Band, Roger A., John P. Pryor, David F. Gaieski, Edward T. Dickinson, Daniel Cummings, and Brendan G. Carr. 2011. Injury-adjusted mortality of patients transported by police following penetrating trauma. *Academic Emergency Medicine* 18 (1): 32–37.

Band, Roger A., Rama A. Salhi, Daniel N. Holena, Elizabeth Powell, Charles C. Branas, and Brendan G. Carr. 2014. Severity-adjusted mortality in trauma patients transported by police. *Annals of Emergency Medicine* 63 (5). Available from https://doi.org/10.1016/j.annemergmed.2013.11.008.

Bickell, William H., Matthew J. Wall, Paul E. Pepe, R. Russell Martin, Victoria F. Ginger, Mary K. Allen, and Kenneth L. Mattox. 1994. Immediate versus delayed fluid resuscitation for hypotensive patients with penetrating torso injuries. *New England Journal of Medicine*. Available from https://doi.org/10.1056/NEJM199410273311701.

Bores, Sam A., William Pajerowski, Brendan G. Carr, Daniel Holena, Zachary F. Meisel, C. Crawford Mechem, and Roger A. Band. 2018. The association of prehospital intravenous fluids and mortality in patients with penetrating trauma. *Journal of Emergency Medicine*. Available from https://doi.org/10.1016/j.jemermed.2017.12.046.

Bourgois, Philippe. 2001. The power of violence in war and peace: Post-cold war lessons from El Salvador. *Ethnography*. Available from https://doi.org/10.1177/14661380122230803.

Branas, Charles C., Ellen J. MacKenzie, Justin C. Williams, C. William Schwab, Harry M. Teter, Marie C. Flanigan, Alan J. Blatt, and Charles S. ReVelle. 2005. Access to trauma centers in the United States. *JAMA: The Journal of the American Medical Association* 293 (21): 2626–33.

Branas, Charles C., Ronald F. Sing, and Steven J. Davidson. 1995. Urban trauma transport of assaulted patients using nonmedical personnel. *Academic Emergency Medicine* 2 (6): 486–93.

Brunson, Rod K., and Jody Miller. 2006. Young black men and urban policing in the United States. *British Journal of Criminology*. Available from https://doi.org/10.1093/bjc/azi093.

Busch, J. 2013. Shots fired: When a police car becomes an ambulance. In Philadelphia cops can transport penetrating-trauma patients; will other systems follow suit? *EMS World* 42 (5). Available from http://www.scopus.com/inward/record.url?eid=2-s2.0-84880167413&partnerID=40&md5=fbf9e202a17cb37015fe7c527df4af82.

Carr, Brendan, Ariel Bowman, Catherine Wolff, Michael T. Mullen, Daniel Holena, Charles C. Branas, and Douglas Wiebe. 2017. Disparities in access to trauma care in the United States: A population-based analysis. *Injury* 48 (2): 332–38.

Carr, Brendan G., Joel M. Caplan, John P. Pryor, and Charles C. Branas. 2006. A meta-analysis of prehospital care times for trauma. *Prehospital Emergency Care*. Available from https://doi.org/10.1080/10903120500541324.

Collier, Paul. 2007. *The bottom billion: Why the poorest countries are failing and what can be done about it*. New York, NY: Oxford University Press.

Crandall, Marie, Douglas Sharp, Erin Unger, David Straus, Karen Brasel, Renee Hsia, and Thomas Esposito. 2013. Trauma deserts: Distance from a trauma center, transport times, and mortality from gunshot wounds in Chicago. *American Journal of Public Health* 103 (6): 1103–9.

Desmond, M., A. V. Papachristos, and D. S. Kirk. 2016. Police violence and citizen crime reporting in the black community. *American Sociological Review*. Available from https://doi.org/10.1177/0003122416663494.

Fishman, P. E., and C. C. Branas. 2004. Urban trauma transport- no need for medical personnel at all? *Presented at the 6th European Congress of Trauma and Emergency Surgery*, September, Rotterdam.

Ghobarah, Hazem Adam, Paul Huth, and Bruce Russett. 2003. Civil wars kill and maim people – long after the shooting stops. *American Political Science Review*. Available from https://doi.org/10.1017/S0003055403000613.

Haas, Barbara, and Avery B Nathens. 2008. Pro/con debate: Is the scoop and run approach the best approach to trauma services organization? *Critical Care* 12 (5). Available from https://doi.org/10.1186/cc6980.

Harmsen, A. M. K., G. F. Giannakopoulos, P. R. Moerbeek, E. P. Jansma, H. J. Bonjer, and F. W. Bloemers. 2015. The influence of prehospital time on trauma patients outcome: A systematic review. *Injury*. Available from https://doi.org/10.1016/j.injury.2015.01.008.

Hashmi, Zain G., Molly P. Jarman, Tarsicio Uribe-Leitz, Eric Goralnick, Craig D. Newgard, Ali Salim, Edward Cornwell, and Adil H. Haider. 2019. Access delayed is access denied: Relationship between access to trauma center care and pre-hospital death. *Journal of the American College of Surgeons*. Available from https://doi.org/10.1016/j.jamcollsurg.2018.09.015.

Holena, Daniel N., Sara F. Jacoby, and Patrick M. Reilly. 2017. Towards a broader view of police prehospital transport. *Journal of Trauma and Acute Care Surgery* 82 (4). Available from https://doi.org/10.1097/TA.0000000000001376.

Hughes, Tom "Tad." 2003. Chavez V. Martinez, the Fifth Amendment, and police questioning: "No one watches as the ambulance pulls away." *Criminal Justice Studies* 16 (4): 339–53.

International Association of Chiefs of Police. 2017. *National consensus policy and discussion paper on use of force.* Alexandria, VA: International Association of Chiefs of Police.

Isom, Deena. 2016. An air of injustice? An integrated approach to understanding the link between police injustices and neighborhood rates of violence. *Journal of Ethnicity in Criminal Justice* 14 (4): 371–92.

Jacoby, Sara F., Therese S. Richmond, Daniel N. Holena, and Elinore J. Kaufman. 2017. A safe haven for the injured? Urban trauma care at the intersection of healthcare, law enforcement, and race. *Social Science & Medicine.* Available from https://doi.org/10.1016/j.socscimed.2017.05.037.

Johnson, Karl E. 2004. Police-black community relations in postwar Philadelphia: Race and criminalization in urban social spaces, 1945–1960. *Journal of African American History* 89 (2): 118–34.

Kaufman, Elinore J., Sara F. Jacoby, Catherine E. Sharoky, Brendan G. Carr, M. Kit Delgado, Patrick M. Reilly, and Daniel N. Holena. 2017. Patient characteristics and temporal trends in police transport of blunt trauma patients: A multicenter retrospective cohort study. *Prehospital Emergency Care.* Available from https://doi.org/10.1080/10903127.2017.1332127.

Liberman, Moishe, David Mulder, André Lavoie, Ronald Denis, and John S. Sampalis. 2003. Multicenter Canadian study of prehospital trauma care. *Annals of Surgery.* Available from https://doi.org/10.1097/00000658-200302000-00001.

Liebschutz, Jane, Sonia Schwartz, Joel Hoyte, Lauren Conoscenti, Anthony B. Christian, Leroy Muhammad, Derrick Harper, and Thea James. 2010. A chasm between injury and care: Experiences of black male victims of violence. *Journal of Trauma: Injury, Infection, and Critical Care* 69 (6): 1372–78.

MacKenzie, Ellen J., David B. Hoyt, John C. Sacra, Gregory J. Jurkovich, Anthony R. Carlini, Sandra D. Teitelbaum, and Harry Teter. 2013. *Hospital Trauma Centers* 289 (12): 1515–22.

MacKenzie, Ellen J., Frederick P. Rivara, Gregory J. Jurkovich, Avery B. Nathens, Katherine P. Frey, Brian L. Egleston, David S. Salkever, and Daniel O. Scharfstein. 2006. A national evaluation of the effect of trauma-center care on mortality. *New England Journal of Medicine.* Available from https://doi.org/10.1056/NEJMsa052049.

Maher, Zoe, Amy J. Goldberg, and Lewis Katz. 2016. Welcoming the Philadelphia immediate transport in penetrating trauma trial! Available from https://tashq.org/wp-content/uploads/2016/11/Oct2016ZMaherEditorial.pdf.

Möller, Anders, Luke Hunter, Lisa Kurland, Sa'ad Lahri, and Daniël J. van Hoving. 2018. The association between hospital arrival time, transport method, prehospital time intervals, and in-hospital mortality in trauma patients presenting to Khayelitsha Hospital, Cape Town. *African Journal of Emergency Medicine* 8 (3): 89–94.

Nagin, Daniel S. 2020. Firearm availability and fatal police shootings. *The ANNALS of the American Academy of Political and Social Science* (this volume).

National Highway Traffic Safety Administration and U.S. Department of Transportation. 2011. EMS system demographics. In *Traffic safety facts: EMS research note.* Available from https://www.ems.gov/pdf/National_EMS_Assessment_Demographics_2011.pdf.

Neely, Keith W., Robert Norton, Ed Bartkus, and John Schriver. 1990. The effect of base station contact on ambulance destination. *Annals of Emergency Medicine.* Available from https://doi.org/10.1016/S0196-0644(05)81568-9.

Patton, Desmond, Aparna Sodhi, Steven Affinati, Jooyoung Lee, and Marie Crandall. 2016. Post-discharge needs of victims of gun violence in Chicago. *Journal of Interpersonal Violence.* Available from https://doi.org/10.1177/0886260516669545.

Philadelphia Police Department. 2010. Directive 3.14 Subject: Hospital cases. Available from http://www.phillypolice.com/assets/directives/D3.14-HospitalCases.pdf.

Puac-Polanco, Victor D., Victor A. Lopez-Soto, Robert Kohn, Dawei Xie, Therese S. Richmond, and Charles C. Branas. 2015. Previous violent events and mental health outcomes in Guatemala. *American Journal of Public Health.* Available from https://doi.org/10.2105/AJPH.2014.302328.

Reed, Jeffrey W., Kevin J. Krizman, Brian D. Woerner, and Theodore S. Rappaport. 1998. An overview of the challenges and progress in meeting the e-911 requirement for location service. *IEEE Communications Magazine.* Available from https://doi.org/10.1109/35.667410.

Rogers, Frederick B., Katelyn J. Rittenhouse, and Brian W. Gross. 2015. The golden hour in trauma: Dogma or medical folklore? *Injury*. Available from https://doi.org/10.1016/j.injury.2014.08.043.

Ryynänen, Olli-Pekka, Timo Iirola, Janne Reitala, Heikki Pälve, and Antti Malmivaara. 2010. Is advanced life support better than basic life support in prehospital care? A systematic review. *Scandinavian Journal of Trauma, Resuscitation and Emergency Medicine* 18 (November). Available from https://doi.org/10.1186/1757-7241-18-62.

Sakran, Joseph V., Ambar Mehta, Ryan Fransman, Avery B. Nathens, Bellal Joseph, Alistair Kent, Elliott R. Haut, and David T. Efron. 2018. Nationwide trends in mortality following penetrating trauma: Are we up for the challenge? *Journal of Trauma & Acute Care Surgery*. Available from https://doi.org/10.1097/TA.0000000000001907.

Seamon, M. J., C. A. Fisher, J. Gaughan, M. Lloyd, K. M. Bradley, T. A. Santora, A. S. Pathak, and A. J. Goldberg. 2007. Prehospital procedures before emergency department thoracotomy: "Scoop and run" saves lives. *Journal of Trauma - Injury, Infection and Critical Care* 63 (1): 113–20.

Smith, R. Malcolm, and Alasdair K. T. Conn. 2009. Prehospital care – Scoop and run or stay and play? *Injury* 40 (Suppl. 4). Available from https://doi.org/10.1016/j.injury.2009.10.033.

Smith, R. M., C. Manifold, and D. Wampler. 2013. San Antonio Police Department launches tactical medic program. specially trained officers can deliver emergency care until EMS takes over. *EMS World* 42 (11): 45–49.

Tung, Elizabeth L., David A. Hampton, Marynia Kolak, Selwyn O. Rogers, Joyce P. Yang, and Monica E. Peek. 2019. Race/ethnicity and geographic access to urban trauma care. *JAMA Network Open* 2 (3). Available from https://doi.org/10.1001/jamanetworkopen.2019.0138.

Van Brocklin, Elizabeth. 19 November 2018 (2018a). "Scoop and run" can save lives. Why don't more police departments try it? *The Trace*.

Van Brocklin, Elizabeth. 14 November 2018 (2018b). Where cop cars double as ambulances. *The Trace*.

Waisbord, Silvio, Eissa Saeed, and Tina Tucker. 2017. The sociological eye in the news. In *News of Baltimore: Race, rage, and the city*, eds. Linda Steiner and Silvio Waisbord, 62–80. New York, NY: Routledge.

Wandling, Michael W., Avery B. Nathens, Michael B. Shapiro, and Elliott R. Haut. 2016. Police transport versus ground EMS. *Journal of Trauma and Acute Care Surgery* 81 (5): 931–35.

Whelan, Aubrey. 17 May 2016. Philly's use of cops to ferry derailment victims did no harm, NTSB finds. *Philadelphia Inquirer*.

World Health Organization (WHO). 2005. *Prehospital trauma care systems*. Geneva: WHO. Available from https://www.who.int/violence_injury_prevention/publications/services/39162_oms_new.pdf.

Wood, Jennifer D., Amy C. Watson, and Anjali J Fulambarker. 2017. The "gray zone" of police work during mental health encounters: Findings from an observational study in Chicago. *Police Quarterly* 20 (1): 81–105.

Zafar, Syed Nabeel, Adil H. Haider, Kent A. Stevens, Nik Ray-Mazumder, Mehreen T. Kisat, Eric B. Schneider, Albert Chi, Samuel M. Glavagno, Edward E. Cornwell, David Thomas Efron, and Elliott Haut. 2014. Increased mortality associated with EMS transport of gunshot wound victims when compared to private vehicle transport. *Injury* 45:1320–26.

Zakrison, Tanya L., Paul A. Hamel, and Stephen W. Hwang. 2004. Homeless people's trust and interactions with police and paramedics. *Journal of Urban Health*. Available from https://doi.org/10.1093/jurban/jth143.

Reconciling Police and Communities with Apologies, Acknowledgements, or Both: A Controlled Experiment

By
THOMAS C. O'BRIEN,
TRACEY L. MEARES
and
TOM R. TYLER

When police officers harm civilians, police leadership almost invariably makes a public statement about the incident, and these communications usually address issues of public mistrust in the police. In addressing public mistrust, political pressures may motivate police leadership to avoid acknowledging the role of police in creating that distrust. The study reported in this article examines the consequences of avoiding versus acknowledging responsibility for the role of police in creating mistrust, along with issuing an apology or not issuing an apology, in public statements. How do these various kinds of gestures shape public cooperation with police? This study reports on an experiment designed to answer that question, with our analysis focusing on the impact of these various kinds of statements on the people who are least likely to trust police. The evidence suggests that police leaders should combine acknowledgement of responsibility for the mistrust with an apology if they want to enlist the cooperation of people who are least likely to trust the police.

Keywords: legitimacy; trust; intergroup apologies; conflict resolution; reconciliation; procedural justice

O ne way to address violence between police and civilians is to ask why some interactions between police and members of the public ever escalate into violence. This is an important question regardless of whether one determines that an officer in the particular incident used force that ultimately is determined to be legally

Thomas C. O'Brien is a psychologist and a postdoctoral research associate in the Department of Psychology at the University of Illinois at Urbana-Champaign and an affiliated scholar of the Justice Collaboratory. His research examines strategies that authorities can take to build legitimacy with communities.

Tracey L. Meares is Walton Hale Hamilton Professor of Law at Yale Law School, where she cofounded the Justice Collaboratory. In addition to her research and teaching, and her career as a federal prosecutor, she has served on national committees including President Obama's Task Force on 21st Century Policing.

Correspondence: tcobrien@illinois.edu

DOI: 10.1177/0002716220904659

acceptable. As Chuck Wexler, the executive director of the Police Executive Research Forum (PERF) explains, this issue is "about the sanctity of all human life—the lives of police officers and the lives of the people they serve and protect" (PERF 2016, 4). Reducing harm to members of the public is an important goal regardless of whether that harm ultimately is found to be legally justifiable, and in recognition of this, policing agencies across the country have undertaken efforts to address such harms. For example, agencies have invested in new policies and added training on how officers can de-escalate incidents that put both officers and members of the public at risk of injury and death. Some agencies have even instituted awards to recognize efforts that officers take to avoid tragic consequences (Chang 2018). But few have focused on broader factors of community perception of the police, factors that contribute to the risk of fatal incidents in the first place. Nor have scholars focused on what steps police leaders can take with members of the public that might disrupt the dynamics that contribute to these fatal incidents. Promoting perceptions of police legitimacy by enhancing procedural justice might be helpful in this regard because people who view the police as legitimate are more willing to accept police authority and cooperate in police efforts to maintain order in their communities.

Research demonstrates that when people view authorities as procedurally just, they view them as more legitimate. This includes three defining components of legitimacy: a basic obligation to obey, trust and confidence, and a sense that authorities share values with the community (Tyler and Jackson 2014). These three components of legitimacy enable a better-functioning system, as people become more likely to comply with the law (Tyler 2005) and more likely to go out of their way to cooperate with authorities by reporting or discussing crime (Tyler and Huo 2002). Procedural justice is a key part of people's psychological connection to their communities (Bradford 2014) and of community members' collective willingness to help each other (Jackson et al. 2012). A consensual relationship between authorities and communities helps to guard against the situations that lead to violent incidents between police and members of the public. Conversely, a lack of trust exacerbates the dynamics that escalate situations to violence in the first place.

Research supports the conclusion that a climate of illegitimacy and distrust leads to situations in which police are more likely to use potentially fatal force in ways that are highly contested (Trinkner, Tyler, and Goff 2016). Surveys show a large trust gap in the level of trust that whites on one hand have in police compared to nonwhites (Gallup 2017; Tyler 2005). With the vast racial disparities in the U.S. criminal justice system (Alexander 2010) and evidence of racial differences in how policing is carried out, especially differences that include disrespectful treatment of young men of color by police in particular, this trust gap is not especially surprising (Fagan et al. 2009; Voight et al. 2017). There is research

Tom R. Tyler is Macklin Fleming Professor of Law and a professor of psychology at Yale Law School, where he cofounded the Justice Collaboratory. He is the author of several books on how people make decisions about legal authorities, including Why People Obey the Law *(Princeton University Press 2006) and* Why People Cooperate *(Princeton University Press 2011).*

demonstrating that there is a lack of trust in police especially on the part of non-whites, and that this lack of trust is foundationally related to interactions that individuals have with particular officers. Yet these more general findings do not necessarily lead to the conclusion that distrust inflames particular incidents of police-citizen violence, though such an outcome is plausible.

For example, Trinkner and Goff (2016) have provided a review of relevant psychological research interpreting social psychological studies pertinent to "identity threats." They note that when police engage with people they consider to be disrespectful or when people do not comply with their instructions, some police interpret these actions as challenges to their masculine identity. Uses of violence, Trinkner and Goff suggest, are a method that officers use to address masculine identity threat. Further empirical work by Trinkner, Kerrison, and Goff supports the finding that officers' fear of being perceived as racist motivates them to use violence. When police believe that the person they are dealing with believes they are acting out of illegitimate motives, their propensity to use force increases (Trinkner, Kerrison, and Goff 2019). In this way, an officer's awareness of the public's perception of her or his lack of legitimacy can be directly linked to uses of force in particular incidents. From this, it follows that repeated and frequent incidents of violence between police and community members can fuel perceptions of illegitimacy, leading to a spiraling cycle of declining legitimacy.

A consensual authority-community relationship may guard against this negative spiral. In a community where people feel that authorities ensure their security, want to help them, and do so through fair processes, people feel more secure. Under such conditions, people approach interactions with police with more trust. Yet building this relationship with police in communities with a long history—or even recent history—of negative police-citizens interactions is a challenge.

Reconciliation as a Process to Build Consensus

If law enforcement were beginning a new relationship with communities devoid of historical context, demonstrating procedural justice would likely be sufficient to earn public trust. As many in law enforcement know, however, legal authorities in America are not operating outside of a historical context. There is a historical context in North America and other parts of the world that makes clear why many communities would not view criminal justice authorities as a source of security and help (Kendi 2016). The lessons of this history are reinforced through extreme incidents of abusive authority that affect the mental health of African Americans through vicarious experience (Bor et al. 2018). Additionally, that history is reinforced through less dramatic but highly consequential personal experiences with authorities (Tyler, Fagan, and Geller 2014) and nonovert lessons about the status of African Americans within the state (Justice and Meares 2014). Both laws and broader inequality have enforced norms that subjugate individuals of darker skin tones living in America, with particular subjugation of blacks and African Americans. Despite attempts at progress through law, racial inequality has plagued the United States and its criminal justice system (Alexander 2010).

For authorities to work toward a consensual relationship with all people that the criminal justice system is charged with serving, it must begin to address this history. Research suggests that the community-level actions authorities take to build trust with communities are related to more legitimacy and cooperation when people perceive them to be sincere in their intention to help the community (O'Brien, Tyler, and Meares 2019). Experimental research among African Americans in particular suggests that inviting community participation in how authorities reform is crucial for people to see those initiatives as sincerely intended to help the community (O'Brien and Tyler 2020).

The research discussed here builds on psychological studies of reconciliation, which demonstrate that empowerment promotes willingness to reconcile among groups who have been disempowered through conflict (Shnabel and Nadler 2015). The police-community reconciliation research is consistent with evaluations of community policing efforts (Gill et al. 2014; Skogan 2006), as well as with research on participation as a form of empowerment in government (Fung 2009; Fung and Wright 2003). Reconciliation is not, however, a process that occurs in isolation; it occurs as part of a process that begins with reforms *acknowledging* injustice (O'Brien and Tyler 2019).

Sincerity is central to the process of reconciliation. Communities must perceive that initiatives to build trust are sincere; otherwise they may backfire and reduce legitimacy (O'Brien, Tyler, and Meares 2019). Part of what shapes perceptions of sincerity is people's preexisting beliefs about whether authorities are procedurally just. The way in which authorities go about undertaking initiatives to improve their relationship with communities is also important to shaping these perceptions (O'Brien and Tyler 2020).

One strategy for reaching out to communities in the reconciliation process is for authorities to offer public apologies. Police have used public apologies, in a variety of contexts, as a strategy to reach out to communities and address racial discrimination in policing. A police chief in Alabama, for example, apologized in person and on camera to a congressman who had been part of a civil rights protest group that the police force had failed to protect a half century earlier (Giammona 2013). Such statements have the advantage of addressing the history and current grievances of an entire community at one time. The use of public apologies, however, may or may not fully address the reasons for distrusting police. If they do not, such apologies may undermine reconciliation rather than enhance it. One example of this risk dates from 2016, when the head of a major policing organization issued a statement in which he said his organization must

> acknowledge and apologize for the actions of the past and the role that our profession has played in society's historical mistreatment of communities of color. . . . At the same time, those who denounce the police must also acknowledge that today's officers are not to blame for the injustices of the past.

There are two key messages here. The first is conciliatory: an apology for "the past." The second is defensive: as he refers to "the past," the chief separates the admitted injustice of the past from the present and defends the modern institution of policing. Later in the speech, the chief makes an argument for removing responsibility from law enforcement of "the past" by emphasizing that they were doing their job to enforce laws that they did not create (see International Association of Chiefs of Police 2016). Thus, despite the conciliatory language in the apology, the message as a whole could be interpreted as largely defensive.

Political pressure may make intergroup apologies in the real world partial (see Dhami 2017), in that the apology does not acknowledge the scope of the relevant injustice or acknowledge responsibility for it. Perhaps this is because apologies that acknowledge specific faults might admit culpability that could lead to criminal charges or lawsuits (see Robbennolt 2003). Moreover, an admission of guilt may also end up angering those who feel unjustly blamed, bringing political heat on the public official. These dynamics lead to a common pattern in which government officials express regret without acknowledging responsibility: an apology that avoids responsibility, or what we call here a "partial apology," to be distinguished from a case in which an official neither apologizes nor acknowledges responsibility by doing nothing.

Our Research

The current research examines whether such "partial apologies" can backfire among those who are less likely to trust the police, the very people for whom these apologies are most relevant. As police know well, how members of the public interpret what police do and say involves both the actual behavior of police and people's views of police. One factor is race: on average, black and African Americans trust police less than other groups in the United States (Gallup 2017); they view them as less fair and respectful (Tyler 2005), reflecting the historical role of law enforcement as well as modern disparities. Despite these factors, there is of course variation in how black and African Americans view police, which is why we split our sample according to those participants who view police as fair and respectful (procedurally just) and those who do not view police as fair and respectful (procedurally unjust). We do this so that readers can see how people's prior views of the police, and in particular how the people least likely to trust them (black and African Americans who view police as unfair and disrespectful), will react to two kinds of apologies—apologies with acknowledgment of responsibility for distrust in the police and those without.

This article summarizes analyses of an experiment we undertook that tested the hypothesis with 678 blacks and African Americans. We also conducted an experiment among a general U.S. sample not limited to blacks and African Americans. The results of this other experiment with 421 participants are available in the appendix, which is available online, and they support the results we present here. We focus here on the results with blacks and African Americans because of the particular challenge that law enforcement have building trust with this group—a group that is disproportionately affected by police violence and that, given the historical context of the United States and ongoing disparities within its criminal justice system, trust police less than other groups in the United States.

We focus our analyses on how apology and acknowledgment impact people's willingness to reach out to police as a source of help and offer police help in solving crime. People's willingness to reach out and report crime or talk with police when they are not legally compelled to do so indicates that they view police as a source of help rather than harm. Past research has also examined how beliefs about procedural justice impact legitimacy and the willingness to voluntarily cooperate with the police (Tyler and Fagan 2008; Tyler and Jackson 2014). Since research has already established that people who believe that police are fair and respectful will cooperate with police more, the research presented here is focused on understanding how apology and acknowledgment will impact cooperation. Our particular focus is on those people who do not view the police as fair. These are the people who do not trust police. They should be the central focus of efforts at trust building.

Research Methods

The experiments for this article were conducted using participants recruited and paid through a company called "TurkPrime" through their paneling service. TurkPrime is an online platform through which researchers can recruit participants specifying specific parameters (e.g., nationality, race, ethnicity; Litman, Robinson, and Abberbock 2017). TurkPrime allows anonymous participants to fill out surveys on an internet webpage, for compensation, and in response to various stimuli. In these experiments, we recruited participants, instructed them to read one of four scenarios about a police chief making a public statement, and then asked them to answer structured questions after they read the scenario.

Participants

The experiment recruited 678 participants, all of whom identified as African American. The sample sizes were selected based on a statistical power analysis (using GPower software; Faul et al. 2009) for detecting a small-to-medium size effect with interactions. The participants included 362 men, 346 women, and 4 participants who identified as "Other," ranging in age from 18 to 84, with an average age of 36 ($SD = 14.94$).[1]

Materials and procedure

Following their consent, participants were presented with information about the context and existing levels of distrust between the police and the community (complete materials appear in the online appendix). The survey instructed participants to imagine "that this was happening in your community" and to reflect on this in writing. The next block showed one of four scenarios. Participants were randomly assigned to one of the four conditions.

In all scenarios, the chief "recognize(d) distrust" between police and the community and called for initiatives to build trust. In the scenario described on the far right of Figure 1, that is all the police chief did; this is to say that the statement acknowledged distrust but neither apologized for it nor acknowledged agency responsibility in its creation. In the second scenario from the far right, the chief *acknowledged* agency responsibility for community distrust of police *but did not apologize*. In the third scenario from the far right, the chief *apologized* for the distrust but did *not acknowledge* police responsibility in creating the distrust. The apology without acknowledgment focused on "the distrust in the relationship between police and members of many communities, especially black and African American communities, from the past." The intention of this statement was to make clear that the chief was apologizing but not taking responsibility for the cause of distrust. In the fourth and final scenario (far left), the chief both *acknowledged* police responsibility for public distrust of the force *and apologized* for that distrust.

Measures

The participants were asked to read one of the four scenarios that had been assigned to them randomly. When they finished reading the scenario, participants were presented with a block of measures assessing cooperative behavior and beliefs about the procedural justice of police in their own community (proposed moderator). All measures were on 1 (*very unlikely/strongly disagree*) to 9 (*strongly disagree/strongly agree*) scales. These measures were constructed as described below.

Cooperation. To assess cooperation, the survey instructed participants to indicate how likely they would be (from *very unlikely* to *very likely*) to act in the following ways: *Answer questions from police about someone in your neighborhood suspected of a crime? Report dangerous or suspicious activity? Call the police to report a crime in which you were the victim? Report a nonviolent crime in your community such as vandalism? Report a violent crime in your community such as assault?* The questions were adapted largely from past research (e.g., Tyler and Huo 2002), with the last two items added to introduce variation in severity of situations (O'Brien, Tyler, and Meares 2019). The average score for these items was 7 out of 9.

Procedural justice. Toward the end of the questions, the survey instructed participants to indicate their agreement (from *strongly disagree* to *strongly agree*) to three statements about procedural justice: *The police: use fair procedures when making decisions about what to do; treat people fairly;* and *treat*

FIGURE 1
Differential Impact of Acknowledgment and Apology on Cooperation

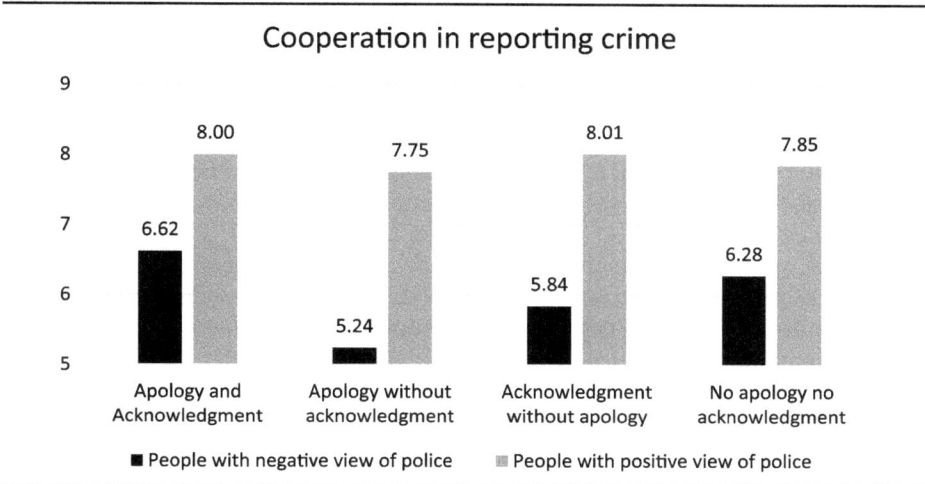

Cooperation in reporting crime

people with courtesy and respect. The average score for these measures in the experiment was 4 out of 9.

Results

We focus our discussion on the results for those who do not view police as procedurally just. The presentation of our results here illustrates the differences in impact of the different kinds of gestures police make to the public when those gestures are perceived by people who have low trust in the police compared to people who have relatively high trust.[2] These results are supported by a more detailed statistical analysis, which, for purposes of brevity, we do not report in this article but which makes us more confident in our results (see the online appendix).

As Figure 1 shows, the people with the least positive views of police as procedurally just (presented in black bars) generally show less cooperation than those with strongly positive views of police. People with the least positive views of police also respond differently than those with strong positive views to variations in the chief's public statement regarding community distrust: the most positive response is among those who received both an apology and an acknowledgment, and the most negative response is among those who received a kind of partial apology—an apology for the distrust itself but no acknowledgment of the role of police. The other kind of partial apology we tested—acknowledgment without an apology—was slightly more positive but not as positive as the acknowledgment combined with an apology.

Among people who already have strong positive views of procedural justice, there is little variation between the condition with both apology and acknowledgment and the acknowledgment only condition. People are least positive in the apology without acknowledgment condition and the condition where police neither apologize nor acknowledge.

The analysis suggests two findings. First, among those with a negative view of the police, the responses vary substantially across the four ways in which a police chief makes a statement. Second, it is only the combination of apology and acknowledgement that motivates a higher level of cooperation than doing nothing. On the contrary, partial efforts are less helpful than doing nothing. This finding is consistent with prior evidence that these types of efforts at reconciliation will enhance cooperation (O'Brien and Tyler 2020; O'Brien, Tyler, and Meares 2019). The research design advances our understanding of reconciliation because it allows us to make inferences about the differences between apologies that include or do not include an apology and acknowledgments that include or do not include an apology.

Discussion

The results reported in this study demonstrate the potential for apologies without acknowledgment or acknowledgment without an apology to backfire among the parts of the population with whom police most need to build trust. The experiment demonstrated this effect among those with less positive beliefs about procedural justice represented by a sample of online participants identifying as black and African American. The results of this experiment and the one reported in the online appendix demonstrate that half-hearted attempts at reconciliation through partial apologies to the public may backfire among those for whom they are most important: members of the population that are least likely to trust police.

The results do not suggest that police apologies are negative; rather, they make clearer the kinds of public statements that agency leaders ought to offer. When agency leaders attempt reconciliation efforts with the community by issuing public apologies, those apologies should be paired with an acknowledgment of responsibility. The results emphasize the point that efforts to build a consensual strategy to be effective must not adopt alternative motives, such as appeasing those who may insist that police have nothing to apologize for. The results suggest, especially in the analyses among people perceiving low levels of procedural justice, that denial of the problem further distances communities from authorities, making it more difficult for them to benefit from community cooperation.

It may seem as though partial apologies would never happen. However, in reality they are common. Once officials decide they will make some kind of overture that addresses reasons for distrust, there are political motivations to avoid full acceptance of responsibility, which is why these "partial apologies" are ubiquitous in the real word (Dhami 2017). Officials balance the interest of reaching out to communities with the interest of appeasing those who want the institution to avoid any blame.

This refusal to acknowledge institutional responsibility can always devolve into a conversation about specific incidents and whether they are indicative of bias. Yet the impact of racial inequality in the United States and its criminal justice system transcends conversations about individual incidents. Racial inequality in the criminal justice system goes far beyond the question of whether an individual officer demonstrates racial bias; it goes back at least as far as the historical factors that have left African Americans as a group at large disadvantage both in terms of economic, educational, and housing opportunities and in terms of disproportionate contact with the criminal justice system (Munger and Seron 2017). Individual actions do have strong impact on the relationship between authorities and communities; the brutal beating of Frank Jude, for example, was linked to a drop of 911 calls to police in Milwaukee, particularly in African American neighborhoods (Desmond, Papachristos, and Kirk 2016). Of course, this example and others like it are not isolated incidents, they are incidents that happen in the context of a history of inequality and pervasive discrimination both at the level of law and policy and in individuals' behaviors toward blacks and African Americans. Beyond the question of whether they as individuals are biased against particular groups, employees of the criminal justice system represent an institution that has demonstrated procedural injustice. That historical context of injustice has created estrangement between authorities and communities (Bell 2016).

Acknowledging responsibility for community distrust on behalf of the police can be politically difficult. Officers, unions, and political activists may react with anger, feeling that innocent officers are being blamed for the actions of a few, or for historical reasons for which they are not responsible. Indeed, at one funeral of New York City Police Department officers, officers turned their backs to Mayor Bill de Blasio, apparently in retaliation for remarks he had made on a separate occasion about conversations he has had with his own son (who has an African American mother and a white American father) about "dangers that he may face" (Altman 2014).

We argue that the response from leaders should not be dictated by the potential for internal opposition. Instead, if policing is fundamentally about serving communities, leaders should seek to promote consciousness of the factors that shape beliefs about policing. Instead of fearing that some will dislike acknowledgment of injustice, police leaders should promote a commitment among their ranks to building trust with communities, which includes recognizing why many distrust police. Irrespective of what officials ought to do, these findings suggest that unless they are willing to both apologize and acknowledge responsibility they are unlikely to achieve the gains they hope for in trust and cooperation from the public.

Although the specific study we presented on apologies does not offer a clear solution for how police leaders can best issue an apology beyond acknowledging responsibility, our other research (O'Brien, Tyler, and Meares 2019; O'Brien and Tyler 2020) suggests that taking proactive measures to address distrust helps to build legitimacy and cooperation. These initiatives are part of a process, not a one-off event that dispels the distrust that is built both through specific incidents and through the larger context of our national history. Taken together with our other research, we recommend following an apology with inviting community participation in initiatives to build trust with the community, whereby the community can have an active role in shaping how police manage crime (O'Brien, Tyler, and Meares 2019; O'Brien and Tyler 2020).

Conclusion

Police need to build trust with communities for their work to be sustainable, and that is not an easy process particularly in contexts of distrust. The results presented here emphasize that reconciliation is not an easy process that can be achieved with a speech. Reconciliation between police and communities will require that people see real improvements in how police treat members of the public. This means that people will need to see both that individual officers treat members of the community with respect when dealing with them one-on-one and that the department as a whole demonstrates respect to the community as a whole. Seeing these changes as the "new normal" will necessarily take time (O'Brien and Tyler 2019). Notably, the effects that the experiment demonstrated were on the decision to cooperate. We measured but did not find effects on beliefs about legitimacy beyond its relationship to beliefs about procedural justice. This has been consistent in experimental research that we conduct (e.g., O'Brien and Tyler 2020): short-term knowledge impacts the decision about whether to cooperate in reporting crime but does not change personal beliefs about authorities. This is also consistent with other psychological research suggesting that behaviors can change *before* personal beliefs (Paluck 2009). It is an important point because it suggests that people might first decide to cooperate with police, and then begin seeing police as more legitimate once they have procedurally just experiences as they are cooperating. In other words, the willingness to cooperate creates contact with the police, which provides an opportunity for the police to act in ways that further promote trust. The process of reconciliation may be cyclical, with the development of trust hinging on community members experiencing procedural justice, following initiatives that acknowledge the barriers to trust.

Following through with the necessary steps for promoting trust will require considerable investment from police departments. However, if authorities succeed in transforming the relationship between authorities and communities to one of consensual authority, the benefits would far outweigh costs. Such a transformation would help to create self-sustaining governance through legitimacy and informal social controls (Meares 2009; Tyler 2016). Research demonstrates that gestures people perceive as sincere may promote both legitimacy and cooperation (O'Brien et al. 2019; O'Brien and Tyler 2019). With higher legitimacy in the eyes of the public, officers will less often find themselves in negative interactions, much less in situations that call for the use of force.

If American police departments are to succeed in transforming their relationship with communities to a consensual style of authority, they must undertake a long-term strategy that involves understanding what gestures communities will perceive as sincere. The data presented in this article suggest that gestures that do not make deep investments are not a viable route to achieving these gains. Authorities will need to take the route of acknowledging responsibility for why communities, in particular black and African American communities, may distrust police. Understanding precisely how to make such gestures may require community participation to better understand their views, which may in itself promote a more trusting relationship (Fung 2009; O'Brien and Tyler 2020; O'Brien, Tyler, and Meares 2019).

Notes

1. The experiment originally also included a sample of participants identifying as white. The sample is irrelevant to the present analyses for reasons that we explain in the online appendix.

2. The color of the bars represents participants' views of police generally, not their response to what the chief says (apologizing or not, acknowledging responsibility or not). The height of the bars represents their level of cooperation, which is shaped by whether the chief apologizes and whether the chief acknowledges responsibility. The colors of the bars differentiate participants based on those who view police generally as unfair (the mean values for these participants are in black, representing people who expressed the most negative views of police, at or below a value of 2.27 on a scale of 1–9) in contrast to those who believe that police are fair (grey bars, representing people who marked near the most positive possible value, 7.80 or above). The graph shows that people who generally think that police are unfair respond most positively to the chief apologizing and acknowledging responsibility, and most negatively to an apology without an acknowledgment.

References

Alexander, Michelle. 2010. *The New Jim Crow: Mass incarceration in the age of colorblindness*. New York, NY: New Press.

Altman, Alex. 22 December 2014. Why New York cops turned their backs on Mayor de Blasio. *Time*.

Bell, Monica, C. 2016. Police reform and the dismantling of legal estrangement. *Yale Law Journal* 126:2054–2150.

Bor, Jacob, Atheendar S. Venkataramani, David R. Williams, and Alexander C. Tsai. 2018. Police killings and their spillover effects on the mental health of black Americans: A population-based, quasi-experimental study. *Lancet* 392 (10144): 302–10.

Bradford, Ben. 2014. Policing and social identity: Procedural justice, inclusion and cooperation between police and public. *Policing and Society* 24 (1): 22–43.

Chang, Cindy. 27 September 2018. LAPD hands out annual awards for bravery and "preservation of life." *Los Angeles Times*.

Desmond, Matthew, Andrew V. Papachristos, and David S. Kirk. 2016. Police violence and citizen crime reporting in the black community. *American Sociological Review* 81 (5): 857–76.

Dhami, Mandeep, K. 2017. An empirical note on perceptions of partial apologies. *Oñati Socio-Legal Series* 7:408–20.

Fagan, Jeffrey, Amanda Geller, Garth Davies, and Valerie West. 2009. Street stops and broken windows revisited: The demography and logic of proactive policing in a safe and changing city. Columbia Public Law Research Paper No. 09-203, Columbia University, New York, NY.

Faul, Franz, Edgar Erdfelder, Axel Buchner, and Albert-Georg Lang. 2009. Statistical power analyses using G*Power 3.1: Tests for correlation and regression analyses. *Behavior Research Methods* 41:1149–60.

Fung, Archon. 2009. *Empowered participation: Reinventing urban democracy.* Princeton, NJ: Princeton University Press.

Fung, Archon, and Erik O. Wright. 2003. *Deepening democracy: Institutional innovations in empowered participatory governance.* Vol. 4. New York, NY: Verso.

Gallup. 10 July 2017. Confidence in police back at historical average. Gallup.com. Available from https://news.gallup.com/poll/213869/confidence-police-back-historical-average.aspx.

Giammona, C. 3 March 2013. Alabama police chief apologizes to Freedom Rider congressman. *NBC News*.

Gill, Charlotte, David Weisburd, Cody W. Telep, Zoe Vitter, and Trevor Bennett. 2014. Community-oriented policing to reduce crime, disorder and fear and increase satisfaction and legitimacy among citizens: A systematic review. *Journal of Experimental Criminology* 10 (4): 399–428.

International Association of Chiefs of Police. 16 October 2016. IACP president makes historic statement. Available from https://www.youtube.com/watch?v=weFWdIl9Nuc.

Jackson, Jonathan, Ben Bradford, Betsy Stanko, and Katrin Hohl. 2012. *Just authority? Trust in the police in England and Wales.* New York, NY: Routledge.

Justice, Benjamin, and Tracey L. Meares. 2014. How the criminal justice system educates citizens. *The ANNALS of the American Academy of Political and Social Science* 651:159–77.

Kendi, Ibram X. 2016. *Stamped from the beginning: The definitive history of racist ideas in America.* New York, NY: Random House.

Litman, Leib, Jonathan Robinson, and Tzvi Abberbock. 2017. TurkPrime.com: A versatile crowdsourcing data acquisition platform for the behavioral sciences. *Behavior Research Methods* 49 (2): 433–42.

Meares, Tracey L. 2009. The legitimacy of police among young African-American men. *Marquette Law Review* 92 (4): 651–66.

Munger, Frank W., and Carroll Seron. 2017. Race, law, and inequality, 50 years after the civil rights era. *Annual Review of Law and Social Science* 13:331–50.

O'Brien, Thomas C., and Tom R. Tyler. 2020. Authorities and communities: Can authorities shape cooperation with communities on a group level? *Psychology, Public Policy, and Law.* Advance online publication. Available from https://doi.org/10.1037/law0000202.

O'Brien, Thomas C., and Tom R. Tyler. 2019. Rebuilding trust between police & communities through procedural justice & reconciliation. *Behavioral Science & Policy* 5 (1): 35–50.

O'Brien, Thomas C., Tom R. Tyler, and Tracey L. Meares. 2019. A community level model of authority: Building popular legitimacy with reconciliatory gestures and participation. *Regulation & Governance.* Available from https://doi.org/10.1111/rego.12264.

Paluck, Elizabeth L. 2009. Reducing intergroup prejudice and conflict using the media: A field experiment in Rwanda. *Journal of Personality and Social Psychology* 96 (3): 574–87.

Police Executive Research Forum. 2016. *Guiding principles on use of force.* Available from http://arks.princeton.edu/ark:/88435/dsp01zs25xc211.

Robbennolt, Jennifer K. 2003. Apologies and legal settlement: An empirical examination. *Michigan Law Review* 102 (3): 460–516.

Shnabel, Nurit, and Arie Nadler. 2015. The role of agency and morality in reconciliation processes: The perspective of the needs-based model. *Current Directions in Psychological Science* 24 (6): 477–83.

Skogan, Wesley G. 2006. *Police and community in Chicago: A tale of three cities.* New York, NY: Oxford University Press.

Trinkner, Rick, and Phillip Atiba Goff. 2016. The color of safety: The psychology of race & policing. In *The Sage handbook of global policing,* eds. Ben Bradford, Beatrice Jauregui, Ian Loader, and Jonny Steinberg, 61–81. Thousand Oaks, CA: Sage Publications.

Trinkner, Rick, Erin M. Kerrison, and Phillip Atiba Goff. 2019. The force of fear: Police stereotype threat, self-legitimacy, and support for excessive force. *Law and Human Behavior* 43 (5): 421–35.

Trinkner, Rick, Tom R. Tyler, and Philip Atiba Goff. 2016. Justice from within: The relations between a procedurally just organizational climate and police organizational efficiency, endorsement of democratic policing, and officer well-being. *Psychology, Public Policy, and Law* 22 (2): 158–72.

Tyler, Tom R. 2005. Policing in black and white: Ethnic group differences in trust and confidence in the police. *Police Quarterly* 8 (3): 322–42.

Tyler, Tom R. 2016. From harm reduction to community engagement: Redefining the goals of American policing in the twenty-first century. *Northwestern University Law Review* 111 (6): 1537–65.

Tyler, Tom R., and Jeffrey Fagan. 2008. Legitimacy and cooperation: Why do people help the police fight crime in their communities? *Ohio State Journal of Criminal Law* 6:231–67.

Tyler, Tom R., Jeffrey Fagan, and Amanda Geller. 2014. Street stops and police legitimacy: Teachable moments in young urban men's legal socialization. *Journal of Empirical Legal Studies* 11 (4): 751–85.

Tyler, Tom R., and Yuen Huo. 2002. *Trust in the law: Encouraging public cooperation with the police and courts.* New York, NY: Russell Sage Foundation.

Tyler, Tom R., and Jonathan Jackson. 2014. Popular legitimacy and the exercise of legal authority: Motivating compliance, cooperation, and engagement. *Psychology, Public Policy, and Law* 20 (1): 78–95.

Voight, Rob, Nicholas P. Camp, Vinodkumar Prabhakaran, William L. Hamilton, Rebecca C. Hetey, Camilla M. Griffiths, David Jurgens, Dan Jurafsky, and Jennifer L. Eberhardt. 2017. Language from police body camera footage shows racial disparities in officer respect. *Proceedings of the National Academy of Sciences* 114 (25): 6521–26.

The global problem of fatal encounters between police and citizens is a massive challenge for both public health and public safety. This volume focuses on a wide range of ideas and evidence about what might be done to save lives in police-citizen encounters, at least in the United States. I focus on three ideas that could make the most difference, most quickly. Each of the ideas is supported by both substantial research evidence and a feasibility assessment of which ideas might be adopted. Three ideas that can transcend political gridlock, appeal to both supporters and critics of the American police, and appeal to police officers themselves are presented: (1) empowering police to take away legally possessed guns from manifestly dangerous people, (2) supporting police in emergency first aid and medical treatment of anyone who is injured by gunfire, and (3) developing implementation strategies based on research on the interactional tactics associated with fatalities and their prevention.

Keywords: police; deadly force; prevention; first aid; shooting victims; red flag laws

Preventing Avoidable Deaths in Police Encounters with Citizens: Immediate Priorities

By
LAWRENCE W. SHERMAN

The global narrative of fatal police shootings has continued to intensify in the two years this volume has been in production. As the volume goes to press, the *New York Times* reports that Brazilian police kill at least sixty-two hundred people a year, or ten times as many deaths per million population (thirty) as in the United States (three) (Ahmed 2019). The police of Hyderabad, in India's newest state of Telangana, shot to death four suspects in a horrific rape/murder case (Gettleman 2019). Both Brazilian

Lawrence W. Sherman is director of the Cambridge Centre for Evidence-Based Policing Ltd., where he serves as editor-in-chief of the Cambridge Journal of Evidence-Based Policing. *He is also Wolfson Professor of Criminology Emeritus at the University of Cambridge Institute of Criminology, where he is chair of the Cambridge Police Executive Programme. Until 2019, he served as a distinguished university professor at the University of Maryland.*

Correspondence: ls434@camb.ac.uk

DOI: 10.1177/0002716220904048

and Hyderabadi police were praised by many citizens for such "speedy justice" that makes communities "safer." In an era in which maintaining a rule of law faces increasing challenges, fatal police shootings in the United States must be seen in a context of contestability. A political consensus about when police should and should not be allowed to kill citizens seems to be in short supply.

Yet seeking political consensus is the only way democracy can work. Since 1889, *The ANNALS* has used its pages to seek such consensus, on issues ranging from racial equality to preventing war with Japan. It is fitting to close this volume with the three proposals from these pages that seem to have the greatest chance of winning a political consensus, and then winning implementation. Each one should save lives of minorities, majorities, police, the mentally ill, and the most dangerous people at large in U.S. communities. These proposals are

1) to empower police to seize guns without a court order, as may appear necessary to them in a "split-second decision";
2) to develop the core tactics underlying systems that seek to reduce "tight coupling" that creates "split-second decisions" and leave too little time to save lives; and
3) to equip police with more powerful first aid strategies, from hi-tech bandages in every police car to policies enabling police to "scoop and run" with every shooting or stabbing victim.

Each of these proposals *could* be endorsed by a wide range of political interests, even if there is no guarantee that they *would* be. But the potential is great for all of them, since they could save police lives as well as citizens'.

The Indiana "Red Flag" Law: In Jake Laird's Memory

Here's how it works: Even without a warrant or judge's signature, police can temporarily confiscate firearms from people who are threatening to harm themselves or others. (Martin 2019)

On the evening of August 18, 2004, residents of a Southside Indianapolis neighborhood called 911 to report that a man was walking down Dietz Street, firing an assault rifle (Mack 2019). Police were dispatched to the scene, even before they knew that the 33-year-old shooter, Kenneth Charles Anderson, had already shot his mother to death in her home. Nor did they know that just eight months earlier, Indianapolis officers had confiscated Anderson's cache of weapons when putting him under "immediate attention" due to his mental health. He was reportedly diagnosed on January 20, 2004, as schizophrenic, when police seized nine guns and more than two hundred bullets. At that time, he said that his two brothers and their families had been murdered, and that the murderers were coming for him and his mother next. None of that was true.

Absent any legal basis for having seized Anderson's property, Indianapolis Police decided they had to return the guns and ammunition to him in March 2004.

After several days of increasing signs of distress, Anderson walked out of his house after dark and started shooting. The 911 calls poured in, and multiple police units were dispatched. When police arrived, he started shooting at their cars, wounding four out of six officers who responded. The third officer to arrive was 31-year-old Timothy "Jake" Laird. Shooting from a concealed location, Anderson's bullet hit Jake Laird fatally just above his bullet-proof vest line.

Returning fire despite being wounded, SWAT officer Peter Koe then shot Anderson fatally and ended the encounter with three dead: Anderson, his mother, and Officer Laird.

Arguably, not one of those fatalities would have occurred had there been a system in place to separate a diagnosed schizophrenic from his guns and bullets. That is just what the Indiana legislature concluded. In 2005, the General Assembly voted to approve the "Jake Laird Law" by overwhelming margins. The House vote was 91-0 in favor; the Senate vote was 48-1.

"Red Flag" laws and police powers

After the mass shootings in El Paso, Texas, and Dayton, Ohio, in summer 2019, President Trump issued a statement:

> "We must make sure that those judged to pose a grave risk to public safety do not have access to firearms and that if they do those firearms can be taken through rapid due process," Trump said, according to *USA TODAY*. "That is why I have called for red flag laws, also known as extreme risk protection orders." (Martin 2019)

The U.S. Congress has yet to pass a federal "red flag" law (as of late 2019), and it is not clear that President Trump would actually sign such a bill if Congress did pass one. But the mere discussion of the proposal came closer to action than any recent proposal for federal endorsement of more local police powers, especially about guns. With support from such Republican senators as Lindsey Graham and Marco Rubio, as well as Republican members of the U.S. House of Representatives, the mere usage of the phrase "red flag law" seemed to soar that summer, even without clarity about what such a law means.

What it always does seem to mean (T. Williams 2019) is that the government can somehow take weapons away from people who possess them legally, if they are shown to pose an "extreme risk." What it seems *not* to mean anywhere but in Indiana is a police power to seize a gun without a court order, immediately and on the spot, with the burden on the gun owner to recover it from the police.

The distinction is crucial. The Indiana version can reduce extreme risk immediately. All other red flag laws require a court order and give up to several weeks for courts to decide. As Officer Jake Laird's death proves, many people can die very quickly if such lengthy delays are allowed.

There are many different forms of red flag laws; all these laws, however, are so different from Indiana's Jake Laird Law that they should not even have the same name. Names of such red flag laws include extreme risk protection orders (ERPOs) (in Oregon, Washington, Maryland, and Vermont), risk protection orders (in Florida), gun violence restraining orders (GVROs) (in California), risk warrants (in Connecticut), and proceedings for the seizure and retention of a firearm (in Indiana). I use the term *red flag laws* here to start a discussion, but I propose a new and better name: a "safety first law."

A red flag law is often defined as any gun control law that allows a *court* to order the temporary removal of firearms from anyone who appears inclined to use it illegally. These definitions include the requirement that a judge should decide to issue the order, not the police acting alone.

How is the Indiana law different from this generic description? This is how the *Indianapolis Star* described the way that the Jake Laird Law has worked since its enactment in 2005:

> It works by allowing police to temporarily confiscate firearms from people who are threatening to harm themselves or others without a warrant or judge's signature. After the warrantless seizure, the officer who recognizes the potential red flags has to submit a written statement to the court describing why the person is considered dangerous. Judges have 14 days to review seizures, and gun owners can fight it in in court. If a judge finds that probable cause exists, the law enforcement agency can retain custody of the guns. If not, the firearms are returned. (Mack 2019)

The Indiana law gives the judge 14 days to decide whether to *return* the gun to a person police decided was at extreme risk. The first red flag law in the United States, however—passed in Connecticut in 1999—gave 14 days to judges to decide whether to *allow police to seize* the weapons before they did so (CONN. GEN. STAT. 1999, cited in Swanson et al. 2017). With requirements to have multiple officers sign a statement recommending removal, the requirements *de jure* reportedly led to minimal use of the law by the police (Swanson et al. 2017). Upon closer examination, however, some officers (in some agencies) found ways to create a *de facto* practice that evolved in Connecticut to include a seize-guns-first-go-to-court-later strategy, as described in a major study of that law (Swanson et al. 2017, 198):

> [A Connecticut] police supervisor explained how [Connecticut] police officers often circumvented the risk-warrant process out of an immediate concern for safety at the scene. In pressing circumstances, it seems that police have other justifications for removing guns, and may need the risk-warrant only to continue holding the weapons once the immediate risk of the scene has passed [as the officer explained to the authors, in his own words, quoted as follows]:
> *The process of obtaining control over firearms [can] happen very quickly . . . in the absence of a warrant, as a matter of fact. It can happen that way. What we end up doing is following up with one of these warrants [after seizing the guns], and then we serve it on ourselves, basically. We serve it on the caretaker of the records department. She has control of the guns once we get them here, and we end up serving her with the warrant. And then that starts the documentation of what we did. . . . "This is what we seized as a result of this warrant," and then we file it with the court. . . . We are at that point compelled to complete the return of service, provide the copy of the entire thing to the subject of the warrant. Our guy is going to be locked up in evaluation at that point in time. . . . So we have to go to the civil court clerk . . . and so the civil clerk would get a copy of our warrant now. They stamp the receiving of the warrant, and create a record, where the*

individual who is the subject of the warrant now gets notification that in two weeks, this day, you're going to have a hearing about these guns.

Regarding the *de jure* problem of delay in obtaining a gun seizure warrant, Swanson and colleagues (2017, 207) concluded that it could be solved by a relatively simple legislative amendment: "to allow police to remove guns immediately with probable cause; this would be similar to current practice in domestic violence situations where a gun surrender requirement is triggered by an ex parte temporary order of protection."

Is there an impact of red flag laws on fatal police shootings?

There is apparently no direct evidence of an effect of any kind of red flag laws on fatal police shootings. There are, in fact, many known cases of police officers killing, or being killed by, persons from whom they are trying to seize weapons lawfully. There is a clear possibility that more red flag laws may increase the number of violent encounters between police and citizens. Why, then, should this policy proposal top this article's list of things that can be done quickly to reduce the count of unnecessary fatal police shootings?

There are three reasons to make this recommendation. The first is that there is some evidence that such laws have reduced suicides. Swanson and colleagues (2017, 204, Table 2) estimated that even with Connecticut's de facto approximation of Indiana's *de jure* police powers of immediate gun seizure, the Connecticut law prevented one suicide death per 10.6 gun seizures. Kivisto and Phalen (2018) estimated that the Connecticut law reduced the firearms suicide rate by 13.7 percent after its implementation (number of gun seizures) rose substantially following the Virginia Tech mass murder in 2007. They also estimated that the Indiana law reduced firearms suicide by 7.5 percent in the 10 years after enactment. This evidence is weak, especially in relation to the question of the proportion of opportunities police had to use the laws in which they actually seized the guns. Yet if there are fewer *repeat* encounters of police with mentally troubled people with guns, there may well be fewer encounters in which someone dies—as in the Jake Laird case.

A second reason to promote red flag laws as a solution to fatal police shootings of citizens is that, as Daniel Nagin's article in this volume shows, the rate of fatal police shootings is strongly correlated, across all fifty states, with the use of guns for suicide. As of 2015 through 2018, with the red flag laws in both Connecticut and Indiana, Nagin shows that the rate of fatal police shootings per ten thousand residents is lower than predicted in both states—and substantially so in Connecticut. While many other factors could explain that variance, it is at least consistent with the hypothesis that such laws could reduce fatal police shootings.

A third reason to promote red flag laws as a leading policy response is the broad political support that the idea has attracted, even in states as conservative as Indiana. Nationally, public opinion polls have found high levels of public support for such laws. A PBS News Hour poll (Santhanam 2019), for example, found that 72 percent of Americans supported the passage of a federal red flag law, while 23 percent were opposed. A national poll of registered voters a year earlier (DeBonis and Guskin 2018) reported that 71 percent "strongly supported" the passage of laws that would "allow the police to take guns away from people who have been found by a judge to be a danger to themselves or others." The idea of identifying "dangerous people with guns" seems to cut across the usual gun control divide. Given the role of gun density in shaping the rates of fatal police shootings, it seems to be in everyone's interest to use this leverage for change—as long as it does not backfire when police start taking guns away.

Hence the third reason for this proposal must be qualified by the need for more evidence. That evidence can come from the second proposal in this article.

Preventing Systems Crashes

As David Klinger's article in this volume observes, there are immense complexities in police systems that can "cascade" into a narrowing of options for police to protect themselves other than shooting someone. Those systems are not the fault of the police officer, nor of the citizen. They are the responsibility of the governments that create police agencies, especially—as Franklin Zimring's article spells out—the state governments. Yet the design of better policing systems is not something at which states are skilled (Sherman 2015). That is why Zimring focused on a modest, federally funded research and development effort as the fastest way to save lives. As Laurie Robinson points out in her commentary, there are good reasons to question the practical impact of this idea. Yet Klinger's article provides a way to shape its focus, which would be all-important for its success.

To take "normal accident theory" (NAT) seriously, it would need to be tested in field experiments. There is no shortage of hypotheses about how to slow down the decision-making that results in fatal police shootings (Klinger 2005, this volume; Sherman 2018). The shortage we confront is a lack of research. Take, for example, the hypothesis advanced four decades ago by Albert J. Reiss, Jr., in *The ANNALS* (1980). His claim was that systems of supervisory oversight for high-speed chases could be applied, with life-saving results, to supervisory oversight of specified police-citizen encounters. This claim seems all the stronger with new technology, especially the potential for on-scene body cameras to transmit real-time images to supervisors in a police command center. Rather than accepting that "no one is in command" at a police encounter, Reiss suggested that a command and control system could be established at a wide range of police-citizen encounters.

This idea, while only one of many innovations that could be field tested in police agencies willing to work with the National Institute of Justice, is one that can be applied directly to the most recent U.S. Supreme Court case on police use of deadly force. This case allowed a police officer to decide to shoot someone solely on the individual officer's discretion, in the presence of other officers who did not shoot—and then pronounced the decision as unreviewable by the federal courts.

The need for supervisory review in cases may be clearest—as Reiss (1980) discussed—where no one is actively shooting, but someone is not responding to police orders to drop a knife. Indeed, Reiss's article in *The ANNALS*, and his proposal for radio-linked supervisory approval for decisions to shoot, almost directly anticipated the facts in this recent Supreme Court ruling (*Kisela v. Hughes* 2018). As the facts in that case were described in the order of the Supreme Court,

> In May 2010, somebody in Hughes' neighborhood called 911 to report that a woman was hacking a tree with a kitchen knife. Kisela and another police officer, Alex Garcia, heard about the report over the radio in their patrol car and responded. A few minutes later the person who had called 911 flagged down the officers; gave them a description of the woman with the knife; and told them the woman had been acting erratically. About the same time, a third police officer, Lindsay Kunz, arrived on her bicycle.
>
> Garcia spotted a woman, later identified as Sharon Chadwick, standing next to a car in the driveway of a nearby house. A chain-link fence with a locked gate separated Chadwick from the officers. The officers then saw another woman, Hughes, emerge from the house carrying a large knife at her side. Hughes matched the description of the woman who had been seen hacking a tree. Hughes walked toward Chadwick and stopped no more than six feet from her. All three officers drew their guns. At least twice they told Hughes to drop the knife. Viewing the record in the light most favorable to Hughes, Chadwick said "take it easy" to both Hughes and the officers. Hughes appeared calm, but she did not acknowledge the officers' presence or drop the knife. The top bar of the chain-link fence blocked Kisela's line of fire, so he dropped to the ground and shot Hughes four times through the fence. Then the officers jumped the fence, handcuffed Hughes, and called paramedics, who transported her to a hospital. There she was treated for non-life-threatening injuries. Less than a minute had transpired from the moment the officers saw Chadwick to the moment Kisela fired shots.

In this case, seven judges of the U.S. Supreme Court overruled the Ninth Circuit U.S. Court of Appeal, which had reversed a lower court's decision to dismiss a constitutional challenge to Kisela's shooting of Hughes; the highest court upheld the lowest, declaring once again that "split second decisions" are unreviewable. Professor Reiss did not claim they were reviewable by a court *ex post facto*. He claimed they were reviewable in advance. The "better systems" proposal of this article does not lie at the boundary of lawful use of force. It depends on finding ways to protect lives.

The Supreme Court said that the shooting was "lawful." Yet many observers consider that shooting to have been "awful"—or at least avoidable. What is clear from the Court's summary is how quickly it all happened. The Court went on to note that

> all three of the officers later said that at the time of the shooting they subjectively believed Hughes to be a threat to Chadwick. After the shooting, the officers discovered that Chadwick and Hughes were roommates, that Hughes had a history of mental illness, and that Hughes had been upset with Chadwick over a $20 debt.

What is not clear to the public is whether this threat had to be resolved by immediate gunfire, or whether some other systems could have been in place to avoid a shoot-or-not decision as the only two alternatives. That question cannot be resolved through mere speculation and hypothetical discussion. But it can be resolved by the development and testing of systems for providing alternative ways to protect life.

As Reiss (1980) suggested, there could, in such situations, be a threshold for engaging supervisory oversight. The report of a woman carrying a kitchen knife would fit under a threshold of "carrying a lethal weapon in public"—just as it would have when the fatal encounter with Officer Jake Laird began in Indianapolis. Events of that description are rare enough so that there would not be a huge burden on supervisory time—especially in comparison to the cost of litigating a police decision to the U.S. Supreme Court, or even a state court. Had a supervisor been linked to the body camera of the Tucson officer, the supervisor might have ordered all officers at the scene by radio to "prepare to use your Taser," or use pepper-spray, or a net-gun, or any other less-lethal weaponry. The decision would then be in the supervisor's hands, and not subject to the judgment of any one officer at the scene.

Comparing the shooting of Ms. Hughes by Officer Kisela to the shootings discussed in the article in this volume by Greg Ridgeway, it is important to note that only Kisela fired a gun. Neither Officer Garcia nor Officer Kunz fired their guns. Perhaps they would have if Kisela had not; that is speculation. But it is not speculation to say that Kisela was not in "command" of the situation. No one was. All three officers were coequal in rank. All three had equal powers under law to shoot. That is the system by which the State of Arizona authorizes police officers to kill people. No system existed in Tucson, or in most other U.S. police agencies, to engage a supervisor in a life-and-death decision.

Any proposal of an option to engage a supervisor in such a confrontation would be immediately criticized for a lack of time. Events moved too fast, it would be said, to connect to anyone at headquarters, let alone to call a sergeant to the scene. Yet this is what "tight coupling" means: the lack of "slack" time between when an officer witnesses a threat and the decision to respond to the threat. Not all tight coupling can be loosened up. But training, policies, and discipline in relation to less-lethal weapons are among the ways to loosen the coupling of risk to a shooting. Reiss's proposal to engage a supervisor is only one possible option. Former Camden County Police Chief J. Scott Thomson used other options to discourage shootings when other weapons could be used (Sherman 2018).

Training alone could be tested for different levels of investment. With a randomized experiment, for example, all officers could be assigned to an initial one-day training course on disarming knife-carriers without shooting. A subset of those officers could be assigned to an annual refresher of such training, while the rest would not. Over 10 years or more, there may be sufficient statistical power to discern differences in weapons use. Or if multiple police agencies joined in an experiment with a sample of thousands of officers, an answer could be possible in an even shorter period of time. A similar approach could be taken with the kind of social interaction training described by Scott Wolfe and colleagues in this volume.

Yet the larger point about systems design can easily get lost in a discussion of specific programs, such as training, early-warning, or incident review systems. The core of systems crash avoidance is to map out the current systems, then compare them to possible alternatives. What is "possible" will face many subjective opinions. Yet the core of the problem is too much demand on policing, and not enough time to meet it. Ultimately, the public as well as police must face a choice between "fast policing" of every 911 call to police, or "slow policing" with systems using big data to help predict lower and higher risks of harm. Even the use of rapid video response by an officer in a command center to a caller may be a form of "slow policing," if it saves thousands of hours of police time wasted in driving to locations where the caller has already departed.

The kind of solutions that David Klinger suggests cannot be implemented overnight. Yet there is every reason to invest in the long run. What can happen in the short run is, potentially, some early breakthroughs in systems design that would save lives quickly. One example, with the facts of *Kisela v. Hughes* (2018), would be the adoption of a knife-encounter protocol. This would be a technology-enabled set of procedures for disarming anyone posing a threat with a knife that would use alternatives to firearms. If that assignment was given to an experienced SWAT team with a large budget for less-lethal weapons, there is good reason to believe that the SWAT team could develop such a protocol. And if a SWAT team were to train other officers in the protocol, the other officers might take that training seriously.

To Stop the Bleeding

Of all the ideas about reducing lives lost in police-citizen encounters, one stands out as producing the most immediate benefits. It is, in fact, the prime example of a redesigned police system. That idea is the implementation of immediate police provision of maximum first aid to all persons shot or stabbed, regardless of who was wounded or why. The idea might have prevented the prosecution of an Oklahoma police officer who stood by with her colleagues doing nothing after shooting an unarmed man (Sherman 2018). It might save the lives of many wounded police officers. It might also focus attention on the need to provide better trauma care in the trauma "deserts" where, Daniel Nagin shows in this volume, fatal police encounters are more frequent compared to states with better access to trauma care.

As Sara Jacoby and colleagues show in this volume, the research is not strong on whether deaths are reduced when police "scoop and run" a victim of a stabbing or gunshot wound to a hospital. Yet the technique remains encouraging. So does the prospect of training more police officers in the techniques taught to more than one million citizens for dealing with gunshot wounds—the "Stop the Bleed" program, sponsored by the American College of Surgeons,[1] has trained ordinary citizens in using tourniquets and other battlefield-tested equipment, and those trained have already saved many lives in mass-shooting events, such as the Synagogue slaughter in Pittsburgh (P. Williams 2019). In the latter case, they even saved the life of the mass shooter, despite some reluctance to do so while his dead victims lay around him.

This is precisely the issue that Trinidad Police Commissioner Stephen Williams addressed in 2014 when he boldly equipped more than two hundred police cars with first aid kits and hemostatic bandages for treating anyone bleeding profusely, including those shot by police officers. There were many objections raised by the officers at the time, including fear of being sued for malpractice of medicine—even with assurances in police orders that they would never be held liable for using first aid. Yet the most emotionally powerful objection was that they did not want the people they had shot to live. Having worked through frequent shots fired at police cars, they saw the people they shot as a threat to them, much as Jake Laird's killer was a threat to police after they had to give the killer his guns back. The issue of police medically treating people they have just shot is not an easy one. But it is necessary to reduce the number of fatal shootings in the United States each year.

The people who police would treat in a system that requires "Stop the Bleed" treatment would overwhelmingly be crime and accident victims. The beneficial effects of such actions on police legitimacy would be substantial. Thousands of families could point to a police car and say, "They saved my daughter's life." For every person killed by police, there would be many more whose lives were saved by police.

Yet the question of whether police should apply these methods, or just drive victims to a hospital, or—like the Oklahoma City case and the *Kisela v. Hughes* case—do nothing except call for medical treatment is still to be addressed. More research is needed to determine which policy would work best in different kinds of communities. But the kind of research that is needed is experimental, not descriptive. We cannot answer these questions without substantial investments in first aid kits and police training. Those investments, in turn, need to be linked to randomized clinical trials, or at least strongly matched control groups. We can learn rapidly only by doing rapidly.

That, in the end, is how this volume comes together. By examining the problem from so many different perspectives, the authors have created a new and distinct perspective. They have collectively helped us to think about what to do next, and with what priority. While they may not agree with each other, they might all agree on the benefits of field testing ways to "Stop the Bleed" once people are shot or stabbed. Such a proposal would be anything but a zero-sum game. This is a proposal to save lives of victims, police, and offenders. The professional duty to defend life does not discriminate.

The tragic choice of this final article is the disservice it does to the many other ideas and insights in this volume. The rhetorical decision to focus on three clear ideas that can be widely explained—and perhaps adopted—comes at the great price of limiting attention to the other authors in the volume. There are many ideas in this volume worth serious attention, even though they are very unlikely to lead to policy changes. That, in fact, is the history of *The ANNALS*, which discussed labor unions, women's rights, and social security long before anyone considered them politically possible. So in skirting many other great ideas, such as daily mandatory alcohol testing for some offenders, or better early warning systems for officers at high risk of shooting "awfully" or even unlawfully, this article may miss the most important content in these pages.

The only mitigation this article can offer for the consequences of its focus is to direct the reader's attention back to the Table of Contents of the full volume, so that anyone reading this online can at least see the full range of topics addressed in the volume. There is so much more in this volume that could be implemented, if scholars or activists were to put their backs into those ideas rather than only these ideas. Social science seems unable to predict major shifts in political culture, so it seems unwise to condemn any idea for a lack of feasibility. What the United States needs is more people thinking seriously, and hard, about the complex problems of reducing shootings by the police, of the police, and for all the policed.

Note

1. See https://www.stopthebleed.org/.

References

Ahmed, Azam. 20 December 2019. Where the police wear masks, and the bodies pile up fast. *New York Times*.

DeBonis, Mike, and Emily Guskin. 9 September 2018. Americans of both parties overwhelmingly support "red flag" laws, expanded background checks for gun buyers, Washington Post-ABC News poll finds. *Washington Post*.

Gettleman, Jeffrey. 21 December 2019. In India tech city shocked by gang rape, vigilante justice gets praise. *New York Times*.

Kisela v. Hughes, 138 S. Ct. 1148, 1162 (2018).

Kivisto, Aaron J., and Peter Lee Phalen. 2018. Effects of risk-based firearm seizure laws in Connecticut and Indiana on suicide rates, 1981–2015. *Psychiatric Services* 69:855–62.

Klinger, David. 2005. *Social theory and the street cop: The case of deadly force*. Washington, DC: Police Foundation.

Mack, Justin L. 7 August 2019. Remembering Jake Laird, the officer whose death inspired Indiana's "red flag" law. *Indianapolis Star*. Available from https://eu.indystar.com.

Martin, Ryan. 6 August 2019. Here's what a red flag law is — and how it works in Indiana. *Indianapolis Star*. Available from https://eu.indystar.com.

Reiss, Albert J., Jr. 1980. Controlling police use of deadly force. *The ANNALS of the American Academy of Political and Social Science* 452:122–34.

Santhanam, Laura. 10 September 2019. Most Americans support these 4 types of gun legislation, poll says. *PBS NewsHour*.

Sherman, Lawrence W. 24 February 2015. Statement to the Presidential Task Force on 21st Century Policing. Available from https://www.c-span.org/video/?324520-1/presidents-task-force-hearing-community-policing.

Sherman, Lawrence W. 2018. Reducing fatal police shootings as system crashes: Research, theory, and practice. *Annual Review of Criminology* 1:421–49.

Swanson, Jeffrey W., Michael A. Norko, Marhsiu-Ju Lin, Kelly Alanis-Hirsch, Linda K. Frisman, Madelon V. Baranoski, Michele M. Easter, Allison G. Robertson, Marvin S. Swartz, and Richard J. Bonnie. 2017. Implementation and effectiveness of Connecticut's risk-based gun removal law: Does it prevent suicides? *Law and Contemporary Problems* 80:179–208.

Williams, Paige. 1 April 2019. Turning bystanders into first responders. *The New Yorker*.

Williams, Timothy. 7 August 2019. What are "red flag" laws, and how do they work? *New York Times*.

Afterword: A Policy-Maker's View

Five Years after Ferguson: Reflecting on Police Reform and What's Ahead

By
LAURIE O. ROBINSON

Policing in the United States is not the same profession it was before Michael Brown's death on a street in Ferguson, Missouri, five years ago. Police use of lethal force has become central to the debate triggered by Ferguson. In this article, I review steps taken to implement policing reforms at local, state, and federal levels; note obstacles to reform; and speculate about which proposals advanced by authors in this volume might be implemented by policy-makers at different levels of government. I conclude by suggesting four areas where attention is needed if reform measures are going to be successfully institutionalized, and I comment on current bipartisan attention in Washington to criminal justice that offers the potential for federal action.

Keywords: police reform; lethal force; federal, state, and local government

It is now five years since Michael Brown's death and since a White House Task Force set up in the aftermath of Ferguson issued its recommendations for twenty-first-century policing (President's Task Force on 21st Century Policing 2015). Over those five years, as the preceding articles in this volume make clear, incidents involving police use of lethal force have been at the center of a reshaped landscape in which law enforcement now operates in this country.

As one observer has described it, "However glacial the pace of change, law enforcement is not the same profession it was five years ago"

Laurie O. Robinson is the Clarence J. Robinson Professor of Criminology, Law & Society at George Mason University. In 2014–15, she cochaired the President's Task Force on 21st Century Policing; and for 10 years, in both the Clinton and Obama administrations, she served as the presidentially appointed assistant attorney general heading the U.S. Department of Justice (DOJ) Office of Justice Programs, DOJ's research and grants agency.

Correspondence: lrobin17@gmu.edu

DOI: 10.1177/0002716219887372

ANNALS, *AAPSS*, 687, January 2020

(Smith 2019, A10). One reflection of those shifts is greater receptivity to change among police leaders, as well as examples of leadership among these police chiefs. At the 2016 annual conference of the twenty-three-thousand-member International Association of Chiefs of Police (IACP), for example, IACP President Terrence Cunningham issued a formal apology for the role law enforcement has historically played in mistreating communities of color, a statement that made headlines across the country (Jackman 2016). Another leadership group, the Police Executive Research Forum (PERF), spearheaded a comprehensive reexamination of use of force policies, releasing in 2016 a groundbreaking set of thirty guiding principles on the subject (PERF 2016). And the following year IACP joined with the Fraternal Order of Police (FOP) and nine other law enforcement organizations to issue a separate consensus policy on the same topic (IACP 2017).

The PERF principles see the greatest potential for reducing use of force in two settings: police encounters with individuals with mental health problems, drug addiction, or other conditions that can prompt erratic behavior; and with individuals who are unarmed or armed with a knife or weapon other than a firearm. While the IACP/FOP consensus document also includes elements similar to the PERF proposal such as de-escalation, it takes a different path in terms of emphasis and specifics. For example, it allows in limited circumstances shooting at moving vehicles and firing warning shots.

Larger police agencies are, in fact, taking steps to revise their use of force policies, and it is having an impact. According to a survey of forty-seven of the largest law enforcement agencies in the United States from 2015 to 2017 conducted by the Major Cities Chiefs Association (MCCA) and the National Police Foundation, 39 percent of the departments changed their use of force policies and revised their training to incorporate de-escalation and beef up scenario-based training approaches. Significantly, officer-involved shootings during this period dropped by 21 percent in the agencies surveyed (Stephens 2019).

Other evidence reflects this trend. A small federally funded study of medium-sized and large police departments in the United States and Canada found "robust policies" on use of force in the agencies surveyed. Although varied in their specific provisions, the survey found that most agencies have policies addressing de-escalation, and some have policy and formalize procedures that can be followed to help build community trust (Charbonneau 2019).

The White House Task Force report, issued in early 2015, has also had an impact. "Agencies all over the country," according to one think tank researcher, "are using the task force report as their playbook" (LaVigne 2018). One potential reason for this is that major law enforcement leadership groups, including IACP, PERF, MCCA, and NOBLE (National Organization of Black Law Enforcement Executives), have embraced the report. They sent it to their members and encouraged them to study its recommendations. IACP also set up an Institute for Community-Police Relations shortly after the report was issued to provide technical assistance, targeted to small and rural agencies, on how to implement the task force recommendations.

Barriers to Change

Despite these examples of forward motion—as well as actions by a host of juris-dictions to adopt new training and policies in such areas as procedural justice, implicit bias, body-worn cameras, and use of force—multiple challenges remain. Four broad barriers are worth noting.

First, as several authors in this volume observe, the highly decentralized nature of policing in the United States, with some eighteen thousand state and local independent departments, means that change in this field will not be quick or easy. And that fully half of these agencies are very small—fewer than ten sworn officers—underscores the challenge (Reeves 2011).

Second, the culture of policing, not unlike many other established institutions, has not traditionally been open to change. Real barriers to reform, as one scholar recently put it, are "the norms of the traditional police culture, particularly the 'warrior' mentality that has dominated American policing for decades" (Walker 2018, 1796).

A third challenge relates to science. While a number of the White House Task Force proposals have gained broad support from police leaders—such as training on de-escalation, implicit bias, and procedural justice—scientific support to date has been slim as to whether these interventions work and how best to implement them, as Engel, McManus, and Isaza discuss (this volume). They also correctly acknowledge, however, that police leaders on the front lines responding to crisis cannot wait for more rigorous academic studies to arrive and are, therefore, mov-ing ahead to implement change with the best knowledge available. As they wisely note, "Changes in policing practice are happening now, and police executives cannot wait for the research field to keep pace." It is unfortunate that the research community—five years after Ferguson—has yet to provide needed feedback for practitioners on what training can be effective in these areas. That makes the practical recommendations offered by Wolfe et al. (this volume) on social interaction skills training ones that should be especially noted.

A final challenge comes from Washington. The push for change is more difficult now because the federal government has stepped back from a lead-ership role. A key part of this is certainly the current administration's deci-sion not to pursue civil rights division "pattern or practice" lawsuits against police departments. Equally important, however, is the U.S. Department of Justice's (DOJ) broad role—something both Democratic and Republican administrations have previously pursued—as a leader and convener in polic-ing innovation, policy, and research. A prime example is the work in the Reagan administration by Attorney General Edwin Meese III and National Institute of Justice Director James K. "Chips" Stewart in sponsoring the highly regarded Harvard Executive Sessions on Policing that were instru-mental in shaping the development of community policing in the 1980s and beyond.

The Path Forward: Where Is the Traction for Policy Change?

Considering these and other obstacles, where is the traction for reform? Should we be looking for efforts at the local level, including from police chiefs? Or is state action the answer? Or should we be turning to federal leaders to play a significant role? Where should the *primary* impetus come from?

The role of local government

When it comes to overseeing police use of lethal force in our decentralized federal system, Zimring (this volume) asserts that "local police have become the decision-makers by default." While Zimring appears to offer this statement with limited enthusiasm, many of the nation's larger agency heads have, in fact, stepped forward since Ferguson as leaders. They have embraced changes in use of force policies; instituted new training in such areas as de-escalation and implicit bias; and adopted body-worn cameras, a step now taken by 60 percent of local police departments (Hyland 2018).

Thinking about the ideas offered by authors in this volume, there are many opportunities for police chiefs and elected officials at the local level to press for change.

The focus by Wolfe et al. (this volume) on improving officers' social interaction skills as a way of helping to de-escalate potential use of force incidents is a welcome one and echoes a recommendation from the White House Task Force (President's Task Force on 21st Century Policing 2015). This is an area that has received far too little attention in the past, with academy training traditionally centered on technical skills such as shooting and driving. These authors correctly offer a cautionary note that "policing needs to develop a stronger training culture mentality."

Ridgeway (this volume) helpfully encourages police chiefs to add to our knowledge about officer-involved shootings by collecting data on who is involved, the number of rounds fired, and the characteristics of the officers involved, zeroing in especially on who did *not* shoot. It is data of this kind that can lead to more evidence-informed policies.

Police leaders can also draw important insights from Zhao and Papachristos (this volume) in their analysis of data from the Chicago Police Department and the impact of social networks on officer behavior. Drawing on their work, chiefs should recognize the capacity of officer misconduct to spread within an agency and the importance of officer assignment. At the same time, as the authors point out, those networks can also be leveraged for interventions and prevention. As a side note, I suggest technical articles like this be routinely translated into lay language for police chiefs and policy-makers. Otherwise, most practitioners will likely never access work of this kind.

Turning to another proposal suited for local implementation, Jacoby, Reeping, and Branas (this volume) call for rapid hospital transport by police for victims of violence. (This echoes Nagin's support in this volume for prompt emergency trauma care.) This is a practical step that every local jurisdiction should consider to reduce deaths. Not only can it literally be a lifesaver for victims of serious penetrating injuries but, as Jacoby, Reeping, and Branas note, research has found the practice can also help to build good faith within low-income communities that are often wary of police.

Role of the states

As Zimring asserts in this volume, even though states are responsible for adjudication and incarceration in the vast majority of U.S. criminal cases, they have traditionally chosen to be the "least important level of government in policing." That, however, may be changing. In the post-Ferguson era, and with the federal government retreating from a leadership role, many states have begun stepping up to exercise more authority over police practices:

- Thirty-four states and the District of Columbia adopted seventy-nine laws in 2015 and 2016 addressing a variety of police reforms, ranging from measures addressing racial profiling and use of force to de-escalation training and body-worn cameras, according to a Vera Institute of Justice study (Subramanian and Skrzypiec 2017).
- In 2019, California Governor Gavin Newsom signed the country's most far-reaching state law on police use of force, the product of more than a year of debate and compromise. The law changes the standard for use of deadly force from when it is viewed as "reasonable" to only when it is seen as "necessary" in light of imminent threat of death or serious bodily harm (Thompson 2019). In fact, the National Conference of State Legislatures reports that between 2014 and 2017, sixteen states passed laws addressing police use of force (National Conference of State Legislatures 2018).
- State initiatives can also play a role in reform: Washington State voters approved an initiative in 2018 making it easier to prosecute police use of deadly force cases, mandating independent investigations into such cases, and requiring police to provide first aid. In support of the last provision, the initiative's authors assert that providing first aid to community members can "increase trust and reduce conflicts" (Ballotpedia 2018, 1), mirroring evidence offered by Jacoby, Reeping, and Branas in this volume.
- Numerous states post-Ferguson have also adopted measures on police interaction with individuals with mental illness, a topic ably addressed in this volume by Pollack and Humphreys. Twenty-seven states and D.C. passed new laws from 2014 to 2017 mandating law enforcement training on this topic (National Conference of State Legislatures 2018). Texas, for example, enacted legislation in 2017 requiring all law enforcement officers in the state to receive 40 hours of Crisis Intervention Team (CIT) training for dealing with this population, and a new state law in Minnesota passed in 2018 mandates 16 hours of CIT and de-escalation training for every police officer in the state (Anderson 2017; ABC News 2018). Pollack and

Humphreys observe that questions remain about the ultimate benefits of CIT training for individuals in behavioral crisis, but they state that "CIT provides a welcome alternative to overly aggressive training that might lead officers to escalate ambiguous situations." CIT training was strongly backed by the White House Task Force (President's Task Force on 21st Century Policing 2015) and, significantly, has garnered support in the policing community from both leadership and rank-and-file. The President of IACP in 2016 launched the "One Mind" campaign aimed at improving law enforcement response to people with mental illness; more than five hundred agencies nationally have now taken the "One Mind" pledge to provide CIT training to their officers and develop a sustainable partnership with community mental health organizations (IACP 2019). And over a dozen large city police unions across the country in 2017 announced support for such training, reflecting that this is not a problem recognized solely by management (Mather 2017).

- State attorneys general have also stepped into the fray. As the Trump administration has retreated from pattern or practice lawsuits, state attorneys general in California and Illinois have come forward to serve as monitors for already existing consent decrees in San Francisco and Chicago. And in New Jersey, the attorney general has set up a statewide police use of force database and now requires every police department in the state to regularly submit data to it (Sullivan 2019).

- Action at the state level relating to firearms is more mixed, despite the need spelled out by Nagin (this volume) to discuss the nexus between statewide availability of firearms and police use of lethal force. Among the policy remedies that Nagin advances are background checks, but despite enormous media and public attention in the aftermath of the Parkland, Florida, school shooting, only two states (Vermont and New Jersey) enacted new background check legislation in 2018 (Gun Laws 2019). On the other hand, in an area Pollack and Humphreys (this volume) cite as an important preventive strategy, seventeen states and the District of Columbia have adopted gun violence restraining orders, or so-called red flag laws (Williams 2019), and there is at least potential for action in this area by Congress. Most of these laws allow judges to issue temporary orders barring individuals from possessing or obtaining firearms upon showing they are an imminent danger to themselves or others, and one state (Indiana) allows police to seize guns on that basis by their own authority.

The federal role

Despite these multiple reform efforts underway at local and state levels, what about federal leadership? Support for a federal role in criminal justice improvement goes back to the Johnson Crime Commission in the 1960s, which called for a federal role in research, data collection, and innovation to address crime and system improvement (President's Commission 1967). These recommendations did not reflect partisan politics. They were reaffirmed by the Reagan administration's Task Force on Violent Crime 14 years later (DOJ 1981).

So Zimring's call in this volume for a focused new federal effort to address police use of lethal force is historically grounded. And he identifies appropriate DOJ agencies for involvement—the National Institute of Justice for research; the Community Oriented Policing Services (COPS) Office for programmatic innovation; and the Civil Rights Division to investigate police misconduct. The Bureau of Justice Statistics (BJS) should be added to this list to collect, analyze and disseminate data, along with the Bureau of Justice Assistance (BJA) to support training, technical assistance, and demonstration projects.

The FBI is a player here as well. In early 2019, the Bureau launched a national use-of-force data collection program, recognizing the need for a comprehensive national database on this subject. One police leader has called the initiative "a significant step forward" (Stephens 2019). Because participation is voluntary, all the national law enforcement membership organizations are working with the FBI to encourage police agencies across the United States to participate (Sprouse 2019).

In contemplating DOJ's role, Zimring also advances the notion of creating a new DOJ statistical and research office, modeled after the United Kingdom's Independent Office for Police Conduct. From 40 years' experience in Washington, I suggest it makes more sense to direct efforts toward ensuring strong leadership for the already-established research and statistics agencies, the National Institute of Justice (NIJ) and BJS, than undertaking a likely futile effort to win congressional approval for a new office in DOJ's vast bureaucracy.

Moving beyond DOJ structure to specific initiatives, what ideas proposed in this volume might be fruitfully advanced with federal support? Engel et al. (this volume), for example, point out, as noted earlier, that many of the most widely supported interventions to address police shootings—de-escalation and implicit bias training, as well as civilian oversight—have modest support at best based on empirical evidence. NIJ's investment in a robust research agenda addressing these areas would constitute an important, and needed, contribution. And once research results are in hand, the COPS Office and BJA could provide support for translating those findings into practitioner-friendly language and sharing them aggressively with the field through training and technical assistance. These are all roles that DOJ agencies have played in the past and can play again with the right funding and the right leadership.

Demonstration projects constitute another fruitful avenue for federal support. Klinger's (this volume) call for addressing police-involved violence, building on the work of Perrow, Sherman, and others, is one such area (Perrow 1984; Sherman 2018). Klinger proposes the creation of tactical review boards to broadly examine police-citizen encounters, including those in which no gun is fired or injuries occur, for the purpose of drawing lessons for police tactical performance, toward the goal of building a culture of safety. While the practical logistics and costs of creating such boards need to be addressed, this is an ideal concept to be tested through demonstration projects. And as the White House Task Force noted in discussing incident review boards, the goal should be to focus on the improvement of practices and policy (President's Task Force on 21st Century Policing 2015).

One can also envision other federal initiatives inspired by the authors in this volume. These could include, for example, demonstration projects to test police hospital transport in several cities as proposed by Jacoby et al. (this volume), or an evaluation in a variety of settings of the social interaction training model that Wolfe et al. (this volume) discuss.

Looking Ahead

It is clear from the foregoing review that there is change under way in the policing field and the potential for further action at local, state, and federal levels. As next steps are contemplated, I suggest four considerations are key to moving forward.

Prioritizing community trust and legitimacy

Very few reforms will "stick" unless a foundation of community trust is established. The White House Task Force viewed building trust and legitimacy as the fundamental first step in bridging the divide between citizens and police (President's Task Force on 21st Century Policing 2015). A recent Urban Institute evaluation of efforts in six cities to build such trust found modest gains but underscored the challenges, including wariness about the initiative from both law enforcement and residents (LaVigne et al. 2019).

O'Brien, Meares, and Tyler (this volume) properly underscore the importance of communities' perceiving outreach to them as sincere. They discuss the benefits of transforming the relationship between officials and the community to one of "consensual authority," which in turn can bring greater legitimacy to the outreach projects. A key part of the relationship, they underscore, entails listening to the community and building a collaborative relationship built on trust. And as Goff (this volume) reminds us, police departments will only learn about much misconduct, and be able to ensure officer accountability, if there *is* community trust and open communication. So making this a priority in every jurisdiction is crucial. It is unlikely reform will be lasting without it.

Hiring for the future of policing

When President Obama asked my White House Task Force cochair, Chuck Ramsey, and me if there was one area we would have delved into if given more time, we said that area was recruitment. American policing in the future will be shaped by the men and women now coming into the police academies, yet at a time when there are calls for advancing a "guardian" culture in policing, many training academies are still organized as military-style boot camps emphasizing a "warrior" approach (Rahr and Rice 2015). A focus on social interaction (Wolfe et al., this volume)—rather than solely tactical skills like shooting well—will better meet the needs of twenty-first-century policing (President's Task Force on 21st Century Policing 2015).

Authors in this volume have added to our understanding, as well, about what recruiters might take into account. Ridgeway, in his analysis of New York City Police Department (NYPD) data, finds evidence that officers hired later in their careers are at a lower risk of shooting, and Goff cautions that less confident officers are more likely to approve of excessive force and less likely to embrace their agency's use of force policies. Their findings should be shared with police officials.

Working on buy-in from the front lines

Getting rank-and-file officers on board is key to implementing, and institutionalizing, reforms that can limit unnecessary police shootings. But while many police leaders across the country are embracing change, there has been resistance at the front lines. The years since Ferguson have been hard for police officers. They have taken a toll. A 2016 Pew Research Center survey of police in the United States found that in the post-Ferguson era, more than three-quarters felt more reluctant to use force when appropriate, and fully 93 percent were more concerned for their safety (Morin et al. 2017). And a recent set of focus groups with officers in Baltimore, where the department has been under a federal consent decree, reflects similar themes. Participants cited multiple factors contributing to low morale, including uncertainty about how to operate under new use-of-force rules. They also reported not feeling valued or listened to by leadership (Crime and Justice Institute 2019). That theme also emerged from a session held by the COPS Office with frontline officers several years ago to solicit reactions to the White House Task Force report. "If they had a rank-and-file meeting three years ago," one attendee asserted, "this report wouldn't have been necessary" (Copple and Erb 2016, 11).

It is therefore important to find ways to engage with, and listen to, rank-and-file officers and police unions and to identify areas of mutual concern. Officer safety and wellness is one such area. Here Klinger's (this volume) observations are relevant—that the "normal accident" literature can be helpful in better understanding and reducing not just violence *by* officers, but also violence by citizens *against* the police.

Developing more robust interaction between academia and law enforcement

There have been multiple efforts over the years to build bridges between scholars and police. These go back to Berkeley (CA) police chief August Vollmer's relationship with the University of California at Berkeley in the early twentieth century and, more recently, the work of George Mason University's Center for Evidence-Based Crime Policy, the launching of Research Advisory Committees by both IACP and PERF, and the establishment of ongoing research partnerships with police departments by individual scholars, such as Anthony Braga's longtime

FIVE YEARS AFTER FERGUSON

237

relationship with the Boston Police Department (Braga, Robinson, and Davis 2013). The creation of the American Society of Evidence Based Policing has also been a significant step. But law enforcement and academia largely still operate in different worlds and speak different languages. Few police chiefs attend American Society of Criminology annual meetings, and few criminologists can be found at IACP's annual conference.

The impressive proposals advanced in this volume merit serious consideration, but whether they will ever reach a law enforcement audience is a real question. Few busy police chiefs—or federal, state and local policy-makers—will read this volume. One solution is to translate academic work into less technical and more succinct formats for practitioner audiences and then to ensure that material reaches practitioners in their publications. I applaud Wolfe et al., Jacoby et al., and Pollack and Humphreys (this volume) for offering proposals that are accessible to a practitioner audience.

A second solution is to create more settings for ongoing dialogue so that exchange of ideas between the two "camps" is institutionalized to a greater degree. Criminologists and other academics can play a significant role here if they step outside their comfort zones and start communicating regularly with policy-makers and policing leaders, including the heads of police management associations and police unions and such organizations as the International Association of Directors of Law Enforcement Standards and Training (IADLEST) and the state POSTs (Peace Officer Standards and Training boards and commissions), both of which are instrumental in shaping police training in the United States.

Conclusion

Five years after Ferguson, it is clear that while positive change is under way in many parts of the country, problems still remain. And while it would be ideal to have the federal government more deeply engaged, that is unlikely until administrations change. At the same time, we should recall that, at base, policing in this country is a local enterprise, and there are strong police leaders across the United States committed to reform—with or without someone in the bully pulpit in Washington.

In addition, the 2020 presidential candidates, with their focus on criminal justice, offer an opportunity for consideration of policing at the national level for the first time in years. While the "First Step Act," the criminal justice legislation passed by Congress late in 2018 with strong bipartisan support, contained no police reform provisions, there is talk of follow-up legislation that provides a chance for additional proposals to be considered (James 2019).

So there is reason for some optimism. It will take time, but the policing field, with the benefit of strong leadership and engagement with interested academics, will continue, I believe, to move in the right direction.

References

ABC News. 16 July 2018. New state law requires all officers undergo crisis intervention training. KSTP Minneapolis. Available from https://kstp.com/news/new-state-law-requires-all-officers-undergo-crisis-intervention-training-mental-health/4991356/ (accessed 5 August 2019).

Anderson, Julie. 2017. Senate Bill 1849 – Breaking down the Sandra Bland Act – 85th Legislature. *Texas County Progress*. Available from https://countyprogress.com/senate-bill-1849-breaking-down-the-sandra-bland-act-85th-legislature/ (accessed 26 August 2019).

Ballotpedia. 2018. Washington Initiative 940, police training and criminal liability in cases of deadly force measure. Available from https://ballotpedia.org/Washington_Initiative_940,_Police_Training_and_Criminal_Liability_in_Cases_of_Deadly_Force_Measure_(2018) (accessed 15 July 2019).

Braga, Anthony, Laurie Robinson, and Edward Davis. 2013. Encouraging a broader set of criminologists to form research partnerships with police departments. *The Criminologist* 4:24–27.

Charbonneau, Amanda. 2019. Analyzing police department policies through the lens of community trust. Paper presented at George Mason University Center on Evidence Based Crime Policy symposium, June 27, Arlington, VA.

Copple, James, and Nicola Erb. 2016. *Rank and file: Leaders in building trust and community policing.* Washington, DC: Office of Community-Oriented Policing Services. Available from https://ric-zai-inc.com/Publications/cops-p351-pub.pdf.

Crime and Justice Institute. 2019. *Feedback from the field: A summary of focus groups with Baltimore police officers.* Boston, MA: Crime and Justice Institute. Available from http://www.crj.org/assets/2019/08/Feedback-from-the-Field_A-Summary-of-Focus-Groups-with-Baltimore-Police-Officers_2019.pdf (accessed 29 August 2019).

Gun laws in 2018. 13 February 2019. *Newsday*. Available from https://projects.newsday.com/databases/long-island/gun-laws-in-2018/?where=category° background checks&offset=0 (accessed 20 August 2019).

Hyland, Shelley S. 2018. *Body-worn cameras in law enforcement agencies*, 2016. Washington, DC: Bureau of Justice Statistics. Available from https://www.bjs.gov/content/pub/pdf/bwclea16.pdf (accessed 12 August 2019).

International Association of Chiefs of Policy (IACP). 2017. *National consensus policy on use of force.* Alexandria, VA: IACP. Available from https://www.theiacp.org/sites/default/files/all/n-o/National_Consensus_Policy_On_Use_Of_Force.pdf (accessed 26 August 2019).

International Association of Chiefs of Policy (IACP). 2019. *One mind campaign – Improving police response to persons affected by mental illnesses.* Alexandria, VA: IACP. Available from https://www.theiacp.org/projects/one-mind-campaign (accessed 26 August 2019).

Jackman, Tom. 17 October 2016. U.S. police chiefs group apologizes for "historical mistreatment" of minorities. *Washington Post*.

James, Nathan. 4 March 2019. *The First Step Act of 2018: An overview.* Washington, DC: Congressional Research Service. Available from https://fas.org/sgp/crs/misc/R45558.pdf (accessed 27 August 2019).

LaVigne, Nancy. 2018. Criminal justice policy and practice in the current administration. Panel presentation at American Society of Criminology annual meeting, November 16, San Francisco, CA.

LaVigne, Nancy, Jess Jannetta, Jocelyn Fontaine, Daniel Lawrence, and Sino Esthappan. 2019. *The national initiative for building community trust and justice: Key process and outcome evaluation findings.* Washington, DC: Urban Institute. Available from https://www.urban.org/research/publication/national-initiative-building-community-trust-and-justice (accessed 9 September 2019).

Mather, Kate. 13 July 2017. LAPD union joins national push for feds to help prepare police for contacts with mentally ill. *Los Angeles Times*. Available from https://www.latimes.com.

Morin, Rich, Kim Parker, Renee Stepler, and Andrew Mercer. 2017. *Behind the badge: Amid protests and calls for reform, how police view their jobs, key issues and recent fatal encounters between blacks and police.* Washington, DC: Pew Research Center. Available from https://assets.pewresearch.org/wp-ontent/uploads/sites/3/2017/01/06171402/Police-Report_FINAL_web.pdf (accessed 9 September 2019).

National Conference of State Legislatures. 2018. *State trends in law enforcement legislation: 2014–2017*. Available from http://www.ncsl.org/research/civil-and-criminal-justice/state-trends-in-law-enforcement-legislation-2014-2017.aspx (accessed 20 August 2019).

Perrow, Charles. 1984. *Normal accidents: Living with high risk technologies*. Princeton, NJ: Princeton University Press.

Police Executive Research Forum. 2016. *Guiding principles on use of force*. Washington, DC: Police Executive Research Forum. Available from https://www.policeforum.org/assets/30%20guiding%20 principles.pdf (accessed 26 August 2019).

President's Commission on Law Enforcement and Administration of Justice. 1967. *The challenge of crime in a free society*. Washington, DC: U.S. Government Printing Office. Available from https://www.ncjrs .gov/pdffiles1/nij/42.pdf (accessed 28 August 2019).

President's Task Force on 21st Century Policing. 2015. *Final report of the President's Task Force On 21st Century Policing*. Washington, DC: Office of Community Oriented Policing Services. Available from https://cops.usdoj.gov/pdf/taskforce/taskforce_finalreport.pdf (accessed 27 August 2019).

Rahr, Sue, and Stephen Rice. 2015. *From warriors to guardians: Recommitting American police culture to democratic ideals*. Washington, DC: National Institute of Justice. Available from https://www.ncjrs.gov/ pdffiles1/nij/248654.pdf (accessed 29 August 2019).

Reeves, Brian A. 2011. *Census of state and local law enforcement agencies, 2008*. Washington, DC: Bureau of Justice Statistics. Available from https://www.bjs.gov/content/pub/pdf/csllea08.pdf (accessed 27 August 2019).

Sherman, Lawrence W. 2018. Reducing fatal police shootings as system crashes: Research, theory, and practice. *Annual Review of Criminology* 1:421–49.

Smith, Mitch. 8 August 2019. More scrutiny and cameras, but how much has policing changed? *New York Times*.

Sprouse, Jennifer Kniceley. June 2019. The national use-of-force data collection. *Police Chief Magazine*. Available from https://www.policechiefmagazine.org/national-use-of-force-data-collection/ (accessed 28 August 2019).

Stephens, Darrel W. 2019. *Officer involved shootings: Incident executive summary*. Washington, DC: National Police Foundation & Major Cities Chiefs Association. Available from https://www.police-foundation.org/publication/officer-involved-shootings-incident-executive-summary/ (accessed 6 September 2019).

Subramanian, Ram, and Leah Skrzypiec. 2017. *To protect and serve: New trends in state-level policing reform, 2015–2016*. Brooklyn, NY: Vera Institute of Justice. Available from https://storage.googleapis .com/vera-web-assets/downloads/Publications/protect-and-serve-policing-trends-2015-2016/legacy_ downloads/041417-PolicingTrendsReport-web.pdf (accessed 1 September 2019).

Sullivan, S. P. 7 May 2019. AG investigating cops identified in NJ.com investigation of police use of force. *NJ Advance Media for NJ.com*. Available from https://www.nj.com/politics/2019/05/ag-investigating-cops-identified-in-njcom-investigation-of-police-use-of-force.html (accessed 1 September 2019).

Thompson, Don. 19 August 2019. California governor signs law to limit shootings by police. *The Washington Post*.

U.S. Department of Justice. 1981. *Attorney General's Task Force on Violent Crime, final report*. Washington, DC: U.S. Department of Justice. Available from https://babel.hathitrust.org/cgi/pt?id=uc 1.31210024703504&view=1up&seq=3.

Walker, Samuel. 2018. "Not dead yet": The national police crisis: A new conversation about policing, and the prospects for accountability-related police reform. *University of Illinois Law Review* 5:1777–1841.

Williams, Timothy. 7 August 2019. What are "red flag" laws, and how do they work? *New York Times*.

THE IMPACT OF THE SOCIAL SCIENCES: How Academics and their Research Make a Difference

Simon Bastow, Patrick Dunleavy, and Jane Tinkler, *all from London School of Economics*

Foreword by Kenneth Prewitt, *Columbia University*

In the modern globalized world, some estimates suggest that around 40 million people now work in jobs that 'translate' or mediate advances in social science research for use in business, government and public agencies, health care systems, and civil society organizations. Many large corporations and organizations across these sectors in the United States are increasingly prioritizing access to social science knowledge. Yet, the impact of university social science continues to be fiercely disputed. This key study demonstrates the essential role of university social science in the 'human-dominated' and 'human-influenced' systems now central to our civilization. It focuses empirically on Britain, the second most influential country for social science research after the US. Using in-depth research, the authors show how the growth of a services economy, and the success of previous scientific interventions, mean that key areas of advance for corporations, public policy-makers, and citizens alike now depend on our ability to understand our complex societies and economies. This is a landmark study in the evidence-based analysis of social science impact.

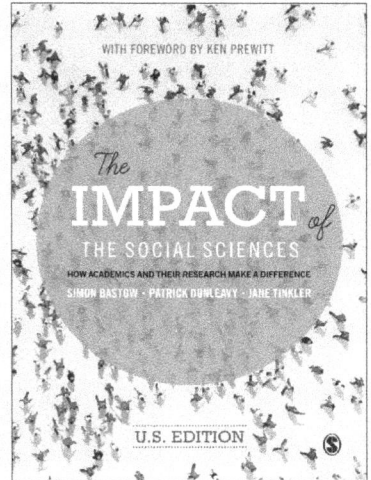

PAPERBACK ISBN: 978-1-4462-8262-5 • FEBRUARY 2014 • 326 PAGES

LEARN MORE AT SAGEPUB.COM!

In compliance with GPSR, should you have any concerns about the safety of this product, please advise: International Associates Auditing & Certification Limited The Black Church, St Mary's Place, Dublin 7, D07 P4AX Ireland EUAR@ie.ia-net.com

www.ingramcontent.com/pod-product-compliance
Lightning Source LLC
Chambersburg PA
CBHW060316030426
42336CB00011B/1071